Exam Ref 70-741 Networking with Windows Server 2016

Andrew Warren

Exam Ref 70-741 Networking with Windows Server 2016

Published with the authorization of Microsoft Corporation by:
Pearson Education, Inc.

Copyright © 2017 by Andrew James Warren

All rights reserved. Printed in the United States of America. This publication is protected by copyright, and permission must be obtained from the publisher prior to any prohibited reproduction, storage in a retrieval system, or transmission in any form or by any means, electronic, mechanical, photocopying, recording, or likewise. For information regarding permissions, request forms, and the appropriate contacts within the Pearson Education Global Rights & Permissions Department, please visit www.pearsoned.com/permissions/. No patent liability is assumed with respect to the use of the information contained herein. Although every precaution has been taken in the preparation of this book, the publisher and author assume no responsibility for errors or omissions. Nor is any liability assumed for damages resulting from the use of the information contained herein.

ISBN-13: 978-0-7356-9742-3
ISBN-10: 0-7356-9742-6

Library of Congress Control Number: 2016959968

5 18

Trademarks

Microsoft and the trademarks listed at https://www.microsoft.com on the "Trademarks" webpage are trademarks of the Microsoft group of companies. All other marks are property of their respective owners.

Warning and Disclaimer

Every effort has been made to make this book as complete and as accurate as possible, but no warranty or fitness is implied. The information provided is on an "as is" basis. The authors, the publisher, and Microsoft Corporation shall have neither liability nor responsibility to any person or entity with respect to any loss or damages arising from the information contained in this book or programs accompanying it.

Special Sales

For information about buying this title in bulk quantities, or for special sales opportunities (which may include electronic versions; custom cover designs; and content particular to your business, training goals, marketing focus, or branding interests), please contact our corporate sales department at corpsales@pearsoned.com or (800) 382-3419.

For government sales inquiries, please contact governmentsales@pearsoned.com.

For questions about sales outside the U.S., please contact intlcs@pearson.com.

Editor-in-Chief	Greg Wiegand
Acquisitions Editor	Trina MacDonald
Development Editor	Rick Kughen
Managing Editor	Sandra Schroeder
Senior Project Editor	Tracey Croom
Editorial Production	Backstop Media, Troy Mott
Copy Editor	Kristin Dudley
Indexer	Julie Grady
Proofreader	Christina Rudloff
Technical Editor	Byron Wright
Cover Designer	Twist Creative, Seattle

Contents at a glance

	Introduction	xxii
	Preparing for the exam	xi
CHAPTER 1	Implement Domain Name System	1
CHAPTER 2	Implement DHCP	57
CHAPTER 3	Implement IP address management	101
CHAPTER 4	Implement network connectivity and remote access solutions	155
CHAPTER 5	Implement core and distributed network solutions	227
CHAPTER 6	Implement an advanced network infrastructure	281
	Index	317

Contents

Introduction   xi

    Organization of this book   xi
    Microsoft certifications   xii
    Acknowledgments   xii
    Free ebooks from Microsoft Press   xii
    Microsoft Virtual Academy   xii
    Quick access to online references   xiii
    Errata, updates, & book support   xiii
    We want to hear from you   xiii
    Stay in touch   xiii
    Preparing for the exam   xv

Chapter 1   Implement Domain Name System   **1**

    Skill 1.1 Install and configure DNS servers 1

        Overview of name resolution   2
        Determine DNS installation requirements   3
        Install the DNS server role   3
        Determine supported DNS deployment scenarios on Nano Server   5
        Configure forwarders, root hints, recursion, and delegation   6
        Configure advanced DNS settings   13
        Administering DNS   19

    Skill 1.2: Create and configure DNS zones and records 26

        Overview of DNS zones   26

What do you think of this book? We want to hear from you!

Microsoft is interested in hearing your feedback so we can continually improve our books and learning resources for you. To participate in a brief online survey, please visit:

https://aka.ms/tellpress

	Configure DNS zones	27
	Configure DNS records	42
	Configure DNS scopes	50
	Monitor DNS	51
	Summary	54

Thought experiment. 55

Thought experiment answers 56

Chapter 2 Implement DHCP   57

Skill 2.1: Install and configure DHCP 57

Overview of DHCP	57
Install DHCP	59
Create and manage DHCP scopes	61
Configure DHCP relay agent and PXE boot	78
Export, import and migrate a DHCP server	80

Skill 2.2: Manage and maintain DHCP. 81

Configure high availability using DHCP failover	82
Backup and restore the DHCP database	89
Troubleshoot DHCP	91
Summary	98

Thought experiment. 98

Thought experiment answer 99

Chapter 3 Implement IP address management (IPAM)   101

Skill 3.1: Install and configure IP address management. 101

Architecture	102
Requirements and planning considerations	103
Configure IPAM database storage using SQL Server	104
Provision IPAM manually or by using Group Policy	106
Configure server discovery	114
Create and manage IP blocks and ranges	118
Monitor utilization of IP address space	123
Migrate existing workloads to IPAM	124

Determine scenarios for using IPAM with System Center
VMM for physical and virtual IP address space management   125

Skill 3.2: Manage DNS and DHCP using IPAM 126
Manage DHCP with IPAM   126
Manage DNS with IPAM   136
Manage DNS and DHCP servers in multiple Active Directory
forests   141
Delegate administration for DNS and DHCP using RBAC   142

Skill 3.3: Audit IPAM 147
Audit the changes performed on the DNS and DHCP servers   148
Audit the IPAM address usage trail   149
Audit DHCP lease events and user logon events   150
Chapter summary   153

Thought experiment 153

Thought experiment answers 154

Chapter 4 Implement network connectivity and remote access solutions   155

Skill 4.1 Implement network connectivity solutions 155
Implement NAT   157
Configure routing   164

Skill 4.2: Implement VPN and DirectAccess solutions 165
Overview of VPNs   165
Determine when to use remote access VPN and S2S
VPN and to configure appropriate protocols   169
Implement DirectAccess   189
Troubleshoot DirectAccess   198

Skill 4.3 Implement NPS 199
Configure RADIUS   199
Configure NPS templates   209
Configure NPS policies   213
Configure certificates   220
Summary   223

Contents   **vii**

Thought experiment......................................224

Thought experiment answers..............................225

Chapter 5 Implement core and distributed network solutions 227

Skill 5.1: Implement IPv4 and IPv6 addressing 227

- Implement IPv4 addressing — 227
- Implement IPv6 addressing — 235
- Configure interoperability between IPv4 and IPv6 — 241
- Configure IPv4 and IPv6 routing — 245
- Configure BGP — 249

Skill 5.2: Implement DFS and branch office solutions................250

- Install and configure DFS namespaces — 251
- Configure DFS replication — 260
- Configure DFS fault tolerance — 270
- Manage DFS databases — 270
- Implement BranchCache — 271
- Chapter summary — 278

Thought experiment......................................278

Thought experiment answers..............................279

Chapter 6 Implement an advanced network infrastructure 281

Skill 6.1: Implement high performance network solutions 281

- Implement NIC teaming or the SET solution and identify when to use each — 282
- Enable and configure Receive Side Scaling (RSS) — 287
- Enable and configure network QoS with Data Center Bridging (DCB) — 291
- Enable and configure SMB Direct on RDMA-enabled network adapters — 294
- Enable and configure SR-IOV on a supported network adapter — 296

Skill 6.2: Determine scenarios and requirements for
   implementing SDN 298

   Determine requirements and scenarios for
   implementing HNV   302

   Deploying Network Controller   305

   Chapter summary   315

Thought experiment. 315

Thought experiment answers 316

Index   *317*

What do you think of this book? We want to hear from you!

Microsoft is interested in hearing your feedback so we can continually improve our books and learning resources for you. To participate in a brief online survey, please visit:

https://aka.ms/tellpress

Introduction

The 70-741 exam focuses on the networking features and functionality available in Windows Server 2016. It covers DNS, DHCP, and IPAM implementations as well as remote access solutions such as VPN and Direct Access. It also covers DFS and branch cache solutions, high performance network features and functionality, and implementation of Software Defined Networking (SDN) solutions such as Hyper-V Network Virtualization (HNV) and Network Controller.

The 70-741 exam is geared toward network administrators that are looking to reinforce their existing skills and learn about new networking technology changes and functionality in Windows Server 2016.

This book covers every major topic area found on the exam, but it does not cover every exam question. Only the Microsoft exam team has access to the exam questions, and Microsoft regularly adds new questions to the exam, making it impossible to cover specific questions. You should consider this book a supplement to your relevant real-world experience and other study materials. If you encounter a topic in this book that you do not feel completely comfortable with, use the "Need more review?" links you'll find in the text to find more information and take the time to research and study the topic. Great information is available on MSDN, TechNet, and in blogs and forums.

Organization of this book

This book is organized by the "Skills measured" list published for the exam. The "Skills measured" list is available for each exam on the Microsoft Learning website: *https://aka.ms/examlist*. Each chapter in this book corresponds to a major topic area in the list, and the technical tasks in each topic area determine a chapter's organization. If an exam covers six major topic areas, for example, the book will contain six chapters.

Microsoft certifications

Microsoft certifications distinguish you by proving your command of a broad set of skills and experience with current Microsoft products and technologies. The exams and corresponding certifications are developed to validate your mastery of critical competencies as you design and develop, or implement and support, solutions with Microsoft products and technologies both on-premises and in the cloud. Certification brings a variety of benefits to the individual and to employers and organizations.

> **MORE INFO** **ALL MICROSOFT CERTIFICATIONS**
>
> For information about Microsoft certifications, including a full list of available certifications, go to *https://www.microsoft.com/learning*.

Acknowledgments

Andrew Warren Writing a book is a collaborative effort, and so I would like to thank my editor, Trina MacDonald, for her guidance. I'd also like to thank my wife, Naomi, and daughter, Amelia, for their patience while I spent the summer locked away in my office following that guidance.

Free ebooks from Microsoft Press

From technical overviews to in-depth information on special topics, the free ebooks from Microsoft Press cover a wide range of topics. These ebooks are available in PDF, EPUB, and Mobi for Kindle formats, ready for you to download at:

https://aka.ms/mspressfree

Check back often to see what is new!

Microsoft Virtual Academy

Build your knowledge of Microsoft technologies with free expert-led online training from Microsoft Virtual Academy (MVA). MVA offers a comprehensive library of videos, live events, and more to help you learn the latest technologies and prepare for certification exams. You'll find what you need here:

https://www.microsoftvirtualacademy.com

Quick access to online references

Throughout this book are addresses to webpages that the author has recommended you visit for more information. Some of these addresses (also known as URLs) can be painstaking to type into a web browser, so we've compiled all of them into a single list that readers of the print edition can refer to while they read.

Download the list at *https://aka.ms/examref741/downloads*.

The URLs are organized by chapter and heading. Every time you come across a URL in the book, find the hyperlink in the list to go directly to the webpage.

Errata, updates, & book support

We've made every effort to ensure the accuracy of this book and its companion content. You can access updates to this book—in the form of a list of submitted errata and their related corrections—at:

https://aka.ms/examref741/errata

If you discover an error that is not already listed, please submit it to us at the same page.

If you need additional support, email Microsoft Press Book Support at *mspinput@microsoft.com*.

Please note that product support for Microsoft software and hardware is not offered through the previous addresses. For help with Microsoft software or hardware, go to *https://support.microsoft.com*.

We want to hear from you

At Microsoft Press, your satisfaction is our top priority, and your feedback our most valuable asset. Please tell us what you think of this book at:

https://aka.ms/tellpress

We know you're busy, so we've kept it short with just a few questions. Your answers go directly to the editors at Microsoft Press. (No personal information will be requested.) Thanks in advance for your input!

Stay in touch

Let's keep the conversation going! We're on Twitter: *https://twitter.com/MicrosoftPress*.

Important: How to use this book to study for the exam

Certification exams validate your on-the-job experience and product knowledge. To gauge your readiness to take an exam, use this Exam Ref to help you check your understanding of the skills tested by the exam. Determine the topics you know well and the areas in which you need more experience. To help you refresh your skills in specific areas, we have also provided "Need more review?" pointers, which direct you to more in-depth information outside the book.

The Exam Ref is not a substitute for hands-on experience. This book is not designed to teach you new skills.

We recommend that you round out your exam preparation by using a combination of available study materials and courses. Learn more about available classroom training at *https://www.microsoft.com/learning*. Microsoft Official Practice Tests are available for many exams at *https://aka.ms/practicetests*. You can also find free online courses and live events from Microsoft Virtual Academy at *https://www.microsoftvirtualacademy.com*.

This book is organized by the "Skills measured" list published for the exam. The "Skills measured" list for each exam is available on the Microsoft Learning website: *https://aka.ms/examlist*.

Note that this Exam Ref is based on this publicly available information and the author's experience. To safeguard the integrity of the exam, authors do not have access to the exam questions.

CHAPTER 1

Implement Domain Name System

Typically, users and computers use host names rather than Internet Protocol version 4 (IPv4) or Internet Protocol version 6 (IPv6) network addresses to communicate with other hosts and services on networks. A Windows Server 2016 service, known as the Domain Name System (DNS) server role, resolves these names into IPv4 or IPv6 addresses.

Since many important apps and services rely on the DNS server role, it is important that you know how to install and configure Windows Server 2016 name resolution using the DNS server role. As a result, the 70-741 Networking Windows Server 2016 exam covers how to install and configure the DNS server role on Windows Server 2016.

> **IMPORTANT**
> **Have you read page xv?**
> It contains valuable information regarding the skills you need to pass the exam.

The 70-741 Networking Windows Server 2016 exam also covers how to implement zones and Domain Name System records using the DNS server role. It is therefore important that you know how to create and manage DNS zones using the Windows Server 2016 DNS server role, and how to create and manage host and service-related records within these zones.

Skills in this chapter:
- Install and configure DNS servers
- Create and configure DNS zones and records

Skill 1.1: Install and configure DNS servers

Windows Server 2016 provides the DNS server role to enable you to provide name resolution services to devices and computers in your organization's network infrastructure. The first stage to provide name resolution is to deploy the DNS server role on Windows Server 2016 server computers.

Overview of name resolution

Although IP addressing is not especially complex, it is easier for users to work with host names rather than with the IPv4 or IPv6 addresses of hosts, such as websites, to which they want to connect. When an application, such as Microsoft Edge, references a website name, the name in the URL is converted into the underlying IPv4 or IPv6 address using a process known as name resolution. Windows 10 and Windows Server 2016 computers can use two types of names. These are:

- **Host names**   A host name, up to 255 characters in length, contains only alphanumeric characters, periods, and hyphens. A host name is an alias combined with a DNS domain name. For example, the alias *computer1*, is prefixed to the domain name, Contoso.com, to create the host name, or Fully Qualified Domain Name (FQDN), *computer1*.contoso.com.

- **NetBIOS names**   Less relevant today, NetBIOS names use a nonhierarchical structure based on a 16-character name. The sixteenth character identifies a particular service running on the computer named by the preceding 15 characters. Thus, LON-SVR1[20h] is the NetBIOS server service on the computer named LON-SVR1.

The method in which a Windows 10 or Windows Server 2016 computer resolves names varies based on its configuration, but it typically works as shown in Figure 1-1.

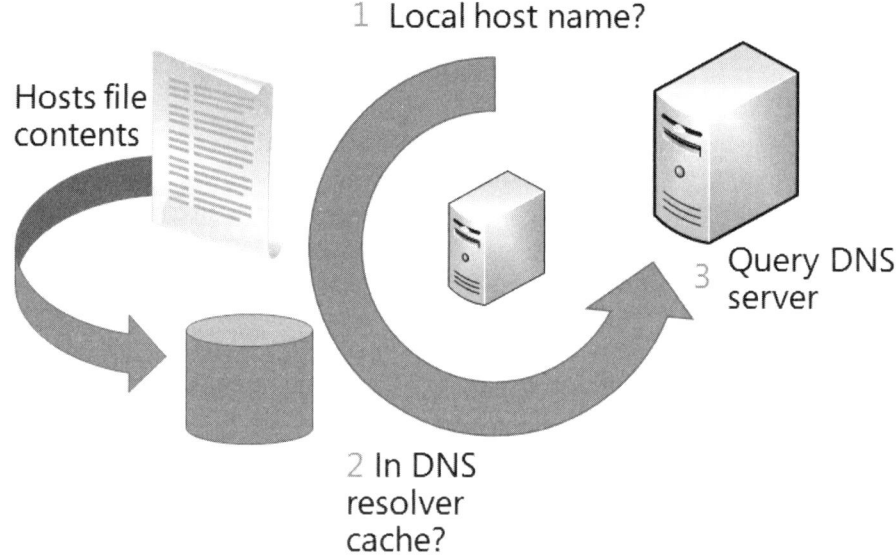

FIGURE 1-1 Typical stages of name resolution in a Windows Server computer

The following process identifies the typical stages of name resolution for a Windows 10 or Windows Server 2016 computer.

1. Determine whether the queried host name is the same as the local host name.

2. Search the local DNS resolver cache for the queried host name. The cache is updated when records are successfully resolved. In addition, the content of the local Hosts file is added to the resolver cache.

3. Petition a DNS server for the required host name.

> **NEED MORE REVIEW? IPV4 NAME RESOLUTION**
>
> To review further details about IPv4 name resolution, refer to the Microsoft TechNet website at *https://technet.microsoft.com/library/dd379505(v=ws.10).aspx*.

Of course, name resolution in Windows Server 2016 does more than just provide for simple name to IP mapping. The DNS server role is also used by computers to locate services within the network infrastructure. For example, when a computer starts up, the user must sign-in to the Active Directory Domain Services (AD DS) domain and perhaps open Microsoft Office Outlook. This means that the client computer must locate a server that can provide authentication services in the local AD DS site, and furthermore, locate the appropriate Microsoft Exchange mailbox server for the user. These processes require DNS.

Determine DNS installation requirements

Before you can install the DNS server role, you must verify that your server computer meets the installation requirements of the role.

The DNS server role installation requirements are:

- **Security** You must sign in on the server computer as a member of the local Administrators group.
- **IP configuration** The server must have a statically assigned IPv4 and/or IPv6 configuration. This ensures that client computers can locate the DNS server role by using its IP address.

In addition to these server requirements, you must also be prepared to answer questions that relate to your organization's network infrastructure. These organizational questions pertain to your Internet presence, and the registered domain names that you intend to use publicly. Although you need not define these domain names during DNS role installation, you must provide this information when you configure the DNS role.

Install the DNS server role

You can install the DNS server role by using Server Manager, or by using Windows PowerShell.

Installing DNS with Server Manager

To install the DNS server role with Server Manager, use the following procedure:

1. Sign in to the target server as a local administrator.
2. Open Server Manager.

3. In Server Manager, click Manage and then click Add Roles And Features.
4. In the Add Roles And Features Wizard's Before You Begin page, click Next.
5. On the Select Installation Type page, click Role-Based or Feature-Based Installation, and click Next.
6. On the Select Destination Server page, select the server from the Server Pool list, and click Next.
7. In the Roles list on the Select Server Roles page, select the DNS Server (see Figure 1-2).
8. In the Add Roles And Features Wizard pop-up dialog box, click Add Features, and then click Next.
9. On the Select features page, click Next.
10. On the DNS Server page, click Next.
11. On the Confirm Installation Selections page, click Install. When the installation is complete, click Close.

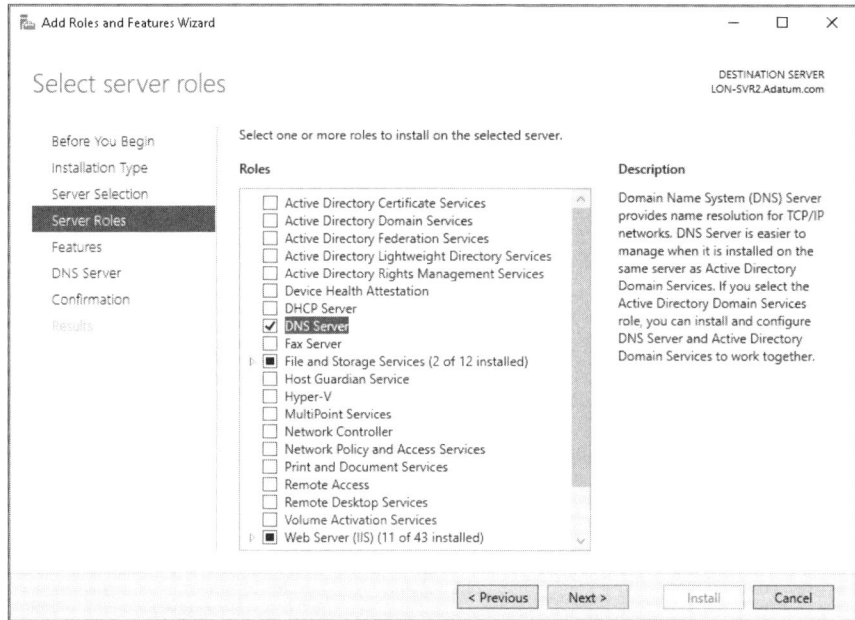

FIGURE 1-2 Installing the DNS Server role by using Server Manager

Installing DNS with Windows PowerShell

Although using Server Manager to install server roles and features is simple, it is not always the quickest method. To install the DNS server role and all related management tools by using Windows PowerShell, use the following procedure:

1. Sign in to the target server as a local administrator.

2. Open an elevated Windows PowerShell window.
3. At the Windows PowerShell prompt, as shown in Figure 1-3, type the following command and press Enter:

   Add-WindowsFeature DNS -IncludeManagementTools

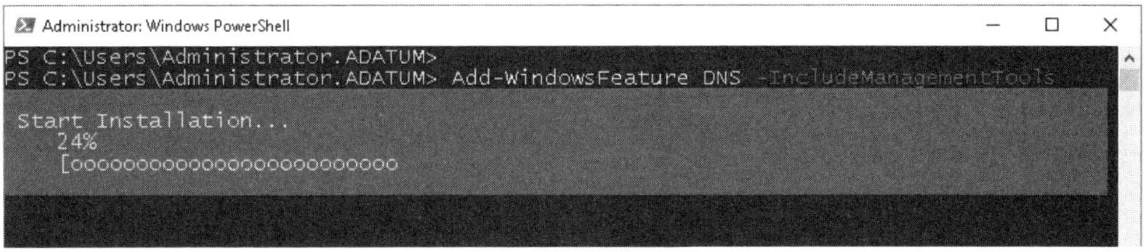

FIGURE 1-3 Installing the DNS Server with Windows PowerShell

Determine supported DNS deployment scenarios on Nano Server

Nano Server is a new Windows Server 2016 deployment option. It is similar to Windows Server Core, but has much smaller hardware requirements. Nano Server also has very limited local sign-in capabilities and local administration function, and supports only 64-bit apps, agents, and tools.

There are a number of situations when you should consider choosing Nano Server over other Windows Server deployment options. For example, Nano Server provides a good platform for a web server running Internet Information Services (IIS). Also, Nano Server is ideally suited to run the DNS server role.

> **NEED MORE REVIEW? GETTING STARTED WITH NANO SERVER**
>
> To review further details about working with Nano Server, refer to the Microsoft TechNet website at *https://technet.microsoft.com/windows-server-docs/compute/nano-server/getting-started-with-nano-server*.

To install the DNS server role on Nano Server, you can use one of the following two strategies.

- **Install the DNS server role as part of the Nano Server deployment** When you deploy Nano Server with the New-NanoServerImage cmdlet, you can use the -Packages Microsoft-NanoServer-DNS-Package parameter to install the DNS server role.
- **Add the role after deployment** After you have deployed Nano Server, you can add the DNS server role by using either Server Manager or Windows PowerShell. However, since Nano Server is a headless server platform with very little local management capability, you must remotely manage the server.

You can add the role to Nano server using one of the following methods:

- From Server Manager, use the Add Other Servers To Manage option to add the Nano Server as a manageable server. Then add the DNS Server role to the server using the procedure outlined earlier in this chapter (see "Installing DNS with Server Manager").
- Establish a Windows PowerShell remoting session with the Nano Server by using the Enter-PSSession cmdlet. You can then use Windows PowerShell cmdlets to install the DNS server role, as described earlier in this chapter. For example, to add the DNS role to a Nano Server from a Windows PowerShell remote session, use the following command:

```
Enable-WindowsOptionalFeature -Online -FeatureName DNS-Server-Full-Role
```

EXAM TIP

Active Directory integrated DNS is not supported on Nano Server, which means that you can implement file-based DNS only on Nano Server.

> *NEED MORE REVIEW?* **ENABLE AND USE REMOTE COMMANDS IN WINDOWS POWERSHELL**
>
> To review further details about using Windows PowerShell remoting, refer to the Microsoft TechNet website at *https://technet.microsoft.com/magazine/ff700227.aspx*.

Configure forwarders, root hints, recursion, and delegation

After you have installed the DNS server role on your Windows Server 2016 server computer, you must configure it. This involves configuring forwarding, root hints, recursion, and delegation.

Configure forwarders

DNS forwarding enables you to define what happens to a DNS query when the petitioned DNS server is unable to resolve that DNS query. For example, you can configure and use DNS forwarding to control the flow of DNS requests throughout your organization so that only specific DNS servers are used to handle Internet DNS queries.

With DNS forwarding, you can:

- Configure a DNS server only to respond to those queries that it can satisfy by reference to locally stored zone information. For all other requests, the petitioned DNS server must forward the request to another DNS server.
- Define the forwarding behavior for specific DNS domains by configuring DNS conditional forwarding. In this scenario, if the DNS query contains a specific domain name, for example Contoso.com, then it is forwarded to a specific DNS server.

To configure forwarding, use the following procedure:

1. In Server Manager, click Tools, and then click DNS.
2. In DNS Manager, right-click the DNS server in the navigation pane and click Properties.
3. In the Server Properties dialog box, on the Forwarders tab, click Edit.
4. In the IP Address list located in the Edit Forwarders dialog box, enter the IP address of the server to which you want to forward all DNS queries, and then click OK. You can configure several DNS servers here; those servers are petitioned in preference order. You can also set a timeout value, in seconds, after which the query is timed out
5. In the Server Properties dialog box on the Forwarders tab you can view and edit the list of DNS forwarders, as shown in Figure 1-4. You can also determine what happens when no DNS forwarders can be contacted. By default, when forwarders cannot be contacted, root hints are used. Root hints are discussed in the next section. Click OK to complete configuration.

FIGURE 1-4 Configuring DNS forwarding

EXAM TIP

You can also configure forwarding by using the Add-DnsServerForwarder Windows PowerShell cmdlet.

To enable and configure conditional forwarding, use the following procedure:

1. In DNS Manager, right-click the Conditional Forwarders node in the navigation pane, and then click New Conditional Forwarder.

2. On the New Conditional Forwarder dialog box, in the DNS Domain box, type the domain name for which you want to create a conditional forward, as shown in Figure 1-5. Next, in the IP address of the master servers list, enter the IP address of the server to use as a forwarder for this domain; press Enter.

3. Optionally, specify the Number of Seconds Before Forward Queries Time Out value. The default value is 5 seconds.

4. Click OK.

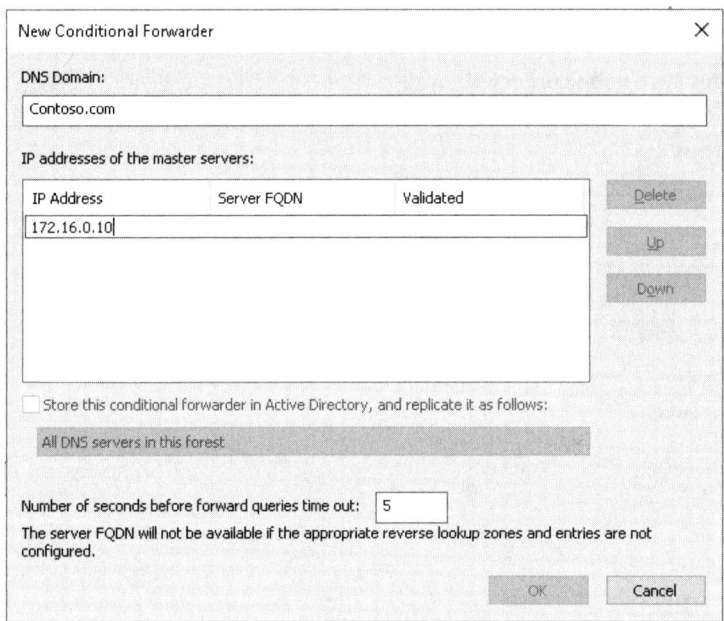

FIGURE 1-5 Configuring conditional DNS forwarding

EXAM TIP

You can use the Add-DnsServerConditionalForwarderZone Windows PowerShell cmdlet to configure conditional forwarding.

Configure root hints

If you do not specify DNS forwarding, then when a petitioned DNS server is unable to satisfy a DNS query, it uses root hints to determine how to resolve it. Before we look at root hints, it is important that you understand how an Internet DNS query is handled.

HOW AN INTERNET DNS QUERY IS HANDLED

A client app, such as Microsoft Edge, wants to resolve a name (like www.contoso.com) to the relevant IPv4 address. This app is referred to as a DNS client. The process used to resolve this name is described next and is shown in Figure 1-6.

1. The DNS client petitions its configured DNS server for the required record (for example, www.contoso.com) using a recursive query.

> **EXAM TIP**
>
> When a DNS server receives a recursive query, it either returns the required result, or it returns an error; the DNS server does not refer the DNS client to another server.

- The petitioned DNS server checks to see if it is authoritative for the required record. If it is, it returns the requested information.
- If it is not authoritative, the DNS server checks its local cache to determine if the record was recently resolved. If the record exists in cache, it is returned to the petitioning client.

2. If the record is not cached, then the DNS server uses a series of iterative queries to other DNS servers in which it requests the petitioned record. It starts with the root server.

> **EXAM TIP**
>
> When a DNS server receives an iterative query, it either returns the required result, or it returns a referral to another server that might be authoritative for the requested record.

3. The record returns it if the root server is authoritative for the requested record. Otherwise, the root server returns the IP address of a DNS server authoritative for the next down-level domain, in this instance .com.
4. The original DNS server petitions the specified .com DNS server using another iterative query.
5. The .com DNS server is not authoritative, and so returns the IP address of the Contoso.com DNS server.
6. The original DNS server petitions the specified Contoso.com DNS server using another iterative query.
7. The Contoso.com DNS server is authoritative, and so returns the required information—in this case, the IPv4 address for www.contoso.com.
8. The original DNS server caches the record and returns the requested information to the DNS client.

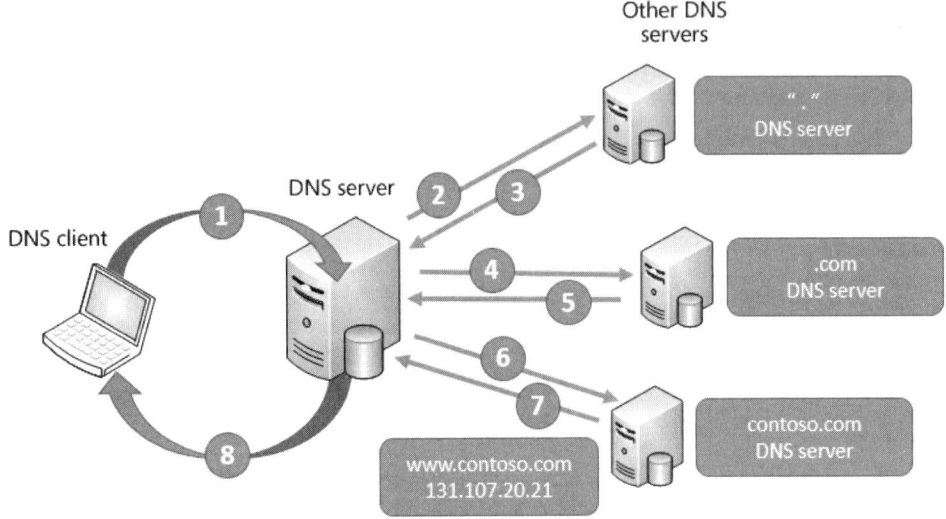

FIGURE 1-6 How Internet DNS queries work

HOW ROOT HINTS ARE USED

As you can see in the preceding explanation and diagram, if a DNS server is not authoritative and holds no cache for that DNS domain, it petitions a root server to start the process of determining which server is authoritative for the petitioned record. However, without the IP address of the root name servers, this process cannot begin.

Root hints are used by DNS servers to enable them to navigate the DNS hierarchy on the Internet, starting at the root. Microsoft DNS servers are preconfigured with the relevant root hint records. However, you can modify the list of root hint servers by using the DNS Manager console or by using Windows PowerShell.

 EXAM TIP

By default, the DNS Server service implements root hints by using a file, CACHE.DNS, that is stored in the %systemroot%\System32\dns folder on the server computer.

You might consider editing the root hints information if you want to configure the flow of DNS query traffic within your internal network. This is also useful between your internal network and the boundary network, which sits between your internal network and the Internet.

EDITING ROOT HINTS

To modify the root hints information using DNS Manager, use the following procedure:

1. In Server Manager, click Tools, and then click DNS.
2. In the DNS Manager console, locate the appropriate DNS server. Right-click the server and click Properties.

3. In the server Properties dialog box, click the Root Hints tab, as shown in Figure 1-7.
4. You can then add new records, or edit or remove any existing records. You can also click Copy From Server to import the root hints from another online DNS server. Click OK when you have finished editing root hints.

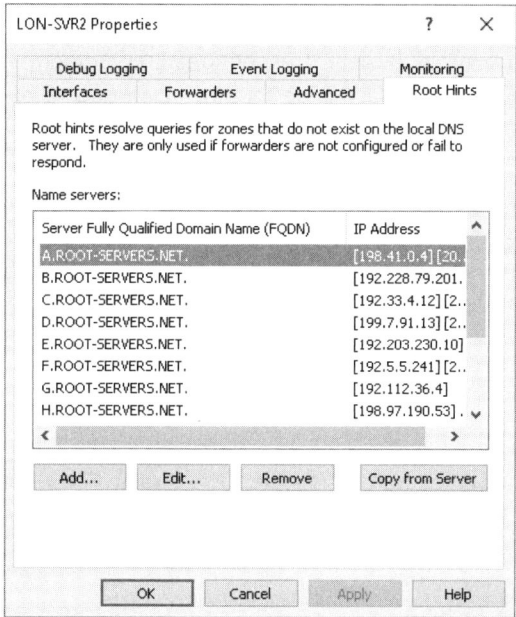

FIGURE 1-7 Configuring root hints

Also, you can use Windows PowerShell to modify the root hints information on your DNS server. The following cmdlets are available to manage root hints:

- **Add-DnsServerRootHint** Enables you to add new root hints records.
- **Remove-DnsServerRootHint** Enables you to delete root hints records.
- **Set-DnsServerRootHint** Enables you to edit existing root hints records. You can also use the Get-DnsServerRootHint cmdlet to retrieve the required record for editing.
- **Import-DnsServerRootHint** Enables you to copy the root hints information from another online DNS server.

For example, to update the value for the root hints assigned to H.Root-servers.adatum.com, use the following two Windows PowerShell commands:

```
$hint = (Get-DnsServerRootHint | Where-Object {$_.NameServer.RecordData.NameServer
 -eq "H.Root-Servers.Adatum.com."} )

$hint.IPAddress[0].RecordData.Ipv4address = "10.24.60.254"
```

The first command obtains the H.Root-servers.adatum.com root hint and assigns it to the variable $hint. The Get-DnsServerRootHint cmdlet obtains the list of all root hints, and the Where-Object cmdlet filters the results to get only the root hint for H.Root-servers.adatum.com.

Configure recursion

Recursion is the name resolution process when a petitioned DNS server queries other DNS servers to resolve a DNS query on behalf of a requesting client. The petitioned server then returns the answer to the DNS client. By default, all DNS servers perform recursive queries on behalf of their DNS clients and other DNS servers that have forwarded DNS client queries to them.

However, since malicious people can use recursion as a means to attempt a denial of service attack on your DNS servers, you should consider disabling recursion on any DNS server in your network that is not intended to receive recursive queries.

To disable recursion, use the following procedure:

1. From Server Manager, click Tools, and then click DNS.
2. In the DNS Manager console, right-click the appropriate server, and then click Properties.
3. Click the Advanced tab, and then in the Server options list, select the Disable Recursion (Also Disables Forwarders) check box, as shown in Figure 1-8, and then click OK.

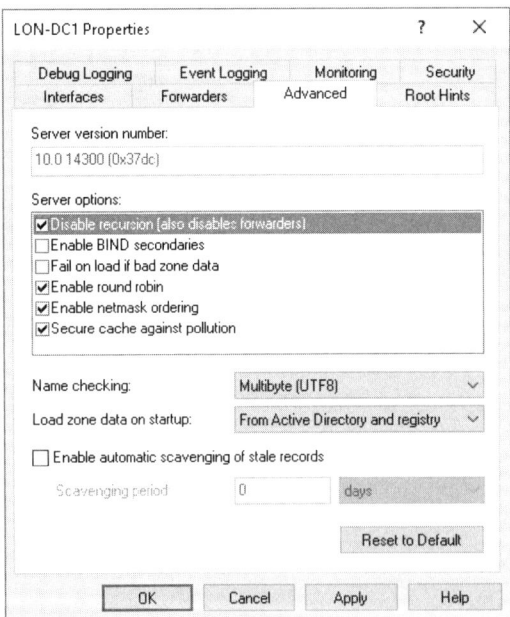

FIGURE 1-8 Disabling recursion

RECURSION SCOPES

While it might seem like a good idea to disable recursion, there are servers that must perform recursion for their clients and other DNS servers. However, these are still at risk from malicious network attacks. Windows Server 2016 supports a feature known as *recursion scopes*, which allow you to control recursive query behavior. To do this, you must use DNS Server Policies.

For example, you might have a DNS server that should be able to perform recursive queries for internal clients within the Adatum.com domain, but should not accept any recursive queries from Internet-based computers. To configure this behavior, open Windows PowerShell and then run the following two commands:

```
Set-DnsServerRecursionScope -Name . -EnableRecursion $False

Add-DnsServerRecursionScope -Name "InternalAdatumClients" -EnableRecursion $True
```

The first command disables recursion for the default recursion scope, which as a result, turns off recursion. The default scope consists of the server-level recursion and forwarding settings that we previously discussed (see "Configure forwarders, root hints, recursion, and delegation," in this chapter).

The second command creates a new recursion scope called InternalAdatumClients. Recursion is enabled for clients in this scope. Next, you must define which clients are part of the recursion scope. Use the following Windows PowerShell command to achieve this:

```
Add-DnsServerQueryResolutionPolicy -Name "RecursionControlPolicy" -Action ALLOW
-ApplyOnRecursion -RecursionScope "InternalAdatumClients" -ServerInterfaceIP
"EQ,10.24.60.254"
```

In this example, client requests received on the DNS server interface with the IP 10.24.60.254 are evaluated as belonging to InternalAdatumClients, and recursion is enabled. For client requests received on other server interfaces, recursion is disabled.

> **NEED MORE REVIEW?** **ADD-DNSSERVERQUERYRESOLUTIONPOLICY**
>
> For more information about using Windows PowerShell to configure recursion scopes, visit the TechNet website at *https://technet.microsoft.com/library/mt126273.aspx*.

Configure delegation

This content is covered in Chapter 1, Implement Domain Name System: "Configure delegation."

Configure advanced DNS settings

Configuring forwarding, recursion, and root hints enables you to control the fundamentals of how DNS queries are processed within your organization. After you have configured these settings, you can move on to enable and configure more advanced settings.

Configure DNSSEC

DNSSEC is a security setting for DNS that enables all the DNS records in a DNS zone to be digitally signed so DNS clients are able to verify the identity of the DNS server. DNSSEC helps ensure that the DNS client is communicating with a genuine DNS server.

> **NOTE DNS ZONES**
> Creating and managing DNS zones is covered in "Create DNS Zones."

When a client queries a DNS server that has been configured with DNSSEC, the server returns any DNS results along with a digital signature. To ensure that the signature is valid, the DNS client obtains the public key of the public/private key pair associated with this signature from a *trust anchor*. In order for this to work, you must configure your DNS clients with a trust anchor for the signed DNS zone.

TRUST ANCHORS

To implement DNSSEC, you must create a TrustAnchors zone. This zone is used to store public keys associated with specific DNS zones. You must create a trust anchor from the secured zone on every DNS server that hosts the zone.

NAME RESOLUTION POLICY TABLE

Additionally, you must create, configure, and distribute a Name Resolution Policy Table (NRPT). A DNSSEC rule in the NRPT is used by clients to determine DNS client behavior and is used by DNSSEC to instruct the client to request validation through the use of a signature.

> **EXAM TIP**
> It is usual in Active Directory Domain Services (AD DS) environments to use Group Policy Objects (GPOs) to distribute the NRPT.

IMPLEMENTING DNSSEC

After installing Windows Server 2016 and deploying the DNS server role to the server, use the following procedure to implement DNSSEC:

1. Launch the DNSSEC Configuration Wizard from the DNS Manager console to sign the DNS zone. In DNS Manager, right-click the desired zone, point to DNSSEC, and then click Sign The Zone. When you sign the zone, as shown in Figure 1-9, you can choose between three options.

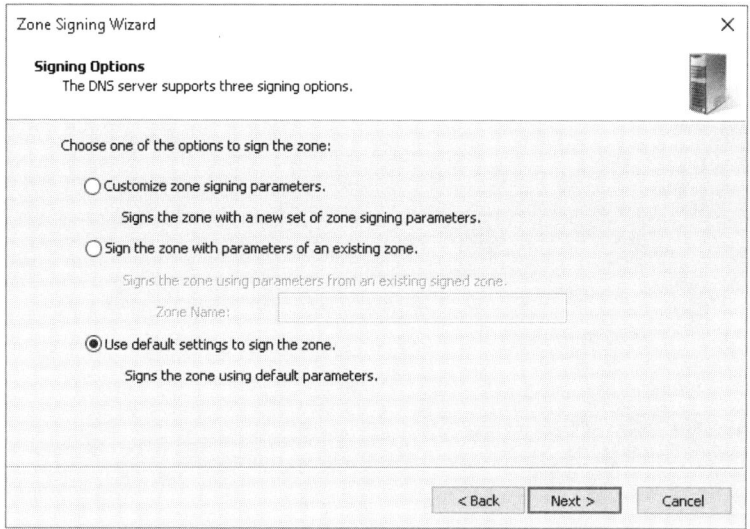

FIGURE 1-9 Signing a DNS zone

- **Customize Zone Signing Parameters**   Enables you to configure all values for the Key Signing Key (KSK) and the Zone Signing Key (ZSK).
- **Sign The Zone With Parameters Of An Existing Zone**   Enables you to use the same values and options as an existing signed zone.
- **Use Default Settings To Sign The Zone**   Signs the zone using default values.

2. Configure Trust Anchor Distribution Points   You can choose this option if you select the Customize Zone Signing Parameters option above. Otherwise, after you have signed the zone, use the following procedure to configure trust anchor distribution points:

   A. In DNS Manager, right-click the desired zone, point to DNSSEC, and then click Properties.

   B. In the DNSSEC Properties For Selected Zone dialog box, on the Trust Anchor tab, as shown in Figure 1-10, select the Enable The Distribution Of Trust Anchors For This Zone check box, and click OK. When prompted, click Yes, and then click OK.

   C. Verify that the Trust Points node exists and contains the relevant DNS KEY (DNSKEY) records. To do this, in DNS Manager, expand the Server node and then expand Trust Points. It contains sub nodes for your DNS zones, which contain two DNS KEY (DNSKEY) records.

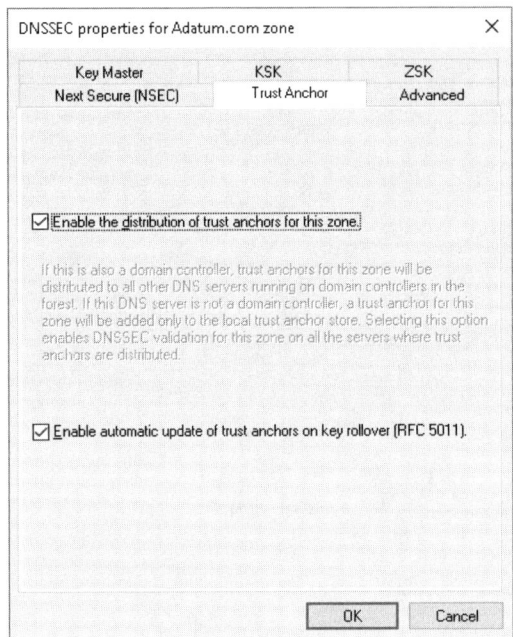

FIGURE 1-10 Enabling trust anchor distribution

3. **Configure the NRPT on the client computers** You must distribute the NRPT to all client computers so that they know to request validation using DNSSEC. The easiest way to achieve this is to use GPO distribution:

   A. Open Group Policy Management and locate the Default Domain Policy.

   B. Open this policy for editing and navigate to Computer Configuration / Policies / Windows Settings / Name Resolution Policy, as shown in Figure 1-11.

   C. In the Create Rules section, type the name of your domain (for example, Adatum.com) in the Suffix text box; doing so applies the rule to the suffix of that namespace.

   D. Select the Enable DNSSEC in this Rule check box, select the Require DNS Clients To Check That The Name And Address Data Has Been Validated By The DNS Server check box, and then click Create.

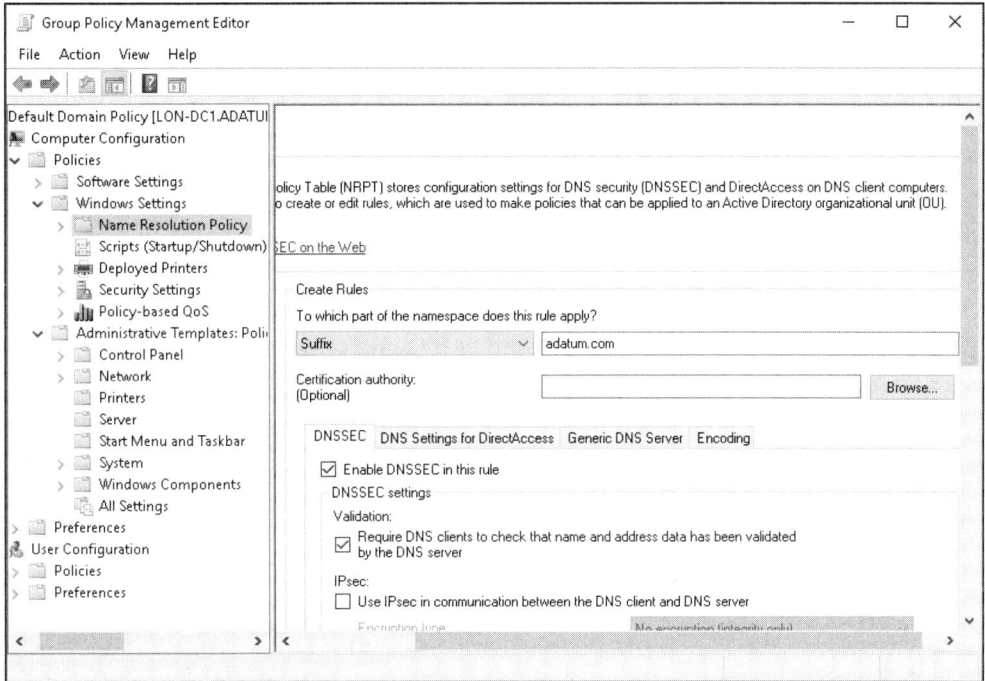

FIGURE 1-11 Creating the NRPT GPO

> **NEED MORE REVIEW? STEP-BY-STEP: DEMONSTRATE DNSSEC IN A TEST LAB**
>
> For more information about implementing DNSSEC, refer to the Microsoft TechNet website at *https://technet.microsoft.com/library/hh831411(v=ws.11).aspx*.

Configure DNS socket pool

You can use the DNS socket pool to enable a DNS server to use a random source port when issuing DNS queries. If you enable DNS socket pool the DNS server selects a source port from a pool of available sockets when the DNS service starts. This means that the DNS server avoids using well-known ports. This can help to secure the DNS server because a malicious person must guess both the source port of a DNS query and a random transaction ID to successfully run a malicious attack.

You can use the DNSCMD.exe command-line tool to configure the DNS socket pool size.

From an elevated command prompt, run the dnscmd /Config /SocketPoolSize <value> command and then restart the DNS server. You can configure the socket pool size from 0 through 10,000. The default pool size is 2,500.

Configure cache locking

When a DNS client queries a recursive DNS server, the server caches the result so that it can respond more quickly to other DNS clients querying the same information. The amount of time that a record resides in cache is determined by the Time To Live (TTL) value of the record.

During the TTL, a record can be overwritten if more recent data is available for the record. However, this potentially exposes a security issue. A malicious person might be able to overwrite the record in cache with information that could redirect clients to a site containing unsafe content.

To mitigate this risk in Windows Server 2016, you can use cache locking to determine when information in the DNS resolver cache can be overwritten. When you enable cache locking, the DNS server does not allow updates to cached records until the TTL expires.

To configure cache locking, on your DNS server, run the Set-DnsServerCache –LockingPercent <value> Windows PowerShell command. The <value> you enter is a percentage of the TTL. For example, if you type 75, then the DNS server does not allow updates to the cached record until at least 75 percent of the TTL has expired.

EXAM TIP

By default, the cache locking percentage value is 100, which means that cached entries cannot be overwritten for the entire duration of the TTL.

Enable response rate limiting

Another security feature you can use in Windows Server 2016 is response rate limiting, which is as a defense against DNS denial-of-service attacks. One common DNS denial-of-service attack is to fool DNS servers into sending large amounts of DNS traffic to particular DNS servers, thus overloading the target servers.

When a configured DNS server with response rate limiting identifies potentially malicious requests, it ignores them instead of propagating them. The DNS server can identify potentially malicious requests because many identical requests in a short time period from the same source are suspicious.

By default, response rate limiting is disabled. To enable response rate limiting, run the Set-DnsServerResponseRateLimiting Windows PowerShell command. This enables response rate limiting using the default values. You can also supply command parameters to customize response rate limiting.

NEED MORE REVIEW? SET-DNSSERVERRESPONSERATELIMITING

For more information about configuring DNS response rate limiting, refer to the Microsoft TechNet website at *https://technet.microsoft.com/library/mt422603.aspx*.

Configure DNS-based authentication of named entities

Windows Server 2016 supports a new feature known as DNS-Based Authentication of Named Entities (DANE). This feature relies on using Transport Layer Security Authentication (TLSA) and can help reduce man-in-the-middle type attacks on your network.

DANE works by informing DNS clients requesting records from your domain from which Certification Authority (CA) they must expect digital certificates to be issued. For example, suppose a DNS client requests the IPv4 address relating to the record https://www.adatum.com. The DNS server provides the requested IPv4 address and related information. However, the DNS server also provides information that the certificate used to authenticate the identity of the webserver www.adatum.com is provided by a particular CA.

Administering DNS

It is important that you know how to administer your DNS servers. You can use tools such as Windows PowerShell and the DNS Manager console to interactively administer the DNS servers in your organization. However, in large enterprise environments, it can be difficult to keep on top of administration of such a critical service. In these circumstances, you can consider implementing DNS policies, delegating DNS administration to a specialist team, and using DNS logging as an indicator of potential problems with DNS.

Implement DNS policies

DNS Policy is a new feature in Windows Server 2016 that enables you to control how a DNS server behaves in a particular set of circumstances. For example, we have already seen how you can implement recursion scopes to control DNS recursion based on certain factors; this is an example of a DNS policy in action.

You can create one or several DNS policies as your organizational needs dictate. However, common reasons for implementing DNS policies include:

- **Application high availability**   The DNS server redirects clients to the healthiest endpoint for an application based, for example, on high availability factors in a failover cluster.
- **Traffic management**   The DNS server redirects clients to the nearest server or datacenter.
- **Split-brain DNS**   The DNS server responds to clients based on whether the client is external or internal to your organization's intranet.
- **Filtering**   The DNS server blocks DNS queries if they are from malicious hosts.
- **Forensics**   The DNS server redirects malicious DNS clients to a sinkhole instead of the host they are attempting to reach.
- **Time-of-day based redirection**   The DNS server redirects clients to servers or datacenters based on the time.

To implement DNS policies, you must use Windows PowerShell commands. However, you must first be able to classify groups of records in a DNS zone, DNS clients on a specific network, or other characteristics that can help identify the DNS clients. You can use the following DNS objects to characterize your DNS clients:

- **Client subnet**   The IPv4 or IPv6 subnet containing the DNS clients.
- **Recursion scope**   The unique instances of a group of settings that control DNS server recursion.
- **Zone scopes**   Contains its own set of DNS resource records. A record can exist in several scopes, each with a different IP address depending on the scope. DNS zones can have multiple zone scopes.

To implement DNS policies, you must first define one or more of the above objects to classify your DNS clients and scopes.

1. For example, to create a subnet for DNS clients in New York, use the following command:

    ```
    Add-DnsServerClientSubnet -Name "NYCSubnet" -IPv4Subnet "172.16.0.0/24"
    ```

2. You need to create multiple client subnet objects based on the IPv4 or IPv6 subnet address.

3. Next, you create a DNS zone scope for New York DNS clients by using the following command:

    ```
    Add-DnsServerZoneScope -ZoneName "Adatum.com" -Name "NYCZoneScope"
    ```

4. Again, you would need to create multiple zone scopes based on your requirements.

5. Next, to create a specific IP address record for clients in the New York City zone scope, run the following command:

    ```
    Add-DnsServerResourceRecord -ZoneName "Adatum.com" -A -Name "www" -IPv4Address "172.16.0.41" -ZoneScope "NYCZoneScope"
    ```

6. Finally, you create the policy that instructs the DNS server to respond based upon the previously defined factors:

    ```
    Add-DnsServerQueryResolutionPolicy -Name "NYCPolicy" -Action ALLOW -ClientSubnet "eq,NYCSubnet" -ZoneScope "NYCZoneScope,1" -ZoneName "Adatum.com"
    ```

Now, if a client in the New York subnet petitions a DNS server for the IPv4 address of the www.adatum.com host, the DNS server responds with the IP address 172.16.0.41. If you create other subnets and zone scopes for other locations, you could instruct the DNS server to respond with a different IP address for client queries from other locations.

> **NEED MORE REVIEW?**   **DNS POLICIES OVERVIEW**
>
> For more information about configuring DNS policies, refer to the Microsoft TechNet website at *https://technet.microsoft.com/windows-server-docs/networking/dns/deploy/dns-policies-overview.*

Configure delegated administration

By default, the following groups have administrative capabilities over your organization's DNS servers:

- **Domain Admins** Has full permissions to manage all aspects of the DNS server in its home domain.
- **Enterprise Admins** Has full permissions to manage all aspects of all DNS servers in any domain in your AD DS forest.
- **DnsAdmins** Can view and modify all DNS data, settings, and configurations of DNS servers in their home domain.

In a small to medium network, it is generally acceptable to use these defaults. However, in large network environments, it can be beneficial to delegate administration for aspects of DNS management to different teams.

If you decide to delegate DNS Server administration to a different user or group, you can add that user or group to the DnsAdmins group for a given domain in the forest. To modify membership of this group, you can use Active Directory Users and Computers or the Windows PowerShell Add-ADGroupMember cmdlet.

To configure DNS administrative permissions, right-click the appropriate DNS server or DNS zone in the DNS Manager console, , and then click Properties. n the Server Properties or Zone Properties dialog box, on the Security tab, you can view and modify permissions for the server or zone, as shown in Figure 1-12.

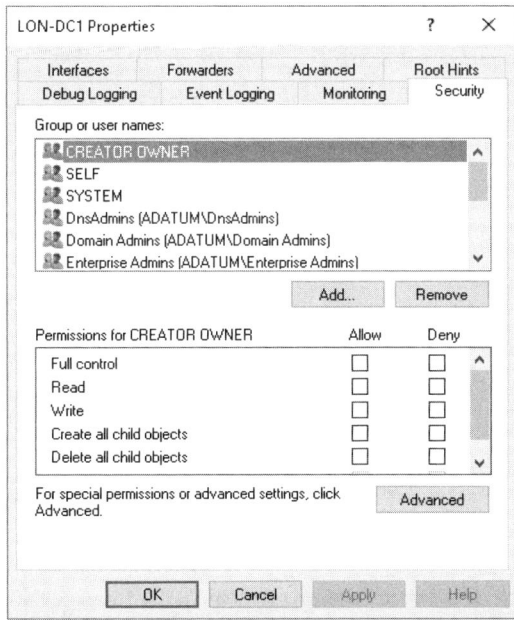

FIGURE 1-12 Delegating DNS administration

Configure DNS logging

Enabling logging can be very beneficial for proactive monitoring, especially when you are investigating poor performance or spurious and unexpected service behavior. By default, DNS records events into a DNS server log that you can review using Event Viewer. The DNS server log is located under the Application and Services Logs node, as shown in Figure 1-13.

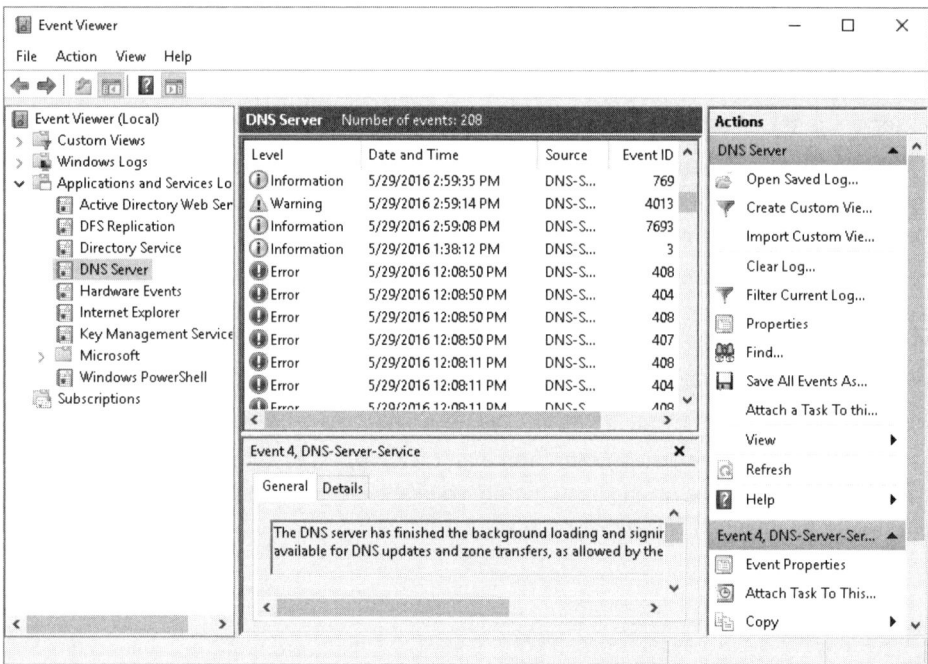

FIGURE 1-13 Viewing the DNS server event log

This log contains common DNS related events, such as service starts and stops, zone signing events, configuration changes, and common warnings and errors.

You can also enable more detailed logging with *debug* logging. However, you should exercise caution when enabling debug logging as it can impose load on the DNS server that might impact service delivery. Debug logging provides the following additional details:

- Packet direction (Outgoing or Incoming)
- Packet contents (Queries/Transfers, Updates, or Notifications)
- Transport protocol (UDP or TCP)
- Packet type (Request or Response)
- Filtering packets by IP address
- Name and location of the log file, which defaults to the %systemroot%\System32\DNS directory
- Log file maximum size limit

To enable debug logging, from the DNS Manager console:

1. Right-click the relevant DNS server, and then click Properties.
2. In the Server Properties dialog box, click the Debug Logging tab, as shown in Figure 1-14, select the Log Packets For Debugging check box, select the events for which you want the DNS server to record debug logging, and then click OK.

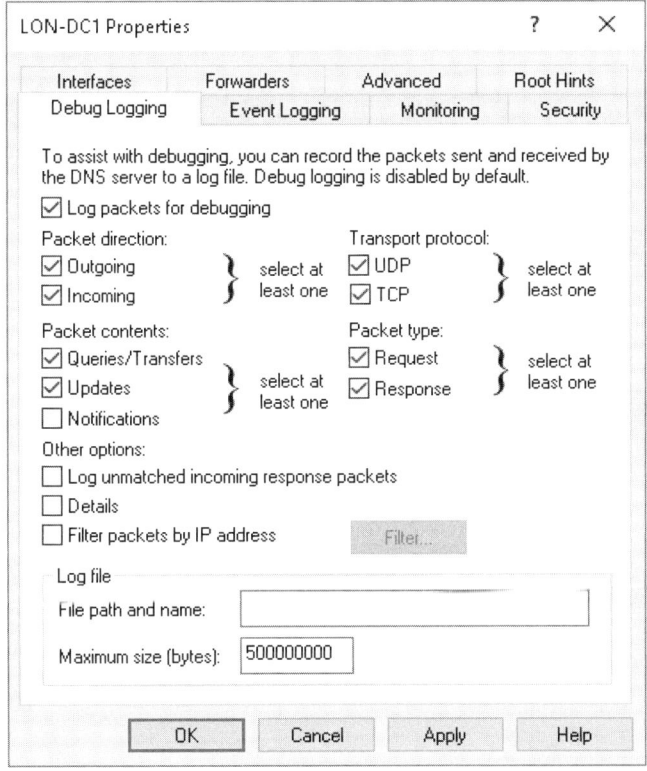

FIGURE 1-14 Configuring DNS Debug logging

Implement DNS performance tuning

The DNS server role, like other server roles and services, can be affected by the poor performance of your server. Poor performance is often caused by lack of server resources: memory, CPU, sufficient disk throughput, and network bandwidth. You can use general tools, such as Performance Monitor, to gauge whether these resources are sufficient in your server and to determine which resources are causing a bottleneck.

When any one or more of these resources is insufficient, a performance bottleneck is created. The solution is to identify which resource has the bottleneck, and to optimize that resource, often by adding more of that resource. The alternative is to distribute the load by adding additional DNS servers.

> **NEED MORE REVIEW? WINDOWS PERFORMANCE MONITOR**
>
> For more information about using Performance Monitor, refer to the Microsoft TechNet website at *https://technet.microsoft.com/library/cc749249(v=ws.11).aspx*.

The two key resources in the DNS server role are CPU and memory. The DNS tab in the Server Manager console provides a Performance pane that you can use to monitor these two critical resources, as shown in Figure 1-15.

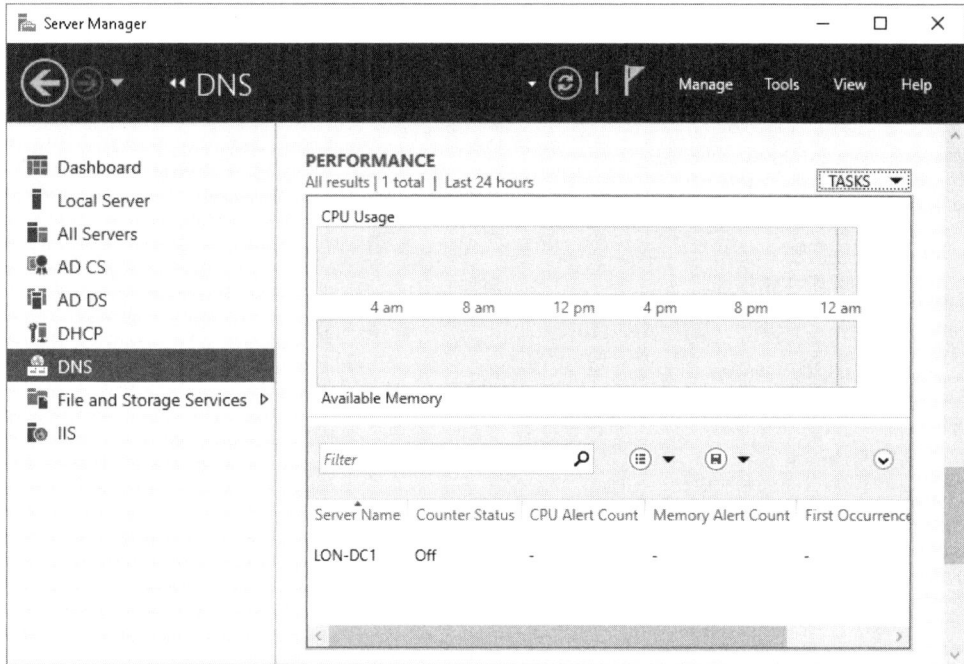

FIGURE 1-15 Monitoring DNS performance

To start monitoring these resources, click Tasks, and then click Configure Performance Alerts. In the DNS Server: Configure Performance Alerts dialog box, you can configure thresholds for alerts for both CPU (percent usage) and Memory (MB available) as shown in Figure 1-16. Click Save when you are ready.

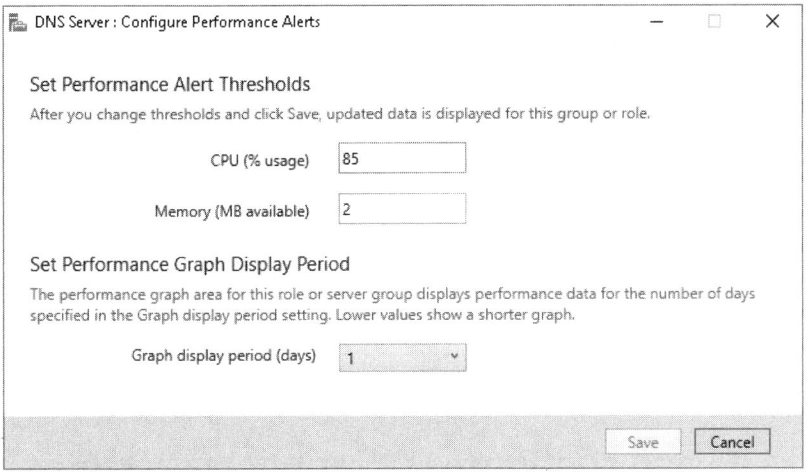

FIGURE 1-16 Configuring DNS performance alerts

Aside from these fundamental server performance characteristics, you can configure the DNS server to help to optimize DNS responsiveness. For example, allowing a DNS server to perform recursion involves imposing additional load on the DNS server when it is unable to provide an authoritative response to a client query. By disabling recursion, you can reduce the load on that DNS server, but at the cost of preventing it from using recursion. Similarly, removing root hints prevents a server from querying the Internet DNS tree on behalf of clients, which reduces workload.

Many of the performance-related decisions you make might have a functionality impact on the way name resolution works within your organization. That means you must consider that impact carefully. To help you plan DNS optimization, you should create a standard DNS server and then perform performance monitoring on the server while it is under a typical query load. You can use tools, such as the industry standard *dnsperf* tool, to help determine the optimum queries per second value for your standard server.

> **NEED MORE REVIEW?** **NAME RESOLUTION PERFORMANCE OF AUTHORITATIVE WINDOWS DNS SERVER**
>
> The following TechNet blog article contains a test procedure for optimizing Microsoft DNS servers at *https://blogs.technet.microsoft.com/networking/2015/08/13/name-resolution-performance-of-authoritative-windows-dns-server-2012-r2/*.

Implement DNS global settings using Windows PowerShell and configure global settings using Windows PowerShell

So far, throughout this chapter, you have seen that you can perform many of the implementation and configuration tasks on DNS servers by using Windows PowerShell. In Skill 1.2: Create and configure DNS zones and records, you explore more Windows PowerShell cmdlets for the DNS server role.

> **NEED MORE REVIEW? DOMAIN NAME SYSTEM (DNS) SERVER CMDLETS**
>
> To review a complete list of Windows PowerShell cmdlets for DNS server, refer to the Microsoft TechNet website at *https://technet.microsoft.com/library/jj649850.aspx*.

Skill 1.2: Create and configure DNS zones and records

Although DNS is based on the concept of domains and subdomains, you store information about these domains and subdomains and the relationship between them in DNS zones. You can consider a DNS zone to be one or more domains and subdomains from your DNS infrastructure.

For example, the domains Adatum.com and sales.adatum.com might both be stored in a DNS zone called Adatum.com, or sales.adatum.com might be stored in a delegated zone called sales.adatum.com, while the parent domain, Adatum.com, is stored in its own zone.

You can store the zone in files on the DNS server or in the Active Directory Domain Services (AD DS) database. It is important that you know how and when to create primary and secondary zones, delegated zones, AD DS–integrated zones, and stub zones.

Overview of DNS zones

Zones are used by DNS servers to resolve client DNS queries. Usually, clients perform forward lookup queries in which a hostname must be resolved into the corresponding Internet Protocol Version 4 (IPv4) or Internet Protocol Version 6 (IPv6) address. Forward lookup queries are resolved by reference to *forward lookup zones*.

Forward lookup zones contain a variety of DNS record type (discussed in the next section) include:

- Host (A) records
- Alias (CNAME) records
- Records that identify which server is hosting a service, such as service (SRV) records and Mail exchanger (MX) records.

Less often, a DNS client queries a DNS server for the name of a host when it has the IPv4 or IPv6 address of the host. This is called a reverse lookup, and is satisfied by reference to a *reverse lookup zone*. Reverse lookup zones contain pointer (PTR) records.

Before you create your zone, you must first determine whether the zone is a forward or reverse lookup zone. Then you must determine whether the zone is primary, secondary, or AD DS–integrated. Strictly speaking, it is not the zone that is primary or secondary. Instead, it is the local copy of the zone that is primary or secondary. In other words, for there to be a secondary zone for Adatum.com, there must already exist a primary zone for Adatum.com on another DNS server from which the secondary can obtain the zone data.

When you first deploy the DNS server role in Windows Server 2016, the DNS Manager console navigation pane contains the server node, and beneath this, nodes for Forward Lookup Zones, Reverse Lookup Zones, Trust Points, and Conditional Forwarders. These nodes are all empty until you start to create zones on the DNS server.

Configure DNS zones

Windows Server 2016 supports a number of different zone types. These include primary zones, secondary zones, and Active Directory integrated zones. It's important that you know how to create and configure these different types of zone..

Create primary zones

A primary zone is a writable copy of a DNS zone that exists on a DNS server. To create a primary zone, in the DNS Manager console, use the following procedure:

1. Right-click the Forward Lookup Zones node, and then click New Zone.
2. In the New Zone Wizard, on the Welcome To The New Zone Wizard page, click Next.
3. On the Zone Type page, select Primary Zone, as shown in Figure 1-17, and then click Next.

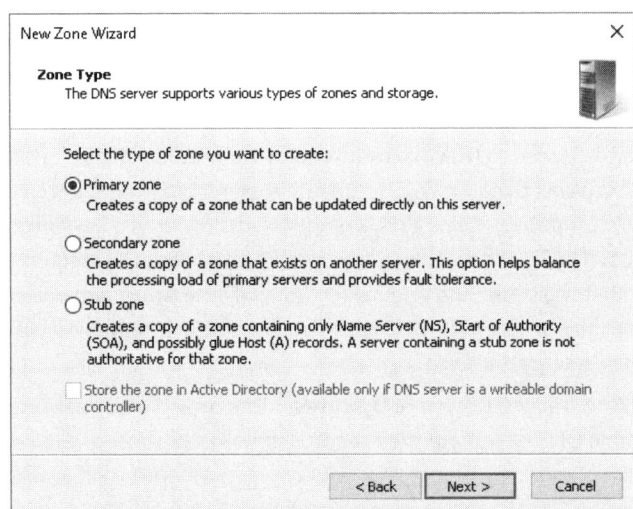

FIGURE 1-17 Creating a primary zone

4. On the Zone Name page, in the Zone name box, type the zone name. For example, type Contoso.com. Click Next.

5. On the Zone File page:
   - If you have a DNS zone file with which to populate your zone (for example, from another DNS server), click Use This Existing File, specify the path to the file, and then click Next.
   - If you do not have an existing zone file, click Create A New File With This File Name and click Next. Figure 1-18 shows the filename that is created automatically when you choose this option.

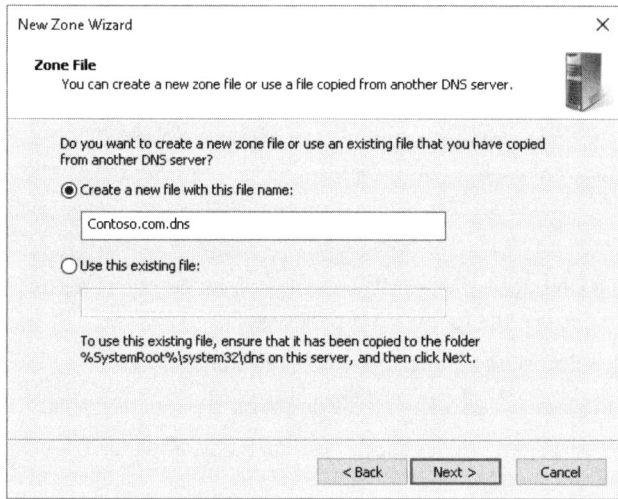

FIGURE 1-18 Defining the zone file

6. On the Dynamic Update page, shown in Figure 1-19, choose one of the following, and then click Next:
   - **Allow Only Secure Dynamic Updates (Recommended For Active Directory)** This option enables clients that support dynamic DNS to update their records in the DNS zone, such as when a client computer obtains a different IPv4 address from a Dynamic Host Configuration Protocol (DHCP) server. This option requires that each DNS record has an owner—the entity that registered the original record. Only the owner can update the record, which helps you secure your DNS records. This option is only available if you are creating an AD DS–integrated zone.
   - **Allow Both Nonsecure And Secure Dynamic Updates** This option also enables clients that support dynamic DNS to update their records in the DNS zone. It also supports nonsecure dynamic updates.
   - **Do Not Allow Dynamic Updates** Choose this option if you want to manually maintain all DNS records.

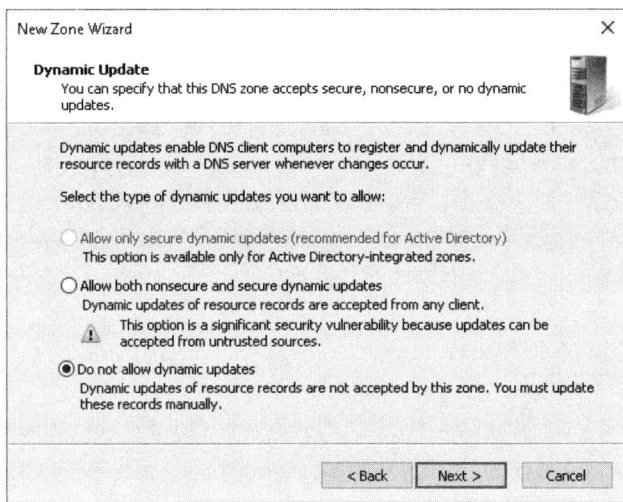

FIGURE 1-19 Choosing dynamic updates

7. On the Completing The New Zone Wizard page, click Finish.

After you have created your primary zone, you can view the initial contents of the zone by using the DNS Manager console, as shown in Figure 1-20. It contains the Start of Authority (SOA) record and a Name Server (NS) record. These two records define which computer(s) are responsible, or authoritative, for the zone.

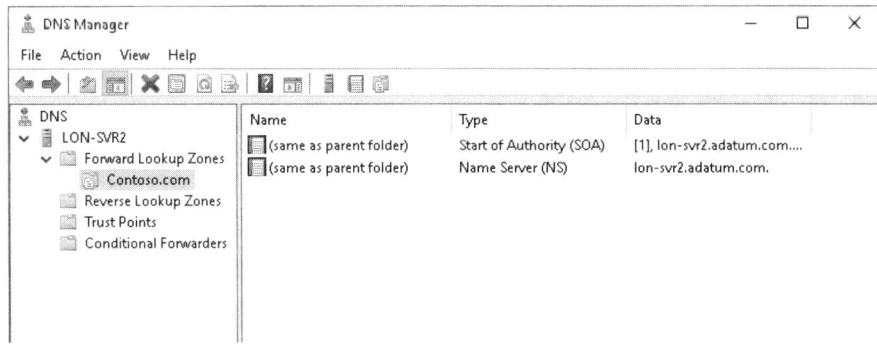

FIGURE 1-20 Viewing the completed Contoso.com zone

You can also add a primary zone by using the Add-DnsServerPrimaryZone Windows PowerShell cmdlet. For example, to complete the same process as in the preceding example by using Windows PowerShell, run the following command:

```
Add-DnsServerPrimaryZone -Name "Contoso.com" -ZoneFile "Contoso.com.dns"
-DynamicUpdate None
```

Skill 1.2: Create and configure DNS zones and records

After you have created the primary zone, you can reconfigure it from the DNS Manager console by right-clicking the zone in the navigation pane and clicking Properties. You can then configure the following properties on each of the following tabs:

- **General** You can change the zone type, zone file name, the dynamic updates setting, and configure aging and scavenging.
- **Start of Authority (SOA)** Shown in Figure 1-21, you can reconfigure the SOA record. This includes the Primary server's Fully Qualified Domain Name (FQDN), the responsible person's contact details, and the Refresh, Retry, and Expire intervals. These intervals determine:
    - **Refresh interval** The frequency with which other DNS servers that host the zone must refresh the zone data.
    - **Retry interval** The interval at which other DNS servers retry a refresh operation.
    - **Expires after** The length of time after failure to refresh zone data other DNS servers assume that the zone data has expired.

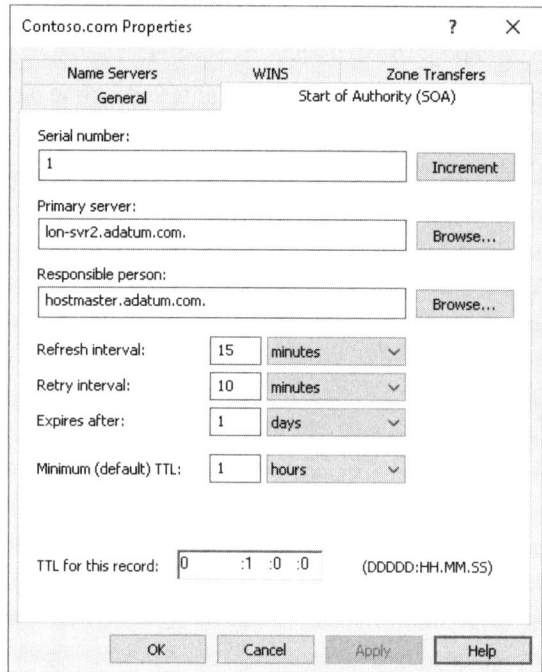

FIGURE 1-21 Editing the Contoso.com DNS zone properties

The Start of Authority (SOA) tab also contains the Minimum (Default) TTL value. This is the value that determines how long records in this zone can be cached by other recursive DNS servers.

- **Name Servers**   Use this tab to add, remove, or edit the name and IP addresses of other DNS servers that host this zone.
- **Zone Transfers**   Use this tab to configure how the zone data is transferred to other name servers hosting copies of the zone.
- **WINS**   Use this tab to configure Windows Internet Name Service (WINS) and DNS integration. WINS supports the resolution of NetBIOS names. Less relevant today, NetBIOS names use a nonhierarchical structure based on a 16-character name. Enabling the Use WINS Forward Lookup option enables the DNS server to respond to requests for NetBIOS names without the client computer having to petition a WINS server directly.

You can configure the zone properties by using the Set-DnsServerPrimaryZone Windows PowerShell cmdlet. For example, to change the Contoso.com Primary Zone Dynamic Update settings with Windows PowerShell, run the following command:

```
Set-DnsServerPrimaryZone -Name "Contoso.com" -DynamicUpdate "NonsecureAndSecure"
```

> **NEED MORE REVIEW? SET-DNSSERVERPRIMARYZONE**
>
> To review further details about modifying primary zone properties with Windows PowerShell, refer to the Microsoft TechNet website at *https://technet.microsoft.com/en-us/library/jj649865.aspx*.

Create and configure secondary zones

Creating a secondary zone is a different process from a primary zone. This is because a secondary zone hosts a read-only copy of a zone, which it obtains from another DNS server.

To create a secondary zone, you must know the name of the zone, and have the name and IP address of a DNS server that hosts a copy of the zone.

> **EXAM TIP**
>
> The name server you specify as a source for a secondary zone does not have to be hosting a primary copy of the zone. You can point one secondary zone server to another secondary zone server. However, somewhere a primary copy of the zone must exist.

You can use the DNS Manager console to create a secondary zone. To do this, use the following procedure:

1. Right-click the Forward Lookup Zones node, and then click New Zone.
2. In the New Zone Wizard, on the Welcome To The New Zone Wizard page, click Next.
3. On the Zone Type page, select Secondary Zone, and then click Next.
4. On the Zone Name page, in the Zone Name box, type the zone name, and click Next.

5. On the Master DNS Servers page, in the Master Servers list, type the FQDN or IP address of the server that hosts a copy of the zone, press Enter, and then click Next, as shown in Figure 1-22.

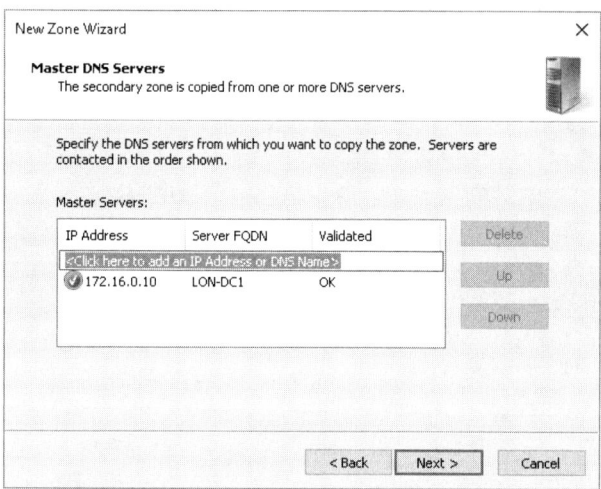

FIGURE 1-22 Defining the master server for a secondary zone

6. On the Completing The New Zone Wizard page, click Finish.

After you have added the secondary zone, it is necessary to configure the master DNS server that you specified. This is to enable zone transfers to your secondary server. To perform this step, switch to the DNS Manager console on the master server and perform the following procedure:

1. Right-click the appropriate zone, and then click Properties.
2. On the Name Servers tab, in the Name servers list, click Add to specify the FQDN and IP address of the DNS server hosting the secondary copy of the zone, as shown in Figure 1-23. Click OK.

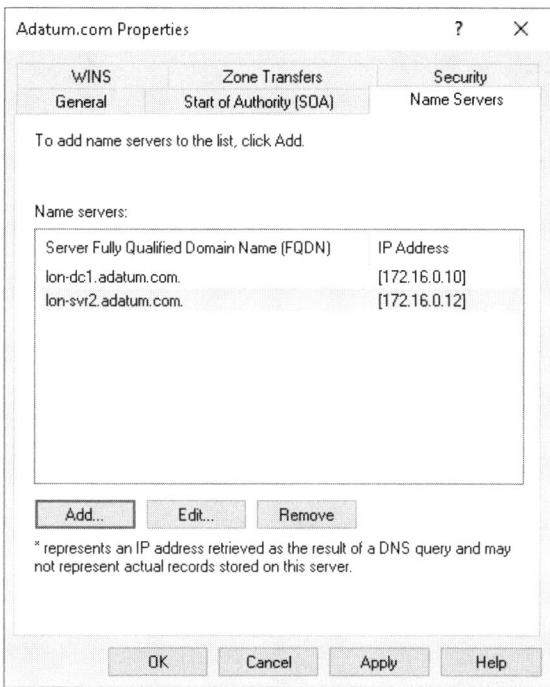

FIGURE 1-23 Configuring the Name Servers list

3. Click the Zone Transfers tab.
4. Select the Allow Zone Transfers check box. Then, as shown in Figure 1-24, choose one of the following:
   - To Any Server.
   - Only To Servers Listed On The Name Servers Tab.
   - Only To The Following Servers (If you choose this option, you must click Edit to specify the list of name servers that you want to allow).

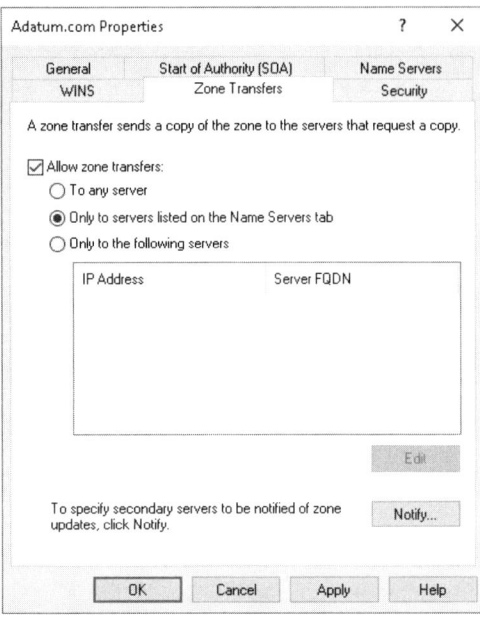

FIGURE 1-24 Configuring zone transfers

5. Click Notify.
6. In the Notify dialog box, either select Servers Listed On The Name Servers Tab, or else click The Following Servers, and then type the IP addresses of the secondary name servers you want to notify.
7. Click OK twice to complete configuration. Next, switch back to the DNS Manager console on the server hosting the secondary zone. You should see the DNS records populate into the secondary zone. If this does not happen immediately, right-click the secondary zone, and then click Transfer From Master.

You can use the Add-DnsServerSecondaryZone Windows PowerShell cmdlet to create a secondary zone. For example, the following command creates a secondary zone for the Adatum.com zone:

```
Add-DnsServerSecondaryZone -Name "Adatum.com" -ZoneFile "Adatum.com.dns"
-MasterServers 172.16.0.10
```

Configure delegation

DNS delegation is when a DNS server delegates authority over a part of its namespace to one or more other DNS servers. For example, Adatum.com and sales.adatum.com could be hosted in the same zone, Adatum.com, with the sales.adatum.com merely being a subdomain record. In this case, the authoritative DNS servers for Adatum.com and sales.adatum.com are the same. There is no need for the DNS servers in Adatum.com to refer recursive DNS servers to another domain.

Alternatively, you could create a separate zone for both Adatum.com and sales.adatum.com, each with their own DNS servers. Because one domain, sales.adatum.com, is a child domain of another domain, Adatum.com, there must exist a method to enable the authoritative name servers for the subdomain to be located. This method is called *delegation*, and is essentially a pointer to the authoritative name servers for a subdomain.

In Figure 1-25, you can see two DNS zones: Adatum.com, which contains a subdomain, marketing.adatum.com, and a second zone, sales.adatum.com, which contains a single domain, sales.adatum.com.

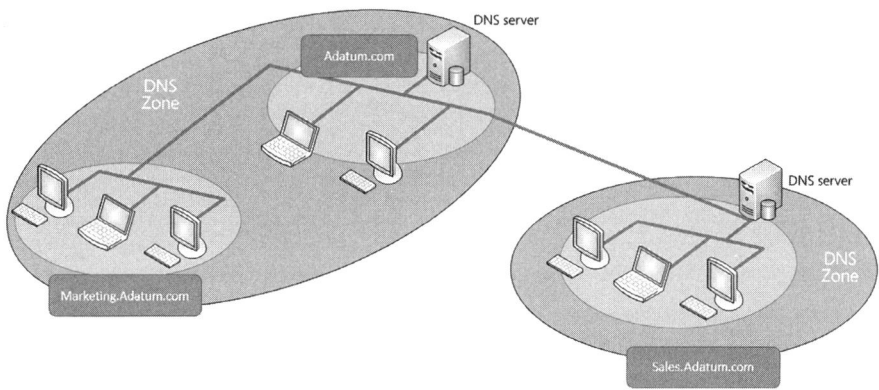

FIGURE 1-25 The Adatum.com DNS namespace separated into two zones

When determining whether to delegate a subdomain, consider the following:

- Your DNS zones are large, and delegation enables you to distribute the zone into smaller pieces across your organization.
- Organizational changes, such as mergers and acquisitions, mean that you have additional subdomains to manage.
- You have a distributed management structure, and want different departments or locations to be responsible for managing their own DNS namespaces.

To create a DNS delegation, in the DNS Manager console, perform the following procedure:

1. Right-click the parent zone. For example, right-click Adatum.com, and then click New Delegation. The New Delegation Wizard launches.
2. In the New Delegation Wizard, on the Welcome page, click Next.
3. On the Delegated Domain Name page, as shown in Figure 1-26, in the Delegated domain box, type the subdomain name. For example, type Sales. The suffix is added automatically. Click Next.

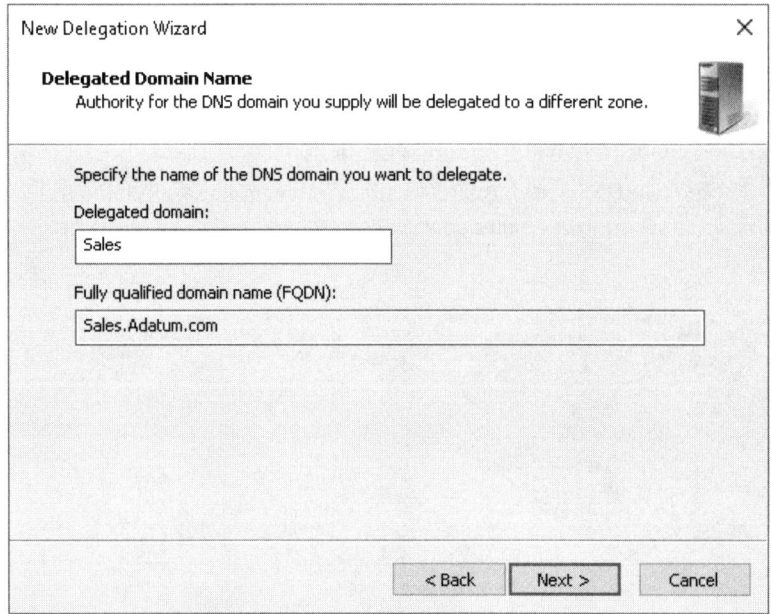

FIGURE 1-26 Delegating the sales.Adatum.com zone

4. On the Name Servers page, click Add.
5. In the New Name Server Record dialog box, on the Server Fully Qualified Domain name (FQDN) box, type the name of the DNS server that hosts the new delegated zone, click Resolve, and then click OK.
6. On the Name Servers page, click Next, and then click Finish.

You can use the Add-DnsServerZoneDelegation Windows PowerShell cmdlet to create a delegated zone in an existing zone. For example, the following command creates the sales.adatum.com delegated zone in the existing Adatum.com zone:

```
Add-DnsServerZoneDelegation -Name "Adatum.com" -ChildZoneName "Sales" -NameServer
"ns1.Sales.Adatum.com" -IPAddress 172.16.0.136
```

After you have completed the delegation, if necessary, you should install DNS on the name server that you specified in the wizard, and create the delegated zone, in this case sales.adatum.com.

> **NEED MORE REVIEW?** **UNDERSTANDING ZONE DELEGATION**
>
> To review further details about delegating DNS zones, refer to the Microsoft TechNet website at *https://technet.microsoft.com/library/cc771640(v=ws.11).aspx*.

Configure Active Directory integration of primary zones

Traditional DNS zones are file-based and are stored in the local file system of the DNS server. DNS servers that host the primary copy of a zone have a writable version of the DNS zone file. Secondary servers have read-only copies of the zone file; they periodically obtain updates by using a zone transfer from their configured master, as you saw in Create and configure secondary zones.

In an AD DS environment, you have the option to create AD DS-integrated zones. In this situation, all copies of the zone data are writable. In addition, the zone data is stored securely in Active Directory and is replicated securely as part of the AD DS database.

The benefits of using AD DS-integrated zones are:

- **Multimaster updates** AD DS-integrated DNS zones are multimaster, and updates can be made to any copy of the zone data. This provides for redundancy in your DNS infrastructure. If your organization implements dynamic updates to the DNS zone, then geographically remote DNS clients can update their records by connecting to the nearest DNS server.
- **Replicated using AD DS replication** AD DS replication is based at the attribute-level. This means that only changed attributes, rather than entire records, are replicated. This means that the volume of zone transfer traffic can be reduced.
- **Secure dynamic updates** You can implement secure dynamic updates in an AD DS–integrated zone. This is discussed in the next section.
- **Improved security** You can delegate administration of AD DS-integrated zone, domains, and resource records with the AD DS object-level Access Control List (ACL) for the zone.

> **EXAM TIP**
>
> When you promote a new domain controller in your AD DS forest, the DNS server role deploys automatically. This is configurable on the Domain Controller Options page of the Active Directory Domain Services Configuration Wizard.

When you create zones on a DNS server that is also a domain controller, you have the option to install an AD DS-integrated zone. To create an AD DS-integrated DNS zone, use the following procedure:

1. On your domain controller, open DNS Manager.
2. Right-click the Forward Lookup Zones node, and then click New Zone.
3. In the New Zone Wizard, on the Welcome To The New Zone Wizard page, click Next.
4. On the Zone Type page, select Primary Zone, as shown in Figure 1-27, select the Store The Zone In Active Directory (Available Only If The DNS Server Is A Writable Domain Controller) check box, and then click Next.

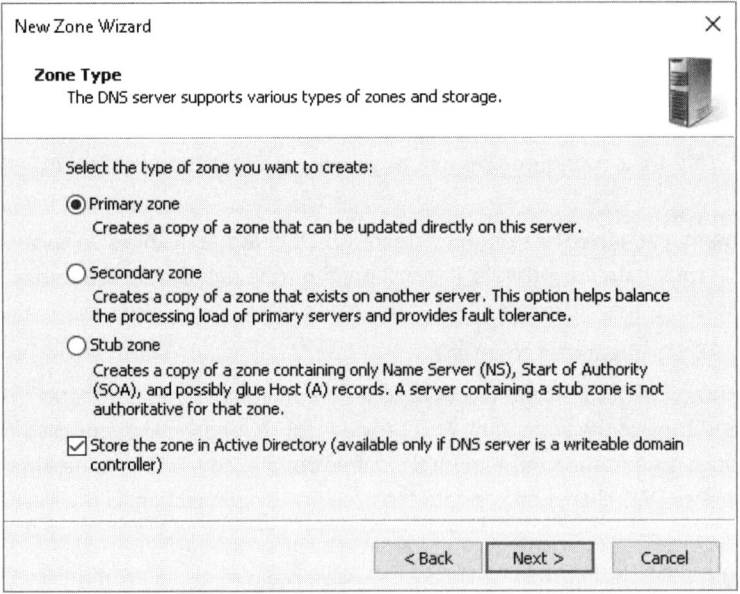

FIGURE 1-27 Selecting the zone type

5. On the Active Directory Zone Replication Scope page, as shown in Figure 1-28, select the appropriate zone replication option from the following:

- **To All DNS Servers Running On Domain Controllers In This Forest**   This option causes the zone data to replicate to all domain controllers running the DNS server role in the forest.

- **To All DNS Servers Running On Domain Controllers In This Domain**   This option (the default) causes the zone data to replicate to all domain controllers running the DNS server role in the current AD DS domain.

- **To All Domain Controllers In This Domain (For Windows 2000 Compatibility)**   This option provides backward compatibility with earlier versions of Windows Server. You would not normally select this option.

- **To All Domain Controllers Specified In The Scope Of This Directory Partition**   Directory partitions enable you to create an AD DS replication boundary that is not restricted to all domain controllers in the forest or local domain. The option is only available if you have created a directory partition before you configure the DNS zone.

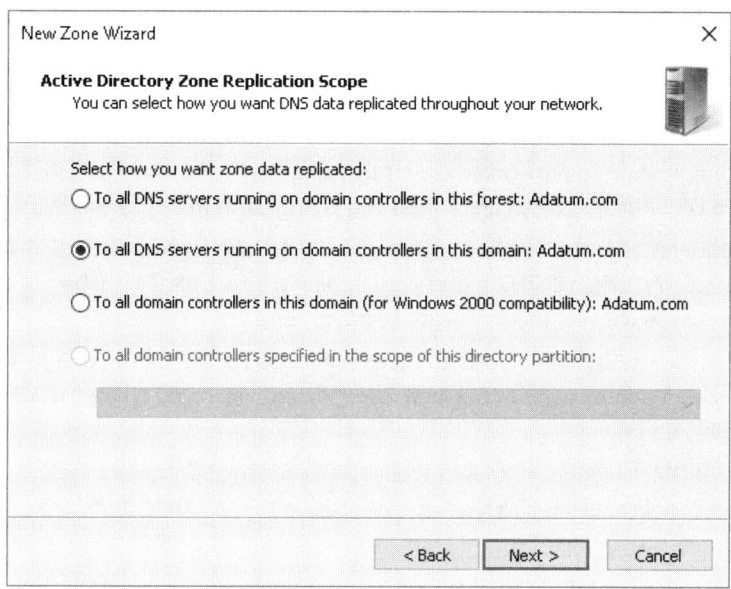

FIGURE 1-28 Specifying the preferred zone replication scope

6. Click Next.
7. On the Zone Name page, in the Zone name box, type the zone name, for example, type Contoso.com. Click Next.
8. On the Dynamic Update page, choose one of the following, and then click Next.
   - Allow Only Secure Dynamic Updates (Recommended For Active Directory)
   - Allow Both Non-Secure And Secure Dynamic Updates
   - Do Not Allow Dynamic Updates
9. On the Completing The New Zone Wizard page, click Finish.

You can also create an AD DS-integrated primary zone by using the Add-DnsServerPrimaryZone Windows PowerShell cmdlet. For example, to complete the same process as in the preceding example by using Windows PowerShell, run the following command:

```
Add-DnsServerPrimaryZone -Name "Contoso.com" -ReplicationScope "Domain"
```

On domain controllers, existing standard primary zones can be converted to AD DS–integrated zones. In DNS Manager, right-click the zone, and then click Properties. On the General page, click Change, and then select the Store The Zone In Active Directory (Available Only If The DNS Server Is A Writable Domain Controller) check box. Click OK twice.

Configure secure dynamic updates

If you have implemented an AD DS-integrated primary zone, you have the option of enabling secure dynamic updates. Dynamic updates is a feature in which DNS clients can update their own DNS records on their configured DNS server. This is particularly convenient when an organization assigns IP configuration to networked clients by using DHCP. If a client obtains a different IP address from a DHCP scope, they can register this change automatically on DNS.

With secure dynamic updates, the DNS server assigns ownership to the registered DNS records, and only the owner—the original DNS client—can update the records. To enable secure dynamic updates, you can choose one of the following options:

- Select the Allow Only Secure Dynamic Updates (Recommended For Active Directory) option on the Dynamic Updates page of the New Zone Wizard when you create an AD DS-integrated primary zone.
- After creating the AD DS-integrated primary zone, in DNS Manager, right-click the DNS zone, and then click Properties. On the General page, in the Dynamic Updates list, click Secure Only.
- After creating the AD DS-integrated primary zone in Windows PowerShell, use the Set-DnsServerPrimaryZone command. For example:

```
Set-DnsServerPrimaryZone -Name "Contoso.com" -DynamicUpdate "Secure"
```

Create and configure stub zones

You can use conditional forwarding as a means to redirect query traffic to a designated DNS server. With conditional forwarding, if a DNS query contains a specific domain name, for example Contoso.com, it is forwarded to a specific DNS server. To learn more about Conditional Forwarding, see "Configure forwarders, root hints, recursion, and delegation."

Alternatively, you can also use a stub zones to achieve a similar result. A stub zone is used by a DNS server to help resolve names between two separate DNS namespaces, such as following a merger or acquisition. A stub zone differs from conditional forwarding in that the stub zone contains the complete list of DNS servers for the other domain.

COMPARING CONDITIONAL FORWARDING WITH STUB ZONES

Imagine that two DNS namespaces, Adatum.com and Contoso.com, are now owned by the A. Datum Corporation following an acquisition. For DNS clients in the Adatum.com domain to locate resources in the Contoso.com domain it requires the use of root hints by Adatum.com DNS servers.

To avoid this, in the Adatum.com domain, you could configure DNS conditional forwarding for the Contoso.com domain. With conditional forwarding, you configure to which DNS server(s) in the Contoso.com domain to forward DNS queries.

You can also use a stub zone for Contoso.com in the Adatum.com domain. This stub zone contains the complete list of DNS server that are authoritative for the foreign domain. This list of servers is updated automatically.

When considering whether to use conditional forwarding or stub zones, remember:

- You must manually maintain conditional forwarding records, while stub zones are maintained automatically.
- With conditional forwarding, you can designate the specific foreign DNS server to forward queries to, but with a stub zone, you cannot.

CREATING A STUB ZONE

You can use the following procedure to create a stub zone. Open DNS Manager, and then:

1. Right-click the Forward Lookup Zones node, and then click New Zone.
2. On the New Zone Wizard, on the Welcome to the New Zone Wizard page, click Next.
3. On the Zone Type page, select Stub Zone, and then click Next.
4. On the Zone Name page, in the Zone name box, type the DNS domain name for the foreign domain, and then click Next.
5. On the Zone File page, if you have a DNS zone file that you use to populate your zone (for example, from another DNS server), click Use This Existing File, specify the path to the file on the Zone File page, and then click Next.
6. On the Master DNS Servers page, in the Master Servers list, type the IP address or FQDN of the DNS server in the foreign domain from which the DNS server obtains zone updates, and then click Next.
7. Click Finish to create the stub zone.

You must now populate the stub zone with the required records that includes the Start of Authority (SOA) record, and the Host (A) and NS records that pertain to the foreign DNS servers, and are retrieved from the specific master server(s). To manually perform this task, in the DNS Manager, right-click the stub zone and then click Transfer from Master.

You can use the Windows PowerShell Add-DnsServerStubZone cmdlet to create a stub zone. For example, to create a stub zone for Contoso.com, use the following command:

```
Add-DnsServerStubZone -Name "Contoso.com" -MasterServers "172.16.0.66" -ZoneFile "Contoso.dns"
```

EXAM TIP

You can create AD DS-integrated stub zones, either in the DNS Manager console, or by using Windows PowerShell. To use Windows PowerShell, replace the zonefile parameter with ReplicationScope.

Configure a GlobalNames zone

Some older networked apps rely on a non-hierarchical naming standard known as NetBIOS. In the past, network clients that accessed these apps needed to be able to resolve these single-label NetBIOS names. You can use the WINS server feature to provide for NetBIOS name registration, resolution, and release.

The disadvantages of using WINS are:

- Organizations must maintain two name services, with the resultant administrative overhead.
- Network clients potentially use both DNS and WINS to resolve names, resulting in possible name resolution delay.

As an alternative to WINS, you can use the DNS GlobalNames zone in Windows Server 2016. When clients resolve single-label names, such as LON-SVR2, these names are resolved by reference to the GlobalNames zone. An organization has only a single GlobalNames zone, which you must create manually. Also, you must populate the zone with the required CNAME resource records that point to your organization's server and app resources.

To create the GlobalNames zone, use the following procedure:

1. Open Windows PowerShell.
2. Run the Set-DnsServerGlobalNameZone –AlwaysQueryServer $true command to enable GlobalNames zone support.
3. Run the Add-DnsServerPrimaryZone –Name GlobalNames –ReplicationScope Forest command to create the GlobalNames zone.
4. Open DNS Manager and locate the GlobalNames zone node.
5. Create the required CNAME records for server resources that still use single-label names.

> **NEED MORE REVIEW? DEPLOYING A GLOBALNAMES ZONE**
> To review further details about the GlobalNames zone, refer to the Microsoft TechNet website at *https://technet.microsoft.com/library/cc731744(v=ws.11).aspx*.

Configure DNS records

Zones contain DNS records that point either to name servers, hosts, services, or to other zones. After you have created your zones, you must populate them with records appropriate to your organization's network. You must also be prepared to maintain these records to ensure the accuracy of zone data.

Create and configure DNS resource records

A DNS server exists to provide name resolution for DNS clients. In order for this to be possible, you must populate the DNZ zones that you create with appropriate DNS resource records. These resource records include:

- **Host** A host record—commonly given the abbreviation A—holds the IPv4 address for the specified hostname. AAAA records hold the IPv6 address for the specified hostname. These are probably the most common resource records and are found in forward lookup zones.
- **Pointer** Also known as PTR records, these enable a DNS client to resolve an IPv4 or IPv6 address into a hostname. These records exist in reverse lookup zones.
- **Start of Authority** Created when you create a primary zone, the SOA record contains information about the authoritative server for the zone, contact information for the zone, and other information, including TTL values for resource records in the zone.
- **Name Server** Name server (NS) records identify the authoritative name servers in the zone, including both primary and secondary servers. They also identify name servers for any delegated zones.
- **Service Location** Known as SRV records, these enable you to specify by service, protocol, and DNS domain name, which servers are hosting particular apps or services. If a DNS client is looking for a web server, for example, you can configure SRV records for the http service enabling clients to find all servers providing that service. Clients then use corresponding A or AAAA records to resolve the server names into IP addresses. An SRV record is more complex than many others, and contains the following fields: _Service.Proto.Name TTL Class SRV Priority Weight Port Target. For example: http._tcp.Contoso.com. IN SRV 0 0 80 www.Contoso.com. AD DS services, such as the Kerberos authentication service, use SRV records to advertise themselves to clients in an AD DS network.
- **Alias** CNAME records enable you to create an alias for a host. For example, the server lon-svr2.adatum.com might host a website. You can create an alias for this host with the name www by adding a CNAME record that points to the FQDN of the lon-svr2 server.
- **Mail Exchanger** MX records are used by Simple Mail Transfer Protocol (SMTP) hosts for transferring email around the Internet. In order for an originating SMTP host to route mail to a recipient with the email address Dave@Contoso.com, it is necessary for the originating host to know which hosts can receive the email at Contoso.com. You create MX records in the Contoso.com namespace to advertise which hosts provide this service. To help to ensure a reliable inbound email flow, you can advertise several hosts by using multiple MX records. Each can be assigned the same or different mail server priorities, or preference values. If you implement MX records with the same priority, email is routed to them randomly, distributing the load. If you use different values, the lower value is used first by the originating server, thereby enabling you to specify a preferred inbound server.

> *NOTE* **ENABLING DYNAMIC UPDATES**
>
> Remember that you can enable dynamic updates for your DNS zone in Microsoft DNS. This enables hosts to register and update their own resource records. This is particularly relevant for A, AAAA, PTR, and SRV records that might commonly be expected to change.

> **NEED MORE REVIEW? RESOURCE RECORD TYPES**
>
> To find out more about common DNS resource record types, refer to the Microsoft TechNet website at *https://technet.microsoft.com/library/cc958958.aspx*.

You can create these records manually from the DNS Manager console. Right-click the appropriate forward lookup zone (reverse lookup zone for PTR records), and then click the appropriate option for the record type you want to create, as shown in Figure 1-29.

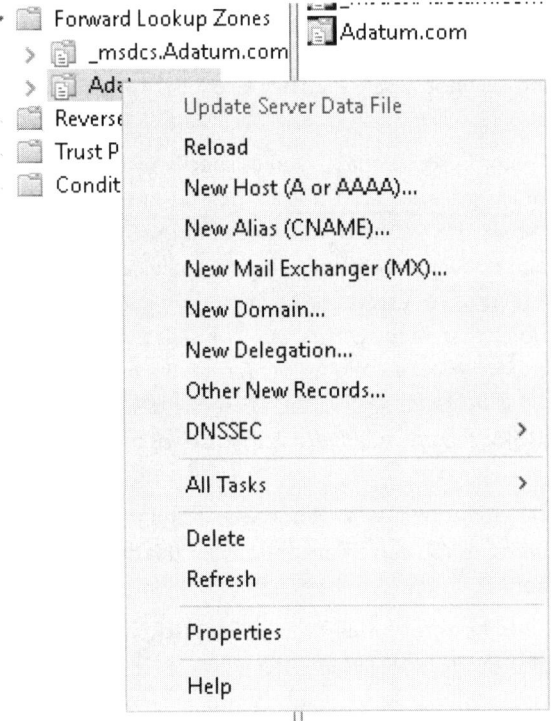

FIGURE 1-29 Creating resource records

Creating the resource records are straightforward, but vary slightly for each record type because you must specify different information for each separately. However, this is a very intuitive process. For example, for a new host record, you must specify the host's name and its IP address. You can also select the option to create a PTR record for the host automatically. For an MX record, you must specify the FQDN of the host that provides SMTP email support, and a Mail server priority value.

If the record type you want is not listed on the context menu, (for example, SRV), select Other New Record from the context menu. Then select the record type you want in the Resource Record Type dialog box, and then click Create Record, shown in Figure 1-30. This list contains all record types, including those used less frequently.

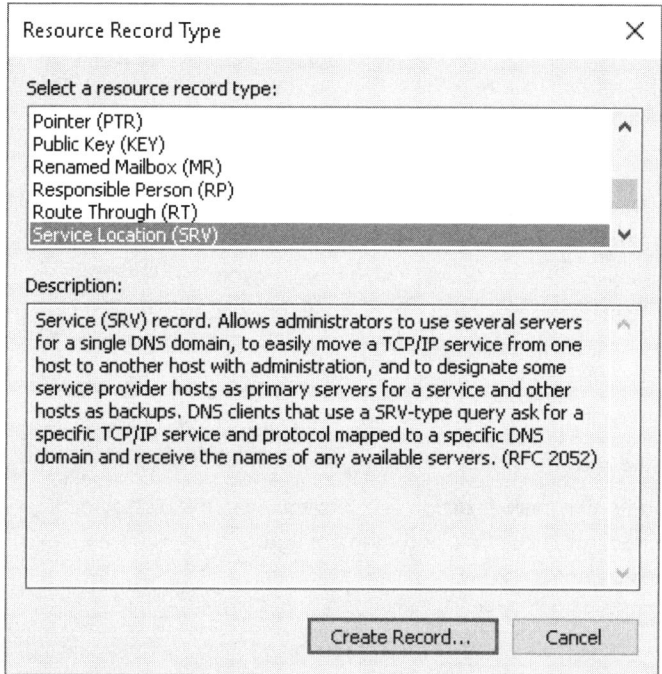

FIGURE 1-30 Selecting resource record types

You can use the Add-DnsServerResourceRecord Windows PowerShell cmdlet to create resource records. For example, the following command creates a host called lon-svr2 in the Contoso.com domain:

```
Add-DnsServerResourceRecord -ZoneName "Contoso.com" -A -Name "lon-svr2"
-AllowUpdateAny -IPv4Address "172.16.0.27" -TimeToLive 01:00:00 -AgeRecord
```

> **NEED MORE REVIEW? ADD-DNSSERVERRESOURCERECORD**
>
> To find out more about adding DNS resource records with Windows PowerShell, refer to the Microsoft TechNet website at *https://technet.microsoft.com/library/jj649925.aspx*.

Configure zone scavenging

Resource records often remain in a DNS zone even though the host that registered the record is no longer active. This is known as a stale record. You can use aging settings to determine when the DNS role can remove a stale record. This removal is known as scavenging.

Two parameters determine scavenging behavior:

- **No-refresh Interval**   The no-refresh interval is the period of time that the record is not eligible to be refreshed. By default, this is also seven days.
- **Refresh Interval**   The refresh interval is the time that the record is eligible to be refreshed by the client. The default is seven days.

Usually, a client host record cannot be refreshed for seven days after it is first registered (or refreshed). But then it must be refreshed within the following seven days. If it is not, the record becomes eligible to be scavenged.

EXAM TIP

By default, aging and scavenging of resource records is disabled.

To enable scavenging, you must enable it on both the DNS zone(s) and on the server(s) that host those zones.

To configure aging and scavenging on a DNS zone:

1. In DNS Manager, right-click the appropriate zone, and then click Properties.
2. On the General tab, click Aging.
3. In the Zone Aging/Scavenging Properties dialog box, shown in Figure 1-31, select the Scavenge Stale Resource Records check box, and then configure your preferred No-Refresh Interval and Refresh Interval values.
4. Click OK twice.

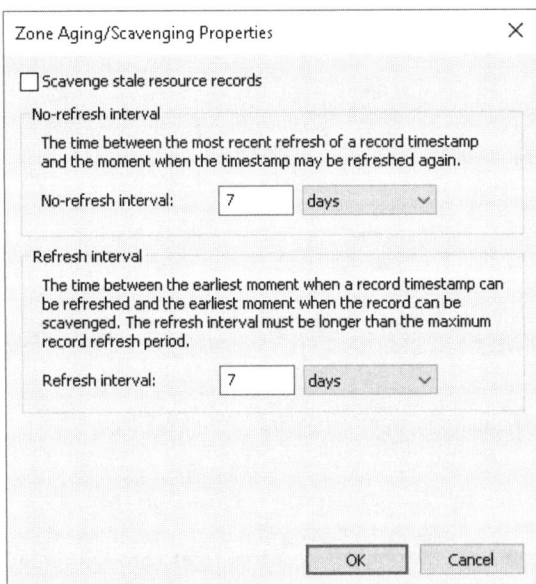

FIGURE 1-31 Enabling and configuring zone aging and scavenging

You can also enable zone aging/scavenging with the Set-DnsServerZoneAging Windows PowerShell cmdlet. For example:

```
Set-DnsServerZoneAging Contoso.com -Aging $True -ScavengeServers 172.16.0.10
```

EXAM TIP

You can configure aging/scavenging for all zones by right-clicking a server in the DNS Manager console and then clicking Set Aging/Scavenging for All Zones.

To configure scavenging on a DNS server, in the DNS Manager console:

1. Right-click the appropriate DNS server and then click Properties.
2. In the Server Properties dialog box, click the Advanced tab.
3. Select the Enable Automatic Scavenging Of Stale Records check box, and then in the Scavenging period box, specify the number of days, and then click OK.

You can enable DNS server aging/scavenging with the Set-DnsServerScavenging Windows PowerShell cmdlet. For example:

```
Set-DnsServerScavenging -RefreshInterval 7.00:00:00
```

EXAM TIP

You can force scavenging to be initiated by right-clicking a server in the DNS Manager console and then clicking Scavenge Stale Resource Records. Alternatively, use the Start-DnsServerScavenging Windows PowerShell command.

> **NEED MORE REVIEW?** **UNDERSTANDING AGING AND SCAVENGING**
>
> To find out more about aging and scavenging, refer to the Microsoft TechNet website at *https://technet.microsoft.com/library/cc771677(v=ws.11).aspx.*

Configure record options

You can configure a number of options for resource records, including preference, weight, priority, and tie to live.

CHANGING PREFERENCE, WEIGHT, AND PRIORITY

Some resource records are assigned preference, weight, and priority values. These are used when there are multiple records that point to the same service or server and you want to control which servers are used first. For example, an AD DS domain controller registers its Kerberos authentication service DNS resource records with a priority value of 0 and a weight of 100, as shown in Figure 1-32.

FIGURE 1-32 Viewing resource record Priority and Weight values

You can adjust these initial values to determine which Kerberos authentication server is used by clients. DNS clients attempt to use the server with the lowest priority value. If multiple servers have the same priority value, clients use the server in proportion to their weight values. Similarly, if multiple MX records exist for an email domain name, then the server with the lowest preference value is used. You can adjust these values using the DNS Manager console or the Windows PowerShell Add-DnsServerResourceRecord or Set-DnsServerResourceRecord cmdlets using the Priority, Weight, and Preference parameters.

CHANGING TIME TO LIVE VALUES

All resource records have a time to live (TTL) value. The TTL is used to determine how long a record can reside in the DNS cache of a DNS client or DNS server that has recently resolved the record. These values should be representative of how frequently resource records change in your organization. If record values are fairly static, a higher TTL is acceptable. If they change frequently, then setting a TTL too high results in DNS cache being out of date, with resultant name resolution errors.

EXAM TIP

To change individual TTL values for resource records in a zone by using the DNS Manager console, you must enable the Advanced view. In DNS Manager, click View, and then click Advanced.

To change the TTL of a record in DNS Manager:

1. Right-click a resource record, and then click Properties.
2. In the Record Properties dialog box, in the Time to live (TTL) box, type the preferred value in days, hours, minutes, and seconds and then click OK.

Alternatively, use the Windows PowerShell Add-DnsServerResourceRecord or Set-DnsServerResourceRecord cmdlets with the -TimetoLive parameter.

Configure unknown record support

Windows Server 2016 adds support in the DNS server role for *Unknown Records*. Unknown Records are resource records with a format that is foreign to the Microsoft DNS server. Support for these unknown records means that you can add the unsupported record types into your zones to support specific apps that require them. The Windows DNS server does not perform record-specific processing for these unknown records, but does respond to DNS client requests for these records.

EXAM TIP
You can use the Add-DnsServerResourceRecord Windows PowerShell cmdlet with the -Unknown parameter to create unknown resource records.

Configure round robin

You can use DNS round robin to help to distribute load across servers providing the same service. For example, if you had three web servers in your network and you wanted to distribute the client load across all three equally, one solution is to configure the same host resource record (www.contoso.com) and point it to three different IP addresses. For example:

www.contoso.com 60 IN A 172.16.0.10

www.contoso.com 60 IN A 172.16.0.12

www.contoso.com 60 IN A 172.16.0.14

Round robin works by responding to each client request for the resolution of www.contoso.com with a differently ordered list of IP addresses. On the first request, the server with the IPv4 address of 172.16.0.10 is returned at the top of the list. Next, 172.16.0.12 is returned first on the list, and so on.

You configure round robin on DNS server on the Advanced server settings dialog box. It is enabled by default. You can also use the Set-DnsServer Windows PowerShell cmdlet.

EXAM TIP
You can also use netmask ordering to achieve a similar result, but in this case, a client receives the result that is most relevant to their location, based on their subnet.

Configure DNS scopes

Windows Server 2016 supports two types of DNS scopes. These are recursion scopes and zone scopes. Recursion scopes are a collection of settings that define recursion behavior in a DNS zone, while zone scopes are collections of resource records. To create, configure, and apply DNS scopes, you must use Windows Server 2016 DNS policies.

> **NOTE RECURSION SCOPES**
> Implementing recursion scopes is covered in the "Configure recursion" section.

Configuring zone scopes

In Windows Server 2016, you can configure your DNS zones to have multiple zone scopes. Each zone scope contains its own set of DNS resource records. A resource record can exist in multiple zone scopes, each with different IP addresses depending on the scope. You can also use the zone scope to control zone transfers, enabling resource records from a zone scope in a primary zone to be transferred to the same zone scope in a secondary zone.

Typically, the first step in creating a zone scope is to create and configure client subnets. You do this in reference to your physical network topology. For example, to create subnet for DNS clients in New York and another for clients in London, use the following Windows PowerShell commands:

```
Add-DnsServerClientSubnet -Name "NYCSubnet" -IPv4Subnet "172.16.0.0/24"
```

```
Add-DnsServerClientSubnet -Name "LONSubnet" -IPv4Subnet "172.16.1.0/24"
```

Next, you create the DNS zone scopes for New York and London DNS clients by using the following commands:

```
Add-DnsServerZoneScope -ZoneName "Adatum.com" -Name "NYCZoneScope"
```

```
Add-DnsServerZoneScope -ZoneName "Adatum.com" -Name "LONZoneScope"
```

Configuring records in zone scopes

After you create the zone scopes, you must populate them with resource records. Again, you must do this with Windows PowerShell. To create a specific IP address record for clients in the New York City zone scope, run the following command:

```
Add-DnsServerResourceRecord -ZoneName "Adatum.com" -A -Name "www" -IPv4Address "172.16.0.41" -ZoneScope "NYCZoneScope"
```

For clients in the London City zone scope, run the following command:

```
Add-DnsServerResourceRecord -ZoneName "Adatum.com" -A -Name "www" -IPv4Address "172.16.1.22" -ZoneScope "LONZoneScope"
```

Configuring policies for zones

Finally, you must create the policies that instruct the DNS servers to respond to client queries based upon the previously defined factors. To configure the DNS servers to respond with resource records from the New York zone scope, create a DNS policy:

```
Add-DnsServerQueryResolutionPolicy -Name "NYCPolicy" -Action ALLOW -ClientSubnet "eq,NYCSubnet" -ZoneScope "NYCZoneScope,1" -ZoneName "Adatum.com"
```

Similarly, for clients based in the London zone scope, you must add another policy:

```
Add-DnsServerQueryResolutionPolicy -Name "LONPolicy" -Action ALLOW -ClientSubnet "eq,LONSubnet" -ZoneScope "LONZoneScope,1" -ZoneName "Adatum.com"
```

Now, if a client in the New York subnet petitions a DNS server for the IPv4 address of the www.adatum.com host, the DNS server responds with the IP address 172.16.0.41. If a client in London requests the same record, the client receives the IPv4 address 172.16.1.22.

> **NOTE DNS POLICIES**
>
> Implementing DNS policies is also covered in "Implement DNS policies."

> **NEED MORE REVIEW? DNS POLICIES OVERVIEW**
>
> For more information about configuring DNS policies, refer to the Microsoft TechNet website at *https://technet.microsoft.com/windows-server-docs/networking/dns/deploy/dns-policies-overview*.

Monitor DNS

Since DNS is such a critical service, providing name resolution and service location for configured clients, it is important that you ensure that DNS is running reliably and is optimized. To help you achieve this, you can use a number of monitoring and auditing tools in Windows Server.

Use DNS audit events and analytical events

Windows Server 2016 can collect a vast amount of logging data. Much of this logging is enabled by default, but features such as Debug logging (discussed in the "Configure DNS logging" section) must first be enabled before you can use them.

You can also use DNS Audit events and DNS Analytic events.

- **DNS Audit Events** These are enabled by default. Use to enable change tracking on your DNS servers. Every time a server, zone, or resource record is edited, an audit event is logged. Event IDs numbered 513 through 582 are logged in this regard, and are explained on the following website.

> **NEED MORE REVIEW? AUDIT EVENTS**
>
> For more information about audit events in Microsoft DNS, refer to the Microsoft TechNet website at *https://technet.microsoft.com/library/dn800669(v=ws.11).aspx#audit*.

- **DNS Analytic Events** These are disabled by default. Windows logs an analytic event every time the DNS server sends or receives DNS information. Event IDs numbered 257 through 280 are logged in this regard, and are explained on the website listed below.

> **NEED MORE REVIEW? ANALYTIC EVENTS**
>
> For more information about analytic events in Microsoft DNS, refer to the Microsoft TechNet website at *https://technet.microsoft.com/library/dn800669(v=ws.11).aspx#analytic*.

VIEWING AUDIT AND ANALYTICAL EVENTS

To view audit events, use the following procedure:

1. Open Event Viewer.
2. Expand Application And Services Logs, expand Microsoft, expand Windows, and then click DNS-Server.
3. Click the Audit folder, as shown in Figure 1-33. You can review events from here.

To view analytic events, use the following procedure:

1. Open Event Viewer.
2. Expand Application And Services Logs, expand Microsoft, expand Windows, and then click DNS-Server.
3. Right-click DNS-Server, click View, and then click Show Analytic And Debug Logs. The Analytical and Audit log folders display, as shown in Figure 1-33.
4. Right-click Analytical and then click Enable Log.
5. In the Event Viewer pop-up dialog box, click OK.

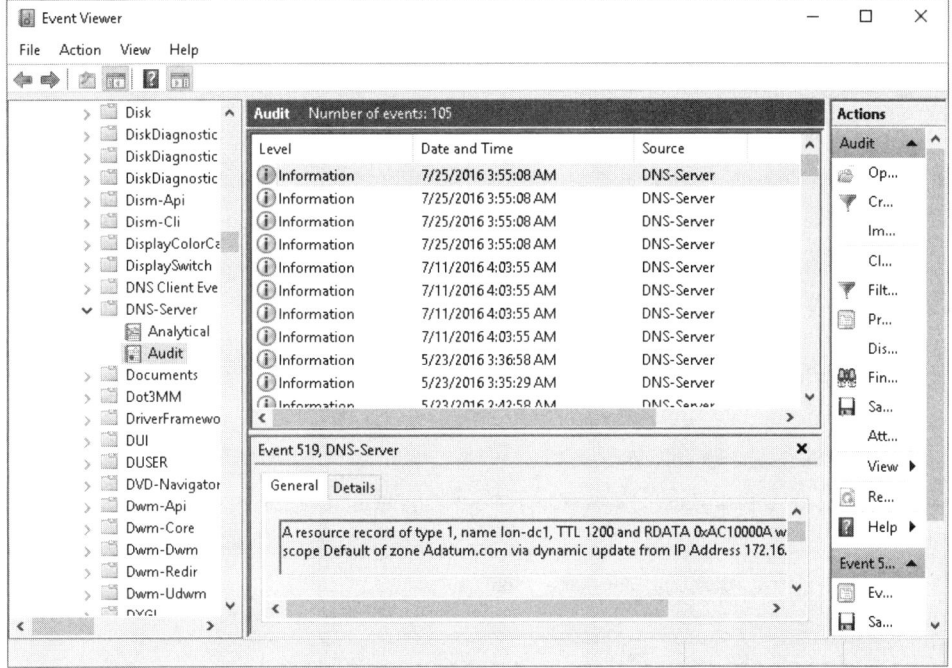

FIGURE 1-33 Viewing Audit events for a DNS server

> **NEED MORE REVIEW? DNS LOGGING AND DIAGNOSTICS**
>
> For more information about logging and diagnostics in Microsoft DNS, refer to the Microsoft TechNet website at *https://technet.microsoft.com/library/dn800669(v=ws.11).aspx*.

Analyze zone level statistics

Introduced in Windows Server 2012 R2, and improved in Windows Server 2016, DNS zone level statistics enable you to understand how a DNS server is being used for each authoritative zone on that server.

You can gather and view the following zone level statistics:

- **Zone queries**   Provides the number of:
    - Queries received
    - Successful responses
    - Failed query responses
    - Name error responses

Skill 1.2: Create and configure DNS zones and records   CHAPTER 1   53

- **Zone transfers**   Provides the number of zone transfer:
    - Requests received when operating as a primary server for a specific zone
    - Requests sent when operating as a secondary server for a specific zone
    - Requests received when operating as a secondary server for a specific zone
- **Zone transfers statistics** also provide the number of zone transfers
    - Received by the DNS Server service when operating as a secondary server for a specific zone
    - Sent by the DNS Server service when operating as a master server for a specific zone
- **Zone updates**   Provides the total number of
    - Dynamic update requests received
    - Dynamic updates rejected

To access these statistics, use the Windows PowerShell Get-DnsServerStatistics cmdlet. For example:

```
Get-DnsServerStatistics -ZoneName "Adatum.com"
```

> **NEED MORE REVIEW? DNS ZONE LEVEL STATISTICS**
>
> For more information about analyzing DNS zone level statistics, refer to the Microsoft TechNet website at *https://blogs.technet.microsoft.com/networking/2013/10/04/dns-zone-level-statistics*.

Chapter summary

- You can install the DNS server role on Windows Server 2016 and Nano Server.
- DNS forwarders, recursion, and root hints enable you to control the flow of DNS query traffic throughout your organization's network.
- You can implement DNSSEC, DNS socket pool, cache locking, DANE, and response rate limiting to help to secure your DNS infrastructure from malicious attacks.
- DNS policies in Windows Server 2016 help you configure DNS behavior throughout your organization without needing to manually configure each DNS server.
- DNS logging can help you to pinpoint problems with the DNS servers in your organization before they can affect your users.
- The DNS server role is affected by CPU and memory resources, and proactive monitoring of these resources can be beneficial.
- Although the DNS namespace is based on domains and subdomains, the data that maintains this namespace is stored in DNS zones.
- Secondary zones receive updates via their configured master server.

- DNS delegation enables a part of your DNS namespace, such as a child domain, to be authoritatively maintained in a separate zone.
- AD DS-integrated zones provide for multimaster updates, secure replication, and secure dynamic updates.
- Conditional forwarding provides similar function to stub zones.
- DNS scopes are based on DNS policies.

Thought experiment

In this thought experiment, demonstrate your skills and knowledge of the topics covered in this chapter. You can find answers to this thought experiment in the next section.

You work in support at A. Datum Corporation. As a consultant for A. Datum, answer the following questions about installing and configuring DNS within the A. Datum organization:

1. You have asked a colleague to deploy the DNS server role to a Nano Server installed as a member of the Adatum.com domain. What must your colleague do?
2. At a branch office, you do not want the local DNS server to perform queries for local clients aside from those for which it is authoritative. How could you address this objective?
3. You want only to allow recursion by your DNS servers for queries received on the internal network and not from Internet-based clients. How could you address this requirement?
4. Managers at A. Datum are concerned with security and your boss has asked that you implement DNSSEC to help to secure DNS. You know that DNSSEC relies on distributing the NRPT. How could you configure NRPT distribution easily?
5. You have installed the DNS server role on a computer running Windows Server 2016. You now want to create zones on the server. You want to store the zone data in AD DS, but the option to store the zone in Active Directory is unavailable. Why might this be?
6. You want to be able to deploy an AD DS–integrated primary zone by using Windows PowerShell. What command should you use?
7. A. Datum has just purchased the Contoso Pharmaceuticals company. Your users are frequently accessing server resources in Contoso's network infrastructure. You need to configure DNS to support this change in circumstances. What two options do you have to more efficiently manage name resolution in this situation?
8. Your network consists of many subnets distributed across the globe. You want to make a web server easily accessible from any location by using the same name. However, you want your users to be directed by DNS to a local web server. What feature of Windows Server 2016 would enable this?

Thought experiment answers

This section contains the solutions to the thought experiment. Each answer explains why the answer choice is correct.

1. To install the DNS server role to an existing Nano Server, your colleague should create a remote Windows PowerShell session to the Nano Server and then use the Enable-WindowsOptionalFeature -Online -FeatureName DNS-Server-Full-Role command to add the DNS role.

2. You could configure the branch DNS server to use forwarding. Specify a DNS server elsewhere in the organization to which it forwards all queries it cannot satisfy locally.

3. You could implement DNS policies. Specifically, you could create a recursion scope so that recursion is enabled when requested on a specific DNS server interface, or from a specific internal subnet. The following three Windows PowerShell commands would enable you to achieve your objective:

   ```
   Set-DnsServerRecursionScope -Name . -EnableRecursion $False

   Add-DnsServerRecursionScope -Name "InternalAdatumClients" -EnableRecursion $True

   Add-DnsServerQueryResolutionPolicy -Name "RecursionControlPolicy" -Action ALLOW
   -ApplyOnRecursion -RecursionScope "InternalAdatumClients" -ServerInterfaceIP
   "EQ,10.24.60.254"
   ```

4. The easiest way to distribute NRPT is to use a GPO. Edit the Default Domain GPO and navigate to Computer Configuration / Policies / Windows Settings / Name Resolution Policy. Create a rule containing the domain suffix you want to distribute for, and then enable both Enable DNSSEC in This Rule and Require DNS Clients to Check that the Name and Address Data Has Been Validated By the DNS Server.

5. The option to store the zone in Active Directory is only available on DNS servers that also have the AD DS server role installed and configured.

6. To deploy an AD DS–integrated primary zone on a DNS server, use the Add-DnsServerPrimaryZone cmdlet with the ReplicationScope parameter. For example: Add-DnsServerPrimaryZone -Name "Contoso.com" -ReplicationScope "Domain"

7. Consider implementing conditional forwarding or a stub zone. Both enable clients to more easily access the name servers for a foreign domain.

8. Use DNS policies and DNS zone scopes to configure this behavior. You can create DNS client subnets and assign these subnets into DNS scopes. Next, you create DNS resource records in the zone scopes. Finally, you would use a DNS policy to determine which records are returned to a DNS client, based on the originating subnet.

CHAPTER 2

Implement DHCP

The Dynamic Host Configuration Protocol (DHCP) server role enables you to more easily configure your network clients by automatically assigning them an Internet Protocol version 4 (IPv4) or Internet Protocol version 6 (IPv6) configuration. The DHCP server role is an essential service, without which, your network clients and devices cannot obtain an IPv4 or IPv6 configuration. This means it is essential that you know how to manage and maintain the DHCP server role. The 70-741 Networking Windows Server 2016 exam covers the installation, configuration, management, and maintenance of the DHCP server role.

Skills in this chapter:
- Install and configure DHCP
- Manage and maintain DHCP

Skill 2.1: Install and configure DHCP

It is relatively straightforward to configure a device with an IPv4 or IPv6 address. However, if you have multiple devices to configure and your network spans multiple subnets and locations, it becomes time-consuming and error-prone.

Overview of DHCP

DHCP enables you to more easily and quickly configure devices with the required IPv4 or IPv6 settings and offers the following advantages to administrators.

- Provides IP addresses automatically
- Ensures correct IP configuration
- Supports device reconfiguration
- Enables efficient use of available IP address pool
- Centralizes IP configuration

To enable DHCP within your organization, you must deploy one or more DHCP servers. Each DHCP server maintains one or more *DHCP scopes*. A DHCP scope contains the relevant IP address pool and supplemental configuration information required to configure a client computer.

After you have completed server setup, the DHCP servers listen for client requests on their configured network interfaces. These client requests originate from client devices that want to obtain an IP configuration. The requests are broadcast-based because the clients do not have a configured IP address needed to communicate directly with a DHCP server. A server responds with the offer of a suitable IP configuration that the client typically accepts. The server completes the process by acknowledging the assignment of the address.

The process is completed through the use of four communication phases:

1. The DHCP client broadcasts a DHCPDISCOVER packet.
2. A DHCP server responds with a DHCPOFFER packet that contains a suggested IP configuration.
3. The client receives the offer and broadcasts a DHCPREQUEST packet that contains a server identifier. This packet indicates that the client wishes to use the offered configuration. If there are multiple DHCP servers, all of them receive the DHCPREQUEST, and they can see from the server identifier that another server is servicing the client request.
4. The server that was identified uses a DHCPACK message to the client to signify that the configuration is live, and that the IP address is now leased by the client.

The client computer now uses the leased IP configuration until the lease duration expires. However, to avoid losing connectivity when the lease expires, clients try a renewal when the lease is 50 percent expired. Clients also attempt to renew the lease and every time the client computer starts up. If the DHCP server is online and accessible, the lease is renewed. This process uses only two messages: a DHCPREQUEST from the client and a DHCPACK from the server.

EXAM TIP

DHCP renewal messages are not broadcast-based because the client has a valid IP configuration with which to use unicast traffic.

If the client cannot communicate with the DHCP server when it attempts renewal at 50 percent lease expired, it tries again at 87.5 percent lease expired. At this time, it starts to use broadcast-based renewal messages. If the client cannot obtain a confirmation of its renewal attempt by 100 percent lease expiration, it switches to the DHCP discovery mode discussed earlier.

It is slightly different if a DHCP client cannot renew during startup. One possible reasons for failing to communicate with a DHCP server might be because the client is no longer in the same subnet. During startup, if a client cannot renew with their configured DHCP server, it sends a message to the configured default gateway. If it does not get a response, the client assumes that it is no longer in the original subnet, and it uses the DHCP discovery phase to obtain a new, valid configuration for the current subnet.

If a Windows-based client cannot renew its DHCP lease, it ceases use of the leased configuration and typically uses an Automatic Private IP Addressing (APIPA) address. APIPA addresses enable basic, local-only subnet communication using an IP address in the range 169.254.0.0/16. Generally, this means that the client is unable to communicate with most, if not all, networked resources.

> **NEED MORE REVIEW?** **HOW DHCP WORKS**
>
> To review further details about how DHCP works, refer to the Microsoft TechNet website at *https://technet.microsoft.com/library/dd183692(v=ws.10).aspx*.

Install DHCP

You can install the DHCP server role by using Server Manager or Windows PowerShell. After you install the DHCP server role, you must authorize it in Active Directory Domain Services (AD DS).

> **EXAM TIP**
>
> You cannot install the DHCP server role on Nano Server.

Install and configure DHCP servers

Before you can install DHCP, you must make sure that you meet the prerequisites, which are:

- Sign in with a local administrative account, or in a domain, sign in as a member of the Domain Admins global security group
- Verify that you are installing to either Windows Server 2016 or Windows Server 2016 Server Core
- Configure the target server with a static IPv4 and/or IPv6 address
- Ensure that all disk volumes are formatted with NTFS. The FAT file system is not secure

> **EXAM TIP**
>
> Avoid installing the DHCP server role on servers that are performing specialized functions such as hosting Web apps, Microsoft Exchange, or Microsoft SQL Server.

To install the DHCP server role, use the following procedure:

1. In Server Manager, click Manage and then click Add Roles And Features.
2. In the Add Roles And Features wizard, on the Before You Begin page, click Next.
3. On the Select Installation Type page and Select Destination Server page, click Next.
4. On the Select Server Roles page, in the Roles list, select the DHCP Server check box.
5. In the Add Features That Are Required For DHCP Server dialog box, click Add Features, and then click Next.
6. On the Select Features page, click Next.
7. On the DHCP Server page, click Next.
8. On the Confirm Installation Selections page, click Install. When the role is installed, click Close.

You can also use the Windows PowerShell Add-WindowsFeature cmdlet to install the DHCP Server role. For example, to install the DHCP Server role with all administrative tools, run the following command:

```
Add-WindowsFeature DHCP -IncludeManagementTools
```

Complete installation and authorize a DHCP server

After you have installed the role, you must complete the installation. This involves creating the required security groups and performing DHCP server authorization. You can complete both these tasks by using the DHCP Post-Install Configuration Wizard. This wizard completes the following tasks:

- Creates the required AD DS security groups that enable delegation of DHCP server administration:
    - DHCP Administrators
    - DHCP Users
- Authorizes the DHCP server role if the computer is domain-joined.

You can access the DHCP Post-Install Configuration Wizard from Server Manager, as shown in Figure 2-1, by following the listed steps.

1. Click Notifications, and then click Complete DHCP configuration.

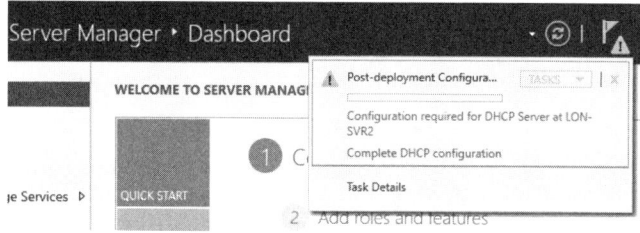

FIGURE 2-1 Completing DHCP Server role installation

2. In the DHCP Post-Install Configuration wizard, on the Description page, click Next.
3. On the Authorization page, specify the credentials required to authorize the server in AD DS. The account you use should be a member of the Domain Admins Global security group. Click Commit to complete authorization and create the required security groups.

> **EXAM TIP**
> You only need to authorize the DHCP server if it is domain-joined.

If you want to authorize the server using a separate task, click Skip AD authorization, as shown in Figure 2-2, and then click Commit. This only creates the required security groups, but you must still authorize DHCP.

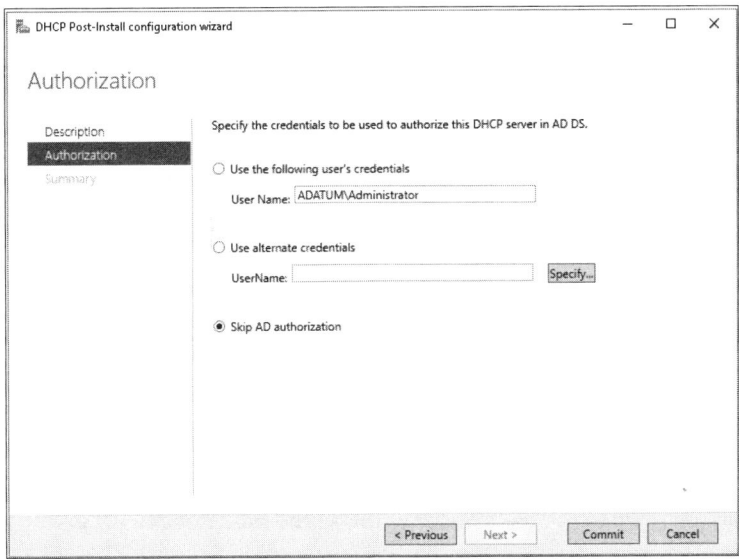

FIGURE 2-2 Skipping AD DS authorization

If you decide not to authorize the DHCP server using the DHCP Post-Install Configuration Wizard, you must do so before enabling the DHCP server. You can use the DHCP console to authorize the DHCP server after installation. To do this, complete the following procedure:

1. In Server Manager, click Tools and then click DHCP.
2. In the DHCP console, right-click the target server and then click Authorize.

You can also use the Windows PowerShell Add-DhcpServerInDC cmdlet to complete this process. For example, the following command authorizes the lon-svr2 server in the contoso.com domain:

```
Add-DhcpServerInDC -DnsName lon-svr2.contoso.com
```

> **NEED MORE REVIEW? DHCP SERVER CMDLETS IN WINDOWS POWERSHELL**
>
> To review further details about using Windows PowerShell to configure DHCP, refer to the Microsoft TechNet website at *https://technet.microsoft.com/library/jj590751(v=wps.630).aspx*.

Create and manage DHCP scopes

After you have installed and authorized your DHCP server, you can begin to create DHCP scopes. Scopes contain the relevant pools of IPv4 or IPv6 addresses and related information that is used to configure your network clients.

Create and configure scopes

A DHCP scope is the fundamental component of the DHCP architecture. A scope contains a pool of IPv4 or IPv6 addresses and supplemental configuration options, such as default gateways, and Domain Name System (DNS) suffixes and DNS servers.

You can create your DHCP scopes by using either the DHCP console or Windows PowerShell. To create a DHCP IPv4 scope using the DHCP console, use the following procedure:

1. In the DHCP console, expand the DHCP server, right-click IPv4, and then click New Scope.
2. In the New Scope Wizard, on the Welcome to the New Scope Wizard page, click Next.
3. On the Scope Name page, provide a name and description for your scope. These should be meaningful. Click Next.
4. On the IP Address Range page, in the Start IP address box, type the first valid IPv4 address in your scope. In the End IP Address box, type the last valid IP address in your scope. In the Length list, click the number of bits in the subnet mask. For example, click 24. The Subnet Mask field is populated for you, as shown in Figure 2-3. Click Next.

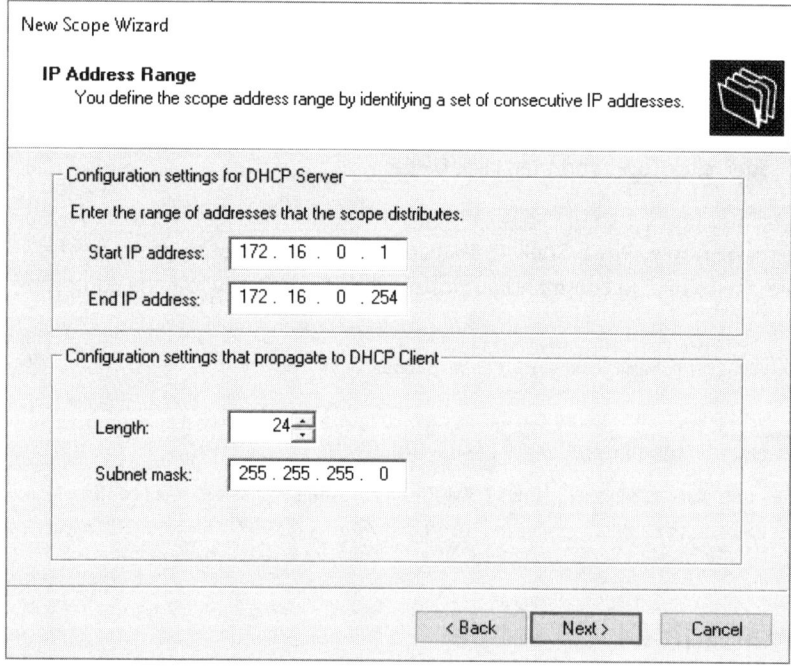

FIGURE 2-3 Defining the scope IP address range and subnet mask

5. On the Add Exclusions and Delay page, in the Start IP Address and End IP address fields, type any ranges of IP addresses that you wish to exclude from the allocation pool and click Add. You can exclude individual IP addresses if you want, as shown in Figure 2-4.

EXAM TIP

You can change the IP address range and DHCP exclusions after you have created the scope.

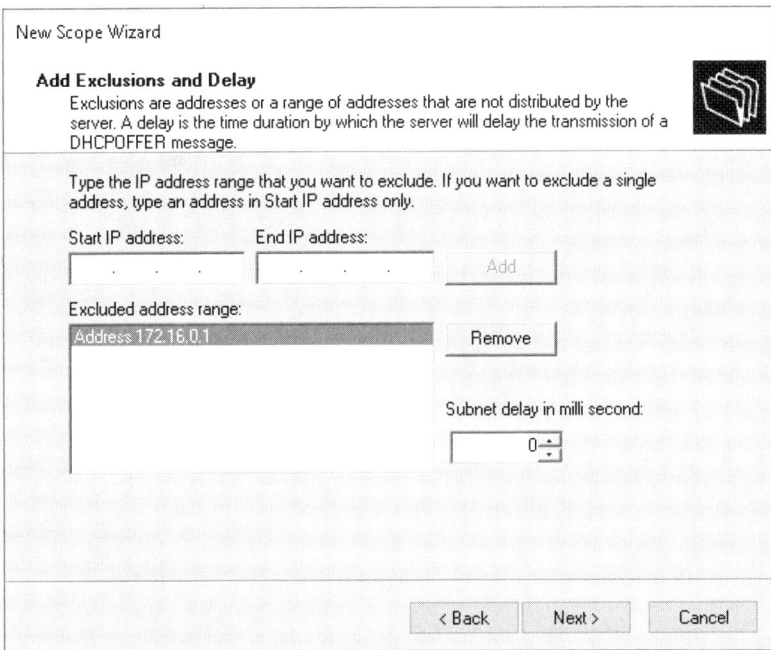

FIGURE 2-4 Adding exclusions to the scope

6. In the Subnet Delay box, enter a value to delay allocation of DHCPOFFER messages to your client computers. Usually, this value is not used. Click Next.

7. On the Lease Duration page, enter the value of the lease period. This is the period that DHCP clients continue to use their allocated IP address before they must renew or release it. The default is eight days. Use a shorter interval for scopes that have limited address capacity, or when clients frequently move between subnets and scopes. Click Next.

8. On the Configure DHCP Options, click Yes, I Want To Configure These Options Now, and then click Next. You can reconfigure these options later in the DHCP console.

9. On the Router (Default Gateway) page, in the IP address box, type the IP address of the default gateway that will service clients in this scope and click Add. You can configure multiple gateways and order them in the list. Click Next.

10. On the Domain Name and DNS Servers page, in the Server Name box, type the fully qualified domain name (FQDN) or IP address of the primary DNS server for clients in this scope, as shown in Figure 2-5, click Add, and then click Next.

> **EXAM TIP**
>
> The Parent Domain Value is automatically populated from the DHCP computer's domain membership or Primary DNS suffix. You can change this as it might not match the DNS domain name for the clients that will use this scope.

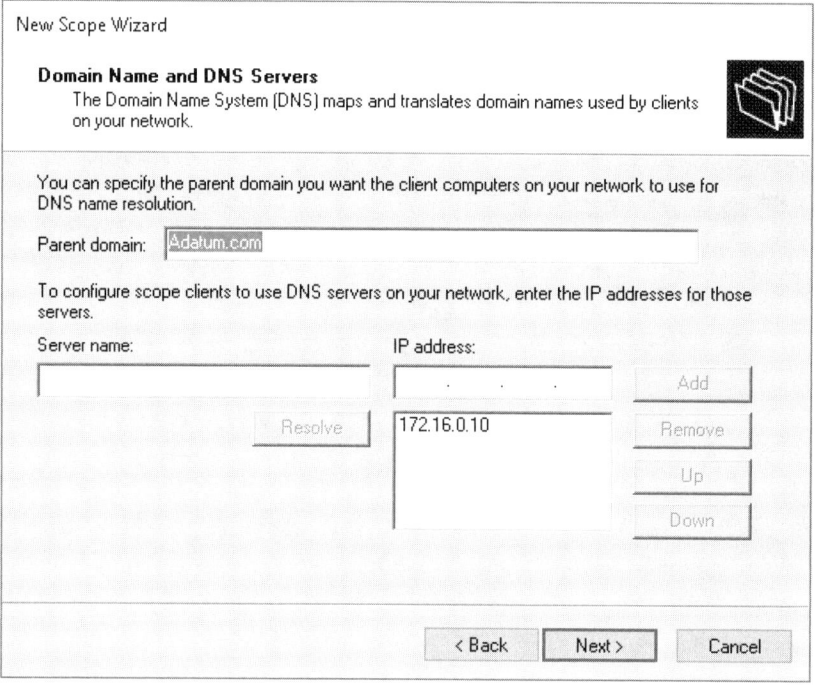

FIGURE 2-5 Configuring the DNS scope options

11. On the WINS Server page, if you use NetBIOS-based apps and do not use a Global-Names zone for single-label name resolution, enter the IP address of one or more WINS servers and then click Next.

12. Finally, on the Activate Scope page, if you are ready to allow clients to obtain IP configurations from the scope, click Yes, I Want To Activate This Scope Now, and click Next. You can activate the scope later from the DHCP console. Click Finish.

To create a DHCP IPv4 scope using Windows PowerShell, use the Add-DhcpServerv4Scope cmdlet. For example, the following command adds a new scope called "London" for the 172.16.0.0/24 subnet on the DHCP server service running on the local computer:

```
Add-DhcpServerv4Scope -Name "London" -StartRange 172.16.0.1 -EndRange 172.16.0.254
 -SubnetMask 255.255.255.0
```

After you have created your scopes, use either the DHCP console or Windows PowerShell to configure them. Let's discuss the configurable options next.

Create and configure superscopes and multicast scopes

The DHCP server role provides two options for more complex scope scenarios. These are superscopes and multicast scopes.

- **Superscopes**   You can use DHCP superscopes to support *multinets*. A multinet is an environment where you have multiple logical networks, or subnets, on a single physical network, such as an Ethernet segment. Superscopes can help in multinet deployment scenarios in the following situations:
    - **Address pool depletion**   You have insufficient IP addresses available in the pool. Since you cannot extend the pool, you must add another scope with its own pool of addresses.
    - **Client migration**   You are migrating client devices to a new DHCP scope, perhaps because you are implementing a new addressing scheme.
    - **Multiple DHCP servers**   You want two or more DHCP servers to service clients on the same physical segment to manage separate logical IP subnets.
- Multicast scopes   A multicast scope, also known as a Multicast Address Dynamic Client Allocation Protocol (MADCAP) scope, supports apps that use multicast transmission to communicate. Addresses from a multicast scope are assigned from class D IP addresses and are in the range from 224.0.0.0 through to 239.255.255.255 (224.0.0.0/3). You use multicast scopes to enable apps to reserve a multicast address for their communications.

EXAM TIP

Multicast transmission enables a server to communicate with multiple client devices efficiently without using broadcasts. Multicast transmission is often used by deployment software, such as Windows Deployment Services.

CREATE A SUPERSCOPE

To create a superscope, you must first have at least one scope on your DHCP server. Then, from the DHCP console, right-click the IPv4 node and then click New Superscope. The New Superscope Wizard starts. You must define the following properties:

- **Name**   A descriptive name for the superscope.
- **Selected scopes**   You must select which scopes are part of the superscope.

After you have created your superscope, the selected scopes appear beneath a newly created Superscope node in the DHCP console, as shown in Figure 2-6.

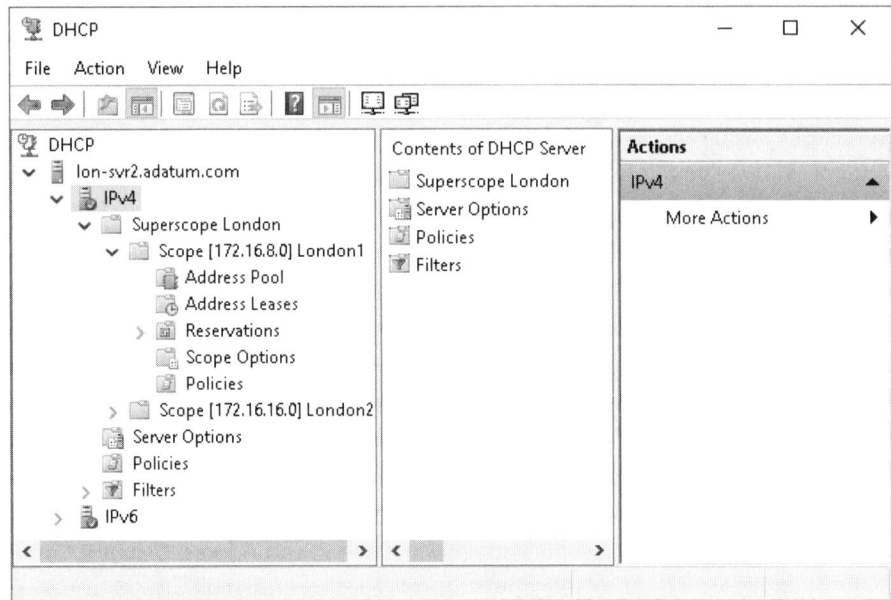

FIGURE 2-6 The Superscope node in the DHCP console

> **EXAM TIP**
>
> To add a scope to an existing Superscope, in the DHCP console, right-click the scope and then click Add To Superscope.

You can use the Add-DhcpServerv4Superscope Windows PowerShell cmdlet to create a superscope. For example, the following command creates the London superscope and combines two scopes in the 172.16.0.0/248 range:

```
Add-DhcpServerv4Superscope -SuperscopeName "London" -ScopeId 172.16.8.0,
172.16.16.0
```

> **NEED MORE REVIEW?** **CONFIGURING A DHCP SUPERSCOPE**
>
> To review further details about DHCP superscopes, refer to the Microsoft TechNet website at *https://technet.microsoft.com/library/dd759168(v=ws.11).aspx*.

CREATE A MULTICAST SCOPE

To create a multicast scope, you must confirm that your application can obtain a multicast address from DHCP. Next, open the DHCP console, right-click the IPv4 node, and then click New Multicast Scope. The New Multicast Scope Wizard starts. You must define the following properties:

- **Name** A descriptive name for the multicast scope.
- **Description** An optional description for the scope.
- **IP Address Range** The range of class D addresses that you want to assign to the scope. Specify a start and end IP address in the range from 239.0.0.0 to 239.255.255.255. The range you specify must allow for at least 256 addresses.
- **Exclusions** As with a standard scope, you can define one or several multicast IP addresses to exclude.
- **Lease duration** The default is 30 days.

After you have created your multicast scope, you can view and configure its properties, as shown in Figure 2-7.

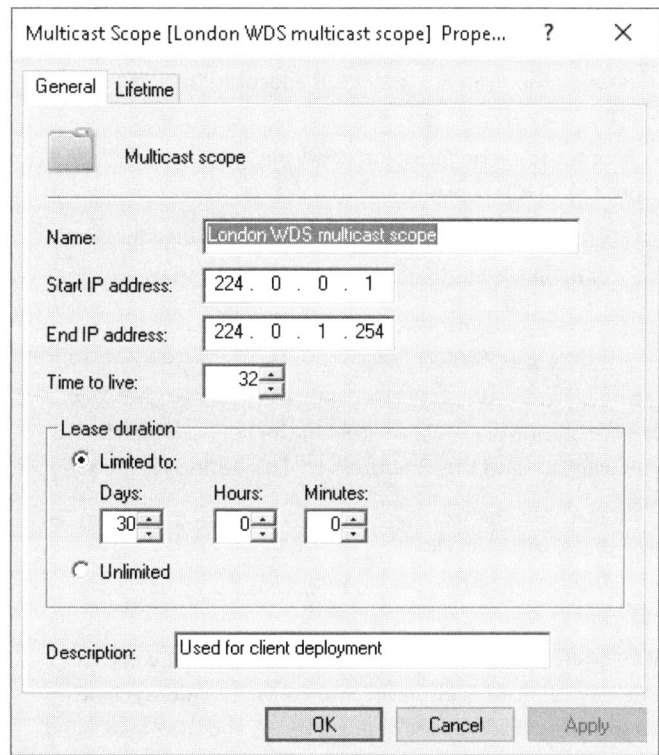

FIGURE 2-7 Configuring multicast scope properties

You can also use the Add-DhcpServerv4MulticastScope Windows PowerShell cmdlet to create multicast scopes. For example, the following command creates the same multicast scope as what is shown in Figure 2-7.

```
Add-DhcpServerv4MulticastScope -ComputerName "lon-svr2.Contoso.com" -Name "London
WDS multicast scope" -StartRange 224.0.0.1 -EndRange 224.0.1.254
```

> **NEED MORE REVIEW?** **CONFIGURING A DHCP MULTICAST SCOPE**
>
> To review further details about DHCP multicast scopes, refer to the Microsoft TechNet website at *https://technet.microsoft.com/library/dd759152(v=ws.11).aspx*.

Configure a DHCP reservation

Imagine that you want to allocate lon-svr3.Contoso.com a specific IPv4 address. While you might consider allocating lon-svr3 a manually assigned IPv4 configuration, you must remember to remove the manually allocated address from any DHCP scopes that contain the address. Also, if you ever want to change the IPv4 configuration for lon-svr3, you must revisit the computer and manually change the address, and then update any scope exclusions.

A DHCP reservation is a method to use so you can allocate a specific IPv4 or IPv6 address from a pool to a designated client device. The advantage of this process is that you:

- Need not exclude any addresses as the reserved address is allocated from the scope's pool of addresses.
- Never need to revisit the computer to reconfigure the IP address as you can reconfigure the reserved address from the DHCP console.

To create a reservation within a scope, you must provide the following information:

- **Reservation name**   A name with which to identify the reservation. Often, the computer name is used.
- **IP address**   The specific IP address you want to allocate to the client from the address pool.
- **MAC address**   The media access control (MAC) address of the network interface in the client computer that you want to bind the IP address to. This address is unique and identifies the client computer.
- **Description**   Optional field to describe the client.

> *EXAM TIP*
>
> You can determine a device's MAC address in a number of ways. For example, if you use the `ipconfig /all` command, the MAC address is displayed in the Physical Address field. You can also use the `arp -a` command to display a list of IP addresses and their associated MAC addresses.

To add a reservation, from the DHCP console, select the appropriate scope, right-click the Reservations node and then click New Reservation. Complete the New Reservation dialog box, as shown in Figure 2-8.

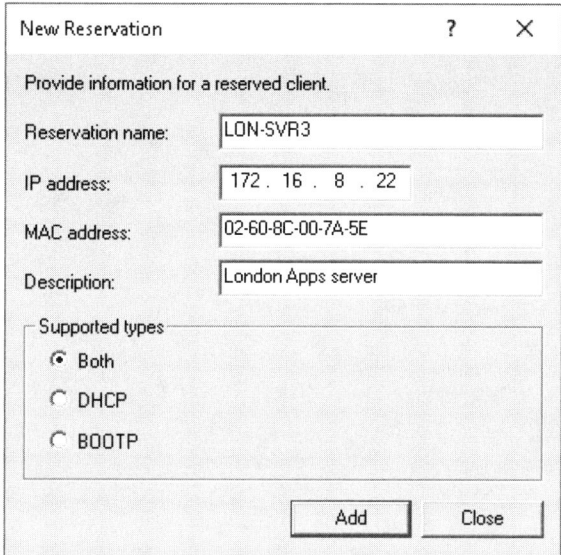

FIGURE 2-8 Adding a reservation

You can also use the Windows PowerShell Add-DhcpServerv4Reservation cmdlet. For example, the following command creates a reservation for the LON-SVR3 client with the MAC address 02-60-8C-00-7A-5E:

    Add-DhcpServerv4Reservation -ScopeId 172.16.8.0 -IPAddress 172.16.8.22 -ClientId
    02-60-8C-00-7A-5E Description "LON-SVR3"

EXAM TIP

Any reservations are displayed in the Address Leases node beneath the Scope node. They are listed as Reservation (inactive) or Reservation (active) depending on whether the configured device is using the reservation.

Configure DHCP options

As part of the configuration of a scope, you are asked if you want to configure scope options. These options enable client computers to obtain a complete IP configuration. Without options, a DHCP client is configured only with an IP address and subnet mask. This does not allow for name resolution, or communications outside of the local subnet.

By using DHCP options, you can allocate additional IP configuration properties with the IP address and subnet mask. There are many options that you can assign but, for the most part, you will configure a default gateway (router) interface, and options that enable name resolution. Table 2-1 shows some of the most common DHCP options.

TABLE 2-1 DHCP options.

Option code	Name
003	Router
004	Time Server
005	Name Servers
006	DNS Servers
015	DNS Domain Name
031	Perform Router Discovery
044	WINS/NBNS Servers
046	WINS/NBT Node Type
047	NetBIOS Scope ID
060	Pre-Boot Execution (PXE) client
066	Boot Server Host Name
067	Bootfile Name

You can configure and apply DHCP options at four different levels:

- **Server**   Assigns options to all DHCP clients of this server.
- **Scope**   Assigns options to DHCP clients of this scope. Scope options override server options.
- **Class**   Assigns options to all clients devices that identify themselves as members of a configured class. Class options override both scope and server options.
- **Reserved client**   Assigns options to a specific DHCP reservation. Reserved client options only apply to devices that have a DHCP reservation and override all other configured options.

When the same option is applied at different levels, the most specific settings overrides any other settings. For example, if you assign the router option at the scope level, but also assign a different router option value for a reserved client, then the reserved client is the effective setting.

CONFIGURE DHCP SERVER OPTIONS

You can configure DHCP server options from the DHCP console. Under the IPv4 or IPv6 nodes, right-click the Server Options node and then click Configure Options. In the Server Options dialog box, as shown in Figure 2-9, you can configure the relevant option by selecting the appropriate option check box, and then configuring the required value(s).

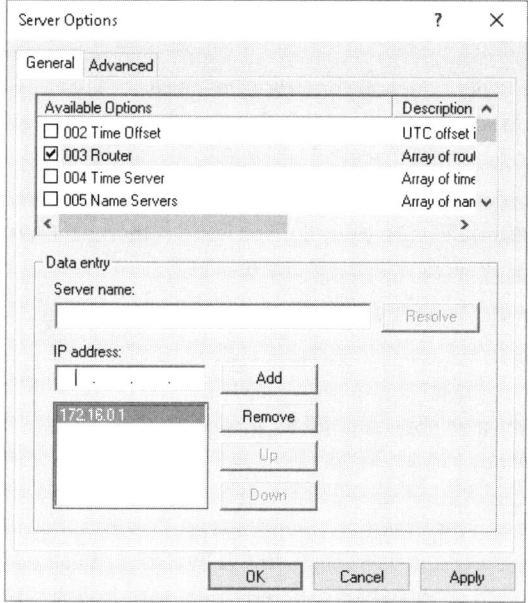

FIGURE 2-9 Configuring DHCP server options

You can also configure DHCP server options with the Set-DhcpServerv4OptionValue Windows PowerShell cmdlet. For example, the following command configures the LON-SVR2 DHCP server with the Router (003), DNS server (006) and DNS domain name (015) server options:

    Set-DhcpServerv4OptionValue -ComputerName LON-SVR2.contoso.com -DnsServer
    172.16.0.10 -DnsDomain contoso.com -Router 172.16.0.1

CONFIGURE DHCP SCOPE OPTIONS

To configure DHCP options at the scope level, in the DHCP console, locate the appropriate scope, right-click the Scope Options node, and then click Configure Options.

You can also configure DHCP scope options with the Set-DhcpServerv4OptionValue Windows PowerShell cmdlet using the -ScopeID parameter. For example, the following command configures the DHCP Router (003), DNS server (006) and DNS domain name (015) scope options on the scope with the ID of 172.16.8.0:

    Set-DhcpServerv4OptionValue -ComputerName LON-SVR2.contoso.com -ScopeId 172.16.8.0
    -DnsServer 172.16.0.10 -DnsDomain contoso.com -Router 172.16.0.1

CONFIGURE CLASS OPTIONS

In addition to server and scope level options, you can also assign class level options to your DHCP clients. Class options are applied when a computer or device has a specific class ID. These classes can be assigned by a vendor, such as Microsoft, or by the DHCP administrator, in which case they are known as user class options.

To implement user class options, you must first create the appropriate user class. You do this by using the following high-level procedure:

1. In the DHCP console by right-click the IPv4 node, and then click Define User Classes. Create the appropriate user class and assign it a unique identifier. For example, you might create a user class for your laptop computers called LAPTOP.
2. On the DHCP client devices, assign the device to the appropriate user class using the IPConfig.exe command-line tool. For example, type IPconfig /setclassid "Ethernet" LAPTOP, where *Ethernet* is the name of the network adapter in the device.
3. Use DHCP policies to assign DHCP options to your defined user classes.

EXAM TIP

You can only define user classes for the whole IPv4 node and not for individual servers or scopes. You cannot define user classes for IPv6.

You use vendor classes to configure client options based on a vendor type. Clients must first identify themselves as being of a particular vendor class. They do this by adding a value in the vendor class ID field of a DHCPREQUEST message when they request a lease from a DHCP server. Vendor classes are determined by a device vendor. As with user classes, you use DHCP policies to assign them. You will learn more about DHCP policies in Skill 2.2.

CONFIGURE DNS OPTIONS FROM WITHIN DHCP

You have seen that you can assign both the name server(s) (option 006) and the DNS domain name (option 015) using DHCP options. You can also configure DHCP and DNS integration. Microsoft DNS supports dynamic updates in which a DNS client can update its host and other records in the DNS zone database. However, you can also configure the DHCP server to automatically update a client's DNS server with the client's host (A) and pointer (PTR) records.

You can configure the following options, as shown in Figure 2-10.

- Dynamically update DNS records only if requested by the DHCP clients (the default option).
- Always dynamically update DNS records.
- Discard A and PTR records when the lease is deleted (selected by default).
- Dynamically update DNS records for DHCP clients that do not request updates (for example, clients running Windows NT 4.0)
- Disable dynamic updates for DNS PTR records.

With the default options, most DHCP clients will update their DNS records themselves. However, the DHCP server always deletes the host and pointer records from the DNS zone when a client lease expires.

You can use the Name Protection option to help protect the DNS zone from incorrect or insecure updates. If the DHCP server attempts to update a DNS name and discovers that another client has registered the name already, the update fails.

EXAM TIP

Your DNS zones must be configured for Secure Dynamic Updates for the Name Protection setting to work.

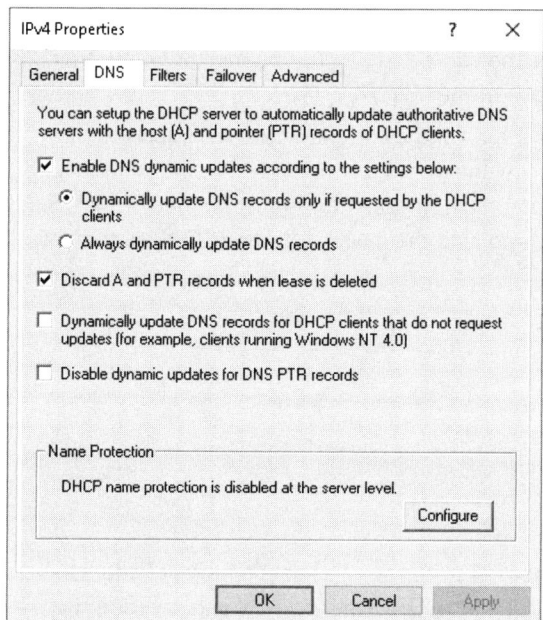

FIGURE 2-10 Configuring DNS options for IPv4

EXAM TIP

You can configure the same DNS settings on the IPv6 node to support your IPv6 clients DNS integration options.

Configure DHCP policies

You can use DHCP policies to assign specific IPv4 options to your DHCP clients. Options are assigned by DHCP based on conditions within your policy, including user and vendor class, MAC address, or other factors. For example, you could create a policy that assigns different ranges of addresses to laptop computers, or assigns longer leases to desktop-based computers.

EXAM TIP

You can create server-level policies that apply to all scopes, or scope-level policies that apply only to a specific scope.

You can use the DHCP console or the Windows PowerShell Add-DhcpServerv4Policy cmdlet to create a DHCP policy. To create a new server-level policy using the DHCP console, under the IPv4 node, right-click the Policies node and then click New Policy. To create a scope-level policy, right-click the Policies node beneath the appropriate scope.

To create a policy, you must provide the following information:

- **Policy Name and Description**   Make the name and description meaningful so that it is easy to identify the purpose and scope of the policy.

- **Conditions**   A condition consists of criteria and an operator, such as Equals or Not Equals, as shown in Figure 2-11. Specify one or more conditions that must be met for the policy to apply. You can define that multiple conditions must be met, or that one of several conditions must be met by combining them with AND and OR operators. You can choose the following criteria:
    - Vendor Class
    - User Class
    - MAC Address
    - Client Identifier
    - Fully Qualified Domain Name
    - Relay Agent Information

- **IP address range**   For scope-level policies only, you can select a range of addresses from those assigned to the scope pool that will be assigned to clients meeting the policy conditions.

- **Options**   For scope-level policies only, you can configure the DHCP options that are assigned to clients meeting the policy conditions: 003 Router, 006 DNS Server, and 015 DNS Domain Name. For server-level policies, you assign the options after creating the policy.

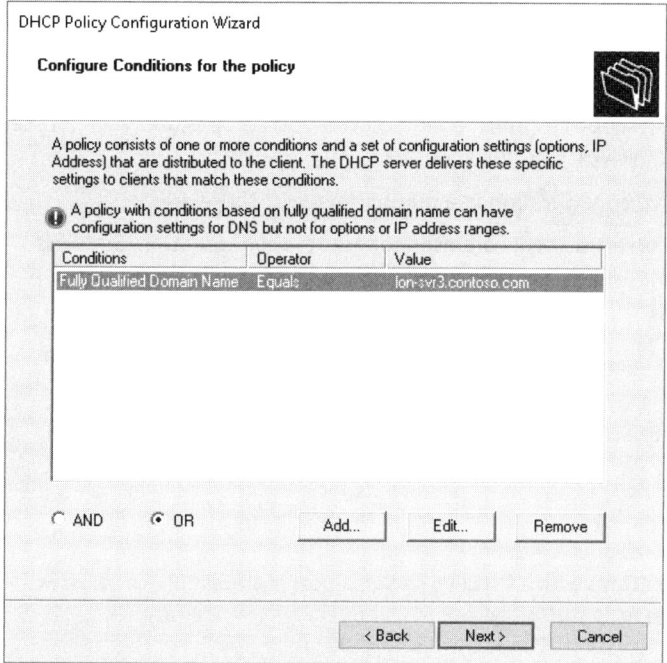

FIGURE 2-11 Creating policy conditions

After you have created the policy, you can configure general DHCP options, such as router and DNS server, and DNS specific settings. To do this, in the DHCP console, right-click your policy in the Policies node, and then click Properties. You can then access the following tabs:

- **General** You can configure the lease duration for the policy. Select the Set Lease Duration For The Policy check box, and then configure the duration.
- **Conditions** You can reconfigure the conditions for the policy.
- IP Address Range For scope-level policies only, you can reconfigure the IP address range.
- **Options** You will find all the standard DHCP options listed here: 003 Router, 006 DNS Server, and 015 DNS Domain Name.
- **DNS** You can reconfigure the DNS integration settings for clients affected by this policy.

> *NEED MORE REVIEW?* **STEP-BY-STEP: CONFIGURE DHCP USING POLICY-BASED ASSIGNMENT**
>
> To review further details about using DHCP policies, refer to the Microsoft TechNet website at *https://technet.microsoft.com/library/hh831538(v=ws.11).aspx*.

Implement IPv6 addressing using DHCPv6

Although IPv6 is not yet very prevalent, it is becoming more widely used, sometimes to enable applications that require it. DHCP fully supports IPv6 through the use of IPv6 scopes. You can configure and manage these scopes as much as you do with IPv4 scopes and you can use both the DHCP console and Windows PowerShell cmdlets.

IPv6 nodes can obtain an IPv6 configuration in a number of ways. These are:

- **Stateless**   Only router advertisements are used for address configuration. Stateless autoconfiguration provides only a router prefix. It does not provide configuration options such as DNS servers.
- **Stateful**   A DHCPv6 server is used to obtain addresses and other configuration options.
- **Both**   The IPv6 client obtains a configuration based on router advertisements and DHCPv6.

EXAM TIP

When an IPv6 device communicates with a DHCPv6 server, it uses multicast IPv6 addresses. IPv4 devices rely on broadcast IPv4 addresses.

To create an IPv6 scope, you must provide the following information:

- **Name and description**   These must be meaningful so that you can easily identify the scope.
- **Prefix**   IPv6 uses prefixes in a similar way to how IPv4 uses subnet masks. Each IPv6 address consists of 128 bits, and the IPv6 prefix states how many of these bits are assigned to information such as IPv6 subnets, routes, and address ranges.

EXAM TIP

IPv6 prefixes are shown in an address/prefix-length notation. For example, 2001:DB5:0:2A4C::/64 is an IPv6 address prefix for a subnet.

- **Preference**   If several DHCPv6 servers offer a client an IPv6 configuration, the client selects the one with the highest preference value. If multiple offers have the same preference value, the client will select the offer with the most options configured in the offer. This setting is not used if you set a preference value of 0 (the default) as shown in Figure 2-12.

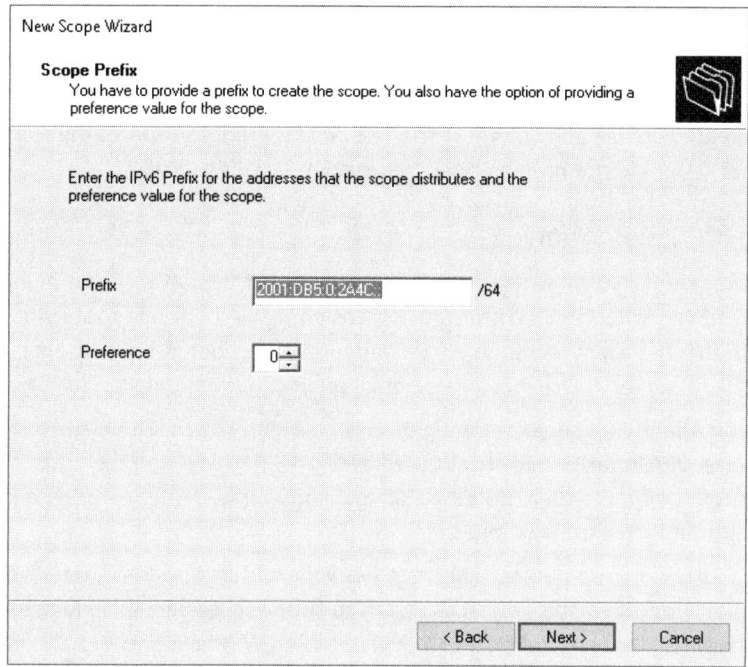

FIGURE 2-12 Configuring the prefix and preference values for a DHCPv6 scope

- **Exclusions** Enter one or more addresses or a range of addresses from the scope that you want to exclude.
- **Lease duration** The default is eight days.

You can also create an IPv6 scope by using the Add-DhcpServerv6Scope Windows PowerShell cmdlet. For example, the following cmdlet creates an IPv6 scope with the prefix of 2001:DB5:0:2A4C:: called LondonScope:

```
Add-DhcpServerv6Scope -Prefix 2001:DB5:0:2A4C:: -Name "LondonScope"
```

Most of the configuration options that you can apply to IPv4 scopes also apply to IPv6 scopes. For example, you can configure IPv6 server options, or apply options at the scope, class, or reservation level. DNS integration options are accessed by using the DNS tab on the IPv6 node properties page, much the same way that you configure these options in IPv4.

> **NOTE**
>
> We will cover IPv6 addressing in more detail in Chapter 11, "Implement IPv4 and IPv6 addressing."

Configure DHCP relay agent and PXE boot

To facilitate specific scenarios, you might need to enable and configure a DHCP Relay Agent in your network to support DHCP clients in subnets that do not host a local DHCP server. You might also need to enable and configure the PXE environment to support the startup of clients' computers, which do not have an operating system installed locally.

Configure DHCP Relay Agent

Much of the traffic in DHCP is broadcast-based. This means that the network communications between a DHCP server and a DHCP client cannot transit a router (typically, routers do not pass broadcast traffic). If a client requiring an IP configuration resides in a subnet that does not host a local DHCP server, the client cannot obtain an IP configuration.

The DHCP Relay Agent enables you to mitigate this problem. The DHCP Relay Agent listens for broadcast-based DHCP traffic on its configured network interfaces and then uses directed communications to forward the client DHCP traffic to a configured DHCP server on another network interface; that is, in another subnet.

This functionality is very often found built-in to network routers nowadays. However, if your routers do not support what is known as *BOOTP forwarding*, as defined in RFC 1542, you can install the DHCP Relay Agent on a computer running Windows Server 2016 on each subnet that does not have a DHCP server.

The DHCP Relay Agent in Windows Server 2016 is a feature of the Routing Role Service in the Remote Access Server role, and not the DHCP Server Role. To install and configure the DHCP Relay Agent, use the following procedure:

1. Install the Remote Access server role with the Server Manager.
2. When prompted by the Add Roles and Features Wizard, on the Select role services page, select the Routing check box.
3. After installation, in Server Manager, click Tools, and then click Routing and Remote Access.
4. In Routing and Remote Access, right-click your server and then click Configure and Enable Routing And Remote Access.
5. In the Routing and Remote Access Server Setup Wizard, choose Custom Configuration, and then choose LAN Routing.
6. Complete the wizard and start the LAN Routing service when prompted.

After you have installed the Routing and Remote Access service, you must enable and configure the DHCP Relay Agent:

1. In Routing and Remote Access, expand the IPv4 node, right-click the General node and then click New Routing Protocol.
2. Select the DHCP Relay Agent and click OK.
3. In the navigation pane, right-click DHCP Relay Agent and then click New Interface. You must add all network interfaces that the relay agent will bind to. This must include

those interfaces that contain DHCP clients without a local DHCP server, and those interfaces with a DHCP server. After you add these interfaces, you can select the properties of each one and set whether the Relay DHCP packets is enabled on the interface.

4. Right-click the DHCP Relay Agent and then click Properties, as shown in Figure 2-13. Enter the IP address of one or more DHCP servers and click Add, and then click OK.

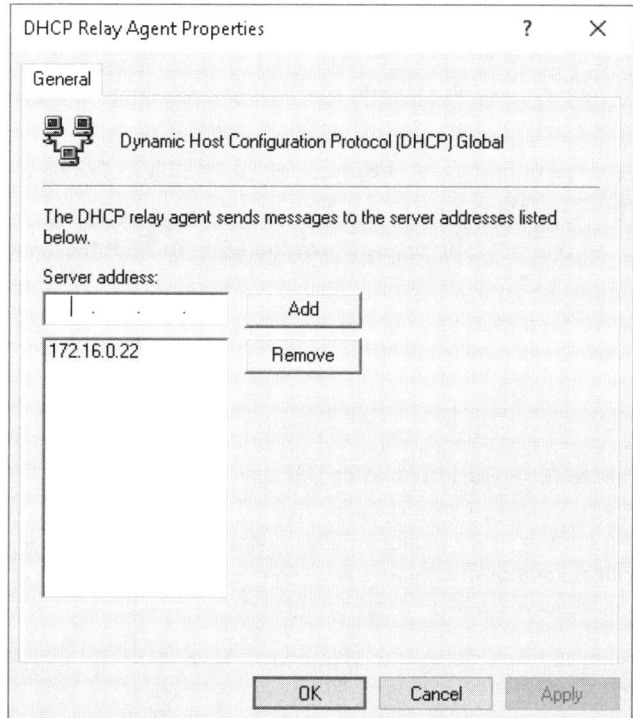

FIGURE 2-13 Configuring the DHCP Relay Agent

Configure PXE boot

Most computers have the capability to startup from a network card without a local operating system installed. This feature might need to be enabled in your computer's BIOS or UEFI firmware. The ability to start from a network card means that a computer can communicate with operating system deployment platforms such as Windows Deployment Services (WDS).

When you decide to implement a deployment service, like Windows Deployment Services, that uses the same communications ports as DHCP. Specifically, DHCPDISCOVER and DHCPOFFER messages use User Datagram Protocol (UDP) ports 67 and 68. These are the same ports as used by the Windows Deployment Services PXE server.

If you install both DHCP and Windows Deployment Services on the same server computer, these ports conflict. To mitigate this issue, you must reconfigure the ports used. You can do this by reconfiguring the 060 Pre-Boot Execution (PXE) client option in DHCP. In fact, you also must change the options 066 Boot Server Host Name and 067 Bootfile Name.

You can use the DHCP console to change options 66 and 67, but you cannot change option 60 with the DHCP console and must use the Netsh.exe command-line tool:

1. Open an elevated command prompt on your DHCP computer.
2. Type **Netsh.exe** and press Enter.
3. At the Netsh prompt, type **dhcp** and press Enter.
4. At the Netsh dhcp prompt, type **server \\servername** and press Enter to connect to the DHCP server. Replace *servername* with the name of your server.
5. At the Netsh dhcp server prompt, type **add optiondef 60 PXEClient String 0 comment=PXE support** and press Enter.
6. At the Netsh dhcp server prompt, type **set optionvalue 60 STRING PXEClient** and press Enter.
7. At the Netsh dhcp server prompt, type **exit** and press Enter, and then close the command prompt.

EXAM TIP
It is advisable to restart the DHCP service after making this change.

You can also add Option 60 in the DHCP Management Console by right-clicking IPv4, selecting Set Predefined Options, and then selecting Add. You can also add this Option using Windows PowerShell:

```
Add-DhcpServerv4OptionDefinition -ComputerName MyDHCPServer -Name PXEClient -Description "PXE Support" -OptionId 060 -Type String
```

And to set the Option value for a scope:

```
Set-DhcpServerv4OptionValue -ComputerName MyDHCPServer -ScopeId "MyScope" -OptionId 060 -Value "PXEClient"
```

Export, import and migrate a DHCP server

From time to time, you might find that you need to move the DHCP server role from one server to another. To perform this server role migration, you must know how to export and import the DHCP server role and data.

Perform export and import of a DHCP server

If you need to export a DHCP server's data, you can use the Windows PowerShell Export-DhcpServer cmdlet. For example, the following command exports the DHCP data to a file called lon-svr2_export:

```
Export-DhcpServer –ComputerName lon-svr2 –Leases -File C:\lon-svr2_export.xml
    -verbose
```

EXAM TIP

You can also the Netsh.exe command-line tool. At the Netsh dhcp server prompt, type **Export C:\lon-svr2_export.txt all**.

If you need to import DHCP server data from a previous export, you can use the Windows PowerShell Import-DhcpServer cmdlet. For example, the following command imports the DHCP data from a file named lon-svr2_export.xml to the new DHCP server named LON-SVR3:

```
Import-DhcpServer –ComputerName LON-SVR3 -Leases –File C:\lon-svr2_export.xml
 -BackupPath C:\ -Verbose
```

EXAM TIP

You can also the Netsh.exe command-line tool. At the Netsh dhcp server> prompt, type **Import C:\lon-svr2_export.txt all**.

Perform DHCP server migration

When you decide to replace an older server, you must migrate the roles that are running on the server, perhaps including the DHCP server role. Migrating the DHCP role is not complicated, but it does require the use of either the Netsh.exe command-line tool, or else Windows PowerShell cmdlets, that are used to export and import the DHCP data.

Use the following high-level procedure to migrate your DHCP server:

1. Deploy the DHCP server role to the new Windows Server 2016 computer.
2. Stop the DHCP service on the old DHCP server.
3. Export the DHCP data from the old server.
4. Copy the DHCP data to the new server.
5. Import the DHCP data on the new server.

Skill 2.2: Manage and maintain DHCP

After you have installed DHCP and created and configured the required DHCP scopes, it is important that you know how to manage the DHCP server role. This includes being able to configure high availability options, manage the DHCP database, and troubleshoot the DHCP role.

NOTE

Configuring a lease period is covered in the "Create and manage DHCP scopes" section.

Configure high availability using DHCP failover

If a DHCP server goes offline, clients continue to use their leased IP configurations, but new clients are unable to obtain a configuration, and clients renewing will fail to do so. For those reasons, it is important that DHCP is highly available in order to service client requests for IPv4 or IPv6 configurations.

High availability options for DHCP

It might seem like the logical thing to ensure high availability is to deploy multiple DHCP servers configured with the same scope(s). But due to the nature of DHCP client-server communications, there is no easy way for DHCP servers to maintain the same range of addresses in their scopes held on another DHCP server. Doing so can result in multiple clients obtaining the same IP configuration from different DHCP servers with no way to resolve the resulting conflict.

Windows Server 2016 provides a number of possible solutions to this problem. They are:

- **Server clustering** You can set up a two-member Windows Server cluster. You can install the DHCP server role on both members of the cluster, and then create an identical scope(s) on each. Install the DHCP data on shared storage in the cluster. If one node fails, then the other node can continue servicing client requests without interruption, shown in Figure 2-14.

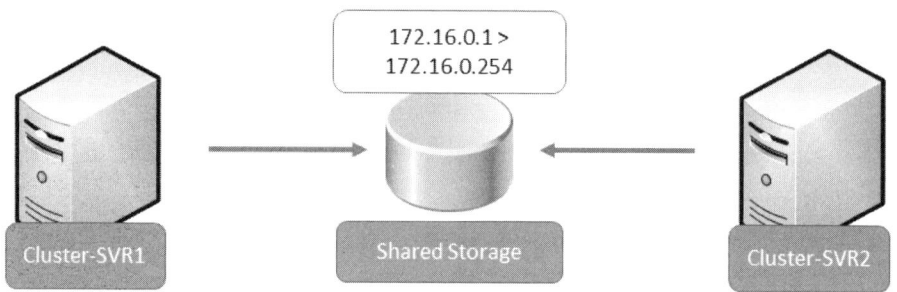

FIGURE 2-14 Server clustering with DHCP

- **Split scopes** You deploy the DHCP server role to two servers. On each server, you configure a subset of available IP addresses for your subnet ensuring that there is no overlap, as shown in Figure 2-15. Next, you use the Delay Configuration option on each server to set a primary server. If the primary fails, the secondary can continue to service client requests.

FIGURE 2-15 Using split scopes with DHCP

- **DHCP failover** With DHCP failover, you can enable two DHCP servers to provide IP configurations to the same subnets. The two DHCP servers replicate lease information between one another, as shown in Figure 2-16. If one of the servers fails, the other server continues providing DHCP services for the subnet(s) for which it is configured.

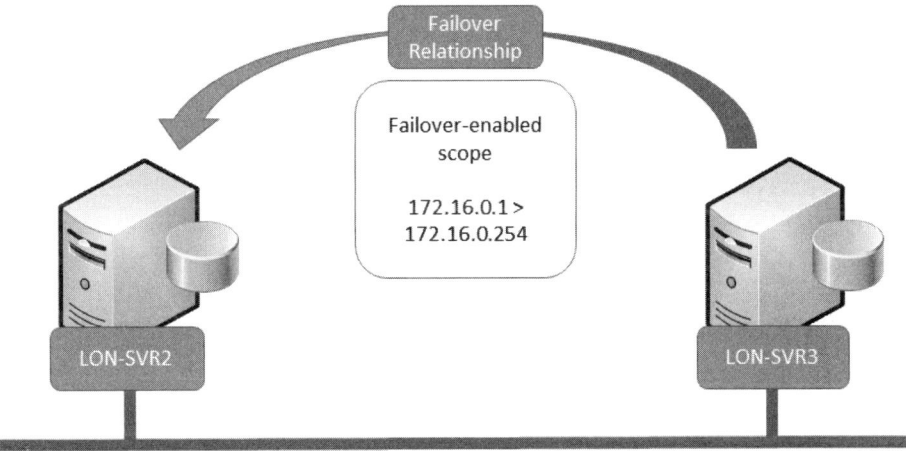

FIGURE 2-16 DHCP failover nodes

Configure split scopes

Implementing DHCP split scopes does not require the more complex configuration of deploying a Windows Server failover cluster. In essence, you configure a similar DHCP scope on each DHCP server, each with the same pool of addresses, but different exclusions.

For example, if you have two DHCP servers, LON-SVR2 and LON-SVR3, and you are using the 172.16.0.0/24 subnet, you have a pool of 254 available IPv4 addresses. Use the following high-level procedure to setup split scope DHCP:

1. Create a scope on one server with the IP address range of 172.16.0.1-172.16.0.254. Do not activate the scope.
2. Run the DHCP Split-Scope Configuration Wizard. This prompts you for:
    - The name of the secondary DHCP server.
    - The split of the scope IP address range between the two DHCP servers.
    - A Delay in DHCP Offer value for each server. This value determines the primary DHCP server.
3. Activate both scopes.

After creating the scope on your primary DHCP server, to enable split scopes, use the following detailed procedure:

1. In the DHCP console, right-click the scope, click Advanced, and then click Split-Scope.
2. In the DHCP Split-Scope Configuration wizard, on the Introduction page, click Next.
3. On the Additional DHCP Server page, in the Additional DHCP Server box, type the fully qualified domain name of the secondary DHCP server, and then click Next.
4. On the Percentage of Split page, shown in Figure 2-17, use the slider to distribute the addresses between the two DHCP servers and then click Next.

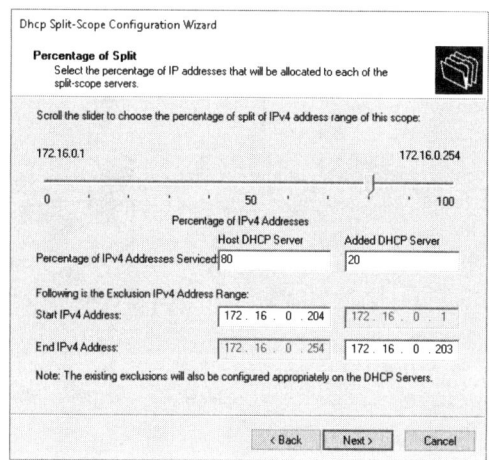

FIGURE 2-17 Defining the DHCP IP address range split

5. On the Delay in DHCP Offer page, shown in Figure 2-18, enter the delay for each server and then click Next. The server with the lowest delay is considered the primary server.

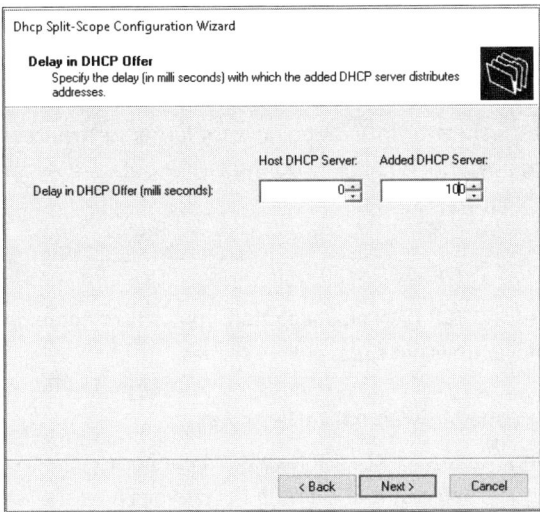

FIGURE 2-18 Defining the master server for a split scope configuration

6. On the Summary of Split-Scope Configuration page, click Finish. As shown in Figure 2-19, you can see that the Split-Scope wizard will create the required scope on the secondary server, and configure exclusions so that only the required range of addresses are allocated. Click Close.

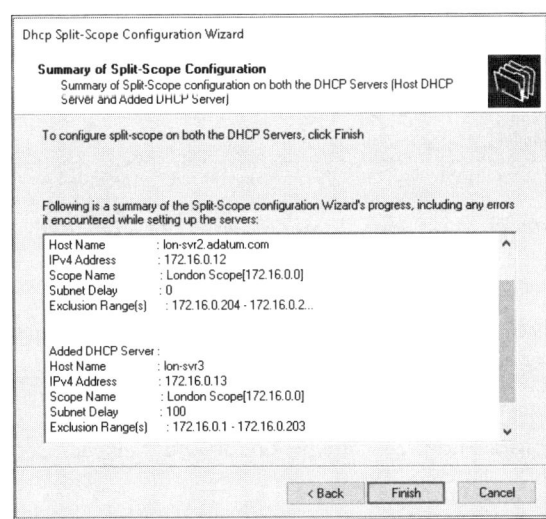

FIGURE 2-19 Viewing the summary information of the split scope

You can create the identical configuration manually by creating matching scopes on each DHCP server, and then manually configuring the exclusion ranges and subnet delay values.

Configure DHCP failover

While DHCP split scope addresses the primary concern of ensuring that there is a DHCP server available to service client requests, it does this by sharing the available address pool between two servers. This can only be a short-term solution, and for larger networks where the address pool is depleted, it might not work effectively during DHCP outages. As an alternative, consider implementing DHCP failover.

EXAM TIP

You can only configure two servers for DHCP failover, In addition, you can configure only IPv4 scopes and subnets. DHCP failover does not support IPv6 scopes.

You can configure DHCP failover in one of two modes. These are:

- **Load Sharing**   In load sharing mode, both DHCP lease IPv4 configurations to clients. Depending on how you configure load distribution ratio determines how the servers responds to IP configuration requests.

EXAM TIP

Load Sharing is the default mode, and the default ratio is 50:50 which means that the servers share the load equally.

- **Hot Standby**   When you implement Hot Standby mode, you designate one server as primary and the other as a secondary. In this mode, only the primary server leases IPv4 configurations to clients. Only when the primary is unavailable does the secondary perform the leasing function.

EXAM TIP

Use Hot Standby mode for deployments where your disaster recovery site is physically separate. However, be aware that for failover messages to transit firewalls, you must enable TCP port 647.

To configure DHCP failover, perform the following steps:

1. Create and configure one or more required scopes on a single DHCP server.
2. On that server, in the DHCP console, right-click the IPv4 node and then click Configure Failover.
3. In the Configure Failover wizard, on the Introduction page, select all DHCP scopes that you want to configure as part of the failover relationship. Click Next.
4. On the Specify the partner server to use for failover page, click Add Server and browse and select the other DHCP server. Click Next.
5. On the Create a new failover relationship page, shown in Figure 2-20, configure the following information, click Next and then click Finish:

- **Relationship Name**   Use this field to identify the relationship.
- **Maximum Client Lead Time**   This value is used in Hot Standby mode. It defines how long the secondary server must wait before taking control of the scope. The default is one hour, and cannot be zero.
- **Mode**   Choose between Load Balance and Hot Standby.
- **Load Balance Percentage**   Used when you enable Load Balance mode. Enables you to determine how much of the address space each server manages. The default is a 50/50 split.
- **Role of Partner Server**   Use this setting when you enable Standby mode. It enables you to define which server is the primary and which the secondary. Choose between Active or Standby.

EXAM TIP

You can configure a single DHCP server to act simultaneously as the primary DHCP server for one scope and also as a secondary DHCP server for another scope.

- **Address reserved for standby server**   Use this value to determine what percentage of addresses within the scope the secondary server can allocate while it waits for the MCLT to expire. This allows the secondary server to allocate a small proportion of addresses while it waits to determine if the primary will come back online. The default is 5 percent of available scope addresses.
- **State Switchover Interval**   When a server loses connectivity with its replication partner, it has no way of determining why this has occurred. You must manually change a partner's status to a down state to indicate to the remaining partner that the other server is unavailable. Setting the State Switchover Value enables you to automate this changed state after a configured time interval. This value is not used by default.
- **Enable Message Authentication**   You can configure message authentication using the shared secret as a password. This means that the failover message traffic between replication partners is authenticated and that helps validate that the failover message originates with the configured failover partner.
- **Shared Secret**   The password used to enable message authentication.

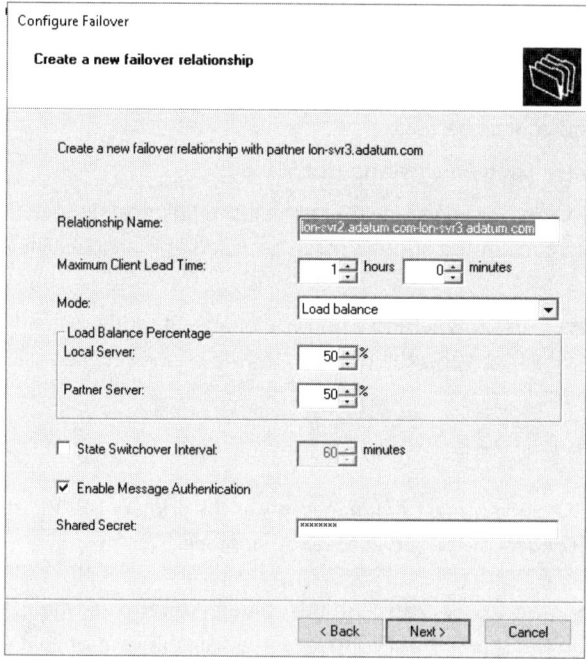

FIGURE 2-20 Configuring DHCP failover

6. On the Progress of Failover Configuration page, click Close.

You can also use the Windows PowerShell Add-DhcpServerv4Failover cmdlet to configure DHCP failover. For example, to create a load balanced DHCP failover relationship between lon-svr2.adatum.com and lon-svr3.adatum.com with the scope 172.16.0.0 being created on the partner computer, lon-svr3.adatum.com, run the following command:

```
Add-DhcpServerv4Failover -ComputerName lon-svr2.adatum.com -Name SFO-SIN-Failover
-PartnerServer lon-svr3.adatum.com -ScopeId 172.16.0.0 -SharedSecret "Pa$$w0rd"
```

> **NEED MORE REVIEW?** **DHCP SERVER CMDLETS IN WINDOWS POWERSHELL**
>
> To review further details about using Windows PowerShell to configure DHCP, refer to the Microsoft TechNet website at *https://technet.microsoft.com/library/jj590751(v=wps.630).aspx*.

After you have configured the failover relationship, you can maintain it by performing the following tasks:

- **Replicate A Scope** Enables you to replicate any changes in a configured scope between the partners in a DHCP failover relationship. To replicate a scope, under the IPv4 node in the DHCP console, right-click the appropriate scope and then click Replicate Scope.

- **Replicate A Scopes** Enables you to replicate all scopes between partners in a DHCP failover relationship. To perform this task, from the DHCP console, right-click the IPv4 node, and then click Replicate Failover Scopes.

> *EXAM TIP*
>
> You can also use the Windows PowerShell Invoke-DhcpServerv4FailoverReplication cmdlet to perform these tasks.

> **NEED MORE REVIEW? UNDERSTAND AND DEPLOY DHCP FAILOVER**
>
> To review further details about DHCP failover, refer to the Microsoft TechNet website at *https://technet.microsoft.com/library/dn338978(v=ws.11).aspx*.

Backup and restore the DHCP database

The DHCP server role stores its data in a database. If the database becomes corrupted, it can lead to service unavailability. Therefore, it is important that you understand how to backup and restore the DHCP database.

Overview of the DHCP database

The DHCP database consists of a number of separate files stored in the %systemroot%\System32\dhcp folder. These are:

- **dhcp.mdb** This is the main DHCP database file.
- **tmp.edb** This is a temporary working file used when indexing and other maintenance operations are being performed on the database file.
- **j50.log** This is a database transaction log. DHCP changes are written to logs and then from the log, the changes are committed to the database. After the records are committed, a pointer in the log moves forward to indicate the transaction is complete. This process helps maintain the integrity of the database during changes. As the transaction log fills, it is renamed and a new transaction log created.
- **j5*.log** These sequentially numbered log files are previous transaction logs.
- **j50.chk** This is the checkpoint file, and it is used to determine which transaction logs have been committed to the database. When the DHCP service starts, an integrity check of the database verifies the database against recent transactions. The checkpoint file expedites that process.
- **j50res00001.jrs and j50res00002.jrs** These two files are reserved database logs, and can be used to store uncommitted transactions destined for the DHCP database

in the event that the system drive runs out of disk space. When they are full, the DHCP service stops so that database integrity is maintained.

Backup and restore the DHCP database

When you back up the DHCP database, the following information is stored in the backup:

- The DHCP scopes, configured reservations and active leases
- Server options, scope options, class and reservation options
- Configuration settings that you configured on the DHCP server properties and any that are stored in the registry.

BACKING UP THE DATABASE

Although the DHCP database is automatically backed up every 60 minutes, you can manually backup the database when you have made significant configuration changes.

> **EXAM TIP**
>
> You can change the default automatic backup interval for DHCP by editing the BackupInterval value in the HKLM\SYSTEM\CurrentControlSet\Services\DHCPServer\Parameters folder in the registry.

To back up the DHCP database, from the DHCP console, right-click the DHCP server and then click Backup, as shown in Figure 2-21. You must specify a folder to store the backup. The default is %systemroot%\System32\dhcp\backup. The database is backed up to the specified location.

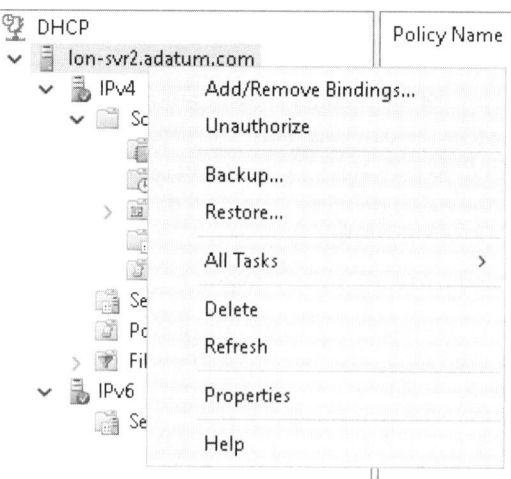

FIGURE 2-21 Performing a manual backup of the DHCP database

EXAM TIP

You can also use the Windows PowerShell Backup-DhcpServer cmdlet to back up the DHCP database.

RESTORING THE DATABASE

If you experience problems with DHCP, and a Restore Operation is indicated, to restore the DHCP database, in the DHCP console, right-click the DHCP server in the DHCP console, and then click Restore. Navigate to the folder that you stored your backup, and then click OK.

The DHCP service must be stopped in order to restore the service. You are prompted to stop and restart the service before the data and settings are restored.

EXAM TIP

You can also use the Windows PowerShell Restore-DhcpServer cmdlet to restore the DHCP database.

NOTE

Configuring DHCP name protection is covered in the "Configure DHCP options" section.

Troubleshoot DHCP

DHCP provides the IP configuration for your network devices, clients, and servers. If this service is unavailable, network connectivity is likely to be affected. It is important to be able to identify common symptoms of DHCP server role problems, and to be able to take corrective action quickly.

Describe common issues with DHCP

DHCP is a reliable service, and when implemented with a properly planned high-availability solution, there are seldom any problems. However, occasionally, issues might occur. Symptoms that you have a problem with the DHCP server role are discussed in Table 2-2.

TABLE 2-2 Symptoms of common DHCP problems.

Symptom	Possible cause	Things to check
DHCP service fails to start	The database might be corrupted.	Perform a restore of the DHCP database and attempt to restart the DHCP service.
DHCP service fails to issue leases	<ul><li>The DHCP service might have failed.</li><li>There might be insufficient IP addresses available in the DHCP scope pool.</li></ul>	<ul><li>Verify that the DHCP service is running.</li><li>Verify that there are sufficient IP addresses available in the pool.</li><li>If the clients are in a different subnet from the DHCP server, verify whether any DHCP relay agent is running and configured correctly.</li></ul>
Client address conflicts	<ul><li>Another device or service is providing DHCP functionality.</li><li>Two overlapping scopes might be servicing requests in the same subnet(s).</li><li>A statically assigned address might be conflicting with a dynamically assigned address.</li></ul>	<ul><li>Determine whether devices, such as wireless access points or hubs, are configured to allocate IP addresses.</li><li>Verify the address pool on adjacent DHCP servers contains no overlap.</li><li>Consider replacing any statically assigned addresses with DHCP reservations – which you can manage centrally, and which are allocated from the pool in a scope.</li></ul>
The DHCP client is unable to lease an address, and falls back to using an Automatic Private IP Addressing (APIPA) address	<ul><li>The DHCP service might have failed.</li><li>There might be insufficient IP addresses available in the DHCP scope pool.</li><li>The DHCP client might be in a subnet without a DHCP server.</li><li>Physical cabling issues.</li></ul>	<ul><li>Verify that the DHCP service is running.</li><li>Verify that there are sufficient IP addresses available in the pool.</li><li>If the clients are in a different subnet from the DHCP server, verify whether any DHCP relay agent is running and configured correctly.</li><li>Ensure that any wired client is correctly connected.</li></ul>

Table 2-2 is not a complete list, but it does contain some of the most common symptoms and causes of DHCP problems. For all other problems, use standard network troubleshooting techniques and processes to work toward a resolution.

Tools to resolve common DHCP issues

It is important that you understand how DHCP works before you can effectively troubleshoot the service. You must be fully conversant with the DHCP messages used both when a client initially obtains a DHCP lease, and afterwards, when the client attempts renewal. Only when you know what to expect, can you then recognize when the process has gone wrong.

USE DHCP AUDIT LOGGING

By default, DHCP Audit Logging is Enabled. You can verify this setting by selecting the Properties of the IPv4 node in the DHCP console, as shown in Figure 2-22. The Enable DHCP Audit Logging check box should be selected.

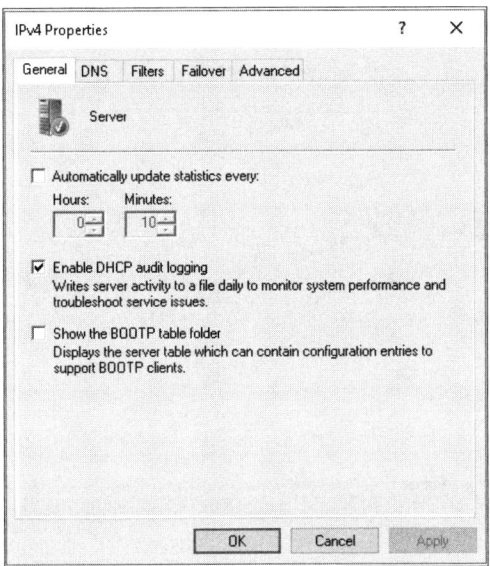

FIGURE 2-22 Enabling DHCP Audit Logging

After enabling this option, you can configure the audit logging path from the Advanced tab, as shown in Figure 2-23. The default folder is %systemroot%\System32\dhcp.

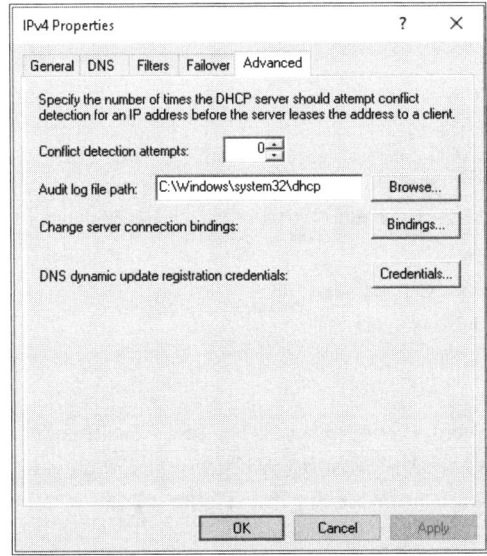

FIGURE 2-23 Configuring the DHCP audit log file path

If this setting is enabled, a log file called DhcpSrvLog – *Day*.log is created in the designated folder, where *Day* represents the day of the week when the log was created.

EXAM TIP

A log called DhcpV6SrvLog – Day.log is created for IPv6-related events.

You can examine this log for DHCP events by using a text editor such a Notepad. The file consists of the fields shown in Table 2-3.

TABLE 2-3 Fields in the DHCP Audit Log.

Field	Explanation
ID	The DHCP event ID code.
Date	Date the event is logged.
Time	Time the event is logged.
Description	A brief explanation of the event.
IP Address	The IP address of the DHCP client.
Host name	The host name of the DHCP client.
MAC Address	The media access control (MAC) address of the DHCP client.

Table 2-4 contains a list of common events.

TABLE 2-4 Common events logged in the DHCP Audit Log

Event ID	Explanation
00	The log started.
01	The log stopped.
02	The log is paused due to low disk space.
10	A client is leased a new IP address.
11	A client renewed a leased address.
12	A client released a leased address.
13	An IP address was found in use on the network.
14	A client lease request was refused because the address pool of the scope is depleted.
15	A lease request was denied.
20	A client leased a Bootstrap Protocol (BOOTP) address.
51	A DHCP server was successfully authorized in AD DS.
54	A DHCP authorization was unsuccessful.

In addition to the audit log, you can also use the Event Viewer to access the DHCP Event Logs. These are located in the Applications and Services Logs \ Microsoft \ Windows \ DHCP-Server\ Microsoft-Windows-DHCP Server Events \ Operational node, as shown in Figure 2-24.

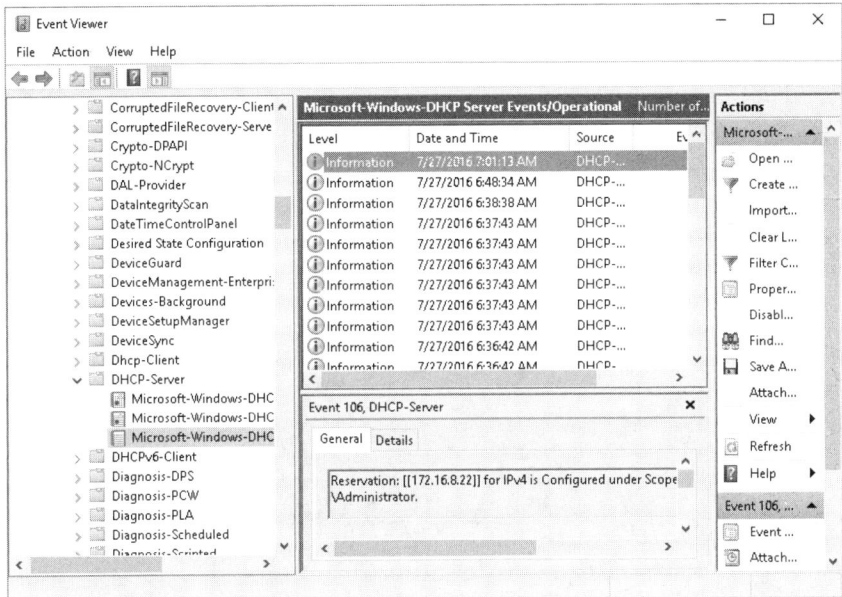

FIGURE 2-24 Event Viewer

> **NEED MORE REVIEW?** **MORE ABOUT DHCP AUDIT AND EVENT LOGGING**
>
> To review further details about DHCP auditing, refer to the Microsoft TechNet website at *https://technet.microsoft.com/library/dd759178(v=ws.11).aspx*.

COMMAND LINE TOOLS

You can use the IPConfig.exe command line tool to help troubleshoot and diagnose DHCP client-related issues, as shown in Table 2-5.

TABLE 2-5 IPconfig.exe commands useful in DHCP troubleshooting.

Command	Usage
ipconfig /all	View complete IP configuration information Use to verify the current IP configuration, including whether the client obtained its configuration from a DHCP server and, if so, which one. This also displays the lease duration.
ipconfig /release	Release the currently leased IP configuration After you release an IP configuration, you can request a new lease and use a packet analyzer, like Microsoft Message Analyzer, to view the process. You can also then view the Address Leases node in the appropriate scope in the DHCP console.
ipconfig /renew	Renew the currently leased IP configuration Enables you to test the lease renewal process.

The output from ipconfig /all is shown in Figure 2-25. In this case, it indicates that the client obtained an IPv4 configuration with the following DHCP characteristics:

- DHCP Enabled says Yes.
- The DHCP server is 172.16.0.10.
- The lease duration expires on Monday, 8, August, 2016.

One common procedure for troubleshooting with ipconfig.exe is to obtain a DHCP lease and repeatedly release and renew the lease while examining the leased addresses in the DHCP console. Used in conjunction with Microsoft Message Analyzer, you can discover what's happening on the physical network when clients try to communicate with a DHCP server.

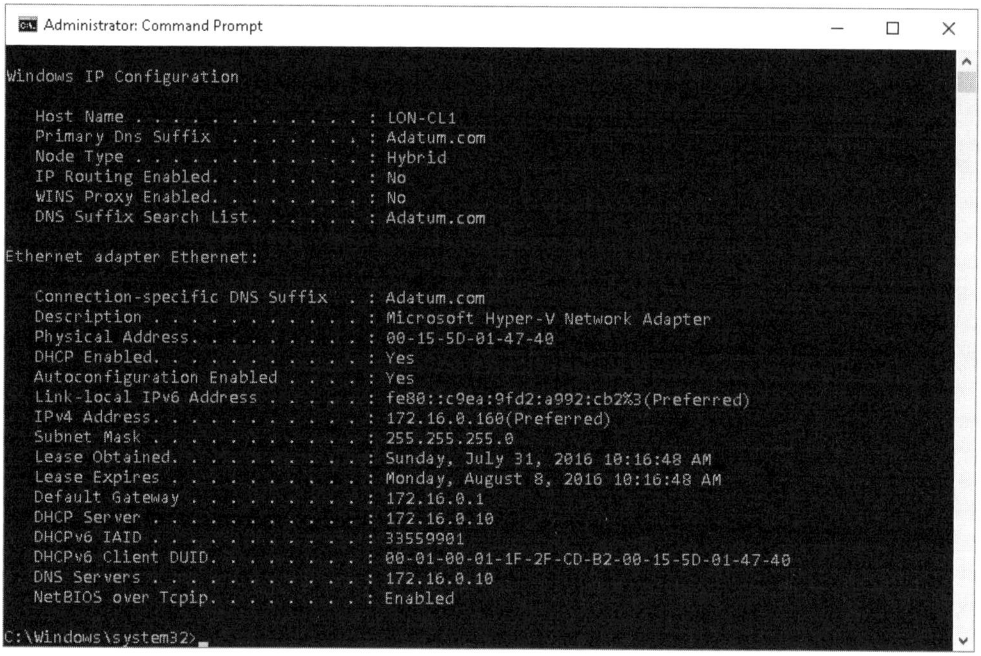

FIGURE 2-25 The output from ipconfig.exe /all

MICROSOFT MESSAGE ANALYZER

Microsoft Message Analyzer enables you to view the messages that pass between networked devices, including a DHCP server and DHCP client, and verify that the traffic is as expected. This is particularly useful when you implement more complex DHCP configurations, such as using a DHCP relay agent, or DHCP failover. After you download and install this network analysis tool, you can view network packets on the local network interfaces to which your computer is connected.

> **NOTE**
>
> You can download Microsoft Message Analyzer from the Microsoft website: *https://www.microsoft.com/download/details.aspx?id=44226*.

When you launch Microsoft Message Analyzer, you can start a local trace. Click the Start Local Trace button in the Start Page. The analyzer begins to collect network messages from the connected network interface(s). You can then analyze these messages and determine if there is a discrepancy in DHCP behavior.

To use Microsoft Message Analyzer to troubleshoot client DHCP issues, start a trace on a client computer, and then attempt to obtain and then renew a DHCP address. You can then review the trace, as shown in Figure 2-26.

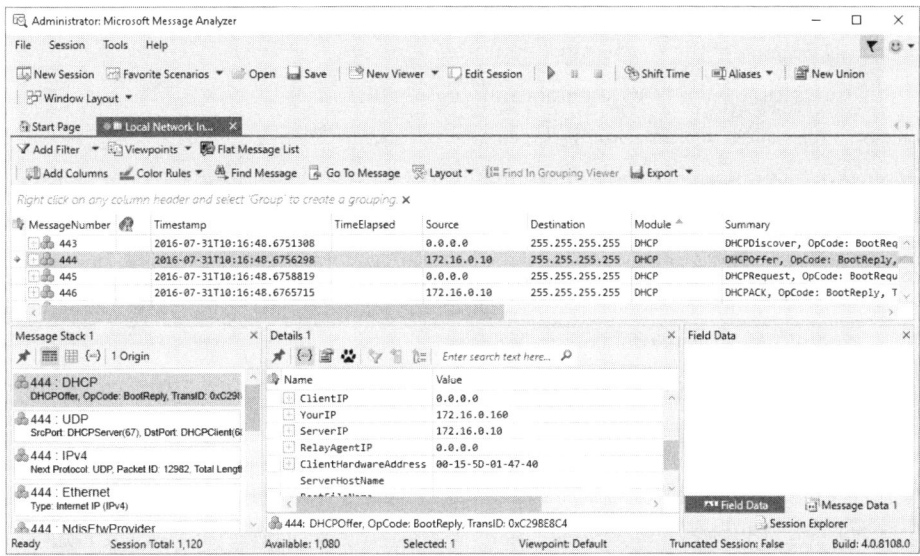

FIGURE 2-26 Microsoft Message Analyzer

As you can see, the expected messages have been captured when the client attempted to obtain a DHCP lease.

> **NOTE**
>
> An explanation of the client-server interaction in DHCP is provided in "An overview of DHCP" in Chapter 3.

Four messages have been isolated from the trace. These are numbered 443 through 446 and represent the DHCPDiscover, DHCPOffer, DHCPRequest, and DHCPACK messages, respectively. The DHCPOffer message is selected, and detail shows that the client has an IPv4 address of 0.0.0.0. This is typical when a client obtains an IP address by lease because it does not have an IPv4 address yet. You can also see from the destination column in the Details pane that the address 255.255.255.255 is used. This is an IPv4 broadcast address, again, as expected for a client obtaining an initial lease.

By examining the trace of a working DHCP dialog, you can identify inconsistencies when the traffic is not flowing as expected.

> **NEED MORE REVIEW? MICROSOFT MESSAGE ANALYZER OPERATING GUIDE**
>
> To review further details how to use Microsoft Message Analyzer, refer to the Microsoft TechNet website at *https://technet.microsoft.com/library/jj649776.aspx*.

Chapter summary

- DHCP simplifies administration of the IPv4 and IPv6 address space in your organization.
- In an AD DS environment, you must authorize your DHCP servers in Active Directory.
- The DHCP scope is the fundamental configuration unit in DHCP.
- Superscopes allow you to address issues arising from multinet configurations.
- Multicast scopes support applications that use multicast transmission to communicate.
- You can assign DHCP options at the server, scope, class, and reservation levels.
- DHCP policies enable you to assign DHCP options based on configurable conditions.
- You can use Windows Server clustering, DHCP split scopes, or DHCP failover to help to provide high-availability options for DHCP.
- DHCP split scopes distribute the available address pool from a scope across two DHCP servers, while DHCP failover replicates the entire scope(s) between configured DHCP failover partners.
- The DHCP database is backed up automatically every 60 minutes.
- DHCP name protection helps protect names registered in DNS by the DHCP service.
- Using tools such as ipconfig.exe in conjunction with Microsoft Message Analyzer is an effective way to verify proper function of DHCP services.

Thought experiment

In this thought experiment, demonstrate your skills and knowledge of the topics covered in this chapter. You can find answer to this thought experiment in the next section.

You work in IT support at A. Datum Corporation. As a consultant for A. Datum, answer the following questions about implementing DHCP within the A. Datum organization:

1. The network at A. Datum consists of multiple subnets. You do not want to deploy a DHCP server into each physical subnet, but want to ensure that all client computers can obtain an IP configuration via a DHCP server. What could you do to facilitate this?
2. You want to deploy the DHCP server role without using the Server Manager console. How could you achieve this?
3. You want to create a scope for an IPv4 subnet with the address 172.16.16.0/255.255.240.0. How many subnet bits must you configure when you create the scope?

4. You want to use a non-Microsoft software deployment package to deploy applications to client computers. The application uses multicast IP. How could DHCP help with this scenario?

5. You want to be able to assign a shorter lease duration to users of Windows tablets. How could you achieve this?

6. Your manager asks you to look into providing DHCP resilience for a branch office. Currently, the network clients obtain an IPv4 configuration from a DHCP server located in the regional HQ in London. Whenever there is a network failure, the clients at the branch are unable to obtain an IPv4 configuration. What possible solutions are available to mitigate this issue, and which would you recommend to your manager?

7. There was an incident recently when a DHCP server failed, and users in London were unable to obtain an IP configuration on their laptop computers. Your manager wants you to ensure that this never happens again. What could you do?

8. Client computers in one part of the London site are failing to obtain an IP configuration. These computers are located in a separate building across the road from the main London HQ offices. You investigate the building and discover that it has no DHCP server locally. What would you do next to start to resolve the problem?

Thought experiment answers

This section contains the solution to the thought experiment. Each answer explains why the answer choice is correct.

1. If your routers support BOOTP forwarding, as defined by RFC 1542, you need do nothing more as the DHCP messages are forwarded between subnets by the routers. However, if your routers do not support this function, you can deploy DHCP Relay Agents on Windows Server 2016 computer by using the Routing and Remote Access console.

2. You can use the Add-WindowsFeature DHCP –IncludeManagementTools Windows PowerShell command to install the DHCP server role and required management tools.

3. A subnet mask of 255.255.240.0 means 20 bits must be assigned when you create the scope.

4. DHCP supports the use of Multicast scopes to support applications and clients that use multicast communications.

5. You can create a scope in DHCP, and then define a user class for tablet devices. Assign the tablets to the user class with the IPconfig.exe tool. Finally, create a DHCP scope-level policy to assign a different lease duration for devices that match the condition of user class = laptop.

6. There are a number of possible solutions. One solution would be to manually assign IPv4 addresses to all clients in the branch. This would negate the need for DHCP, but it does make management of the organization's IP address space more complicated. Us-

ing DHCP, possible solutions include placing a DHCP server at the branch and configuring it with the required scope for that branch. This is probably the simplest solution, and requires no failover configuration. If you preferred to allocate IPv4 addresses from the London offices, then using split scope would work well, with the Delay in DHCP Offer value set higher on the branch DHCP server so that it does not offer addresses unless the London DHCP server is unresponsive. You would need to take care to set this value correctly because obtaining an IP configuration over a wide area network link is slower than over a local area network link.

7. This scenario is probably best resolved by using DHCP failover. Configure a DHCP scope(s) for the London offices on one DHCP server, and then implement DHCP failover in load sharing mode, distributing the scope 50/50. This optimizes performance and helps to ensure high availability.

8. Since client computers are unable to obtain an IP configuration from servers located in the main office, it is the link to the main office that should be investigated. Determine whether any routers are offline. Verify that if a DHCP relay agent is used, it is online and configured correctly. Finally, verify that the DHCP server the clients normally use is online. Also, check that the scope from which they obtain their configurations is active.

CHAPTER 3

Implement IP address management

Networks can be complex, with many components and services combining to provide the environment required to support your organization's users' devices and apps. Windows Server 2016 server roles, such as Dynamic Host Configuration Protocol (DHCP) and Domain Name System (DNS), provide fundamental IP connectivity. Consequently, it is important that you are able to easily manage and maintain these services.

You can use the Windows Server 2016 IP address management (IPAM) server feature to manage and maintain both DHCP and DNS, even in a multiple Active Directory Domain Services (AD DS) forest environment.

Skills in this chapter:
- Install and configure IP address management
- Manage DNS and DHCP using IPAM
- Audit IPAM

Skill 3.1: Install and configure IP address management

It can be time-consuming and sometimes complicated to manage the allocation of IP addressing in medium to large organizations. IPAM enables you to deploy, monitor, and administer your IP infrastructure, and enables you to manage all aspects of deployed DHCP and DNS servers.

> **NOTE MORE IP ADDRESSING**
> Managing IP addressing is covered in Chapter 5: "Implement IPv4 and IPv6 addressing."

If you have more than one DHCP and/or DNS server in your organization, consider implementing IPAM to help implement IP address management. With IPAM, you can perform the following tasks:

- Allocate IPv4 and IPv6 addresses
- Optimize IP address spaces
- Manage DHCP and DNS servers
- Monitor DHCP and DNS servers
- Collect statistics from AD DS domain controllers and Network Policy Servers (NPS)

Architecture

IPAM consists of the following components, shown in Figure 3-1.

- **IPAM client**   A computer installed with Windows 8 or newer, or Windows Server 2012 or newer. The client must have the remote server administration tools (RSAT) installed. The client communicates using the Windows Communication Foundation (WCF) protocol with the IPAM server over TCP port 48885. The client is responsible for providing reporting about the IPAM architecture.

EXAM TIP

You can reconfigure this port with the Windows PowerShell Set-IpamConfiguration cmdlet.

- **IPAM server**   Any domain-member computer installed with Windows Server 2012 or newer. The IPAM server communicates with managed servers, with the IPAM client(s), and with the IPAM database.
    - **IPAM database**   Can be a Windows Internal Database, or you can use a SQL Server database on Windows Server 2012 R2 and newer.
    - **Role-based access control**   Determines what the IPAM administrator can see on their IPAM client console. For example, you can restrict viewing of IP address lease data to a specific set of IPAM administrators by adding their user accounts to the IPAM IP Audit Administrators group.
    - **Scheduled tasks**   Used by the IPAM server to collect statistical data from managed servers at predetermined intervals.

EXAM TIP

You cannot install the IPAM feature on an AD DS domain controller, and it is not recommended that you install the feature on a DHCP server because DHCP discovery is disabled. Ideally, you deploy the IPAM feature on a server dedicated to that purpose.

- **Managed servers**   Domain controllers, NPS, DNS, and DHCP servers running Windows Server 2008 or newer.

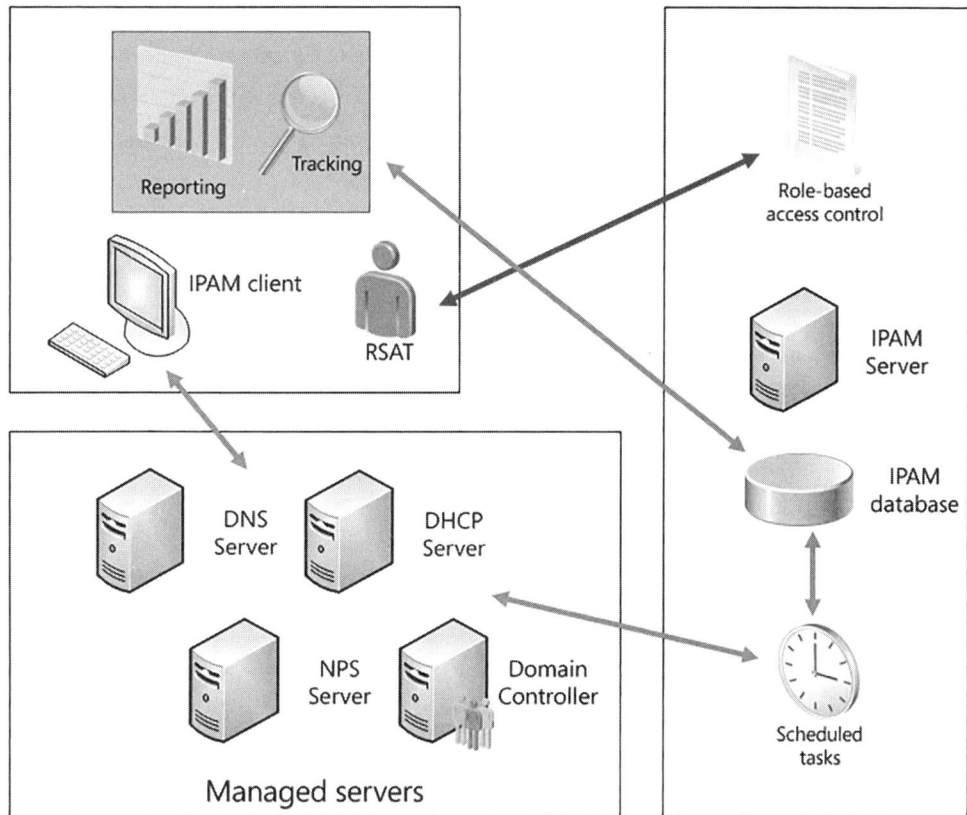

FIGURE 3-1 IPAM architecture

Requirements and planning considerations

Before you deploy IPAM, you must ensure that your IT infrastructure is ready, and that you have chosen a deployment topology. The requirements for deploying IPAM are not complex. They are:

- **Windows Server 2012** You must install the IPAM feature on a server running at least Windows Server 2012.
- **Database** You can use the Windows Internal Database on all versions of Windows Server, but if you implement IPAM on a server running Windows Server 2012 R2 or newer, you can deploy a Microsoft SQL Server database to support IPAM.
- **Network** Your network infrastructure must be in place. IPAM requires access to a domain controller and to an authoritative DNS server.
- **AD DS** You must install IPAM on a domain-member server computer. If you install IPAM on a server computer running Windows Server 2016, IPAM can support discovery across multiple AD DS forests.

When you deploy IPAM, you can choose from three possible topologies. These are:

- **Distributed** You deploy an IPAM server at each physical location, or site.
- **Centralized** You deploy a single IPAM server to support the entire organization.
- **Hybrid** You deploy a central IPAM server at your main datacenter, with dedicated IPAM servers deployed to each site, as shown in Figure 3-2.

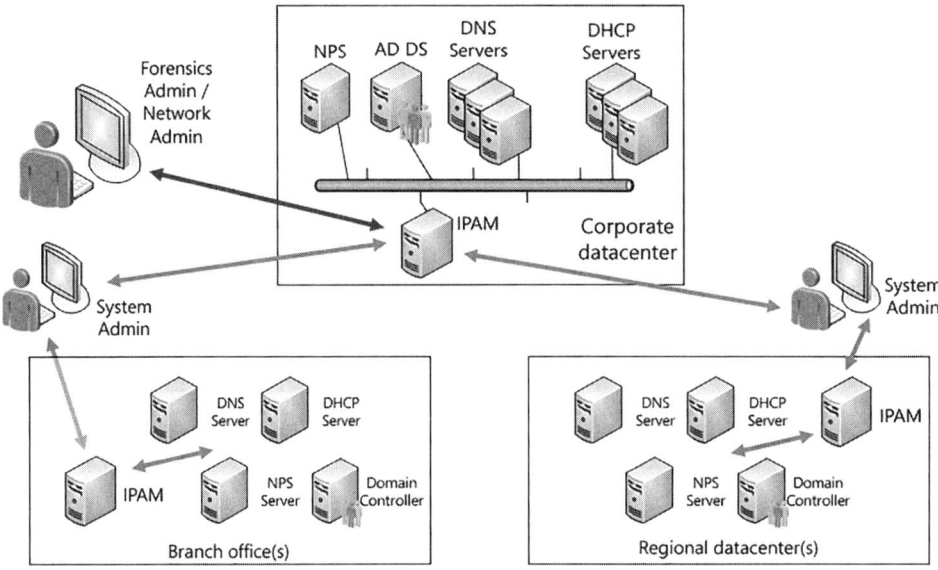

FIGURE 3-2 Hybrid deployment of IPAM

> **NEED MORE REVIEW?** **IP ADDRESS MANAGEMENT (IPAM) OVERVIEW**
>
> To review further details about IPAM, refer to the Microsoft TechNet website at *https://technet.microsoft.com/library/hh831353(v=ws.11).aspx*.

Configure IPAM database storage using SQL Server

If you deploy IPAM on Windows Server 2012 R2 or Windows Server 2016, you can configure the IPAM database as a Windows Internal Database (WID), or you can use an external SQL Server database. Typically, this is a choice you make during initial provisioning of your IPAM server.

When you launch the Provision IPAM Wizard, you are asked whether you want to use WID or a SQL Server database. If you choose WID, you must specify the location of the database and related log files. The default is %WINDIR%\System32\IPAM\Database.

If you want to use a SQL Server database, your SQL Server must be running SQL Server 2008 R2 or newer. You must then specify the:

- Server name
- Database name
- Port (the default is 1433)

You must configure authentication to the SQL Server to support IPAM. The process for this varies depending on whether the SQL Server is running on the same or a different computer to IPAM, and whether you want to use Windows authentication or SQL authentication.

SQL and IPAM on separate computers

To use Windows authentication, open an elevated command prompt, and run SQLCMD. Then run the following commands (where *DOMAIN\IPAM1$* is the AD DS domain name and the IPAM computer name, and *IPAM_DB* is the name of the SQL database):

```
CREATE LOGIN [DOMAIN\IPAM1$] FROM WINDOWS
CREATE DATABASE IPAM_DB
GO
USE IPAM_DB
CREATE USER IPAM FOR LOGIN [DOMAIN\IPAM1$]
ALTER ROLE DB_OWNER ADD MEMBER IPAM
USE MASTER
GRANT VIEW ANY DEFINITION TO [DOMAIN\IPAM1$]
```

To use SQL authentication, at a SQLCMD prompt, run the following commands (where *ipamuser* is a SQL authentication login name, *'password'* is the SQL password for this account, and *IPAM_DB* is the name of the SQL database):

```
CREATE LOGIN ipamuser WITH PASSWORD = 'password'
CREATE DATABASE IPAM_DB
GO
USE IPAM_DB
CREATE USER IPAM FOR LOGIN ipamuser
ALTER ROLE DB_OWNER ADD MEMBER IPAM
GO
USE MASTER
GRANT VIEW ANY DEFINITION TO ipamuser
GO
```

EXAM TIP

The information you enter here must exactly match what you enter in the IPAM provisioning wizard.

SQL and IPAM on the same computer

If SQL and IPAM are deployed on the same computer, to use Windows authentication, open an elevated command prompt and run SQLCMD. Then run the following commands (where *IPAM_DB* is the name of the SQL database):

```
CREATE LOGIN [NT AUTHORITY\Network Service] FROM WINDOWS
CREATE DATABASE IPAM_DB
GO
USE IPAM_DB
CREATE USER IPAM FOR LOGIN [NT AUTHORITY\Network Service]
ALTER ROLE DB_OWNER ADD MEMBER IPAM
GO
USE MASTER
GRANT VIEW ANY DEFINITION TO [NT AUTHORITY\Network Service]
GO
```

To use SQL authentication, at a SQLCMD prompt, run the following commands (where *ipamuser* is a SQL authentication login name, *'password'* is the SQL password for this account, and *IPAM_DB* is the name of the SQL database).

```
CREATE LOGIN ipamuser WITH PASSWORD = 'password'
CREATE DATABASE IPAM_DB
GO
USE IPAM_DB
CREATE USER IPAM FOR LOGIN ipamuser
ALTER ROLE DB_OWNER ADD MEMBER IPAM
GO
USE MASTER
GRANT VIEW ANY DEFINITION TO ipamuser
GO
```

> **EXAM TIP**
> The information you enter here must exactly match what you enter in the IPAM provisioning wizard.

> **NEED MORE REVIEW? CONFIGURE THE SQL DATABASE FOR IPAM**
> To review further details about the SQL Server database for IPAM, refer to the Microsoft TechNet website at *https://technet.microsoft.com/library/dn758115(v=ws.11).aspx*.

Provision IPAM manually or by using Group Policy

Before you can begin using IPAM, you must deploy and then provision the IPAM service.

Deploying IPAM

You can use Windows PowerShell or Server Manager to deploy the IPAM feature. To install the feature using Server Manager, use the following procedure:

1. In Server Manager, click Manage, and then click Add Roles And Features.
2. Click through the Add Roles And Features Wizard, and then, on the Select Features page, select the IP Address Management (IPAM) Server check box.

3. In the Add Features That Are Required For IP Address Management (IPAM) Server? dialog box, click Add Features, and then click Next.
4. Click Install and when the feature has finished installing, click Close.

> **EXAM TIP**
>
> You can also use the Windows PowerShell Install-WindowsFeature IPAM -IncludeManagementTools command to install the IPAM feature.

Provisioning manually

After you have deployed the IPAM server feature, you must provision IPAM. Provisioning is the process of configuring permissions, access settings, and shared folders on managed servers so that your IPAM server can communicate with them.

You can provision the server manually, or by using Group Policy Objects (GPOs). When you launch the Provision IPAM Wizard, you are asked whether you would like to provision manually, or by using GPOs, as shown in Figure 3-4.

To provision IPAM manually, complete the following procedure:

1. In Server Manager, in the navigation pane, click IPAM.
2. In the IPAM Server Tasks pane, shown in Figure 3-3, click Provision The IPAM Server.

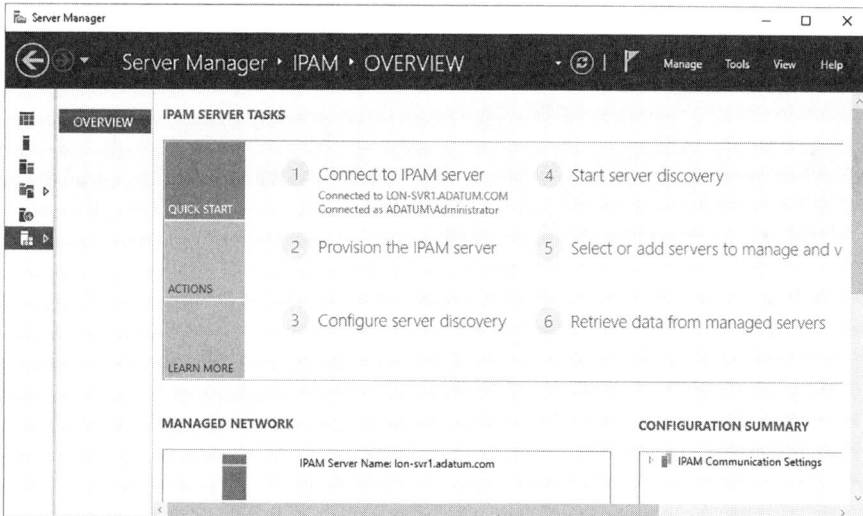

FIGURE 3-3 IPAM server tasks

3. On the Before You Begin page, click Next.
4. On the Configure Database page, shown in Figure 3-4, click either Windows Internal Database (WID) or Microsoft SQL Server. Click Next.

EXAM TIP

If you choose Microsoft SQL Server, you must define the credentials required to connect to the designated database on the Database Credentials page. The details you enter must match those you specified when you configured your SQL Server database to support IPAM.

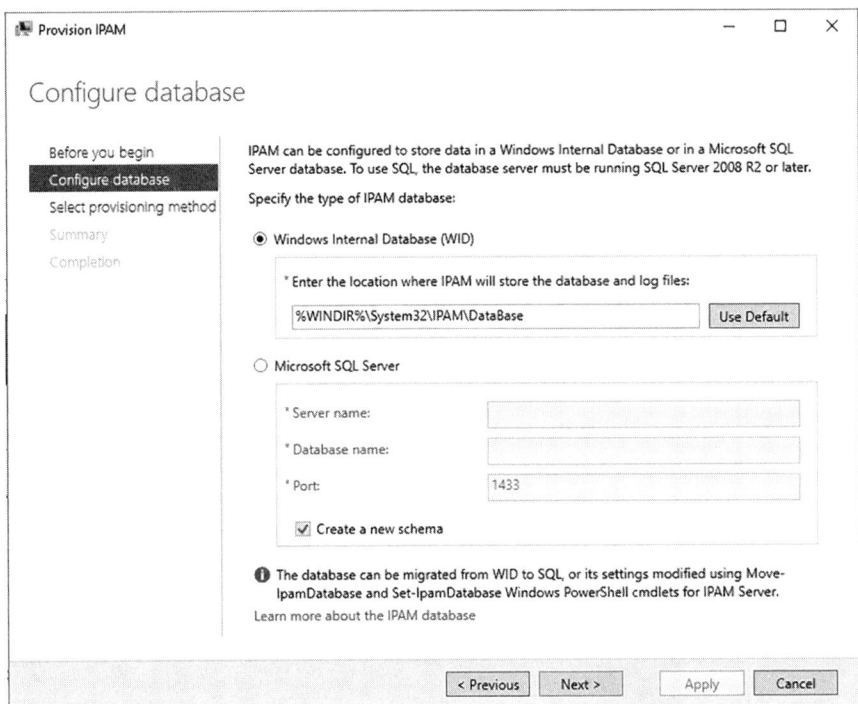

FIGURE 3-4 Configuring the IPAM database

5. On the Select Provisioning Method page, click Manual, as shown in Figure 3-5, and then click Next.

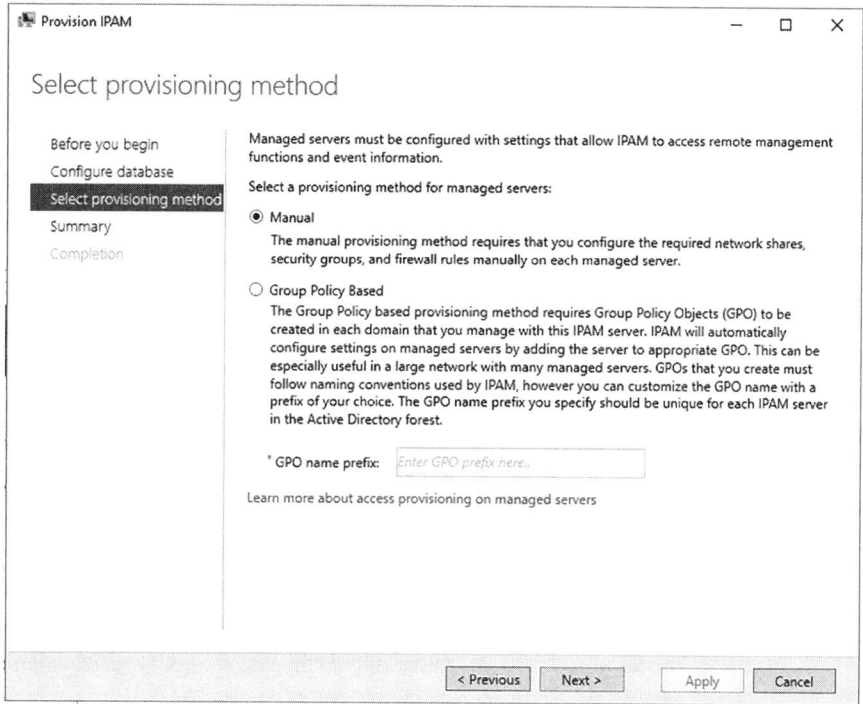

FIGURE 3-5 Selecting a provisioning method

6. Click Apply, and then click Close.

EXAM TIP

Although you cannot change from Group Policy-based provisioning to manual provisioning, you can change from manual to Group Policy-based provisioning by using the Set-IpamConfiguration -ProvisioningMethod Automatic Windows PowerShell command.

After you have completed the Provision IPAM wizard, you must manually provision your managed servers. Now, although you have chosen to perform this process manually, you can still use GPOs to assist with the process. However, unlike using the Group Policy-based provisioning method, the GPOs are not created or applied automatically. Nor are they unapplied when you wish to remove a managed server from IPAM.

NEED MORE REVIEW? CREATE IPAM PROVISIONING GPOS

If you decide to use GPOs to assist with IPAM provisioning, refer to the documentation on the following Microsoft TechNet website at *https://technet.microsoft.com/library/jj878306(v=ws.11).aspx*.

DHCP SERVERS

To manually provision your DHCP managed servers for IPAM, use the following procedure:

1. Configure Windows Firewall on a managed DHCP server. Open Windows Firewall with Advanced Security.
2. Create an inbound rule from a predefined template: In Rule Type, click Predefined, click DHCP Server Management, and then click Next.
3. In Predefined Rules, under Rules, select:
   - DHCP Server (RPCSS-In)
   - DHCP Server (RPC-In)
4. Click Next, click Allow The Connection, and then click Finish.
5. Create another inbound rule from a predefined template. In Rule Type, click Predefined, click File And Printer Sharing, and then click Next.
6. In Predefined Rules, under Rules, select:
   - File And Printer Sharing (NB-Session-In)
   - File And Printer Sharing (SMB-In)
7. Click Next, click Allow The Connection, and then click Finish.
8. Create another inbound rule from a predefined template. In Rule Type, click Predefined, click Remote Event Log Management, and then click Next.
9. In Predefined Rules, under Rules, select:
   - Remote Event Log Management (RPC)
   - Remote Event Log Management (RPC-EPMAP)
10. Click Next, click Allow The Connection, and then click Finish.
11. Create another inbound rule from a predefined template. In Rule Type, click Predefined, click Remote Service Management, and then click Next.
12. In Predefined Rules, under Rules, select:
    - Remote Service Management (RPC)
    - Remote Service Management (RPC-EPMAP)
13. Click Next, click Allow The Connection, and then click Finish.
14. Configure security groups on a managed DHCP server. In your AD DS domain, using Active Directory Users And Computers, create a universal security group called IPAMUG.
15. Add the computer running the DHCP role to this group.
16. On the DHCP server, using Computer Management, locate the DHCP Users group.
17. Add the universal security group IPAMUG to this group.
18. On the DHCP server, using Computer Management, locate the Event Log Readers group. Add the universal security group IPAMUG to this group.

19. Configure a DHCP audit share on a managed DHCP server:
    - Share the %WINDIR%\system32\DHCP folder with the name DHCPAUDIT.
    - Grant the IPAMUG group Read permissions on this shared folder.
20. Restart DHCP.

> **NEED MORE REVIEW? MANUALLY CONFIGURE DHCP ACCESS SETTINGS**
>
> To review further details about manually provisioning your DHCP servers, refer to the Microsoft TechNet website at *https://technet.microsoft.com/library/jj878311(v=ws.11).aspx*.

DNS SERVERS

To manually provision your DNS managed servers for IPAM, use the following procedure:

1. Configure Windows Firewall on a managed DNS server. Open Windows Firewall with Advanced Security. Create an inbound rule from a predefined template.
2. In Rule Type, click Predefined, click DNS Service, and then click Next.
3. In Predefined Rules, under Rules, select:
    - RPC (TCP, Incoming)
    - DNS (UDP, Incoming)
    - DNS (TCP, Incoming)
    - RPC Endpoint Mapper (TCP, Incoming)
4. Click Next, click Allow The Connection, and then click Finish.
5. Create another inbound rule from a predefined template.
6. In Rule Type, click Predefined, click Remote Service Management, and then click Next.
7. In Predefined Rules, under Rules, select:
    - Remote Service Management (RPC-EPMAP)
    - Remote Service Management (NP-In)
    - Remote Service Management (RPC)
8. Click Next, click Allow The Connection, and then click Finish.
9. Create another inbound rule from a predefined template:
10. In Rule Type, click Predefined, click Remote Event Log Management, and then click Next.
11. In Predefined Rules, under Rules, select:
    - Remote Event Log Management (RPC)
    - Remote Event Log Management (RPC-EPMAP)
12. Click Next, click Allow The Connection, and then click Finish.

13. Configure security groups on a managed DNS server. This procedure is the same as for your DHCP servers.

    Enable event log monitoring on a managed DNS server. You can enable Event log monitoring by editing the HKLM\SYSTEM\CurrentControlSet\Services\EventLog\DNS Server\Custom SD value in the registry. Add the Security ID (SID) of your IPAM server to the end of this registry value. Specifically, at the end of the value, type the following (where SID is the SID of your IPAM server. You can determine the SID by running the Get-ADComputer <IPAM_Server_Name> command at a Windows PowerShell command prompt).

    (A;;0x1;;;*SID*)

14. Configure the DNS DACL on a managed DNS server by opening the DNS Manager console.
15. In DNS Manager, right-click the local DNS server, and then click Properties.
16. Click the Security tab, and then add the IPAMUG group.

> **NEED MORE REVIEW? MANUALLY CONFIGURE DNS ACCESS SETTINGS**
>
> To review further details about manually provisioning your DNS servers, refer to the Microsoft TechNet website at *https://technet.microsoft.com/library/jj878346(v=ws.11).aspx*.

NPS AND DOMAIN CONTROLLERS

To manually configure your NPS servers and domain controllers for IPAM, use the following procedure:

1. Configure Windows Firewall on a managed domain controller or NPS server. Create an inbound rule from a predefined template.
2. In Rule Type, click Predefined, click Remote Event Log Management, and then click Next.
3. In Predefined Rules, under Rules, select:
   - Remote Event Log Management (RPC)
   - Remote Event Log Management (RPC-EPMAP)
4. Click Next, click Allow The Connection, and then click Finish.
5. Configure security groups on a managed domain controller or NPS server. This procedure is the same as for your DHCP servers.

> **NEED MORE REVIEW? MANUALLY CONFIGURE DC AND NPS ACCESS SETTINGS**
>
> To review further details about manually provisioning your NPS servers and domain controllers, refer to the Microsoft TechNet website at *https://technet.microsoft.com/library/jj878317(v=ws.11).aspx*.

Provisioning by using GPOs

To provision IPAM by using Group Policy-based provisioning, complete the following procedure:

1. In Server Manager, in the navigation pane, click IPAM.
2. In the IPAM Server Tasks pane, click Provision The IPAM Server.
3. On the Before You Begin page, click Next.
4. On the Configure Database page, click either Windows Internal Database (WID) or Microsoft SQL Server, and then click Next.
5. On the Select Provisioning Method page, click Group Policy Based, as shown in Figure 3-6, in the GPO Name Prefix, type a meaningful prefix, and then click Next.

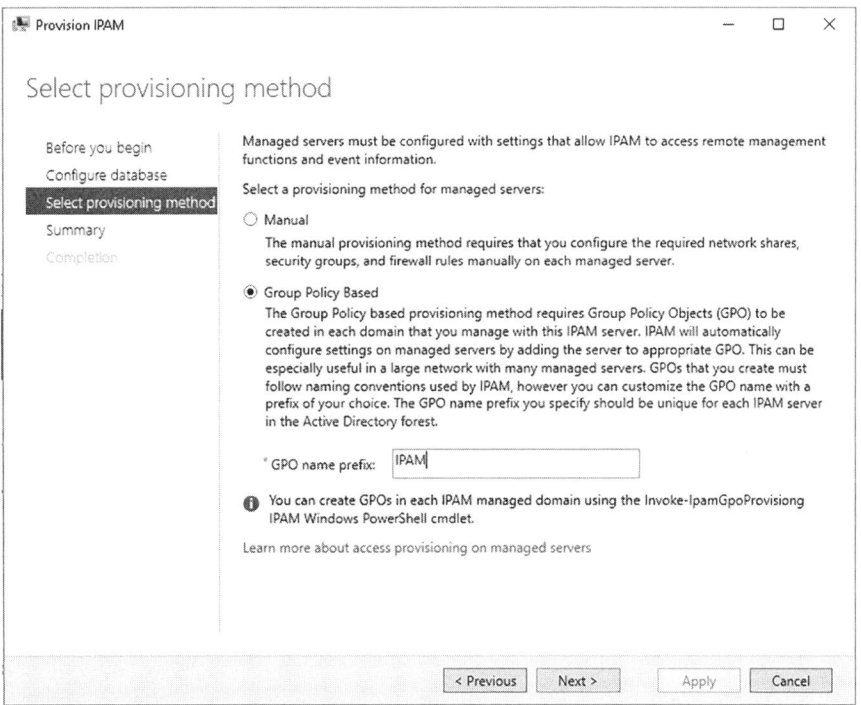

FIGURE 3-6 Configuring Group Policy Based IPAM provisioning

6. Click Apply, and then click Close.

The Completion page displays, as shown in Figure 3-7.

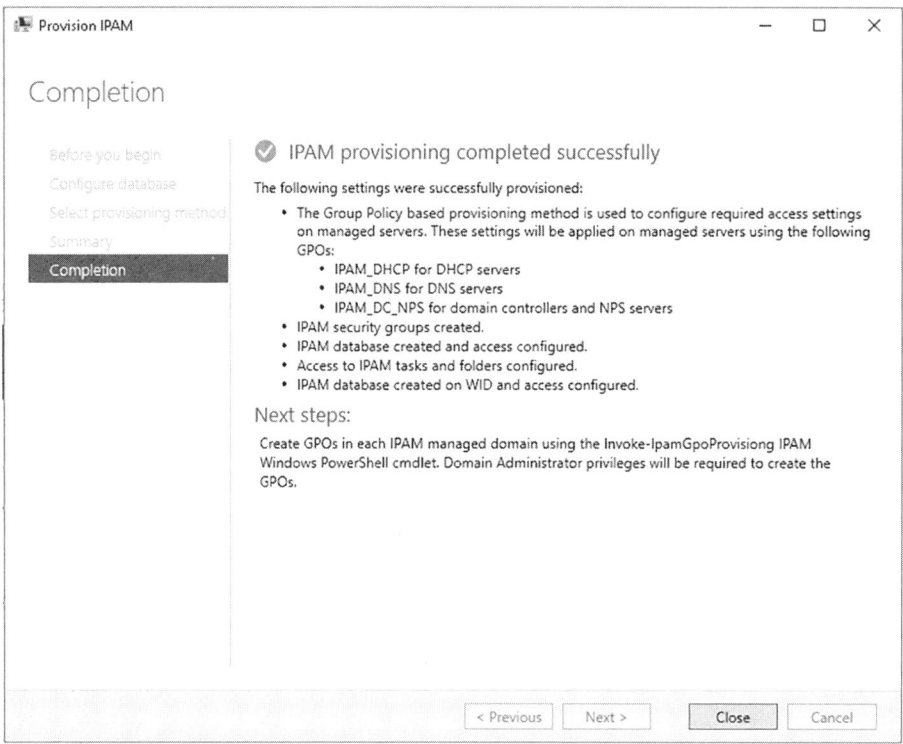

FIGURE 3-7 The IPAM installation summary

Configure server discovery

After provisioning, you must configure and perform server discovery. Discovery enables you to add managed servers to IPAM. To launch discovery, from Server Manager, in the IPAM console, perform the following procedure:

1. On the IPAM Server Tasks page, click Configure Server Discovery.
2. In the Configure Server Discovery dialog box, click Get Forests.
3. In the Configure Server Discovery popup dialog box, click OK. Close the Configure Server Discovery dialog box, and then on the IPAM Server Tasks page, click Configure Server Discovery.
4. The Configure Server Discovery dialog box appears, as shown in Figure 3-8, with the AD DS forest discovered. In the Select Domains To Discover list, click the domains that contain servers that you want to manage, and then click Add.

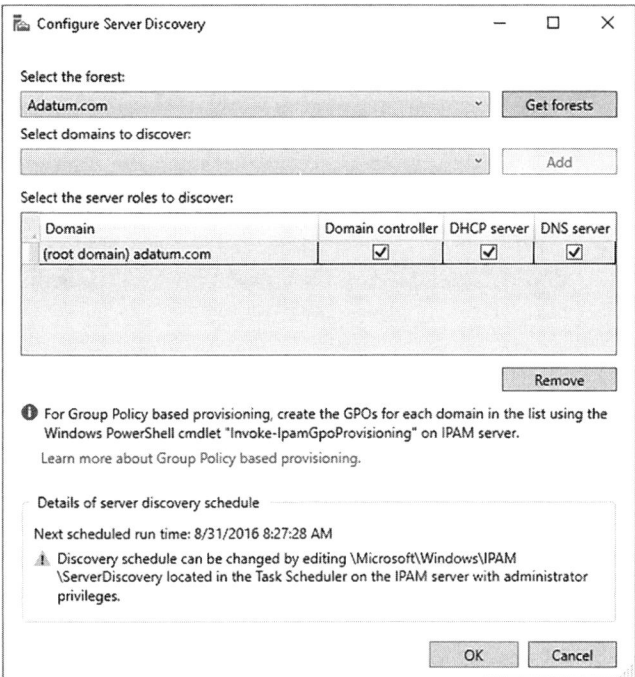

FIGURE 3-8 Configuring server discovery

5. In the Select The Roles To Discover pane, select the roles you want to discover in each domain that you have added. Click OK to begin discovery.

6. In the IPAM Server Tasks pane, click Start Server Discovery. A task to discover servers in the selected domain(s) is launched. Wait until this task has completed, and then click Select of Add Servers To Manage And Verify IPAM Access. Discovery can take 10 minutes to complete, or possibly longer. The yellow bar in Server Manager updates when discovery is complete.

7. The status of your domain controller in discovered domains is displayed. However, the status is reported as blocked, as shown in Figure 3-9.

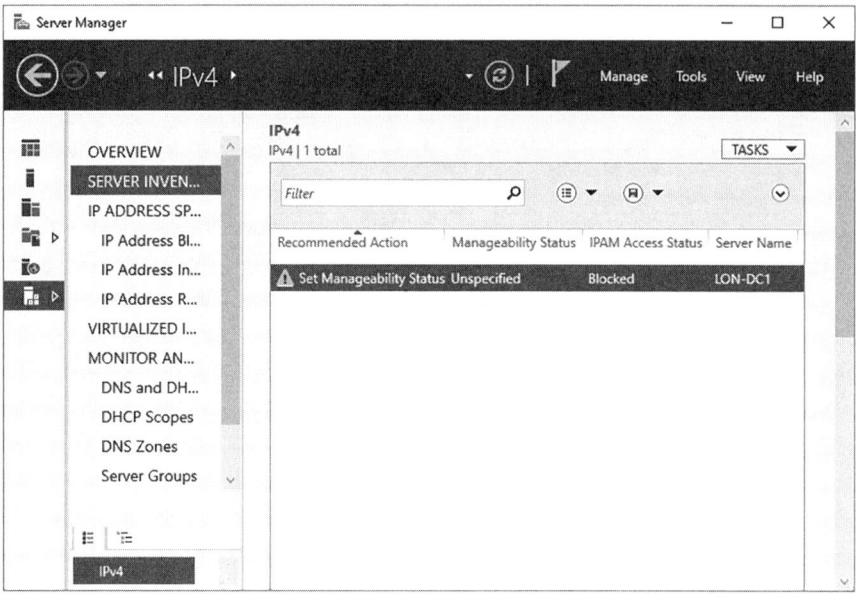

FIGURE 3-9 Viewing IPv4 node in the server inventory

8. To unblock the domain controller, run the following Windows PowerShell command, substituting your domain name, the FQDN of your IPAM server, and the user account name that is delegated management permission:

```
Invoke-IpamGpoProvisioning -Domain Adatum.com -GpoPrefixName IPAM -IpamServerFqdn
LON-SVR1.adatum.com -DelegatedGpoUser Administrator
```

EXAM TIP

You run the Invoke-IpamGpoProvisioning cmdlet to grant the IPAM server the necessary permissions to manage servers in your domain. When you run this command, it creates the GPOs and links them to your domain. These GPOs apply the necessary permissions for the IPAM server to perform management of domain controllers, DNS, and DHCP servers in your domain.

9. When the command has completed, switch to Server Manager and refresh the display: right-click the server and then click Refresh Server Access Status. It can take a few minutes to update the display. The yellow status bar in Server Manager indicates progress.
10. Right-click the server, and then click Edit Server.
11. In the Add Or Edit Server dialog box, shown in Figure 3-10, in the Manageability Status list, click Managed, and then click OK.

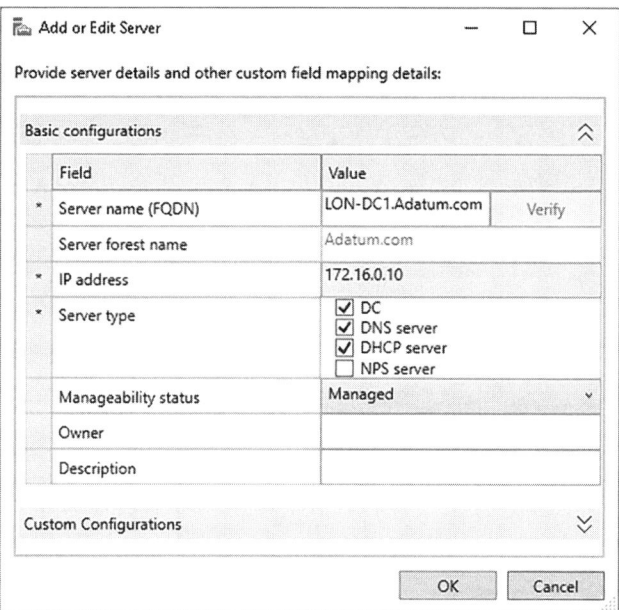

FIGURE 3-10 Configuring a server's manageability status

EXAM TIP

If the status of the server(s) still shows as Blocked, force a GPO update on the managed server(s), and also on the IPAM server. If necessary, you could need to restart the server(s). Use gpupdate /force **to force the GPOs to apply.**

12. If you want to add additional servers, in Server Inventory, right-click Managed Servers, and then click Add Server. In the Add Or Edit Server dialog box, shown in Figure 3-10, type the FQDN of the server and click Verify. In the Server Type list, select all the services that apply. In the Manageability Status list, click Managed, and then click OK.
13. When all server(s) are showing as managed, on the IPAM Server Tasks pane, click Retrieve Data From Managed Servers.

When discovery is complete, on the Manager Servers page, your managed server status should look similar to what you see in Figure 3-11.

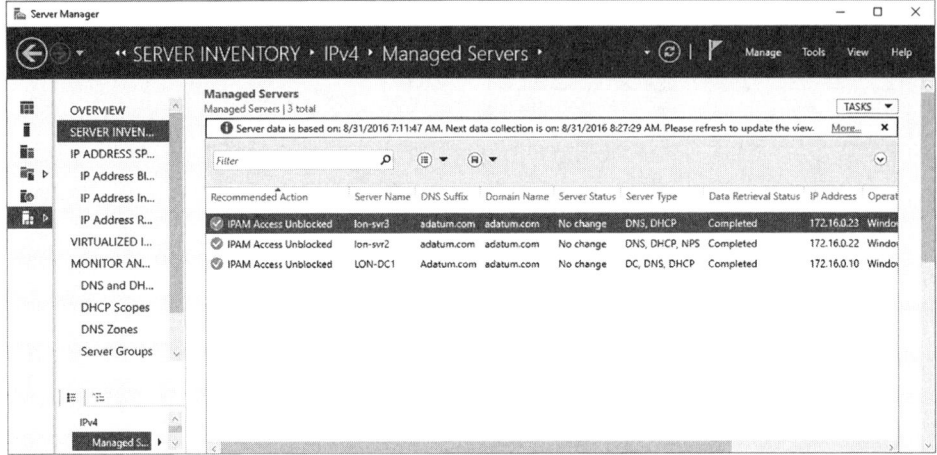

FIGURE 3-11 Viewing managed servers under the IPv4 node

Create and manage IP blocks and ranges

One of the significant advantages of using IPAM is the ability to perform management of your IP address space and related services from a single management interface: the IPAM console. To manage your IP address space, in Server Manager, click IPAM, and then click IP Address Space.

You can then select the following:

- **IP Address Blocks** An IP address block is an IP subnet, and is the highest-level object within your IP address space structure. It consists of a start IP and an end IP address. Use IP address blocks to create IP address ranges on your DHCP server(s). Beneath this node, you can view:
    - **IP Address Subnets** You can view or manage your IP subnets from this node.
    - **IP Address Ranges** You can use this node to view or manage your IP address ranges, as shown in Figure 3-12.
    - **IP Addresses** You can view or manage the individual IP addresses from this node.
- **IP Address Inventory** Provides a logical group that enables you to customize how your address space is displayed enabling efficient management and tracking of IP usage. Enables you to see all IP addresses in your organization together with the related device details, such as type and name.
- **IP Address Range Groups** You can organize your IP address ranges into logical groups using this option. For example, you could organize IP address ranges by location or by business function.

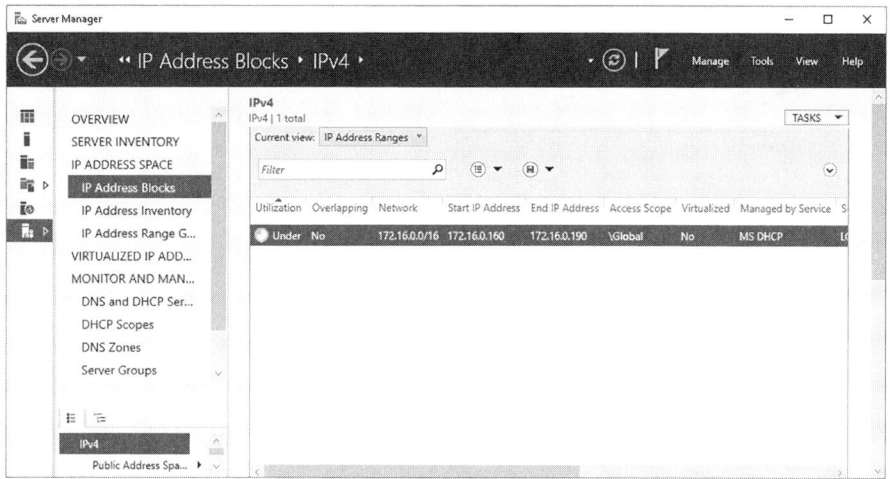

FIGURE 3-12 Viewing IP address ranges

Managing IP address blocks

To create an IP address block, in the IPAM console, under the IP Address Space node, in the navigation pane, click IP Address Blocks. Then complete the following procedure:

1. In the details pane, click Tasks, and then click Add IP Address Block.
2. In the Add Or Edit IPv4 Address Block dialog box, shown in Figure 3-13, enter the following information, and then click OK:

   - **Network ID**   The subnet ID. For example, 192.168.1.0.
   - **Prefix Length**   The number of subnet bits in the network ID. For example, 24.
   - **Automatically Assign Address Values**   Select either Yes or No.
   - **Start IP Address**   The first IP address in the network. The default is the first IP address in the network ID that you specified, but you can change this. For example, 192.168.1.0.
   - **End IP Address**   The last IP address in the network. The default is the last IP address in the network ID that you specified, but you can change this. For example, 192.168.1.255.
   - **Regional Internet Registry (RIR)**   Only valid if you enter a public IPv4 address.
   - **Received Date From RIR**   Only valid if you enter a public IPv4 address.
   - **Description**   Optional. A meaningful description that helps you identify the block.
   - **Last Assigned Date**   Optional.
   - **Owner**   Optional. Enables you to enter text to indicate the owner of the block.

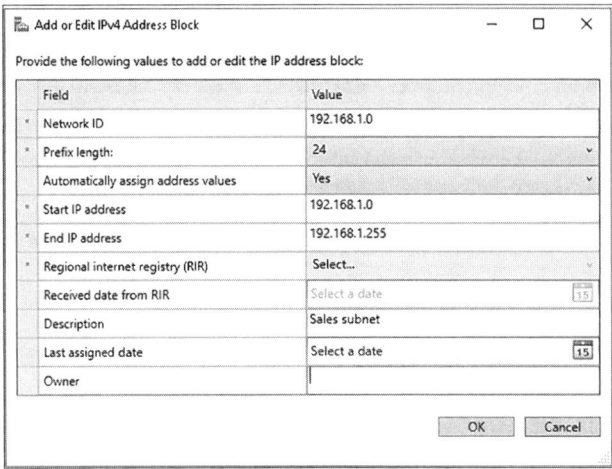

FIGURE 3-13 Adding an IPv4 address block

EXAM TIP

You can also use the Windows PowerShell Add-IpamBlock cmdlet to create an IP address block.

You can complete a similar procedure to add IPv6 address blocks. To create an IPv6 address block, in the IPAM console, under the IP Address Space node, in the navigation pane, click IP Address Blocks, and then click IPv6. In the Tasks list, click Add IP Address Block, and then configure the options in the Add or Edit IPv6 Address Block dialog box, as shown in Figure 3-14.

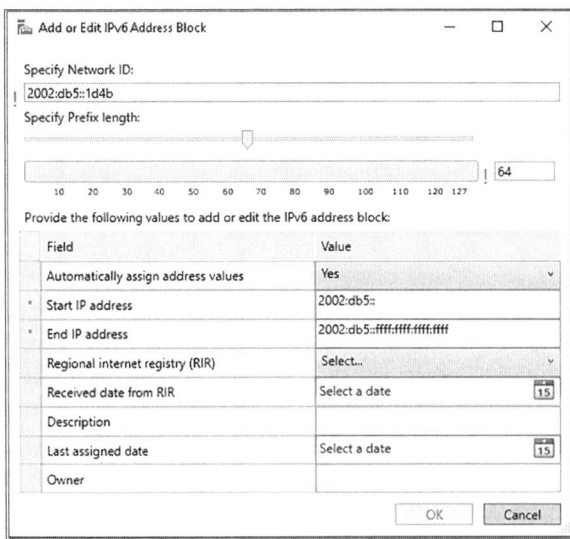

FIGURE 3-14 Adding an IPv6 address block

After you have created your IP Address Block, you can right-click it in the IPAM console and edit the address block.

> **EXAM TIP**
>
> You can also use the Windows PowerShell Set-IpamBlock cmdlet to modify an IP address block.

Managing IP Address ranges

To create an IP address range, in the IPAM console, under the IP Address Space node, in the navigation pane, click IP Address Blocks. In the Current View list, click IP Address Ranges. Then complete the following procedure:

1. In the details pane, click Tasks, and then click Add IP Address Range.
2. In the Add Or Edit IPv4 Address Range dialog box, shown in Figure 3-15, enter the following information, and then click OK:
   - **Network ID**   The subnet ID. For example, 192.168.1.0.
   - **Prefix length (0-32)**   The number of subnet bits in the network ID. For example, 24.
   - **Subnet Mask**   Automatically generated from the prefix length.
   - **Automatically Create IP Address Subnet**   Select this option to create a subnet with the configured values.
   - **Automatically Assign Address Values**   Click Yes or No.
   - **Start IP Address**   The first IP address in the network. The default is the first IP address in the network ID that you specified, but you can change this. For example, 192.168.1.0.
   - **End IP Address**   The last IP address in the network. The default is the last IP address in the network ID that you specified, but you can change this. For example, 192.168.1.255.
   - **Managed By Service**   Choose IPAM (the default), or Non-MS DHCP, or Virtual Machine Manager (VMM).
   - **Service Instance**   Specify which IPAM server is running the service. The default is Localhost.
   - **Assignment Type**   Choose either Static, Dynamic, Auto, VIP, or Reserved.
   - **Description**   Optional.
   - **Owner**   Optional.
   - **Enable Network Virtualization**   Yes or No.
   - **Custom Configurations**   Use these options to define: AD DS site, region or country, device type, and many other properties.

- **WINS and DNS** Configure the name resolution settings for clients obtaining an IP configuration from this range.
- **Gateway** Configure the routing settings for clients obtaining an IP configuration from this range.
- **Reservations** Configure the IP reservations for clients obtaining an IP configuration from this range.

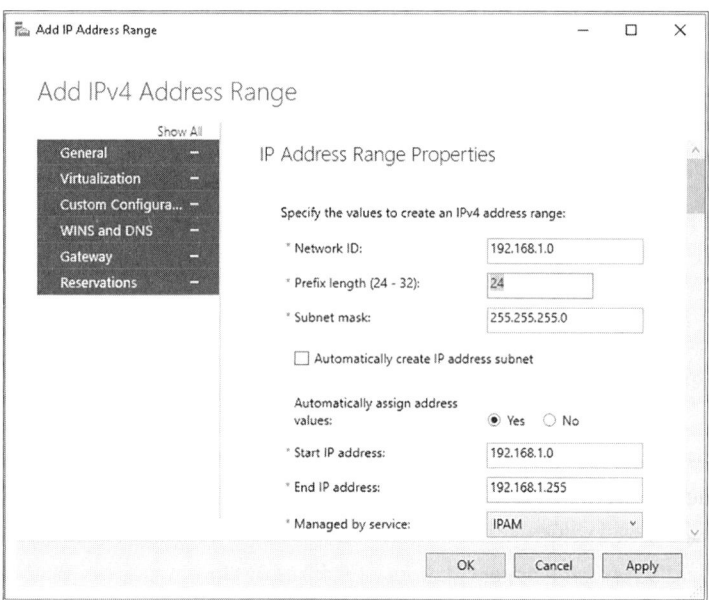

FIGURE 3-15 Adding an IPv4 address range

EXAM TIP

You can also use the Windows PowerShell Add-IpamRange cmdlet to create an IP address block.

You can complete a similar procedure to add IPv6 address ranges. To create an IPv6 address block, in the IPAM console, under the IP Address Space node, in the navigation pane, click IP Address Blocks, and then click IPv6. In the Tasks list, click Add IP Address Range, and then configure the options in the Add IPv6 Address Range dialog box.

After you have added your IP address range(s), you can edit their details from the console. Right-click the appropriate range, and then click Edit IP Address Range.

EXAM TIP

You can also use the Windows PowerShell Set-IpamRange cmdlet to create an IP address block.

> **NEED MORE REVIEW?** **MANAGING IP ADDRESS SPACE**
>
> To review further details about managing the IP address space with IPAM, refer to the Microsoft TechNet website at *https://technet.microsoft.com/library/jj878303(v=ws.11).aspx*.

Monitor utilization of IP address space

It is important to know how your IP address space is being utilized in order to properly plan and maintain your organization's network infrastructure. IPAM enables you to monitor utilization of:

- IP address ranges
- IP address blocks
- IP range groups

You can configure thresholds for utilization of IP address ranges, groups, and blocks either when you create them, or afterwards in the IPAM console. By using a threshold, you can determine over or under utilization of the resource. IPAM displays the utilization information in various places in the console, depending upon the current view.

For example, to view utilization of IP address in an IP address range, in IPAM, click IP Address Space, and then click IP Address Range Groups. In the results pane, shown in Figure 3-16, Over Or Under is shown in the Utilization column for the selected range, and the Percentage Utilized column gives a numerical value for the utilization of the address space. Use the Utilization Trend tab of the Details View to discover more information about utilization over a measured period of time.

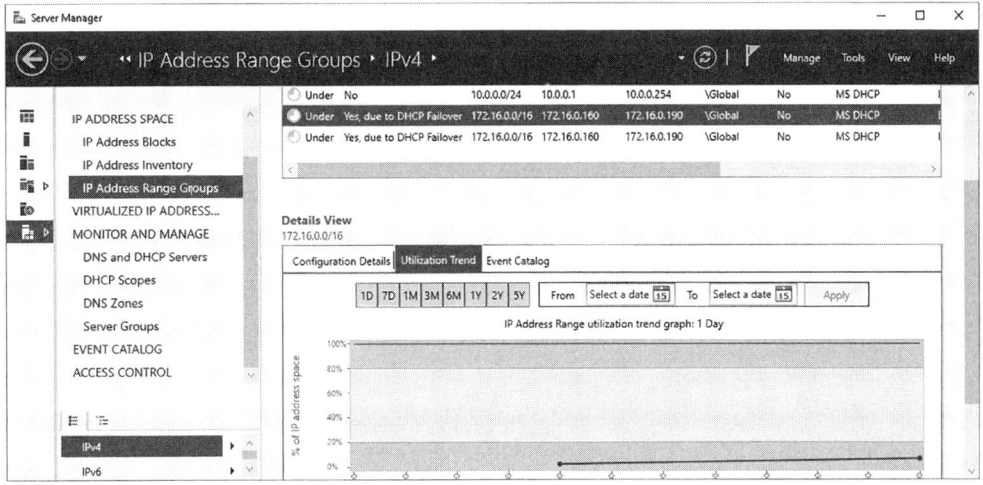

FIGURE 3-16 Viewing IPv4 utilization trend data

> **EXAM TIP**
>
> IPAM only provides IP address utilization trend information for IPv4.

Migrate existing workloads to IPAM

If your organization has invested a lot of effort in IP address management using a non-Microsoft solution, you can migrate your IP address space to IPAM by using an import process based on comma separated value (CSV) files.

When you use a CSV file to import into the IPAM address space, you must populate the first line of the CSV file with a header that contains the field names used in the IPAM console. For example: IP address, managed by service, device type, etc.

To import an IP address range, use the following syntax in your CSV file:

```
Network, Start IP address, End IP address, Managed by service, Assignment Type

192.168.2.0/24, 192.168.2.1, 192.168.2.254, IPAM, dynamic
```

Use the information in Table 3-1 to determine the required fields in your CSV files.

TABLE 3-1 Mandatory import fields

IP address blocks	IP address ranges	IP addresses
- Network - Start IP address - End IP address - RIR	- Network - Start IP address - End IP address - Managed by service - Assignment type	- IP address - Managed by service - Service instance - Device type - IP address state - Assignment type

After you have created your CSV file, to import the records, from the IPAM console:

1. Click IP Address Space, and then click IP Address Ranges.
2. Click Tasks, and then click either:
   - Import IP Address Blocks
   - Import IP Address Subnets
   - Import IP Address Ranges
   - Import IP Addresses
3. In the Open dialog box, locate and double-click the CSV file that contains the data to be imported. Your file is imported and the required records are created in IPAM.

You can also use the Windows PowerShell Import-IpamAddress, Import-IpamRange, and Import-IpamSubnet cmdlets to import your IP addresses, IP address ranges, or IP address blocks.

Determine scenarios for using IPAM with System Center VMM for physical and virtual IP address space management

If your organization creates and manages virtual machine networks, you can consider implementing IPAM and VMM integration. This enables you to have a complete end-to-end view of your entire IP address space, both physical and virtual. This view enables you to avoid the possibility of address space conflicts that can arise if your virtual address space was managed separately from your physical address space.

To enable VMM and IPAM integration, you must add your IPAM server to the resources in VMM. After you have added your IPAM server, the IP address settings in VMM are synchronized with settings that are stored in the IPAM server. These settings relate to logical networks and virtual machine networks (VM networks) in VMM.

> *NOTE* **VM NETWORKS**
>
> VM networks are covered in Chapter 6: "Determine scenarios and requirements for implementing Software Defined Networking."

After you enable the IPAM network service in VMM, you can create or modify logical networks in IPAM and these automatically synchronize to VMM. You can also create or edit a logical network in VMM and then view it in IPAM. Use the following high-level steps to integrate IPAM with VMM:

1. On the IPAM server, create a user account for VMM to communicate with your IPAM server.
2. Add the user account to a group which is a member of the IPAM ASM Administrator role.

> *NOTE* **MORE ON IPAM ROLE-BASED ACCESS**
>
> IPAM role-based access control (RBAC) is discussed in Chapter 3, "Delegate administration for DNS and DHCP using RBAC."

3. In the VMM console, add and configure the Microsoft Windows Server IP Address Management network service in VMM by using the following procedure. In the Fabric workspace, create a network service called IPAM, and then:
   - On the Manufacturer And Model page, select Microsoft and Microsoft Windows Server IP Address Management.
   - Ensure that you configure the IPAM service to run in the context of the user account that you assigned to the IPAM ASM Administrator role.
   - Specify the fully qualified domain name (FQDN) of the IPAM server.
   - Ensure that the configuration provider is Microsoft IP Address Management Provider.

> **NEED MORE REVIEW?** **HOW TO ADD AN IPAM SERVER IN VMM IN SYSTEM CENTER**
>
> To learn how to add an IPAM server in VMM, refer to the Microsoft TechNet website at *https://technet.microsoft.com/library/dn249418.aspx*.

After you have configured the integration of IPAM and VMM, when using the IPAM network service with VMM:

- When you make changes to logical networks in VMM, the virtualized IP address space in IPAM automatically updates.
- When you create logical networks in IPAM, they are added to VMM.

Skill 3.2: Manage DNS and DHCP using IPAM

One of the primary benefits of implementing IPAM is the ability to consolidate management of your DHCP and DNS servers. By using IPAM, you can manage DHCP servers, scopes, policies, and DHCP failover from the IPAM console. You can also manage DNS servers, and DNS zones and records.

Manage DHCP with IPAM

By using the DNS And DHCP Servers page in the IPAM console, shown in Figure 3-17, you can manage the following aspects of your DHCP infrastructure:

- Configure DHCP server properties and options
- Configure DHCP vendor and user classes
- Configure and/or import DHCP policies
- Activate or deactivate DHCP policies
- Add DHCP MAC address filters
- Replicate DHCP servers for failover DHCP configuration
- View DHCP scope information across all servers
- Launch the DHCP management console

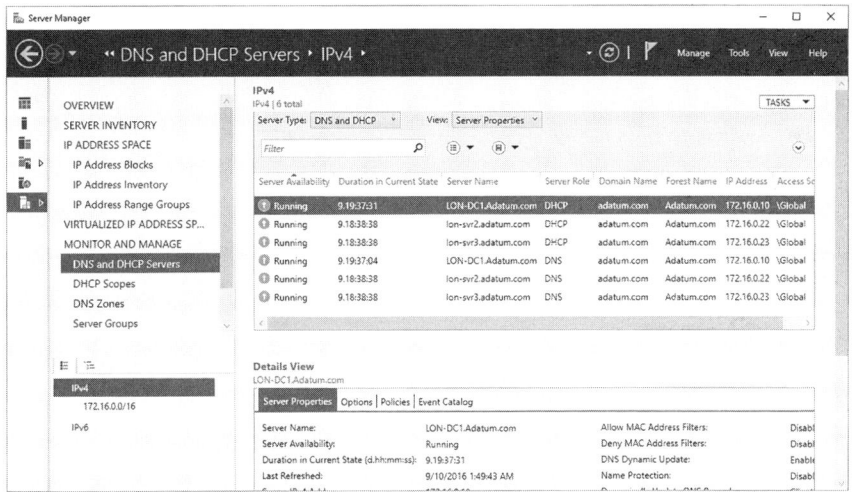

FIGURE 3-17 Viewing DNS and DHCP servers

In addition to server management, you can also manage your DHCP scopes using the IPAM console:

- Activate/deactivate scopes
- Configure scope properties
- Duplicate scopes
- Replicate scopes
- Add/remove a scope from a DHCP superscope
- Create DHCP reservations
- Configure/remove DHCP failover
- Import a DHCP policy
- Activate/deactivate DHCP scope policies

NOTE **MORE ON DHCP**

DHCP is covered in Chapter 2: "Install and configure DHCP."

Manage DHCP server properties using IPAM

To manage your DHCP servers in IPAM, under the Monitor And Manage node, click DNS and DHCP Servers. Then select the server you want to manage in the details pane. Right-click the selected server, as shown in Figure 3-18, and then choose from the following:

- Edit DHCP Server Properties
- Edit DHCP Server Options
- Configure DHCP Policy

- Add DHCP MAC Address Filter
- Launch MMC
- Activate DHCP Policies
- Deactivate DHCP Policies

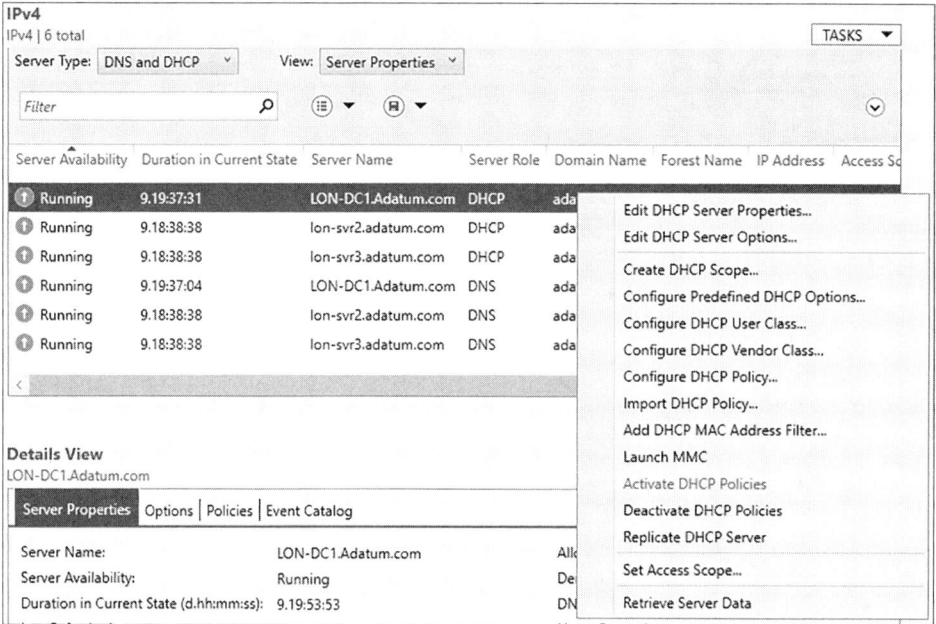

FIGURE 3-18 Configuring a DHCP server

To manage the DHCP server properties, use the following procedure:

1. Under the Monitor and Manage node, click DNS and DHCP Servers.
2. Select the server you want to manage in the details pane.
3. Right-click the selected server, and then click Edit DHCP Server Properties.
4. In the Edit DHCP Server Properties dialog box, shown in Figure 3-19, you can modify the following properties:
   - Enable DHCP Audit Logging
   - Configure DNS Dynamic Updates for DHCP clients
   - Configure DNS Dynamic Update Credentials for DHCP clients
   - Configure MAC Address Filters

These properties are the same that you can configure in the DHCP console when you select the properties of the IPv4 or IPv6 nodes, and are discussed in Chapter 2, "Install and configure DHCP."

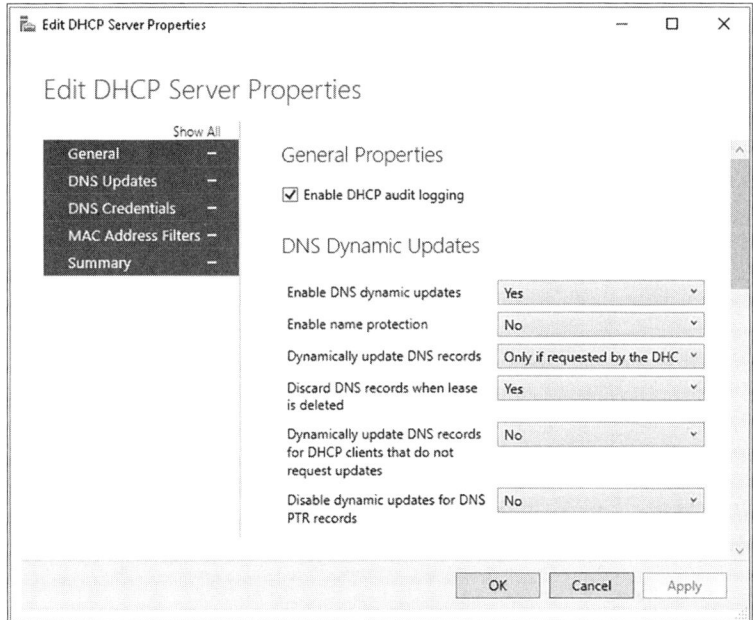

FIGURE 3-19 Configuring DHCP server properties

To edit a DHCP server's options, perform the following procedure:

1. Under the Monitor And Manage node, click DNS And DHCP Servers.
2. Select the server you want to manage in the details pane.
3. Right-click the selected server, and then click Edit DHCP Server Options.
4. In the Edit DHCP Server Options dialog box, shown in Figure 3-20, you can create or modify the DHCP server options. These options are used when a client obtains an IP configuration from the configured server and include settings such as default gateway, DNS settings, and, where configured, user and vendor class options. Server options are overridden by scope options and reservation options.

These options are the same that you can configure in the DHCP console when you select the Server Options node beneath the IPv4 or IPv6 nodes, and are discussed in Chapter 2: "Create and manage DHCP scopes, configure DHCP options."

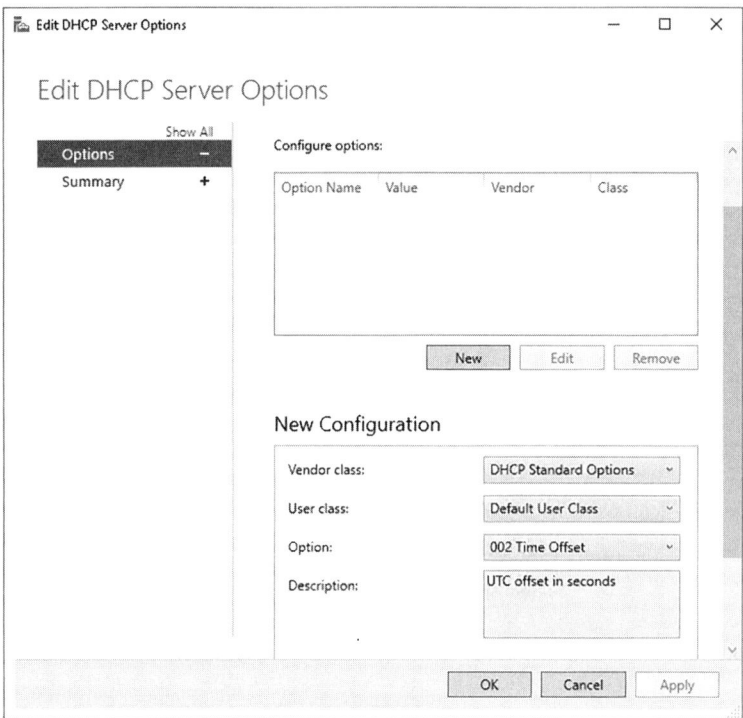

FIGURE 3-20 Configuring DHCP server options

Configure DHCP scopes and options

You can use IPAM to create and configure DHCP scopes and options. This enables you to use the IPAM console to perform virtually all DHCP management tasks.

CREATE A DHCP SCOPE

To use IPAM to create a DHCP scope, on the DNS and DHCP Server page, right-click a DHCP server, and then click Create DHCP Scope. In the Create DHCP Scope dialog box, shown in Figure 3-21, define the following information, and then click OK.

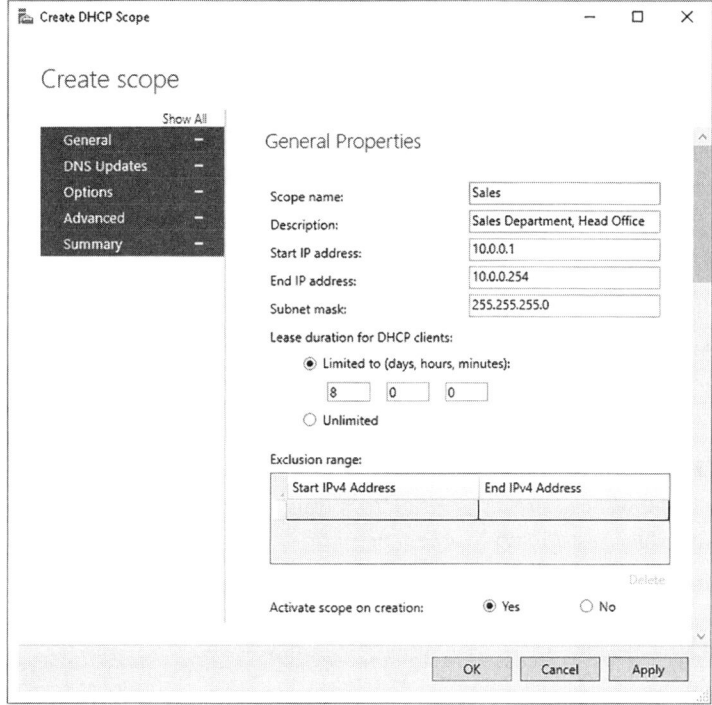

FIGURE 3-21 Adding a DHCP scope

- A scope name and description
- A start and end IP address
- A subnet mask
- A lease duration – 8 days is the default
- Any excluded addresses or range of addresses from the scope
- Whether the scope should be activated after creation
- Dynamic DNS options, including whether dynamic updates are supported for clients, and whether DNS name protection is enabled for clients
- DHCP scope options, such as Router, DNS Servers, and DNS Domain Name
- Advanced properties: whether supported clients are DHCP only, BOOTP only, or both

MANAGE A DHCP SCOPE

You can manage scopes from the IPAM console. In IPAM, under the Monitor And Manage node, click DHCP Scopes. Then, in the details pane, right-click the scope you want to manage. You can then choose from the following options:

- **Edit DHCP Scope** Enables you to reconfigure the scope configuration including start and end IP address, lease duration, exclusions, scope options, and DNS update settings.

- **Duplicate DHCP Scope**   Enables you to create another scope based on the properties of an existing scope. The duplicated scope is initially configured on the same server and with the same name, matching lease duration, duplicate DNS update settings, and DHCP scope options. You can then modify these initial settings to create a new scope.
- **Create DHCP Reservation**   Reservations enable you to create and configure a specific IP address in a scope for a particular client.
- **Add to DHCP Superscope**   Superscopes enable you to combine scopes to support special configurations.
- **Configure DHCP Failover**   DHCP failover provides for high-availability of the DHCP service. This is discussed in the next section.
- **Configure DHCP Policy**   DHCP policies provide a convenient way to manage the properties of multiple scopes. This is discussed in the next section.
- **Import DHCP Policy**   This is discussed in the next section.
- **Deactivate Scope**   If you want to prevent clients from using the scope to obtain an IP configuration, perhaps while performing maintenance, you can deactivate the scope.
- **Activate Scope**   After completing the maintenance on a scope, you can activate it once more.
- **Activate DHCP Policies**   This is discussed in the next section.
- **Deactivate DHCP Policies**   This is discussed in the next section.
- **Set Access Scope**   Enables you to determine the management scope of the DHCP scope. This is discussed later in this chapter under the heading: "Delegate administration for DNS and DHCP using RBAC."

Configure DHCP policies in IPAM

You can use DHCP policies to assign IPv4 options to DHCP clients. These options are assigned by DHCP based on conditions within the policy, including user and vendor class, MAC address, or other factors. You can configure and apply DHCP policies at both the server and scope level.

> *NOTE*   **MORE ON DHCP POLICIES**
>
> DHCP policies is covered in Chapter 2: "Implement DHCP:Configure DHCP policies."

To configure and apply a DHCP server policy using IPAM, in IPAM, under the Monitor And Manage node, click DNS And DHCP Servers. Right-click a DHCP server, and then click Configure DHCP Policy. To configure and apply a DHCP scope policy using IPAM, in IPAM, under the Monitor And Manage node, click DHCP Scopes. Right-click a DHCP scope, and then click Configure DHCP Policy.

To create your policy, in the Create DHCP Policy Wizard, shown in Figure 3-22, configure the following options, and click OK.

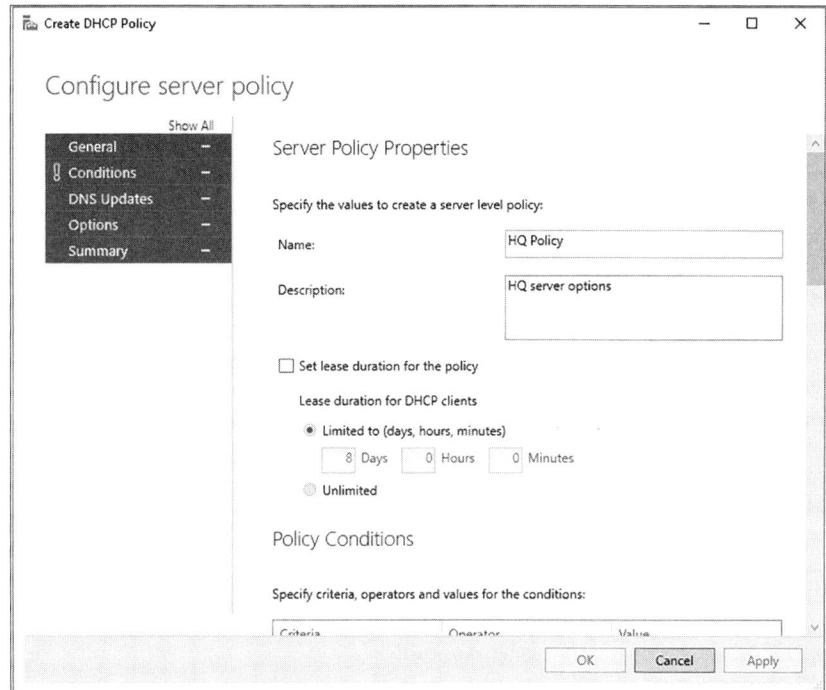

FIGURE 3-22 Creating a server policy

- A policy name and description.
- A lease duration for the policy.
- Policy conditions. A client must meet the condition(s) of the policy for the configured options in the policy to apply. You can configure multiple conditions if you wish.
- Dynamic DNS options, including whether dynamic updates are supported for clients, and whether DNS name protection is enabled for clients.
- DHCP scope options, such as Router, DNS Servers, and DNS Domain Name.

The process for configuring a scope policy is very similar.

If you have previously created a server or scope level policy, you can apply the same policy to another server or scope. To do this, in the IPAM console, right-click the server or scope, and then click Import DHCP Policy. In the Import Policy dialog box, shown in Figure 3-23, click Server or Scope as required, and then select the appropriate policy by using the drop-down lists to identify the source server, scope, and policy.

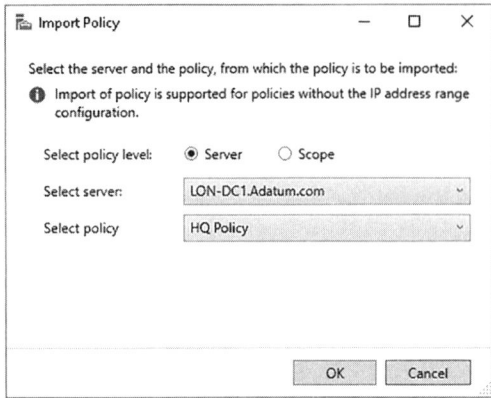

FIGURE 3-23 Importing a server policy

Configure DHCP failover in IPAM

DHCP failover enables you to configure high-availability for DHCP by using two DHCP servers to provide IP configurations to the same subnets. The two DHCP servers replicate lease information between one another. If one of the servers fails, the other server continues providing DHCP services for the subnet(s) for which it is configured.

> **NOTE MORE ON DHCP FAILOVER**
> DHCP failover is discussed in Chapter 2: "Configure DHCP failover."

To configure DHCP failover using IPAM, use the following procedure:

1. In IPAM, under the Monitor And Manage node, click DHCP Scopes.
2. Right-click a DHCP scope, and then click Configure DHCP Failover.
3. In the Configure DHCP Failover Relationship Wizard, on the Configure Failover Relationship page, shown in Figure 3-24, in the Configuration Option list, click Create New Relationship.

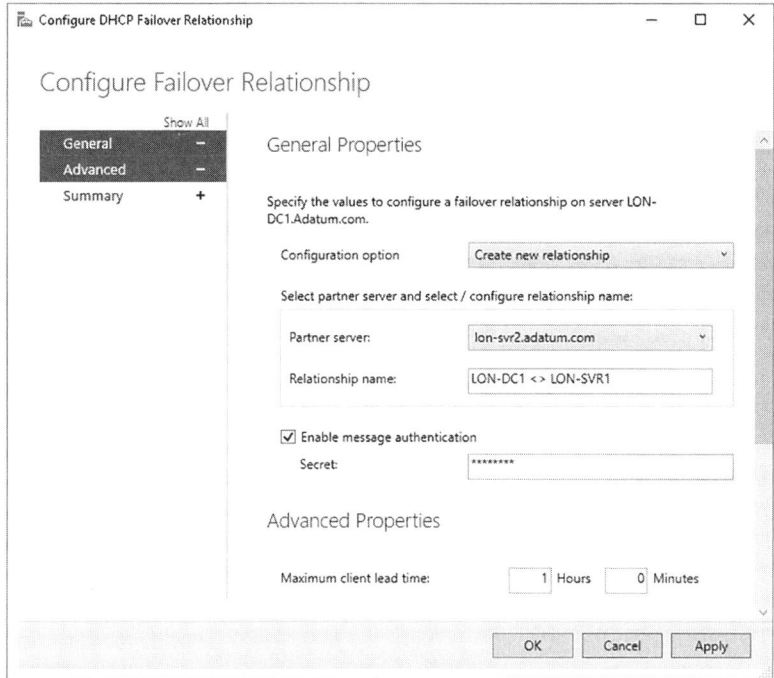

FIGURE 3-24 Configuring failover

1. In the Partner Server list, select another server in the same subnet.
2. Then configure the following options:
   - **Enable Message Authentication**   You can configure message authentication using the secret as a password. This means that the failover message traffic between replication partners is authenticated and that helps validate that the failover message originates with the configured failover partner.
   - **Secret**   The password used to enable message authentication.
   - **Maximum Client Lead Time**   This value is used in Hot standby mode. It defines how long the secondary server must wait before taking control of the scope. The default is one hour, and cannot be zero.
   - **Mode**   Choose between Load Balance and Hot Standby.
   - **Percentages**   Used when you enable Load Balance mode. Enables you to determine how much of the address space each server manages. The default is a 50:50 split.
   - **Role Of Partner Server**   Use this setting when you enable Standby mode. It enables you to define which server is the primary and which the secondary. Choose between Active or Standby.

- **Addresses Reserved For Standby Server** Use this value to determine what percentage of addresses within the scope the secondary server can allocate. This allows the secondary server to allocate a small proportion of addresses while it waits to determine if the primary comes back online. The default is five percent of available scope addresses.
- **State Switchover Interval** When a server loses connectivity with its replication partner, it has no way of determining why this has occurred. You must manually change a partner's status to a down state to indicate to the remaining partner that the other server is unavailable. Setting the State Switchover value enables you to automate this changed state after a configured time interval. This value is not used by default.

3. Click OK.

Using Windows PowerShell

In addition to using the IPAM console to manage your DHCP servers and scopes, you can also use the following Windows PowerShell cmdlets to retrieve information about DHCP servers and scopes:

- **Get-IpamDhcpConfigurationEvent** Retrieves DHCP server configuration events from the IPAM database.
- **Get-IpamDhcpScope** Retrieves information about IPAM DHCP scopes.
- **Get-IpamDhcpServer** Retrieves information about IPAM DHCP servers.
- **Get-IpamDhcpSuperscope** Retrieves information about IPAM DHCP superscopes.

Manage DNS with IPAM

You can use the IPAM console to perform the following DNS management tasks:

- View DNS servers and zones
- Create new zones
- Create DNS records
- Manage conditional forwarders
- Open the DNS management console for a selected server

> **NOTE MORE ON DNS**
> DNS is covered in Chapter 1, "Install and configure DNS servers."

Manage DNS server properties using IPAM

You can use IPAM to manage a number of DNS server properties. To manage a DNS server in IPAM, under the Monitor And Manage node, click DNS And DHCP Servers. Right-click the appropriate DNS server and select one of the following options:

- **Launch MMC** Enables you to load the DNS console for the selected server and perform all DNS management tasks.
- **Create DNS Zone** Enables you to create a DNS zone on the selected DNS server. You can create forward lookup zones, and reverse lookup zones for both IPv4 and IPv6. You can create Primary, secondary, or stub zones. You can define that the zone be Active Directory-integrated, or stored in a file.
- **Create DNS Conditional Forwarder** You can configure conditional forwarding for a DNS server.

To add a new DNS zone, complete the following procedure:

1. Right-click the DNS server that hosts the zone, and then click Create DNS Zone.
2. On the Create DNS Zone page, shown in Figure 3-25, under General Properties, configure the following settings, and then click OK:

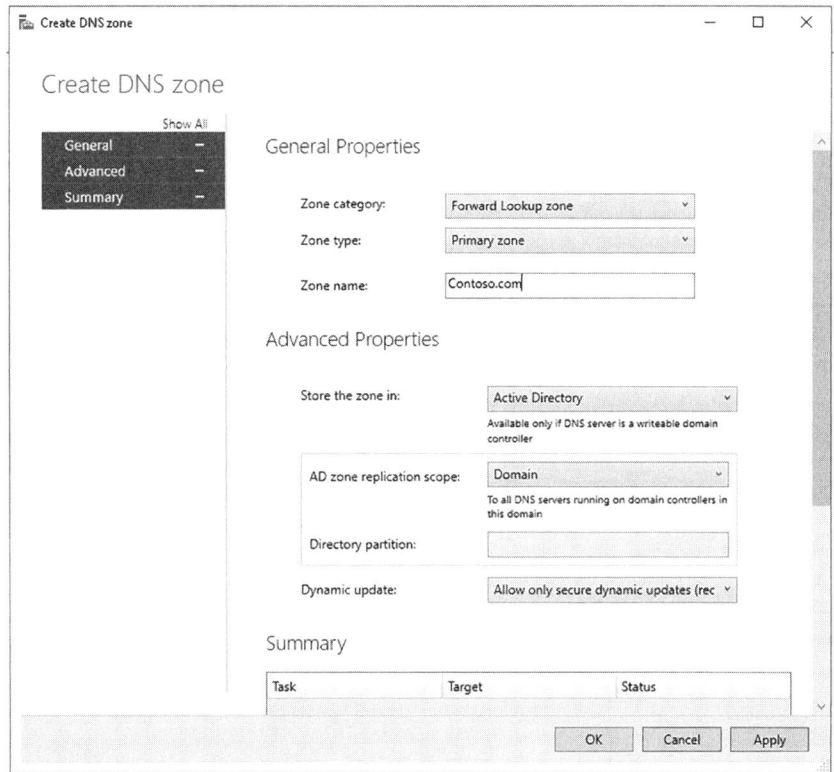

FIGURE 3-25 Adding a DNS zone in IPAM

- **Zone Category** Choose from Forward Lookup zone, IPv4 Reverse Lookup zone, and IPv6 Reverse Lookup zone.

- **Zone Type**   Choose from Primary zone, Secondary zone, and Stub zone. If you select Secondary or Stub, you must define the Master DNS server(s) from which this DNS server obtains its zone data.
- **Zone Name**   This is the FQDN for the DNS domain.
- **Store The Zone In**   Choose between Active Directory or Zone file. If you select Zone file, specify the file name. If you choose Active Directory, you must configure the following two options:
- **AD Zone Replication Scope**   Choose how the zone data is replicated in AD DS. Options are: Domain, Forest, Legacy, and Custom.
- **Directory Partition**   If you choose custom for the AD zone replication scope option, you must define the AD DS application partition name here.
- **Dynamic Update**   Choose how clients update DNS dynamically. Options are: Allow Only Secure Dynamic Updates (recommended for Active Directory), Allow Both Nonsecure And Secure Dynamic Updates, and Do Not Allow Dynamic Updates.

Manage DNS zones and records

You can manage DNS zone and associated records from the IPAM console. Under the Monitor And Manage node, click DNS Zones, as shown in Figure 3-26. You can see a list of available zones.

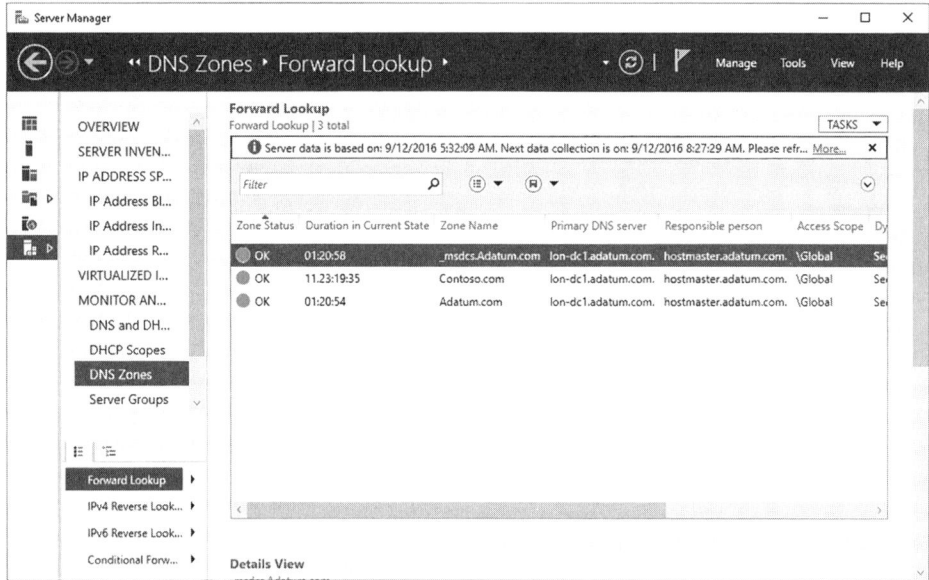

FIGURE 3-26 Using IPAM to view DNS zones

To manage a zone, right-click the zone, and then select one of the following options:

- **Delete DNZ Zone**   Enables you to remove the DNS zone.
- **Add DNS Resource Record**   You can add any DNS resource record to the selected zone. For example, as shown in Figure 3-27, you can create a host (A) record.

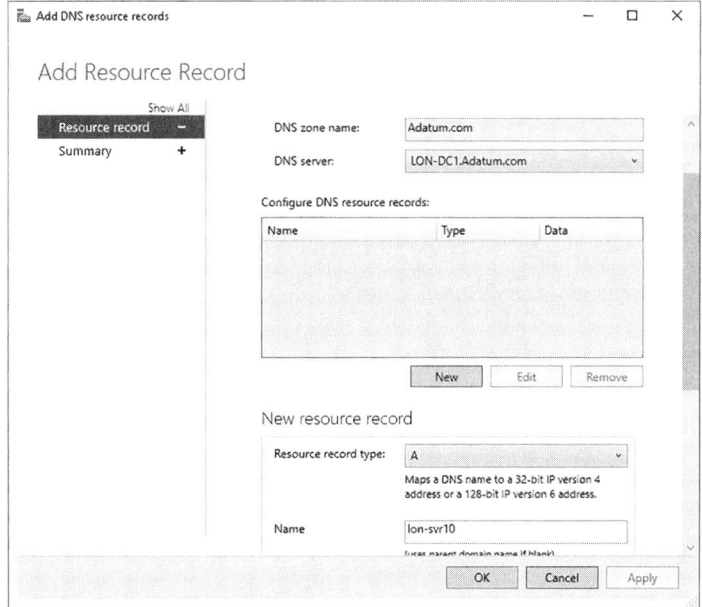

FIGURE 3-27 Adding a resource record

- **Edit DNS Zone**   You can reconfigure the zone properties, as shown in Figure 3-28. Configurable properties are:
    - **Advanced Properties**   Options include where the zone is stored (Active Directory or file), the AD replication scope and partition, whether dynamic updates are enabled for the zone, and zone aging and scavenging options.
    - **Name Servers**   The list of configured name servers for the zone.
    - **SOA**   The Start of Authority information for the zone.
    - **Zone Transfers**   Whether zone transfers are enabled, and to which DNS servers.

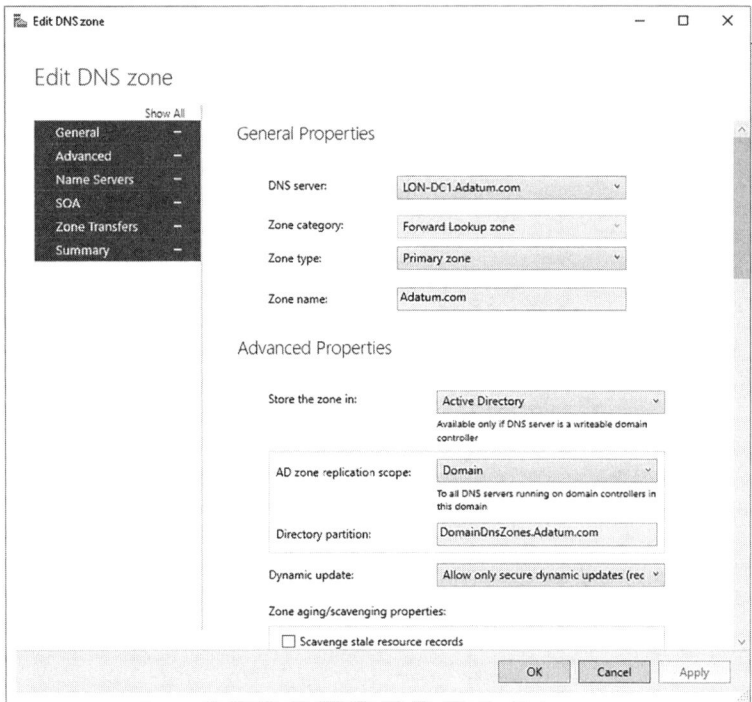

FIGURE 3-28 Editing zone properties

> **NOTE THE DNS ZONE**
>
> These DNS zone options are discussed in Chapter 1, "Create and configure DNS zones and records, configure DNS zones."

Using Windows PowerShell

In addition to using the IPAM console to manage your DNS servers and zones, you can also use the following Windows PowerShell cmdlets to retrieve information about DNS servers and zones:

- **Get-IpamDnsServer** Retrieves information about IPAM DNS servers.
- **Get-IpamDnsZone** Retrieves information about IPAM DNS zones.
- **Get-IpamDnsConditionalForwarder** Retrieves information about IPAM DNS conditional forwarders.
- **Get-IpamDnsResourceRecord** Retrieves IPAM DNS resource records.

Manage DNS and DHCP servers in multiple Active Directory forests

In Windows Server 2016, you can use IPAM to manage your DNS and DHCP servers across multiple AD DS forests so long as a two-way trust relationship exists between the AD DS forest where you installed IPAM and each of the remote AD DS forests.

To manage multiple forests, in the IPAM console, on the IPAM Server Tasks page, click Configure Server Discovery, and then complete the following procedure:

1. In the Configure Server Discovery dialog box, shown in Figure 3-29, click Get Forests. The trusted forests and domains are discovered.
2. Click Configure Server Discovery. The Configure Server Discovery dialog box is displayed once again. In the Select The Forest list, click the forest that you want to manage.
3. In the Select Domain To Discover list, click the domains that you want to manage and click Add. Repeat this process until all domains are listed in the Select The Server Roles To Discover list, and then click OK.
4. Finally, you must run the Windows PowerShell Invoke-IpamGpoProvisioning cmdlet to grant the IPAM server the necessary permissions to manage servers in your domains.

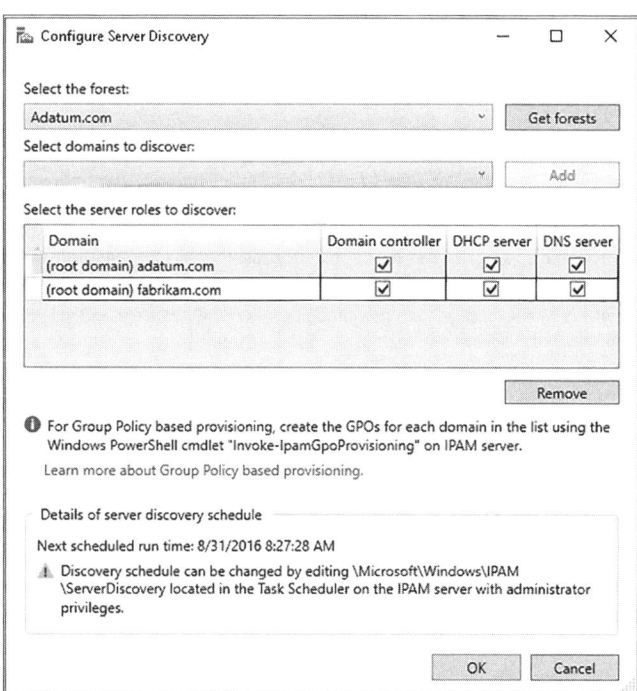

FIGURE 3-29 Configuring server discovery in multiple forests

Delegate administration for DNS and DHCP using RBAC

You can implement role-based access control to help make it easier to administer your IP infrastructure using IPAM. RBAC in IPAM is based on roles, access scopes, and access policies.

- **Roles**   A collection of IPAM operations. There are eight built-in roles available, but you can create your own roles to address your specific administrative requirements. You can associate a built-in or custom role with a Windows user or group account.
- **Access Scopes**   Determines the collection of objects a user has access to thereby enabling you to define administrative boundaries within IPAM. For example, you could create access scopes based on business function or location.
- **Access Policies**   Combines a role and an access scope to assign permissions to a user or group. For example, you could create an access policy for a user with a role called IP Address Range Admin and an access scope called Global\Europe. Therefore, this user has permission to edit and delete IP address ranges that are associated with the Europe access scope.

IPAM has several built-in role-based security groups that you can use for managing your IPAM infrastructure, as shown in Table 3-2.

TABLE 3-2 Built-in IPAM role-based security groups

Group name	Description
IPAM DNS Administrator	Members of this group can manage DNS servers and their associated DNS zones and resource records.
IPAM MSM Administrator	Members of this group can manage DHCP servers, scopes, policies, and DNS servers and associated zones and records.
IPAM ASM Administrator	Members of this group can perform IP address space tasks, in addition to common IPAM management tasks.
IP Address Record Administrator	Members of this group can manage IP addresses, including unallocated addresses, and members can create and delete IP address instances.
IPAM Administrator	Members of this group have privileges to view all IPAM data and to perform all IPAM tasks.
IPAM DHCP Administrator	Completely manages DHCP servers.
IPAM DHCP Reservations Administrator	Manages DHCP reservations.
IPAM DHCP Scope Administrator	Manages DHCP scopes.
DNS Record Administrator	Manages DNS resource records.

To configure RBAC in IPAM, from Server Manager, open the IPAM console, and then click Access Control. Then click either Roles, as shown in Figure 3-30, or Access Scopes or Access Policies.

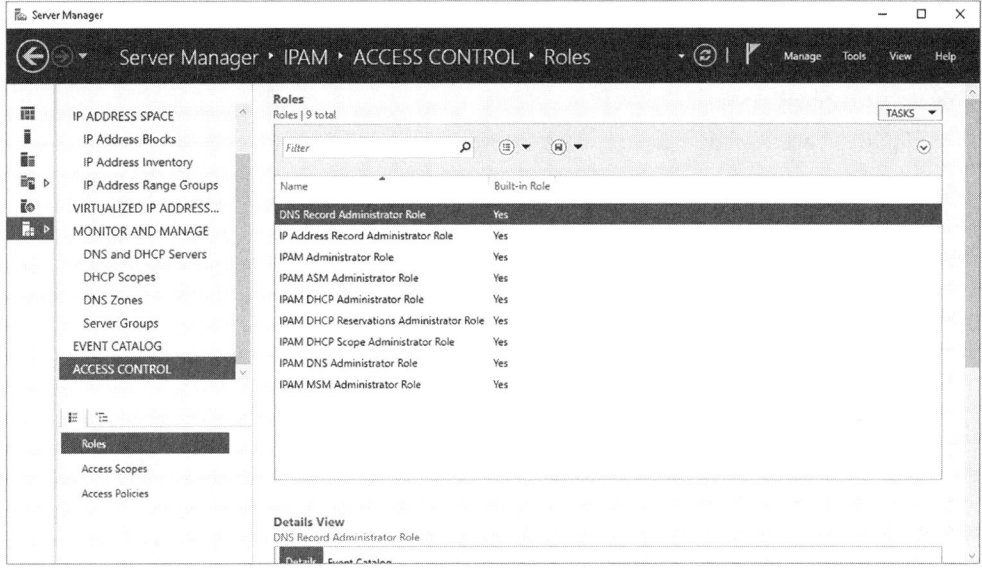

FIGURE 3-30 Viewing RBAC roles

MANAGING ROLES

To configure a new role, perform the following procedure:

1. Under Access Control, in the Roles pane, click Tasks, and then click Add User Role.

2. In the Add Or Edit Role dialog box, type a name and a description for your role. Then, in the Operations list, as shown in Figure 3-31, select the management tasks that the role holders are able to perform, and click OK.

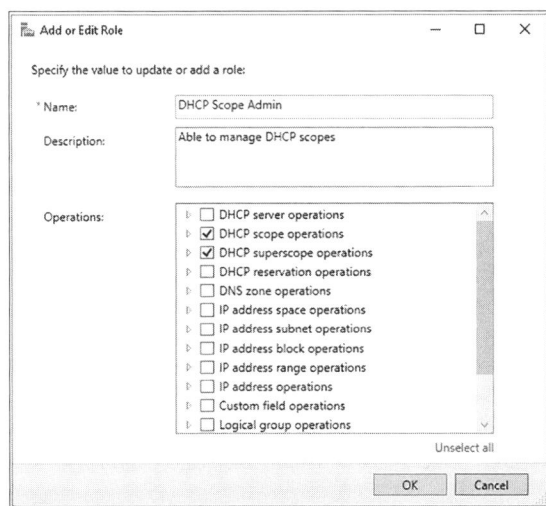

FIGURE 3-31 Adding a new role

Skill 3.2: Manage DNS and DHCP using IPAM   CHAPTER 3   **143**

You can edit any custom role by right-clicking the role and clicking Edit Role. You cannot edit built-in roles.

MANAGING ACCESS SCOPES

To configure an access scope, perform the following procedure:

1. Under Access Control, in the Access Scopes pane, click Tasks, and then click Add Access Scope.
2. In the Add Access Scope dialog box, click New.
3. Type a name and a description, as shown in Figure 3-32, click Add, and then click OK.

FIGURE 3-32 Adding an access scope

EXAM TIP

IPAM includes the Global access scope. Users assigned to Global have access to all objects in IPAM that their role permits. All other access scopes are subsets of Global.

You can edit any custom access scope by right-clicking the access scope and clicking Edit Access Scope. You cannot edit the Global scope.

MANAGING ACCESS POLICIES

No default access policies exist. To create a new access policy, perform the following procedure:

1. Under Access Control, in the Access Policies pane, click Tasks, and then click Add Access Policy.
2. In the Add Access Policy, under User Settings, click Add.

3. In the Select User Or Group dialog box, enter the name of a user or group to which you want to assign the role, and click OK.

EXAM TIP

You should always use groups. That way, if you must later reconfigure the access policy because a user has changed job function, you merely need to remove the user from the AD DS group rather than reconfigure the IPAM access policy.

4. Optionally, enter a description, as shown in Figure 3-33.

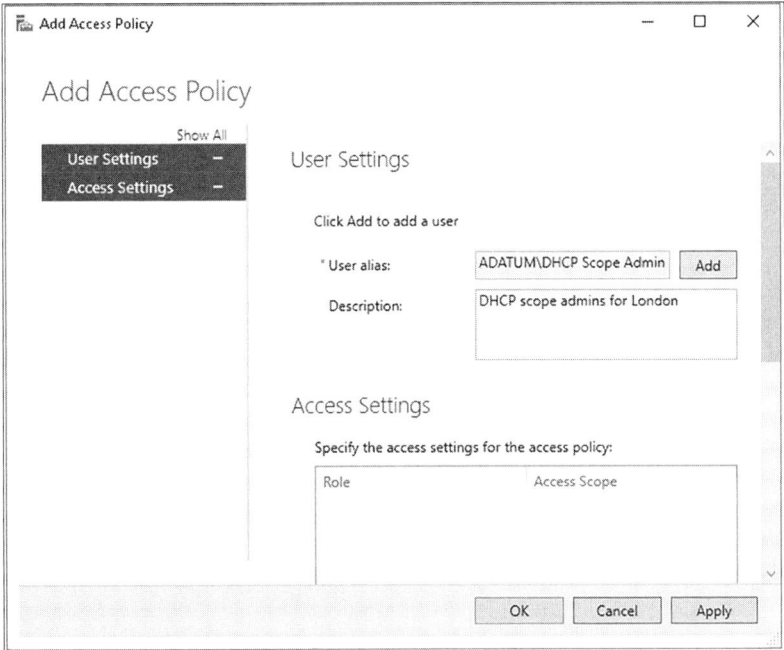

FIGURE 3-33 Adding a group to an access policy

5. Under the Access Settings heading, click New.
6. Under the New Setting heading, in the Select Role list, select either a built-in role or a custom role.
7. In Select The Access Scope For The Role, click the desired scope and then click Add Setting, as shown in Figure 3-34.
8. If you wish to add multiple roles and/or scopes to the policy, repeat the preceding steps. When all roles and access scopes for the policy are configured, click OK.

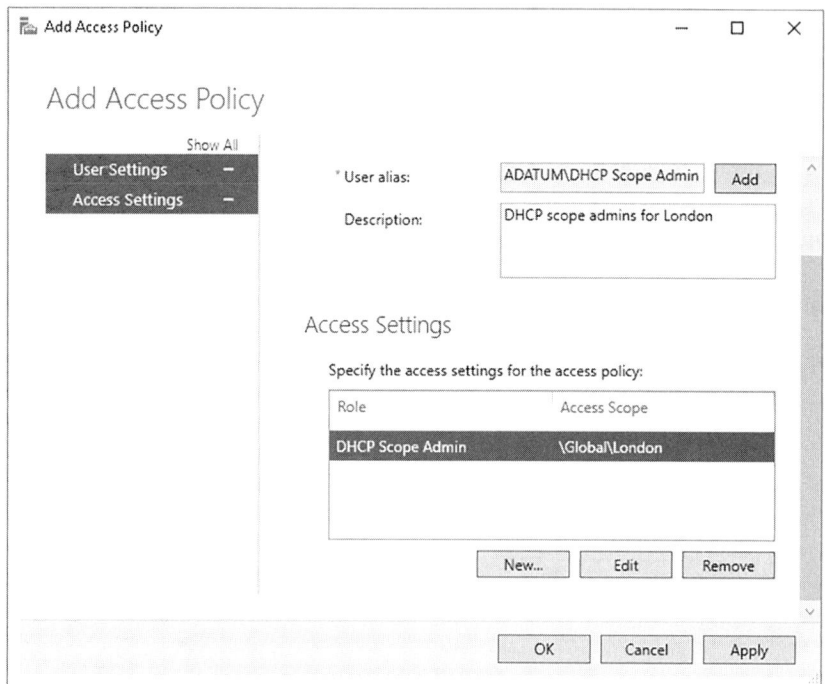

FIGURE 3-34 Configuring an access policy

You can reconfigure your access policies by selecting them in the Access Policies pane under Access Control.

CONFIGURE THE ACCESS SCOPE FOR OBJECTS

You can define the access scope for objects such as servers, DNS zones, and DHCP scopes by selecting the object, right-clicking it, and then clicking Set Access Scope. In the Set Access Scope dialog box, shown in Figure 3-35, clear the Inherit Access Scope From Parent check box, and then, in the Select The Access Scope list, click the appropriate scope, and then click OK.

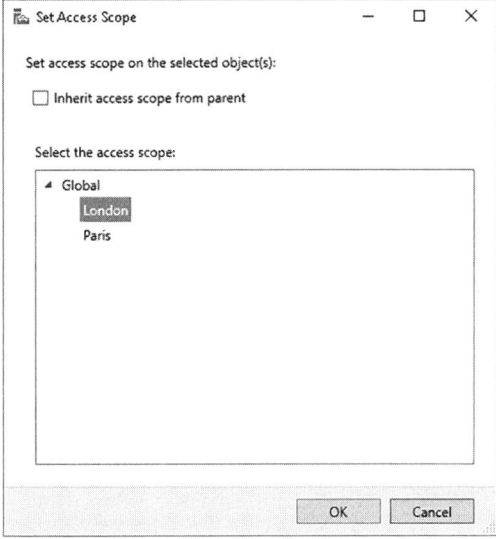

FIGURE 3-35 Configuring an access policy

Skill 3.3: Audit IPAM

IPAM provides extensive monitoring and auditing features that enable you to track IPAM configuration changes, DHCP configuration changes, IP address usage, and other important network infrastructure events.

However, before you view the auditing information, you must be aware of a couple of changes that you should make in order to track events efficiently. These are:

- **Enable Logon Event Auditing**   You must enable Audit account logon events auditing on both AD DS domain controllers and servers running the NPS role. You can configure this by using Group Policies. In the Group Policy Management Editor, navigate to Computer Configuration\Policies\Windows Settings\Security Settings\Local Policies\Audit Policy and enable the Audit Account Logon Events value.

- **Configure Security Event Log Size**   To avoid rollover, you must increase the size of the security event log so that it is large enough to allow the periodic IPAM audit task to complete without overwriting events. Again, you can use GPOs to achieve this change. In the Group Policy Management Editor, navigate to Computer Configuration\Policies\Windows Settings\Security Settings\Event Log and enable, and then configure the Maximum Security Log Size value.

- **Configure Audit Log File Location**   Ensure that the log file location for DHCP IPv4 and IPv6 leases is stored in the same folder. The IPAM audit processes access this information from a single shared folder. By default, both logs are stored in C:\Windows\system32\dhcp.

Audit the changes performed on the DNS and DHCP servers

It is important to be able to track the changes that administrators make to your IPAM server(s) and to the IPAM-managed network services (DHCP, DNS, and NPS). The Event Catalog node in the IPAM console enables you to access auditing information that relates to these events.

To view configuration changes made to DNS or DHCP services, in the IPAM console, click Event Catalog, and then click IPAM Configuration Events, as shown in Figure 3-36. You can identify DNS and DHCP related events from the Keywords column. The Details view provides further insight into the event that you have selected in the IPAM Configuration Events pane.

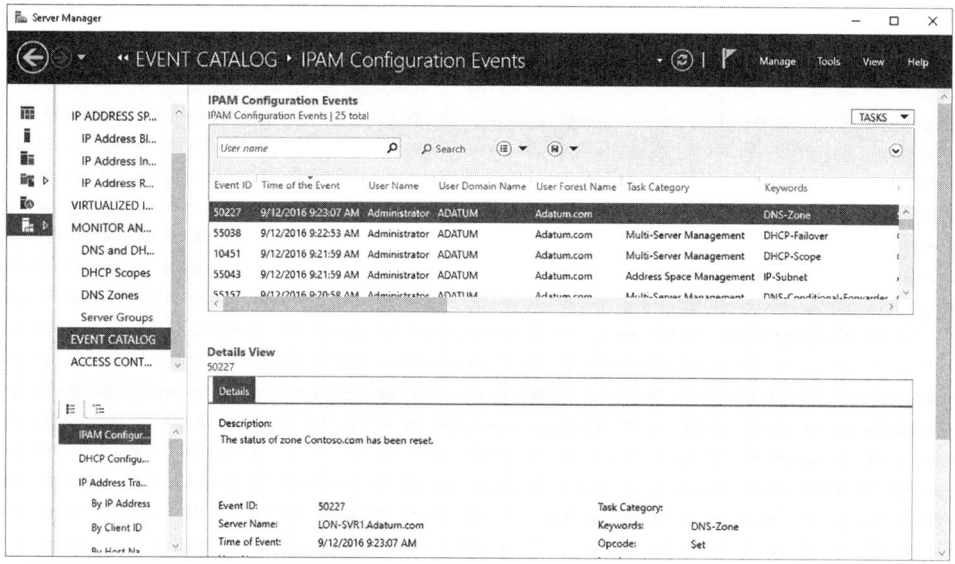

FIGURE 3-36 Viewing IPAM configuration events

The IPAM Configuration Event node lists events that relate to DNS, DHCP, NPS, and IPAM itself, including provisioning, discovery, and address space management. If you want additional information about the DHCP services running in your organization, you can select the DHCP Configuration Events node, as shown in Figure 3-37.

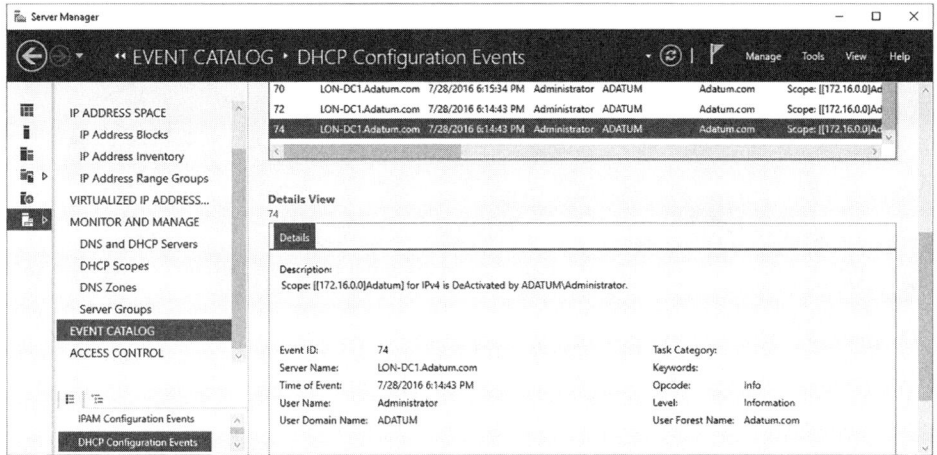

FIGURE 3-37 Viewing DHCP configuration events

The DHCP Configuration Events node lists all DHCP-related events for all discovered and managed servers in your organization that are running the DHCP role.

> **NEED MORE REVIEW?** **OPERATIONAL EVENT TRACKING**
>
> To review further details about operational event tracking in IPAM, refer to the Microsoft TechNet website at *https://technet.microsoft.com/library/jj878322(v=ws.11).aspx*.

Audit the IPAM address usage trail

You can also use the monitoring features of IPAM to determine the IP address usage within your organization. You can access this information from the IP Address Space node in the IPAM console. Then, select either the IP Address Blocks, IP Address Inventory, or IP Address Ranges Groups node.

For example, to view usage of a particular DHCP scope, click the IP Address Range Groups node and select a DHCP scope from the IPv4 pane, as shown in Figure 3-38. The Percentage Utilized column displays how much of the address space is used. Click the Utilization Trend tab in the Details View. You can see the IP Address Range Utilization Trend graph for a selected period, in this case, the last day.

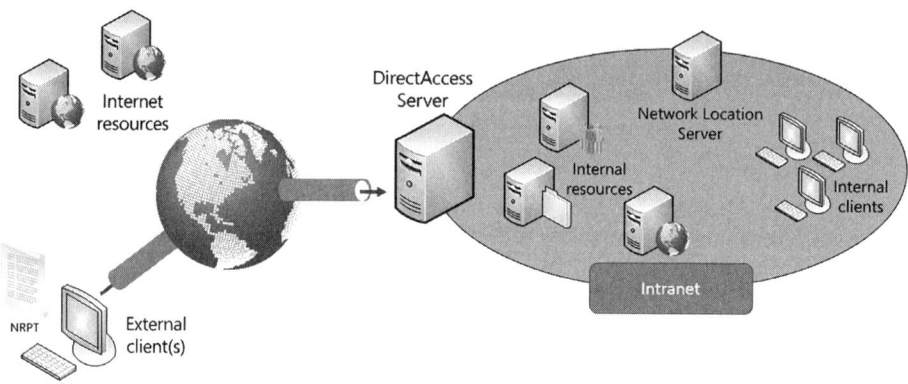

FIGURE 3-38 Viewing the Utilization Trend data for an IP Address Range Group

Audit DHCP lease events and user logon events

IPAM also enables you to centrally track and view events relating to DHCP lease events and user logon events. These are displayed in the Event Catalog in the IP Address Tracking node. You can view this information by:

- IP address
- Client ID
- Host name
- User name

To view DHCP lease events or user logon events by IP address, click the By IP Address node, as shown in Figure 3-39. In the By IP Address pane, in the text box, type the IP address that you want to track and the date range that you are interested in, and then click Search.

> *NOTE* **SEARCH RESULTS**
>
> If you want to widen the search, you needn't enter a date range, or an IP address, and the returned results are for all stored dates and for all IP addresses.

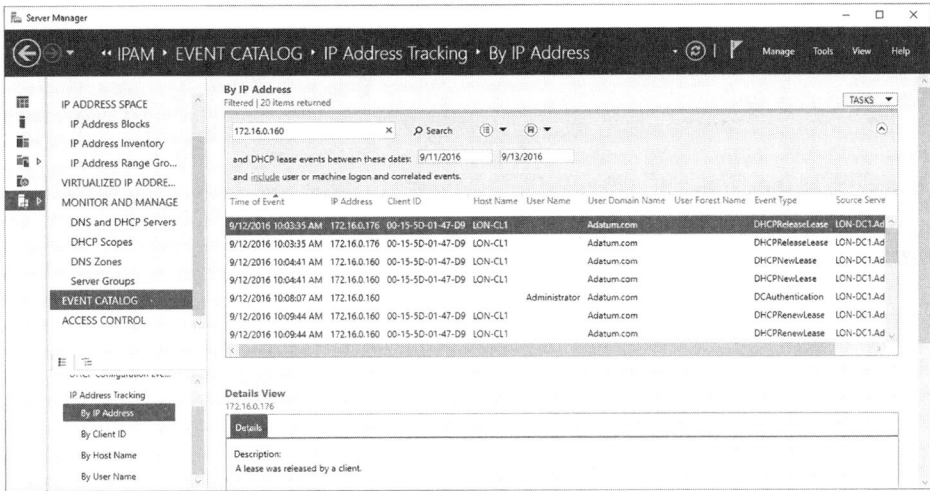

FIGURE 3-39 Viewing IP address tracking by IP address

Click an event in the By IP Address pane, and the Details View provides more information about the selected event. If you would prefer to view the tracked information by client ID, then click the By Client ID node. If you wish to search for a specific client, as shown in Figure 3-40, enter its MAC address in the text box, and then click Search.

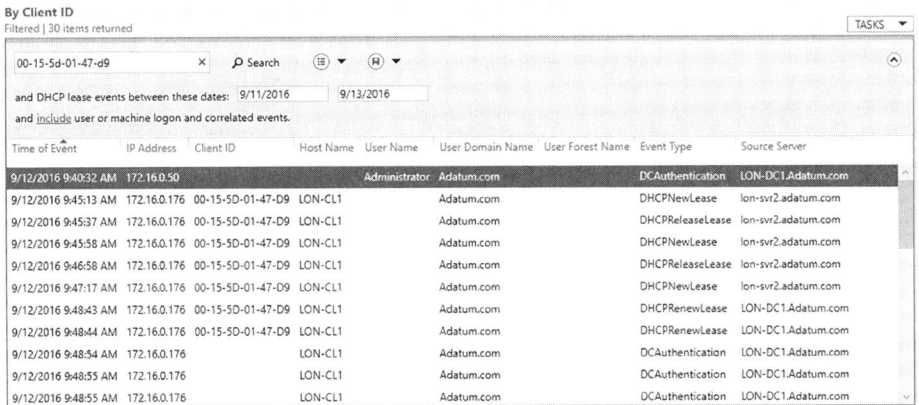

FIGURE 3-40 Searching for lease information by MAC address

You can also search for lease information by host name, as shown in Figure 3-41, or by user name, as shown in Figure 3-42.

FIGURE 3-41 Searching for lease information by host name

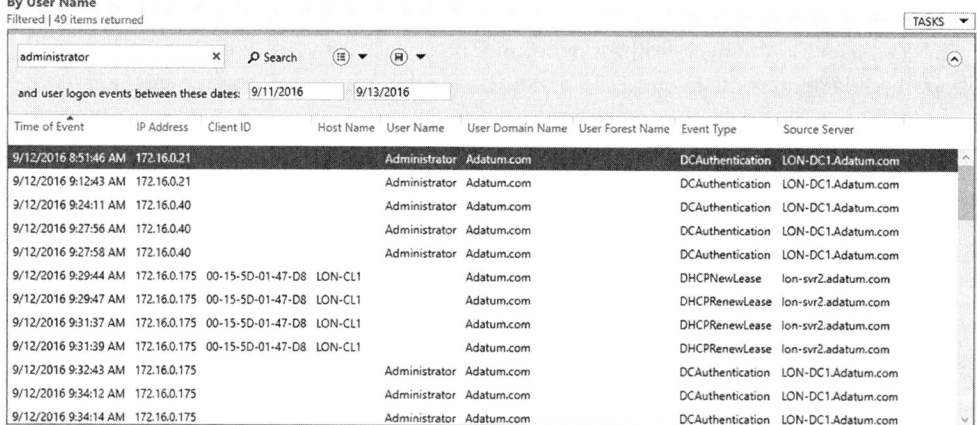

FIGURE 3-42 Searching for lease information by user name

> **NEED MORE REVIEW? IP ADDRESS TRACKING**
>
> To review further details about IP address tracking, refer to the Microsoft TechNet website at *https://technet.microsoft.com/library/jj878332(v=ws.11).aspx#ip*.

Chapter summary

- You can use IPAM to allocate IPv4 and IPv6 addresses, optimize IP address spaces, manage DHCP and DNS servers, monitor DHCP and DNS servers, and collect statistics from AD DS domain controllers and NPS.
- IPAM deployments support both WID and SQL Server databases.
- After installing the IPAM feature, you can provision IPAM either manually, or by using GPOs.
- If you want to manage DHCP and DNS server across AD DS forests, you must enable two-way trusts between those forests and then discover and provision the servers in all forests.
- IPAM enables you to manage DHCP server and scope properties and DNS server and zone properties from a single point.
- RBAC enables you to easily define delegated administration for DNS, DHCP, and IPAM management tasks within the IPAM console.
- You can track IP address usage, DHCP lease events, and user logons by using the IPAM Event Catalog node.

Thought experiment

In this thought experiment, demonstrate your skills and knowledge of the topics covered in this chapter. You can find answers to this thought experiment in the next section.

You work in support at A. Datum. As a consultant for A. Datum, answer the following questions about managing DNS and DHCP by using IPAM within the A. Datum organization:

1. Your manager wants you to determine which computer has obtained the IP address 172.16.16.75. How could you find out using the IPAM console?
2. You have deployed your first IPAM server and performed GPO-based provisioning. You ran the Invoke-IpamGpoProvisioning cmdlet to complete the provision process. What comes next?
3. You want to enable DHCP high-availability by using the IPAM console. What DHCP high-availability option(s) can you configure with the console?
4. What does the Set Access Scope option do when applied to a DHCP scope?

Thought experiment answers

This section contains the solution to the thought experiment. Each answer explains why the answer choice is correct.

1. You could open the IPAM console and select the By IP Address node in the Event Catalog. In the Search box, type the address 172.16.16.75, and click Search. The returned results should indicate which client computer has leased that address.
2. After provisioning, you must configure and complete the server discovery process.
3. You can enable and configure DHCP failover by using the IPAM console.
4. The Set Access Scope option enables you to define the management scope for a DHCP or DNS object. This determines who can manage the object.

CHAPTER 4

Implement network connectivity and remote access solutions

Many apps and services require connectivity to the Internet, so it's important that you understand the network connectivity options available for Windows Server 2016. These options include *Network Address Translation (NAT) and routing.*

Most organizations support users who work away from the office, so the IT department is responsible for facilitating remote connectivity for these users. Windows Server 2016 supports a number of remote access solutions, including Virtual Private Networks (VPNs) and DirectAccess.

You can use the Network Policy Server (NPS) role in Windows Server 2016 to control access to your organization from your remote users by using policy-based security. Also, NPS provides support for the industry standard Remote Authentication Dial-In User Service (RADIUS) protocol.

Skills in this chapter:

- Implement network connectivity solutions
- Implement VPN and DirectAccess solutions
- Implement NPS

Skill 4.1: Implement network connectivity solutions

NAT enables you to implement a private Internet Protocol Version 4 (IPv4) addressing scheme within your organization while still enabling users, apps, and services to access the Internet. NAT is a device, a component in a device, or a software service that enables your organization's computers to access Internet-based resources by translating private IPv4 addresses in your intranet into public IPv4 addresses on the Internet, as shown in Figure 4-1.

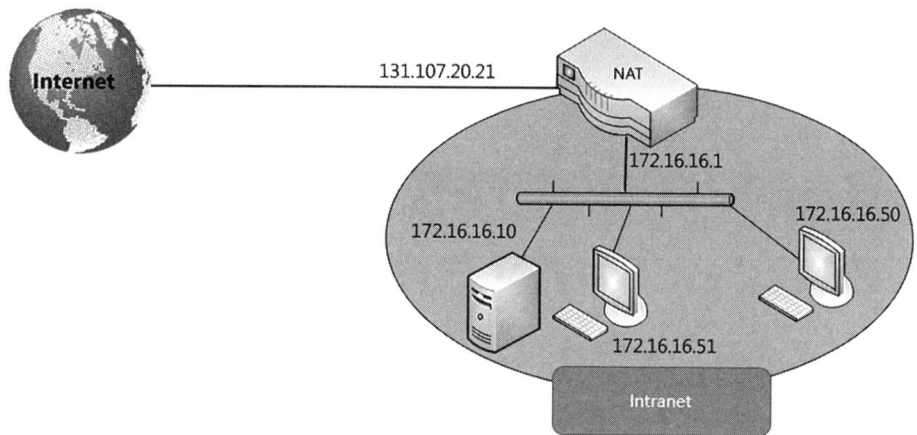

FIGURE 4-1 An illustration shows a NAT device connecting a corporate intranet to the Internet

All devices that connect to the Internet require a unique public IPv4 address. However, there are insufficient public addresses available in the IPv4 address space for all devices that require this type of connection. As a result, organizations use private IPv4 address ranges for devices within their intranets. These addresses are designated by the Internet Assigned Numbers Authority (IANA), and are listed in Table 4-1.

TABLE 4-1 Private IPv4 address ranges

Class	Mask	Range
A	10.0.0.0/8	10.0.0.0–10.255.255.255
B	172.16.0.0/12	172.16.0.0–172.31.255.255
C	192.168.0.0/16	192.168.0.0–192.168.255.255

> **NOTE PRIVATE IPV4 ADDRESSING**
>
> Implementing private IPv4 addressing is covered in Chapter 5, "Implement core and distributed network solutions."

Communications from designated private IPv4 addresses are not routed onto the public Internet. This is where NAT is useful. A NAT device edits the header of IPv4 traffic originating on the private network. It replaces the source IPv4 address in the header with one of its assigned public IPv4 addresses and then routes the traffic on to the Internet.

When return traffic is received on the public interface, the NAT device edits the header. It replaces the public destination's IPv4 address with the appropriate private IPv4 address, and then routes the traffic to the appropriate internal device.

> **EXAM TIP**
>
> A mapping table is maintained by the NAT device to record to which internal client traffic must be routed.

Implement NAT

On a computer running Windows Server 2016, a NAT server is installed with at least two network adapters. You must configure one of these network adapters with a private IPv4 address and connect it to the intranet within your organization. You must configure the second adapter with a public IPv4 address, and connect it to the Internet, either directly, or by configuring routing through your perimeter network to the Internet.

To enable NAT within your organization, you must deploy a NAT device, and then configure client computers to use the NAT device's private IPv4 interface as their configured default gateway.

> **NOTE MORE ON CONFIGURING AN IPV4 HOST**
>
> Configuring an IPv4 host is covered in Chapter 5, " Implement core and distributed network solutions."

The NAT device also helps to secure your organization's network devices by hiding your computers' IPv4 addresses. When a computer on the intranet initiates communications with a server on the Internet, only the NAT device's external IPv4 address is visible to devices on the Internet.

Implement NAT with Windows Server 2016

Before you can configure a Windows Server 2016 computer as a NAT server, you must install the Remote Access server role.

INSTALLING THE REMOTE ACCESS SERVER ROLE

On Windows Server 2016, use the following procedure to enable NAT:

1. Install the Remote Access server role with Server Manager. When prompted by the Add Roles And Features Wizard, on the Select role services page, select the Routing check box.
2. Follow the instructions in the wizard to install the necessary features to support the Remote Access role, as shown in Figure 4-2. Click Close when the installation is complete.

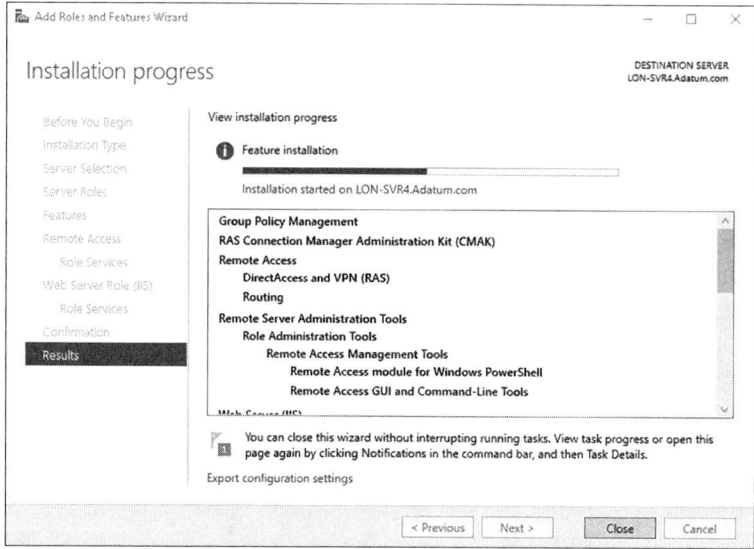

FIGURE 4-2 Installing the Remote Access role

ENABLING NAT IN REMOTE ACCESS

After you have installed the Routing role service, you must enable NAT in Remote Access. Use the following procedure:

1. In Server Manager, click Tools, and then click Routing And Remote Access.
2. In Routing And Remote Access, right-click your server and then click Configure and Enable Routing and Remote Access.
3. In the Routing And Remote Access Server Setup Wizard, choose Network Address Translation (NAT), as shown in Figure 4-3, and then click Next.

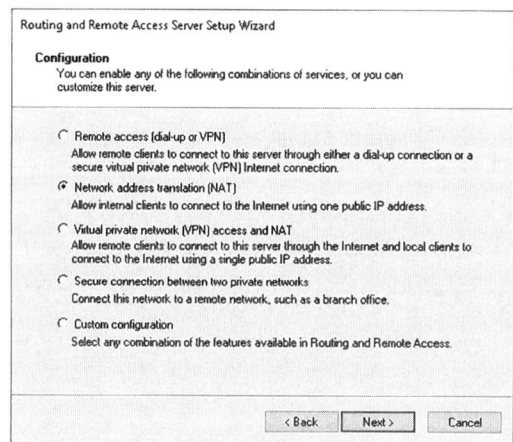

FIGURE 4-3 Configuring the NAT role

4. On the NAT Internet Connection page, select the appropriate network interface and then click Next. This interface must be able to communicate with the Internet and must be assigned a public IPv4 address, as shown in Figure 4-4.

EXAM TIP

It's a good idea to name your network connections so they are easily identifiable. To do this, right-click Start, and then click Network Connections. You can then rename your connections to match their configured purposes.

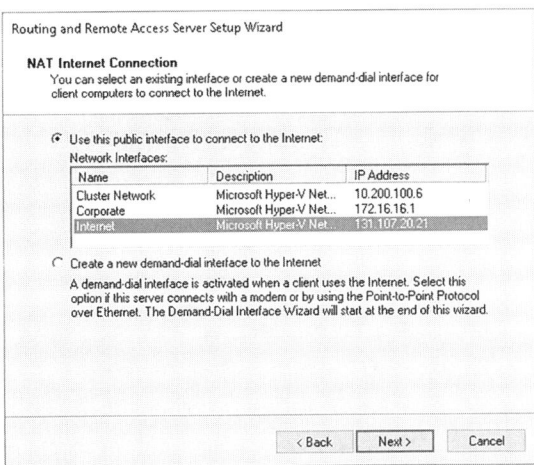

FIGURE 4-4 Selecting the Internet connection for a NAT server

5. On the Network Selection page, select the network connection that this device uses to connect to the intranet, as shown in Figure 4-5. Click Next.

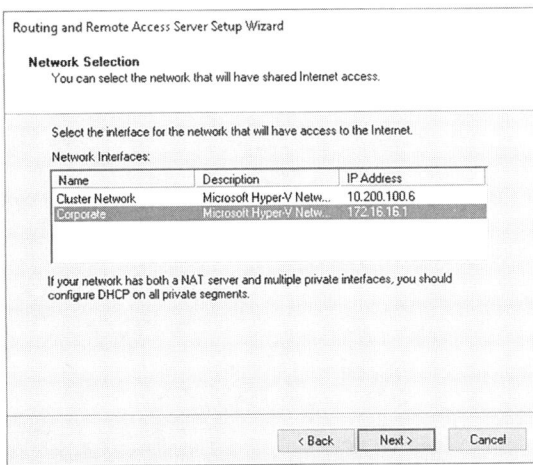

FIGURE 4-5 Selecting the intranet connection

Skill 4.1: Implement network connectivity solutions   CHAPTER 4   **159**

6. Complete the wizard and when prompted, click Finish. The Routing and Remote Access service starts automatically.

CONFIGURING NAT INTERFACES

After you have enabled NAT, you must complete its configuration. In the Routing And Remote Access console, use the following procedure:

1. In the navigation pane, locate the IPv4 node. Beneath it, locate the NAT node, as shown in Figure 4-6.

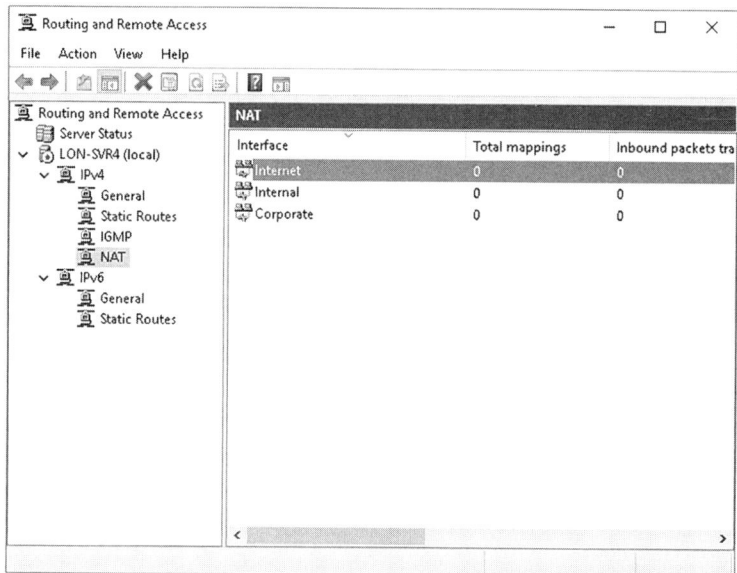

FIGURE 4-6 The NAT node in the Routing and Remote Access console

2. Right-click the interface that you assigned to the Internet and then click Properties. On the NAT page, you can change the type of interface from public to private. You can also disable or enable NAT by selecting the Enable NAT On This Interface check box, as shown in Figure 4-7.

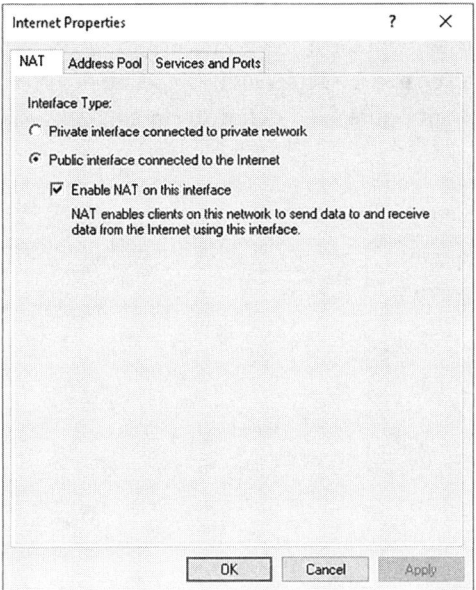

FIGURE 4-7 The properties dialog box of the configure Internet-connected network connection

3. On the Address Pool page, shown in Figure 4-8, you can configure a range of public IPv4 addresses that your ISP has assigned for your use, if required. The Reservations button enables you to configure specific public IPv4 addresses for use by specific private IPv4 clients.

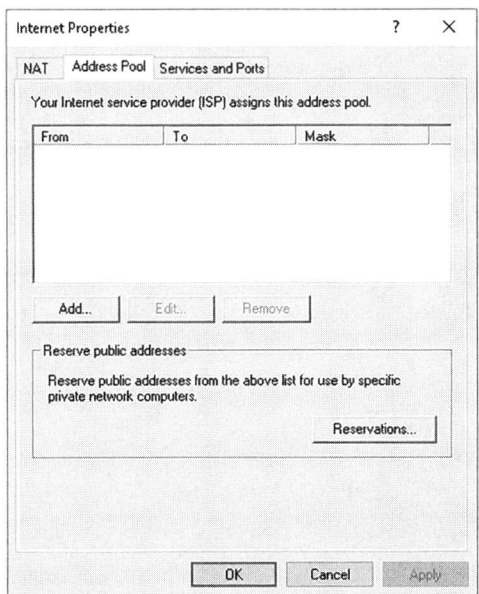

FIGURE 4-8 Configuring the public IPv4 address pool

4. The Services And Ports tab, shown in Figure 4-9, enables you to define how inbound requests are handled. You can define what services you want the NAT server to publish on the Internet. For example, you can enable a web server by selecting the Web Server (HTTP) check box, and then, as shown in Figure 4-10, define the internal server that hosts this web server.

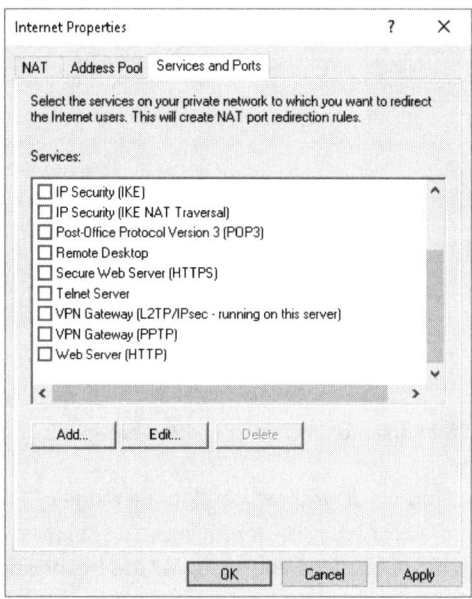

FIGURE 4-9 Configuring inbound services and ports

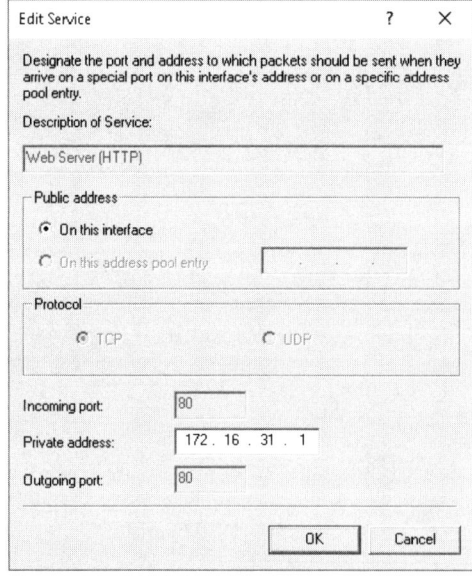

FIGURE 4-10 Adding a publishable service

CONFIGURING THE NAT NODE

You can configure the NAT node in the Routing and Remote Access console. Right-click NAT in the console and then click Properties, as shown in Figure 4-11.

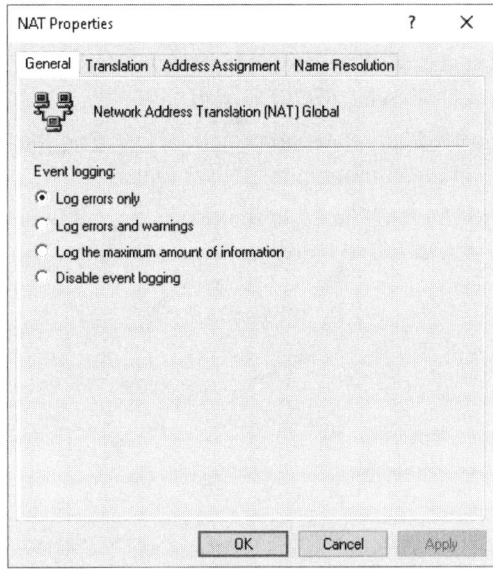

FIGURE 4-11 Configuring the NAT node

Table 4-2 shows the configurable settings.

TABLE 4-2 NAT node configurable options

Tab	Explanation	Options
General	You can configure and control event logging options from the General tab.	Log Errors Only Log Errors And Warnings Log The Maximum Amount Of Information Disable Event Logging
Translation	Translation enables you to control the timeouts after which any TCP or UDP mappings are removed. The mappings are used by NAT to track which internal client is connected to which external resource.	Remove TCP Mapping After (minutes) Remove UDP Mapping After (minutes)
Address Assignment	You can allow the NAT service to allocate IPv4 addresses from a configurable pool. If you are already using a Dynamic Host Configuration Protocol (DHCP) service elsewhere on the private network, do not select this option.	Automatically Assign IP Addresses By Using the DHCP Allocator (If selected, you can then define the IPv4 address pool that the DHCP allocator in NAT should use.)
Name Resolution	You can configure name resolution behavior. Clients might already be configured to use Domain Name System (DNS) resolution so you do not need to enable this option unless you do not have DNS on the private network.	Resolve IP Addresses for Clients Using Domain Name System (DNS) (If selected, you can then define that the NAT service provides DNS resolution for clients. You can optionally configure a demand dial interface to use for resolution.)

Monitoring NAT

After you have installed and configured NAT, and enabled your NAT clients, you must know how to monitor the NAT service. You can do this in the Routing And Remote Access console.

Right-click the NAT node, and then click one of the following:

- **Show DHCP Allocator Information** Displays DHCP-related information. This includes a list of the DHCP messages, such as DISCOVER, REQUEST, and OFFER.
- **Show DNS Proxy Information** Displays the DNS-related information, including the number of queries received from clients and the number of responses sent.

You can also view the live mappings being used by NAT clients. In the NAT node, in the Details pane, right-click the Internet-connected interface, and then click Show Mappings. The following information is displayed:

- Protocol
- Direction
- Private Address
- Private Port
- Public Address
- Remote Address
- Remote Port
- Idle Time

You can also use Event Viewer to view NAT-related events.

> ***NEED MORE REVIEW?*** **NETWORK ADDRESS TRANSLATION**
>
> To review further details about NAT, refer to the Microsoft TechNet website at *https://technet.microsoft.com/library/d151130d-6925-4e43-8f1b-c6bc0d920f5c.aspx*.

Configure routing

Routing is the process of managing the flow of network traffic between subnets. You can configure Windows Server 2016 as both an IPv4 or IPv6 router to connect multiple IP subnets together.

> **NOTE**
>
> Configure routing is covered in Chapter 5, "Implement core and distributed network solutions."

Skill 4.2: Implement VPN and DirectAccess solutions

You can use VPNs to support many of your organization's remote access requirements, including the ability to connect your sites using site-to-site (S2S) connections. Windows Server 2016 also provides support for DirectAccess, an always-on remote access solution that can make connecting remotely as seamless as connecting locally.

Overview of VPNs

Using Windows Server 2016, you can implement a number of different remote access scenarios using VPNs. These are:

- **Remote access** Enables remote users to connect to their workplace securely. The VPN provides a point-to-point connection between the remote user's computer and your organization's server, as shown in Figure 4-12. The fact that the connection is provided through a public network, the Internet, is transparent to the user.

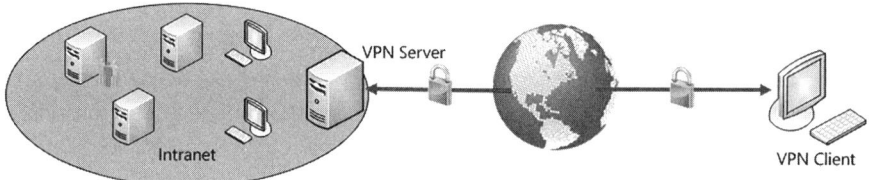

FIGURE 4-12 A remote access VPN

- **Site-to-site** Also known as router-to-router connections, S2S connections enable you to connect your remote sites. As with remote access VPNs, S2S VPNs are built on tunneling protocols that use the Internet to route network packets between your sites, as shown in Figure 4-13.

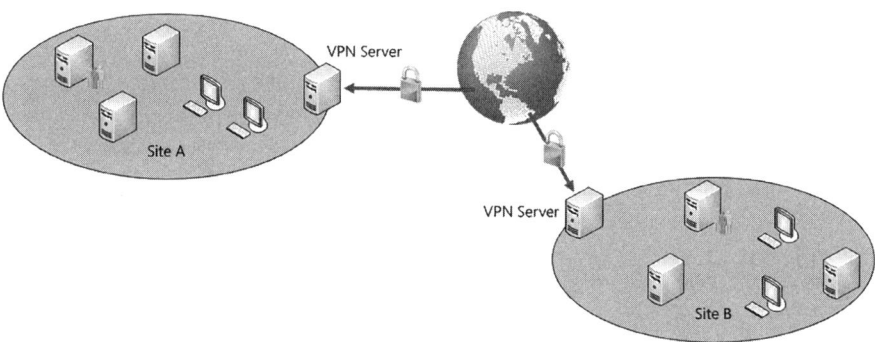

FIGURE 4-13 A site-to-site VPN

Whatever type of VPN you implement, they all share certain characteristics. These include:

- **Authentication**   Helps to ensure that both the VPN client and the VPN server can identify one another. You can choose from a number of different authentication methods depending on the VPN protocol you select, and other network infrastructure factors, such as whether your network provides a public key infrastructure (PKI) enabling the use of digital certificates.

- **Encryption**   Because private data is routed over a public network, it is important to take steps to secure this data in transit. Data encryption is used for this purpose. You can implement a number of different encryption methods, depending on the VPN protocol used, and the specific configuration of your network infrastructure.

- **Encapsulation**   A VPN routes data through a public network by using tunneling protocols. Private data is encapsulated in a structure, with a public header containing the appropriate routing information, which can transit a public network and arrive at the correct private destination.

Configure different VPN protocol options

You can use the following VPN protocols in Windows Server 2016:

- **Point-to-Point Tunneling Protocol (PPTP)**   You can implement both remote access and S2S VPNs with PPTP. PPTP is a widely supported protocol, but is considered less secure than its alternatives. Authentication and encryption is provided by either the Microsoft Challenge Handshake Authentication Protocol version 2 (MS-CHAPv2) or by the Extensible Authentication Protocol-Transport Layer Security (EAP-TLS) authentication methods.

- **Layer 2 Tunneling Protocol with Internet Protocol Security (L2TP/IPsec)**   L2TP combines PPTP and Layer 2 Forwarding (L2F), but unlike PPTP, L2TP requires IPsec in transport mode to provide encryption.

- **Secure Socket Tunneling Protocol (SSTP)**   Based on the HTTPS protocol, SSTP relies on Transmission Control Protocol (TCP) port 443 to pass network traffic. This is a significant benefit, as this port is usually open on firewalls to facilitate web server traffic, whereas both PPTP and L2TP might require firewall reconfiguration.

- **Internet Key Exchange Version 2 (IKEv2)**   Uses IPsec in tunnel mode. This protocol is particularly useful for users using mobile devices, such as phones and tablets, when their links might be dropped. The VPN reconnect feature is available only with this VPN type. IKEv2 supports easy migration between wireless hotspots, and makes using a remote access VPN far easier for mobile users.

EXAM TIP

PPTP requires TCP port 1723. L2TP uses User Datagram Protocol (UDP) port 500, UDP port 1701, and UDP port 4500. IKEv2 relies on UDP port 500.

Configure authentication options

Authentication enables communicating parties to identify one another and is an essential part of any remote access infrastructure. Windows Server 2016 supports the following VPN authentication methods, as shown in Table 4-3.

TABLE 4-3 VPN authentication protocols

Authentication Protocol	Explanation	Comments
PAP	Based on plain text password exchange, this is the least secure authentication method. However, while not recommended in production environments, it can prove useful when testing remote access.	■ This is the least secure method of authentication and it is strongly recommended that you block use of PAP. ■ Provides no protection against client or server impersonation.
CHAP	CHAP is based on challenge and response using MD5 hashing to encrypt the response. In challenge and response authentication, passwords are not exchanged. CHAP does have a weakness, however; it requires that the user's password is stored using reversible encryption.	■ Improves over PAP because the password is not sent over the wire. ■ Requires plain text version of password. ■ Provides no protection against server impersonation.
MS-CHAP-v2	Like CHAP, this protocol relies on challenge and response but is more secure.	■ Stronger security than PAP or CHAP and is the minimum you should use. ■ Useful for clients that do not meet the requirements for EAP.
EAP	Providing the most secure form of authentication for VPNs in Windows Server 2016, EAP is based on a random authentication method negotiated by the remote access client and remote access server.	■ Strongest security available. ■ Flexibility in enabling different authentication methods.

Implement remote access and S2S VPN solutions using RAS gateway

In Windows Server 2016, when you deploy the DirectAccess and VPN (RAS) role service, which is part of the Remote Access server role, then you are deploying the RAS Gateway. RAS Gateway can be deployed in both single tenant and multitenant modes.

Because RAS Gateway is multitenant-aware, you can have multiple virtual networks with overlapping address spaces located on the same virtual infrastructure. This can be useful if you have multiple locations, or multiple business groups, that share the same address spaces and must be able to route traffic to the virtual networks.

RAS Gateway supports the following scenarios:

- **Multitenant-aware VPN gateway** The RAS Gateway is configured as a virtual network-aware VPN gateway enabling you to:
    - Connect to the RAS Gateway by using an S2S VPN from a remote location.
    - Configure individual users with VPN access to the RAS Gateway.

- **Multitenant-aware NAT gateway** The RAS Gateway is configured as a NAT device enabling access to the Internet for virtual machines on virtual networks.
- **Forwarding gateway for internal physical network access** Enables access to server resources on physical networks from your virtual networks.
- **DirectAccess server** Enables you to connect remote users to your network infrastructure without the need for VPNs. DirectAccess is discussed later in this chapter.
- **GRE tunneling** Enables connectivity between tenant virtual networks and external networks.
- **Dynamic routing with BGP** Used in large, enterprise-level networked systems. BGP is often implemented by cloud service providers (CSPs) to connect to their tenants' networked sites. BGP reduces the need to configure manual routes on your routers because it is a dynamic routing protocol. For example, it can automatically learn routes between sites connected with S2S VPNs.

If you intend to deploy RAS Gateway in multitenant mode, you should deploy RAS Gateway only on virtual machines running Windows Server 2016. Consequently, deploying and configuring RAS Gateway in multitenant mode requires advanced knowledge of Hyper-V virtualization, Windows PowerShell, and skills with Virtual Machine Manager (VMM).

Although RAS Gateway is multitenant aware, you can also deploy and configure RAS Gateway in Windows Server 2016 in single tenant mode, either on a physical or virtual server computer. For most organizations, implementing RAS Gateway in single tenant mode is typical and enables you to deploy RAS Gateway as:

- An edge VPN server (both for remote access and S2S VPNs)
- An edge DirectAccess server
- Both edge VPN and edge DirectAccess

> **NEED MORE REVIEW? RAS GATEWAY**
>
> To review further details about RAS Gateway, refer to the Microsoft TechNet website at *https://technet.microsoft.com/windows-server-docs/networking/remote-access/ras-gateway/ras-gateway*.

In Windows Server 2016, you can use Windows PowerShell commands to deploy and configure the RAS Gateway.

> **NEED MORE REVIEW? REMOTE ACCESS CMDLETS**
>
> To review further details about Windows PowerShell cmdlets for RAS Gateway, refer to the Microsoft TechNet website at *https://technet.microsoft.com/library/hh918399.aspx*.

Determine when to use remote access VPN and S2S VPN and to configure appropriate protocols

The choice of when to use a remote access VPN or to implement an S2S VPN is straightforward. If you must connect a single remote user to your organization's network infrastructure, implement a remote access VPN. However, if you must interconnect multiple sites, implement S2S VPNs.

The principles behind these two types of VPNs are broadly similar, as are the tunneling and authentication protocols. However, the method you use for implementation varies.

Implement a remote access VPN

Before you configure your VPN server, you must verify the following:

- **Network interfaces**   Your VPN server requires at least two network interfaces. You must also determine which interface is Internet-facing and which connects to the organization's private network(s).

- **VPN client IP configuration**   You must determine how VPN clients obtain a valid IP configuration. You can use a DHCP server in your organization's private network, or else you can assign addresses from a range of addresses that you define on the VPN server.

> **EXAM TIP**
>
> If you choose DHCP, the VPN server requests blocks of addresses from the DHCP server and allocates VPN clients addresses from that block. If your DHCP scope is low on available addresses, a VPN server might fail to obtain a block and VPN clients will fail to connect.

- **RADIUS configuration**   If you intend to manage authentication and/or accounting centrally for your VPN servers using RADIUS, you must be ready to configure the VPN server as a RADIUS client. This requires that you configure the NPS role in your organization. This is discussed in "Skill 4.3: Implement NPS."

After you have verified these choices, to implement a remote access VPN on Windows Server 2016, complete the following procedure:

1. On the server that you want to act as a VPN server, sign in and open Server Manager.
2. Click Manage and then click Add Roles And Features.
3. Click through the Add Roles And Features Wizard, and on the Server Roles page, select the Remote Access check box. Click Next.
4. On the Select Role Services page, select the DirectAccess and VPN (RAS) check box and click Next. When prompted, click Add Features to install the required features to support the selected role services.
5. Click Next, click Install, and when the role installation is complete, click Close.

After the role is installed, in Server Manager:

1. Click Notifications, and then click open the Getting Started Wizard.
2. In the Getting Started Wizard, on the Welcome To Remote Access page, click Deploy VPN Only, as shown in Figure 4-14.

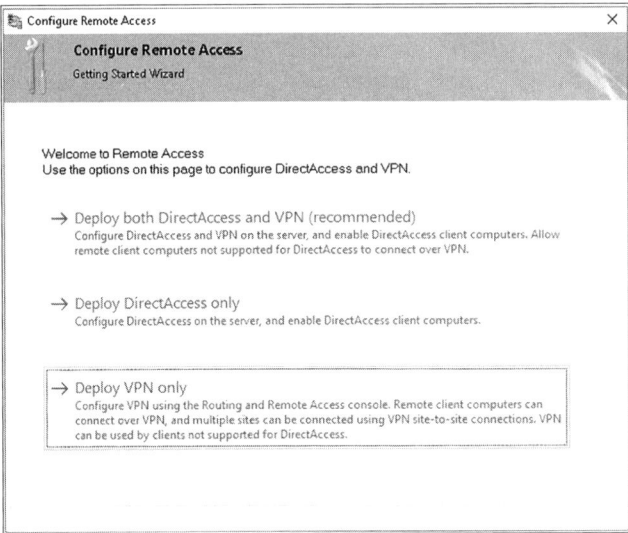

FIGURE 4-14 Enabling VPN only

3. The Routing And Remote Access console opens. Right-click the local server in the navigation pane and then click Configure And Enable Routing and Remote Access.
4. In the Routing And Remote Access Server Setup Wizard, on the Configuration page, as shown in Figure 4-15, click Remote Access (Dial-Up Or VPN) and then click Next.

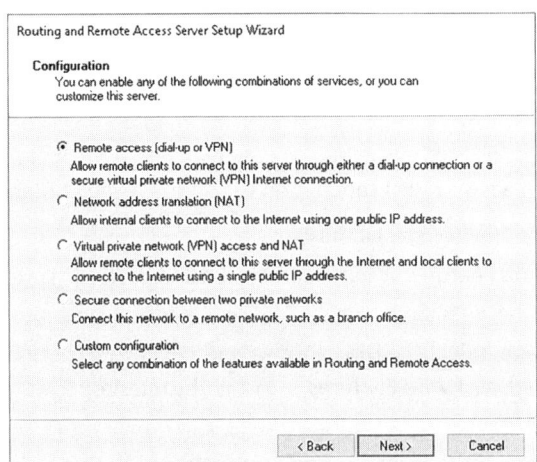

FIGURE 4-15 Selecting the routing and remote access configuration

5. On the Remote Access page, select the VPN check box and then click Next.
6. On the VPN Connection page, in the Network interfaces list, select the network adapter that connects to the Internet, as shown in Figure 4-16, and then click Next.

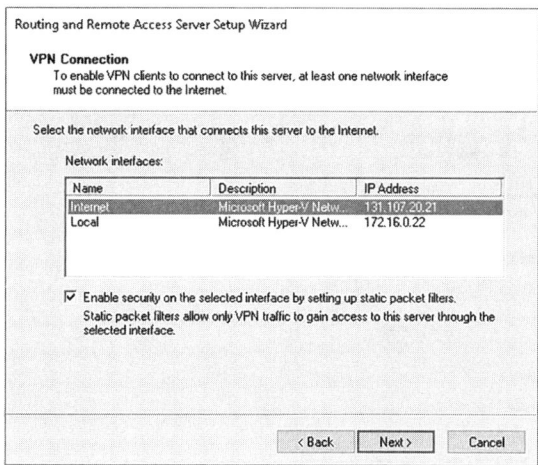

FIGURE 4-16 Selecting the Internet network interface

7. On the IP Address Assignment page, click Automatically if you want an existing DHCP server on the internal network to assign IP addresses to remote clients, or click From a Specified Range of Addresses if you want the remote access server to assign these addresses.
8. If you opted to assign addresses from a specified range, on the IP Address Assignment page, as shown in Figure 4-17, specify the range of addresses you want to allocate. Be careful these do not overlap any addresses that are in use in DHCP, or that might be statically assigned to network clients. Click Next.

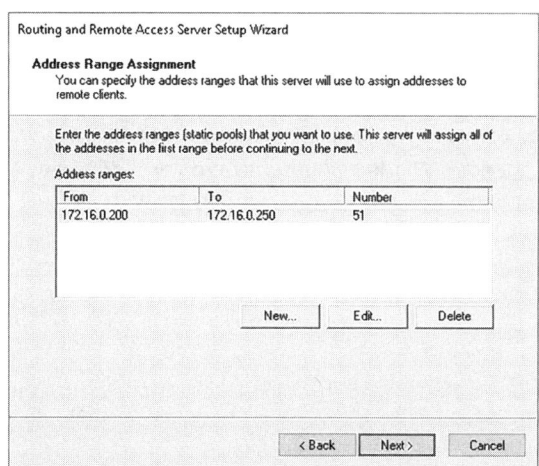

FIGURE 4-17 Configuring address assignment

9. If you have configured NPS, and you want to use this server as a RADIUS client, then on the Managing Multiple Remote Access Servers page, click Yes, Set Up This Server To Work With A RADIUS Server. Otherwise, if this server will perform authentication and authorization of remote access attempts locally, click No, Use Routing And Remote Access To Authenticate Connection Requests, as shown in Figure 4-18.

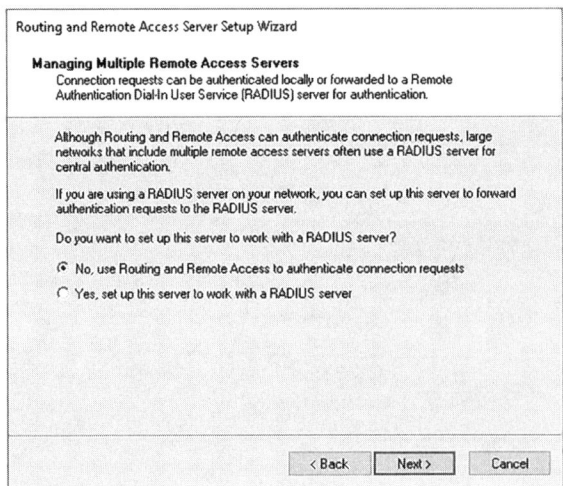

FIGURE 4-18 Configuring whether or not to use RADIUS for authentication

10. Click Finish to complete the process. Routing and Remote access starts.

After completing the wizard, you might want to reconfigure some aspects of your VPN server. From the Routing and Remote Access console, right-click your local server and then click Properties. In the Server Properties dialog box, you can configure the following properties:

- **General** You can enable or disable this server as an IPv4 and IPv6 router. You can also enable or disable this server as an IPv4 or IPv6 remote access server. By default, the server is configured as a LAN and demand-dial routing IPv4 router and IPv4 remote access server.

- **Security** On the Security tab, shown in Figure 4-19, you can specify the authentication provider and accounting provider. Windows Authentication and Windows Accounting are selected by default, but you can choose to use RADIUS.

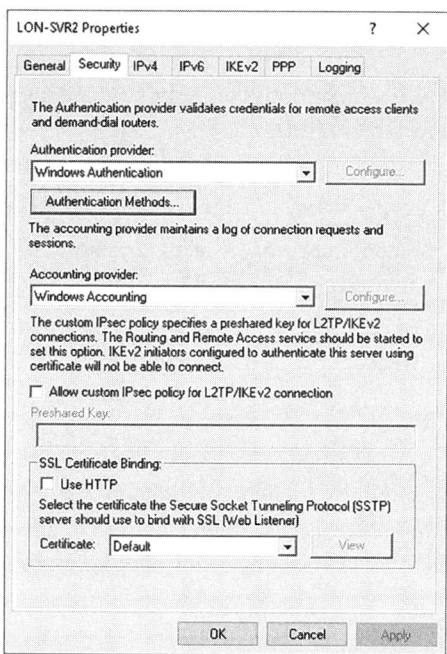

FIGURE 4-19 Configuring security options for your VPN server

You can also configure supported authentication methods, as shown in Figure 4-20. By default, EAP and MS-CHAP-v2 are selected. These are the methods supported by the VPN server and not necessarily those supported by any network policies that you configure in NPS. NPS network policies are discussed in Chapter 4: Implement network connectivity and remote access solutions, "Skill 4.3, Implement NPS, heading "Configure NPS policies."

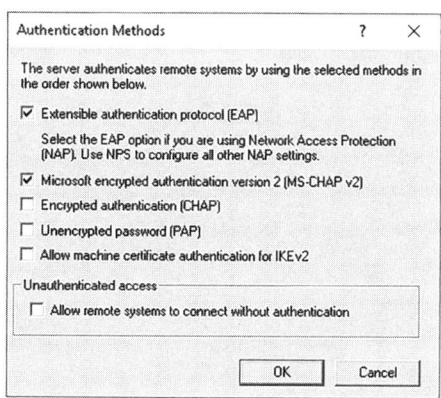

FIGURE 4-20 Selecting an authentication method for your VPN server

- **IPv4**   On the IPv4 tab, configure the IPv4 Address Assignment options, including the Static Address Pool.

- **IPv6** Similarly, the IPv6 tab enables you to configure IPv6 Settings for Remote Access Client.
- **IKEv2** On the IPEv2, configure the IKEv2 Client Settings: Idle Time-Out, Network Outage Time, and Security Association Expiration Control Settings.
- **PPP** The PPP tab enables you to configure the Point-to-Point Settings for your VPN server. These include Allowing Multilink Connections, and Bandwidth Control options.
- **Logging** From the Logging tab, you can configure what level of logging to be recorded by the local server. The default is to use Log Errors and Warnings.

After you have completed the configuration of your VPN server, you must then install and configure the NPS role, including defining your network policies. This is discussed in "Skill 4.3: Implement NPS."

CONFIGURE A CLIENT VPN

To complete the process of configuring a VPN, you must configure the remote client itself. To create a VPN in Windows 10, from the Network And Sharing Center, under Change Your Network Settings, click Set Up A New Connection Or Network and then click Connect To A Workplace.

To configure your VPN connection, in the Connect To A Workplace Wizard, provide the following information.

- **How do you want to connect?** You can connect by using an existing Internet connection or by dialing directly into your workplace.
- **Internet Address** This is the name or IP address of the computer that you connect to at your workplace, as shown in Figure 14-21. Typically, this is an FQDN, such as remote.adatum.com.
- **Destination Name** The name of this VPN connection.

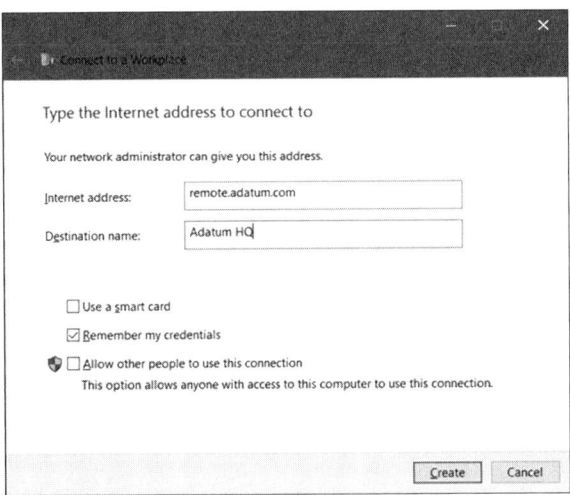

FIGURE 4-21 The Connect To A Workplace Wizard

After you have created the VPN connection, from the Network And Sharing Center, click Change Adapter Settings, right-click your VPN connection, and click Properties. As shown in Figure 4-22, you can then configure additional options as required by your organization's network infrastructure.

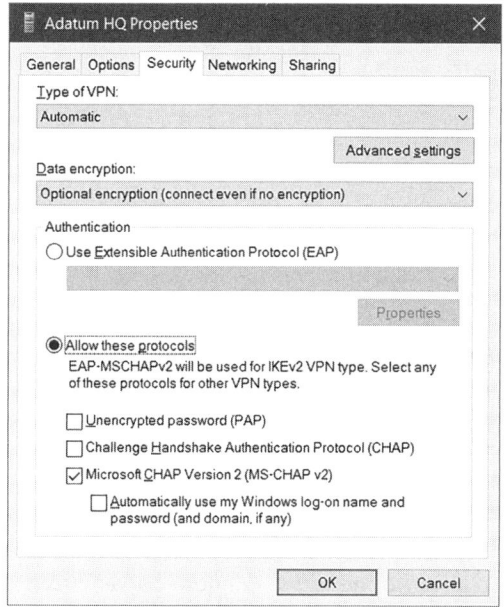

FIGURE 4-22 The Security tab of a VPN connection

These settings must match the VPN server settings, and those defined in any connection request policies or network policies defined in your NPS. NPS is discussed in Chapter 4, "Implement network connectivity and remote access solutions." You can configure the following options:

- **Type Of VPN** Point-to-Point Tunneling Protocol (PPTP), Layer Two Tunneling Protocol with IPsec (L2TP/IPsec), Secure Socket Tunneling Protocol (SSTP), or Internet Key Exchange version 2 (IKEv2).
- **Data Encryption** None, Optional, Required, Maximum Strength.

Under Authentication, you choose either Use Extensible Authentication Protocol (EAP) or Allow These Protocols. If you choose to use EAP, configure one of the following:

- Microsoft Secured Password (EAP-MSCHAP v2) (Encryption Enabled)
- Microsoft Smart Card Or Other Certificate (Encryption Enabled)
- Cisco: EAP-FAST (Encryption Enabled)
- Cisco: LEAP (Encryption Enabled)
- Cisco: PEAP (Encryption Enabled)

If you choose Allow These Protocols, you then configure the following options:

- Unencrypted Password (PAP)
- Challenge Handshake Authentication Protocol (CHAP)
- Microsoft CHAP Version 2 (MS-CHAP v2)
    - Automatically Use My Windows Log-on Name and Password (And Domain name)
- Use Extensible Authentication Protocol (EAP)

CONFIGURE VPN RECONNECT

VPN reconnect enables Windows to reestablish a dropped VPN connection without requiring user intervention. For example, consider a user traveling on a train. The user connects to the workplace using a VPN over an Internet connection established using a mobile broadband card. When the train passes through a tunnel, the broadband connection drops, and the VPN disconnects.

With earlier versions of Windows, when the train emerged from the tunnel, although the mobile broadband reconnects, the VPN required manual intervention. VPN reconnect reestablishes the VPN connection without prompting the user.

In order to implement VPN reconnect, your network infrastructure must meet the following requirements:

- Your VPN server must be running Windows Server 2008 R2 or newer.
- The user's computer must be running Windows 7 or newer, or Windows Server 2008 R2 or newer.
- Your organization must implement a PKI because VPN reconnect requires the use of a computer certificate.
- You must implement an IKEv2 VPN.

APP-TRIGGERED VPNS

Windows 10 supports a new feature called app-triggered VPNs. This feature enables you to configure that a VPN is initiated when a particular app, or set of apps, is started.

To enable app-triggered VPNs, you must first determine the Package Family Name for the universal app(s), or the path for any desktop apps, which will be the trigger for the VPN. While it is fairly easy to determine the path for a desktop app (generally, these are installed in the C Drive in Program Files), you must use the Windows PowerShell Get-AppxPackage cmdlet to find the Package Family Name for universal apps.

For example, to determine the Package Family Name for Microsoft OneNote, examine the output, as shown in Figure 4-23, and locate the PackageFamilyName property. You can see that it is: Microsoft.Office.OneNote_8wekyb3d8bbwe.

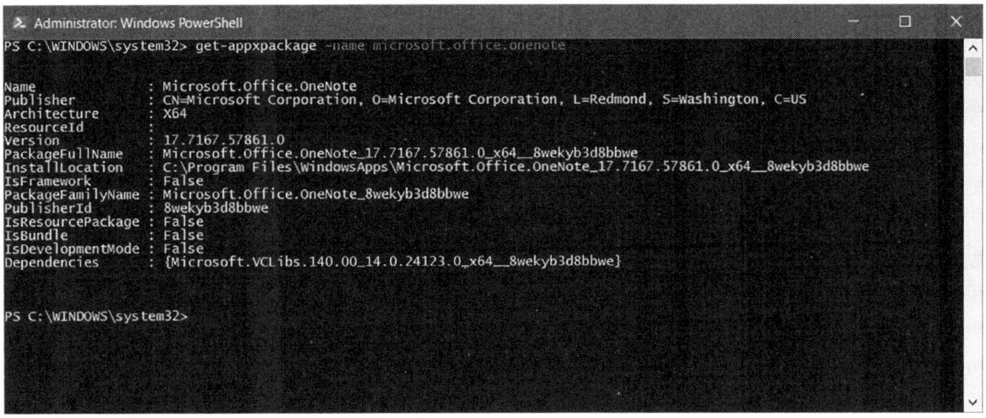

FIGURE 4-23 Determining a universal app's package family name

To configure the app to trigger a VPN, use the Add-VpnConnectionTriggerApplication Windows PowerShell cmdlet. For example, to configure the OneNote app to trigger a VPN called A. Datum HQ, use the following command:

```
Add-VpnConnectionTriggerApplication -ConnectionName "A. Datum HQ" -ApplicationID
Microsoft.Office.OneNote_8wekyb3d8bbwe
```

Alternatively, if you are using the desktop version of OneNote, then you would use the following Windows PowerShell command:

```
Add-VpnConnectionTriggerApplication -ConnectionName "A. Datum HQ" -ApplicationID
"C:\Program Files\Microsoft Office\root\Office16\ONENOTE.EXE"
```

EXAM TIP
You cannot implement app-triggered VPNs on domain-member computers.

CREATE AND CONFIGURE CONNECTION PROFILES
Although manually configuring VPN connections is relatively simple, completing the process on many computers with the same or similar settings is very time-consuming. In these circumstances, it makes sense to create a VPN profile and then distribute the profile to your users' computers.

When you use VPN profiles in Windows Server 2016 or Windows 10, you can take advantage of a number of advanced features. These are:

- **Always On** You can configure the VPN profile so that the VPN initiates when the user signs in or when there has been a change in the network state, such as no longer being connected to the corporate Wi-Fi.
- **App-Triggered VPN** You can configure the VPN profile to respond to a specific set of apps; if a defined app loads, then the VPN initiates.

- **Traffic Filters** With traffic filters, your VPN profiles can be configured to initiate only when certain criteria, defined in policies, are met. For example, you can create app-based rules in which only traffic originating from defined apps can use the VPN. You can also create traffic-based rules that filter based on protocol, address, and port.
- **LockDown VPN** You can configure LockDown to secure your user's device so that only the VPN can be used for network communications.

EXAM TIP

You can find out more about VPN profile options in Windows 10 from the Microsoft TechNet website at *https://technet.microsoft.com/itpro/windows/keep-secure/vpn-profile-options*.

You can create and distribute VPN profiles by using the Connection Manager Administration Kit (CMAK), Microsoft Intune, or Configuration Manager. To use CMAK to distribute the profile, use the following procedure:

1. On your Windows 10 client computer, right-click Start, and then click Programs and Features.
2. In the Programs and Features dialog box, click Turn Windows Features On or Off.
3. In the Windows Features dialog box, select RAS Connection Manager Administration Kit (CMAK), and then click OK.
4. Click Close.
5. Right-click Start, and then click Control Panel.
6. In Control Panel, click System and Security, and then click Administrative Tools.
7. Double-click Connection Manager Administration Kit.
8. On the Welcome to the Connection Manager Administration Kit Wizard page, click Next.
9. On the Select The Target Operating System page, click Windows Vista Or Above, and then click Next.
10. On the Create Or Modify A Connection Manager profile page, click New Profile, and then click Next.
11. On the Specify The Service Name and the File Name page, in the Service name box, type the name for your VPN connection. Your users will see this name when they go to establish the VPN connection. In the File Name box, type the file name you want to call this profile. This filename is used to distribute the profile and is not seen by your users. Click Next.
12. On the Add Support for VPN Connections page, select Phone Book From This Profile.
13. In the VPN server name or IP address text box, type the IP address or FQDN for the VPN server, as shown in Figure 4-24, and then click Next.

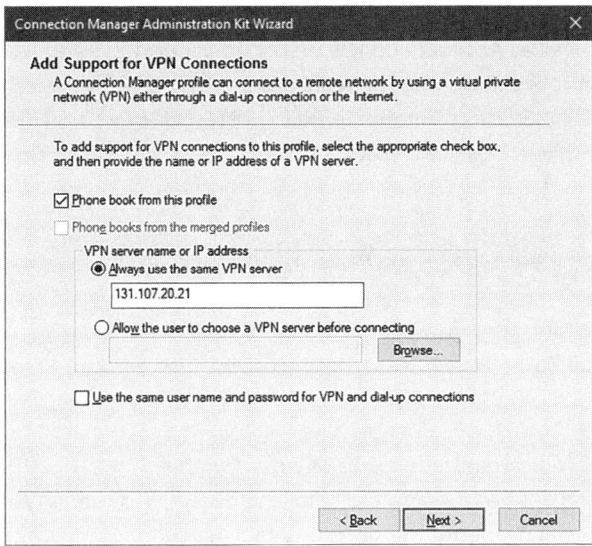

FIGURE 4-24 Defining the VPN server's public IPv4 address in the Connection Manager Administration Kit Wizard

14. On the Create or Modify a VPN Entry page, click Next.
15. On the Add a Custom Phone Book page, clear the Automatically Download Phone Book Updates check box, and then click Next.
16. Click through the rest of the wizard. Then, on the Build The Connection Manager Profile and its Installation Program page, click Next.
17. On the Your Connection Manager Profile Is Complete And Ready to Distribute page, make a note of where the profile will be created, and then click Finish.

Your profiles are stored, by default, in the C drive in Program Files\CMAK\Profiles\Windows Vista and above folder. The profile consists of an executable file, the name of which you defined in the wizard, and supplemental files.

DEPLOYING CONNECTION PROFILES

You can distribute VPN profiles by using the following methods:

- **Distribute with scripts**   Use a Windows PowerShell or other script to distribute the profile to your VPN users.
- **Distribute on removable media**   Copy the CMAK profile to a USB memory stick for users to install.
- **Build as part of desktop image**   Add the CMAK profile to the standard Windows desktop image that you deploy to new workstations.
- **Deploy using automated software distribution**   You can use the following methods to deploy VPN profiles to Windows clients:

- **Microsoft System Center Configuration Manager** You can deploy VPN profiles to Windows clients as well as Android and iOS clients. To support iOS and Android, the devices must be enrolled in Intune. The following profile types can be distributed: Microsoft SSL (SSTP), Microsoft Automatic, IKEv2, PPTP, L2TP, Cisco AnyConnect, Pulse Secure, F5 Edge Client, Dell SonicWALL Mobile Connect, and Check Point Mobile VPN.

> **NEED MORE REVIEW? HOW TO CREATE VPN PROFILES IN SYSTEM CENTER CONFIGURATION MANAGER**
>
> To review further details about distributing VPN profiles with System Center Configuration Manager, refer to the Microsoft TechNet website at *https://technet.microsoft.com/library/mt629189.aspx*.

- **Microsoft Intune** If your organization uses Microsoft Intune, you can distribute VPN profiles to enrolled devices running the following operating systems: Windows, Android, and iOS. You can distribute the same profile types as for Configuration Manager.

> **NEED MORE REVIEW? VPN CONNECTIONS IN MICROSOFT INTUNE**
>
> To review further details about distributing VPN profiles with Intune, refer to the Microsoft TechNet website at *https://docs.microsoft.com/intune/deploy-use/vpn-connections-in-microsoft-intune*.

- **AD DS Group Policy** If your organization uses neither Configuration Manager nor Microsoft Intune, consider using GPOs to deploy your VPN profile. You can use a Windows PowerShell script launched using a GPO logon script to distribute the profiles. The script creates a Group Policy preference to deploy the VPN profile.

> **NEED MORE REVIEW? DEPLOYING VPN CONNECTIONS BY USING POWERSHELL AND GROUP POLICY**
>
> To review further details about using GPOs to distribute VPN profiles, refer to the Microsoft TechNet website at *https://technet.microsoft.com/library/ee431700(v=ws.10).aspx*.

Implement an S2S VPN

You use an S2S VPN to securely connect two parts of your organization over the Internet. There is no difference from a technical standpoint between an S2S VPN connection and a remote access VPN.

When a router in one site initiates a VPN connection to a router in the other site, the initiating router is considered a VPN client, while the responding router is considered the VPN server. You must configure a VPN profile at the initiating router, including a VPN protocol and authentication type and method. These must match the supported VPN protocol and authentication options on the responding router.

Network traffic that crosses the S2S connection does not originate at either of the routers, but rather from the client or server computers at each location. You must therefore define a demand-dial interface on the originating router.

When you create a demand-dial interface, you must define:

- **The Demand-Dial Interface Name** Apart from defining an identifying name, this name is used in authentication. See "Set IP Demand-Dial Filters."
- **Whether the Connection is One-Way or Two-Way** In a one-way connection, only one router initiates the VPN connection and the other router always responds. In a two-way connection, either router can initiate the VPN connection and either can respond.
- **The Credentials Used to Authenticate** You must ensure that the name of the responding router's demand-dial interface matches the name of the user account that the initiating router uses, as shown in Figure 4-25. If you use a two-way connection, then the interface names at each end must match the remote end's user account name.

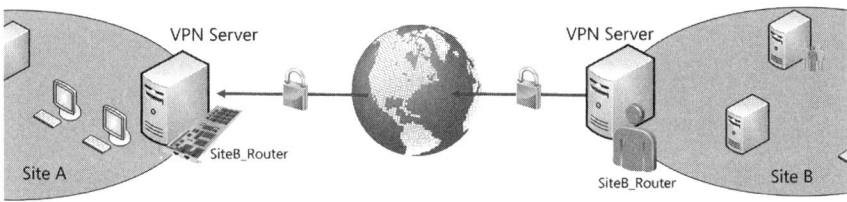

FIGURE 4-25 Configuring the demand-dial interface name

- **What Traffic You Will Allow Over the Connection** You can establish demand-dial interface filters that determine what traffic can initiate a connection. For example, you might configure that only secure web traffic (HTTPS) is allowed over the link. You use the Set IP Demand-Dial Filters property to configure this behavior.
- **What Times of Day the Connection is Allowed** If you only want a connection to be allowed at specified times, you can configure the demand-dial interface's Dial-Out Hours property.
- **Whether the Connection is Persistent** Demand-dial connections can be defined as persistent. That is, once initiated, they stay connected until you manually disconnect them. If a persistent demand-dial interface loses connectivity, the connection is automatically reestablished. If the connection is non-persistent, it is referred to as an on-demand connection. On-demand demand-dial connections drop the connection after a period of inactivity.

CREATING AN S2S CONNECTION

To create an S2S connection using Routing And Remote Access, on both servers that will be configured as S2S routers, perform the following procedure:

1. Install the DirectAccess and VPN (RAS) role service. This is part of the Remote Access server role. After the role is installed, in Server Manager, run the Getting Started Wizard.

2. In the Getting Started Wizard, on the Welcome to Remote Access page, click Deploy VPN Only.

3. The Routing and Remote Access console opens. Right-click the local server in the navigation pane and then click Configure and Enable Routing and Remote Access.

4. In the Routing and Remote Access Server Setup Wizard, on the Configuration page, as shown in Figure 4-26, click Secure Connection Between Two Private Networks and then click Next.

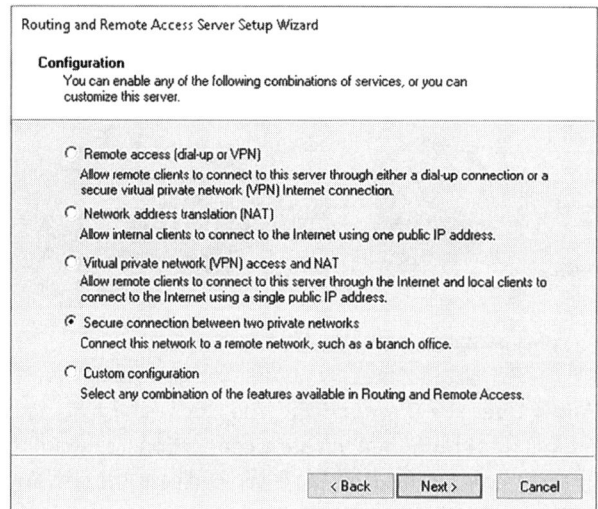

FIGURE 4-26 Selecting the routing and remote access configuration

5. On the Demand-Dial Connections page, when asked if you want to use demand-dial connections, as shown in Figure 4-27, click Yes, and then click Next.

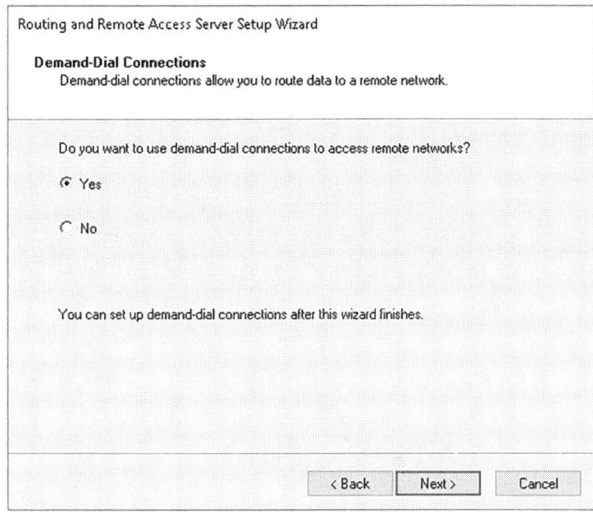

FIGURE 4-27 Enabling demand-dial routing

6. On the IP Address Assignment page, click Automatically if you want an existing DHCP server on the internal network to assign IP addresses to remote clients, or click From A Specified Range Of Addresses if you want the remote access server to assign these addresses.

7. If you opted to assign addresses from a specified range, on the IP Address Assignment page, specify the range of addresses you want to allocate. Be careful these do not overlap any addresses that are in use in DHCP, or that might be statically assigned to network clients. Click Next.

8. Click Finish to complete the process. Routing And Remote access starts.

After you have completed the initial configuration, the Demand-Dial Interface Wizard launches automatically. Use the following procedure to complete configuration:

1. In the Demand-Dial Interface Wizard, click Next.

2. On the Interface Name page, in the Interface name box, type the interface name, as shown in Figure 4-28. Remember that the interface name must match the name of the user account that will be used to authenticate the connection at the remote end, as shown in Figure 4-25. Click Next.

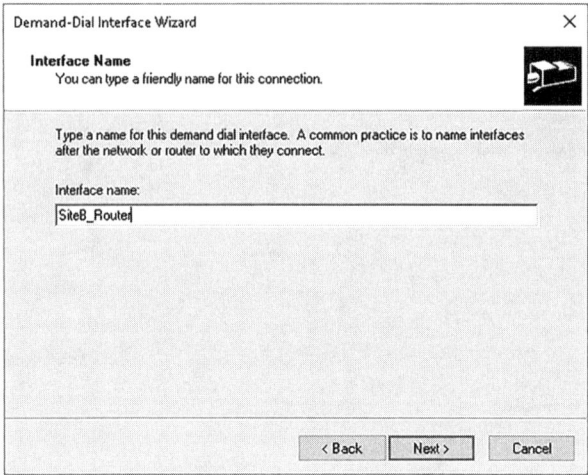

FIGURE 4-28 Defining a demand-dial interface name

3. On the Connection Type page, click Connect Using Virtual Private Network (VPN), as shown in Figure 4-29, and then click Next.

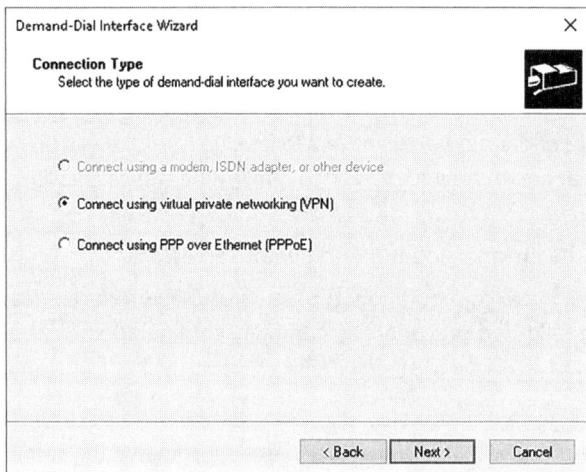

FIGURE 4-29 Selecting the connection type for a demand-dial interface

4. On the VPN Type page, select the VPN protocol you want to use, as shown in Figure 4-30, and then click Next.

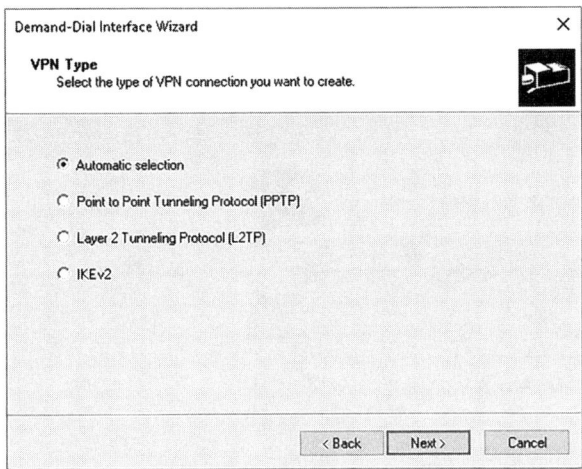

FIGURE 4-30 Selecting the VPN protocol

5. On the Destination address page, type the FQDN or IP address of the remote router and click Next.

6. On the Protocols and Security page, shown in Figure 4-31, select the Route IP Packets On This Interface check box. Optionally, select the Add A User Account So A Remote Router Can Dial-In. Selecting this option establishes this as a two-way connection. Click Next.

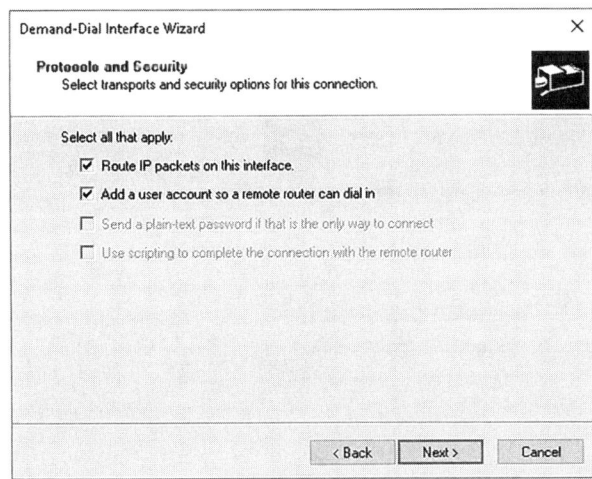

FIGURE 4-31 Configuring protocol and security

7. On the Static Routes For Remote Networks page, configure any routing information required to connect to the remote network and click Next.

8. On the Dial-in Credentials page, shown in Figure 4-32, enter the password for the user account and click Next. You cannot specify the user name because the wizard defines

this to match the local interface name. This means when you configure the remote end, the specified user account at the remote end will match the user account created on this page and also the local interface name.

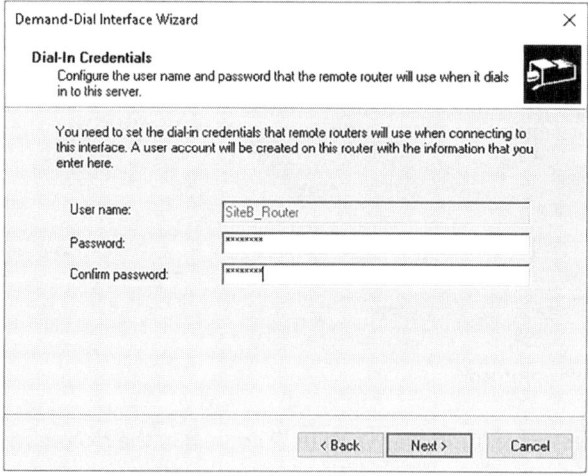

FIGURE 4-32 Configuring dial-in credentials

9. On the Dial-Out Credentials page, shown in Figure 4-33, enter the User Name, Domain Name, and Password needed to connect to the remote router. Once again, the user account specified must match the remote interface name. Click Next and then click Finish.

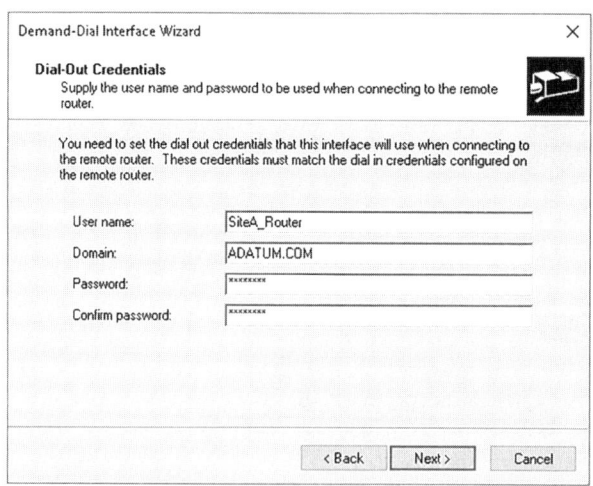

FIGURE 4-33 Configuring Dial-Out Credentials

After you have configured one end of the S2S VPN, you must configure the other end. When that process is complete, you can optionally configure the following properties of the connection:

- **Set IP Demand-dial Filters** Use this option to define the type of traffic that can traverse the demand-dial link. In the Routing and Remote Access console, expand the local server, expand the Network Interfaces node, and then in the detail pane, right-click the demand-dial interface and then click Set IP Demand-Dial Filters, as shown in Figure 4-34. Add the desired filters by defining the network source, destination, protocol, and port. Click OK.

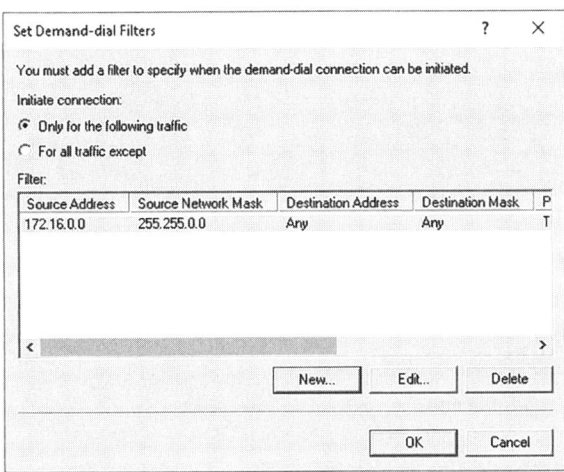

FIGURE 4-34 Configuring Demand-Dial filters

- **Dial-Out hours** To configure when the link can be used, in the Network Interfaces node, right-click the demand-dial interface you want to configure, and then click Dial-Out Hours. Configure the desired availability and click OK, as shown in Figure 4-35.

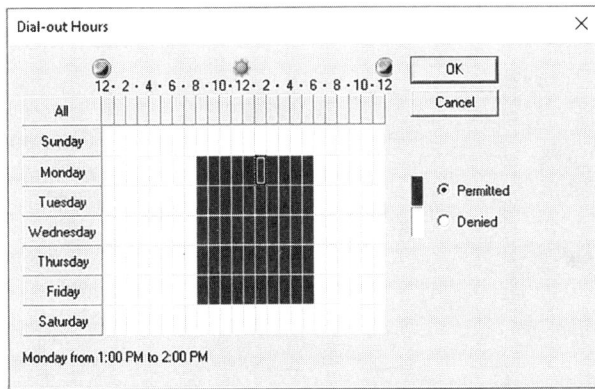

FIGURE 4-35 Configuring demand-dial hours

- **Persistent** To configure a connection as persistent, right-click the Demand-Dial interface and then click Properties. On the Options tab, shown in Figure 4-36, choose Demand-Dial for non-persistent connections, and then configure the Idle Time Before The Connection Is Dropped. Alternatively, for a persistent demand-dial interface, click Persistent Connection.

FIGURE 4-36 Configuring a demand-dial interface to be non-persistent

To configure VPN type or authentication settings for your demand-dial interface, right-click the interface in the Network Interfaces node and then click Properties. Click the Security tab, as shown in Figure 4-37.

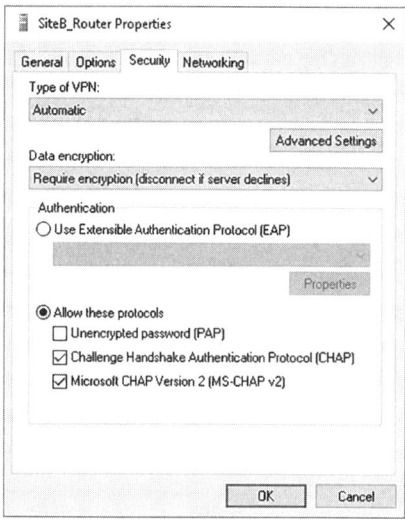

FIGURE 4-37 Configuring the type of VPN and authentication settings

You can configure:

- **Type of VPN**   Select from automatic, PPTP, L2TP, and IKEv2.
- **Data encryption**   Choose from No Encryption Allowed, Optional Encryption, Require Encryption, and Maximum Strength Encryption.
- **Authentication**   Available methods of authentication are EAP, PAP, CHAP, and MS-CHAP-v2.

Implement DirectAccess

DirectAccess is a feature of Windows Server 2016 that enables remote clients to connect to your organization's network infrastructure without needing a VPN.

> **NOTE DIRECTACCESS**
> DirectAccess was first introduced in Windows Server 2008 R2.

Remote client computers connect seamlessly to internal resources, whether they are connecting locally (internally) or remotely (externally). Client computers are able to sense their own location (internal or external) and configure accordingly. Consequently, this simplifies your remote access infrastructure because you do not need to implement RADIUS by using NPS.

To implement DirectAccess, as shown in Figure 4-38, the following components are required:

- **DirectAccess Server**   This Windows Server 2016 server connects to both the internal network and the Internet, and is a gateway for external clients.
- **DirectAccess Clients**   Any domain-joined computer running an Enterprise edition of Windows 7 or newer. The clients connect to the DirectAccess server using IPv6 and IPsec. If a native IPv6 network is unavailable, the clients use an IPv6 transition technology such as 6to4 or Teredo.
- **Network location Server**   DirectAccess clients use the network location server to determine their locations: internal or external. If a client computer can connect to the NLS using HTTPS, it is an internal location and DirectAccess GPOs do not apply.
- **Internal Resources**   These are the IPv6-capable apps and resources that you want to make available to your DirectAccess clients.
- **AD DS**   Provides for authentication and GPO distribution and application.
- **Group Policy**   DirectAccess client and server configuration is based on GPOs.
- **PKI Infrastructure**   This is an optional component, and not displayed in Figure 4-38. Digital certificates can be used to enhance security, and when you deploy client computers running Windows 7, a PKI must be used to complete the deployment.
- **DNS Server**   DNS is used by client computers to locate internal resources.
- **Name Resolution Policy Table**   The NRPT is used by client computers to determine which DNS servers they should use: internal DNS, or external DNS.

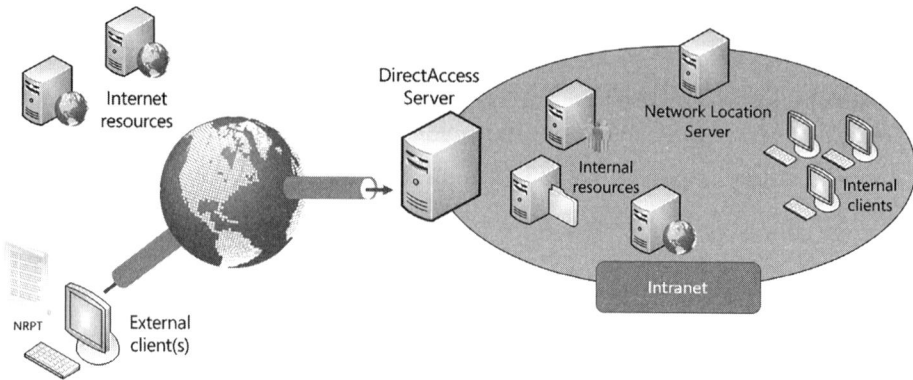

FIGURE 4-38 DirectAccess components

DirectAccess tunneling options

DirectAccess user IPv6 and IPsec to enable connections to internal resources. However, not all organizations have implemented IPv6. Consequently, DirectAccess uses IPv6 transition tunneling options to enable clients to connect to internal resources. The tunneling options include:

- **ISATAP**   Enables DirectAccess clients to connect to the DirectAccess server over IPv4 networks for intranet (internal) communication.
- **6to4**   Enables DirectAccess clients to connect to the DirectAccess server over the IPv4-based Internet for external communication.
- **Teredo**   Enables DirectAccess clients to connect to the DirectAccess server over the IPv4-based Internet if clients are behind a NAT device.
- **IP-HTTPS**   Used by clients that are unable to connect to the DirectAccess server by using the preceding methods.

> *NOTE* **IPV6 TRANSITION OPTIONS**
>
> IPv6 transition options are discussed in more detail in Chapter 5, "Implement core and distributed network solutions."

Server deployment options

You can deploy a DirectAccess server on any Windows Server 2016 server computer that is a member of an AD DS domain using one of three network topology configurations:

- **Edge**   Use this topology if you deployed your firewall software on an edge computer running Windows Server 2016 installed with two network adapters: one connects to the intranet and the other to the Internet.

- **Behind the firewall with two network adapters**   Use if your DirectAccess server is deployed behind a firewall and has two network adapters: one connects to the intranet and the other to the perimeter network.
- **Behind the firewall with one network adapter**   Use of your DirectAccess server is behind your firewall and installed with a single network adapter, which is connected to the Intranet.

EXAM TIP

Although the DirectAccess server must be a domain-member computer, it must not be a domain controller.

ADVANCED DEPLOYMENT OPTIONS

DirectAccess supports a number of advanced deployment options, including:

- **Multiple endpoints**   For clients running Windows 8 or newer, if you implement the DirectAccess Server role on multiple servers in different locations, the DirectAccess clients automatically select the closest endpoint.

EXAM TIP

You must specify the endpoint manually for DirectAccess clients running Windows 7.

- **Multiple domains**   If your organization has multiple domain names, the DirectAccess clients can connect to multiple domains.
- **Deploy behind NAT device**   If required, you can deploy a DirectAccess server behind a NAT device.
- **Off-premise provisioning**   You can use the Djoin.exe tool to provision a non-domain client computer with an AD DS Binary Large Object (BLOB). This enables the computer to join your domain without first being connected to the internal network.

Implement DirectAccess server requirements

Before you can deploy DirectAccess, you must ensure that your DirectAccess server(s) meets the following requirements. The DirectAccess Server must:

- Be a domain member but not a domain controller.
- Have at least one network adapter connected to the internal network.
- Have a public IPv4 address for any Internet-connected adapter, if you have opted for the Edge topology configuration.
- Have the Windows Firewall enabled on all profiles.
- Be installed with the DirectAccess and VPN (RAS) role service, part of the Remote Access server role.

Install and configure DirectAccess

To deploy a DirectAccess server, first deploy the DirectAccess and VPN (RAS) role service using either Windows PowerShell or Server Manager. Then, complete the following procedure:

1. In Server Manager, click Tools and then click Remote Access Management.
2. In the Remote Access Management console, under the Configuration node, click DirectAccess and VPN. In the Details pane, as shown in Figure 4-39, click Run the Getting Started Wizard.

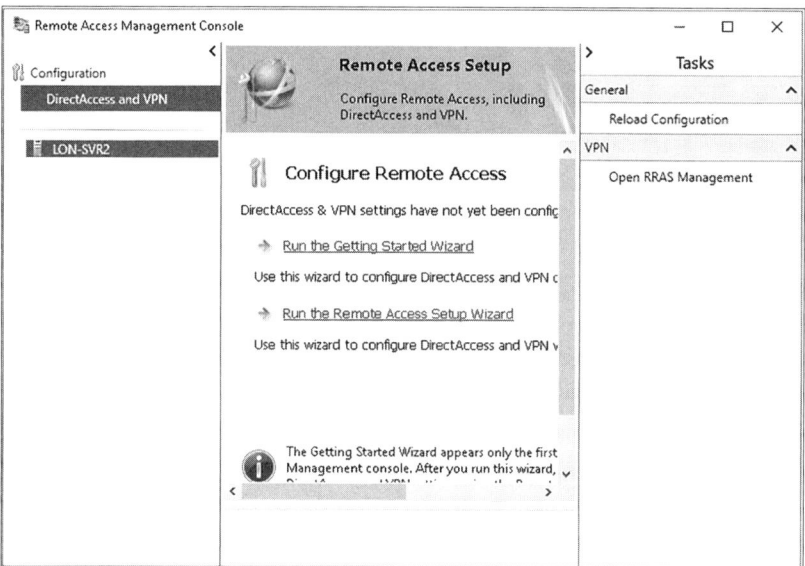

FIGURE 4-39 Running the Getting Started Wizard

EXAM TIP

Using the Getting Started Wizard makes deploying DirectAccess simple. However, it is not recommended for deployments that require any of the advanced deployment options mentioned earlier in this section. It is also not suitable for deployments that support Windows 7 clients.

3. On the Configure Remote Access page, click Deploy DirectAccess Only. Prerequisites are verified.
4. On the Remote Access Server Setup page, shown in Figure 4-40, click the appropriate topology and then type the FQDN or public IPv4 address used by clients to connect to the DirectAccess server. Click Next.

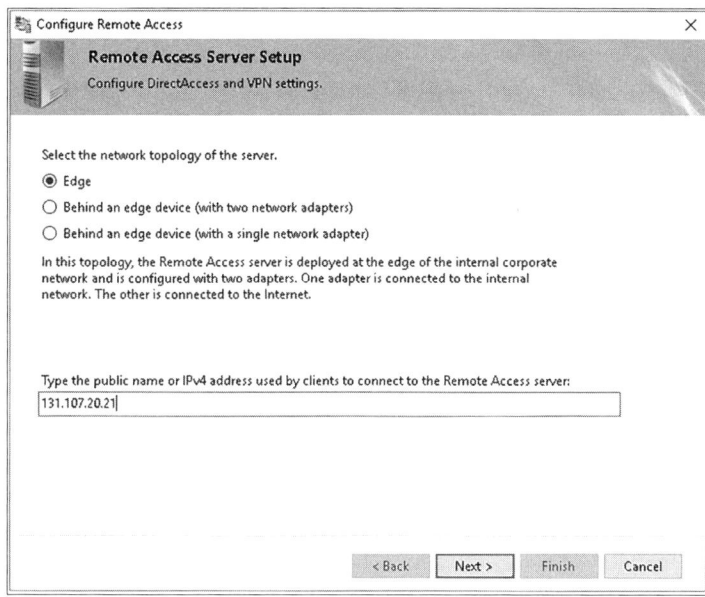

FIGURE 4-40 Configuring the DirectAccess topology

5. On the Remote Access Settings Will Be Applied page, click the Here link to configure GPO settings, DirectAccess client security group settings, server adapter settings, and DNS properties.

6. On the Review The Configuration Settings page, shown in Figure 4-41, next to Remote Clients, click Change.

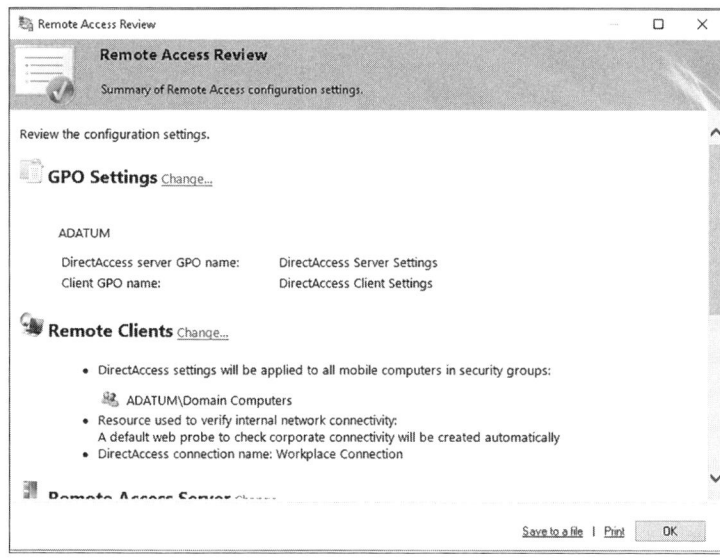

FIGURE 4-41 Configuring the DirectAccess topology

7. In the DirectAccess Client Setup dialog box, on the Select Groups tab, shown in Figure 4-42, define the AD DS objects to which the DirectAccess client GPOs will apply. By default, the GPO is applied to the Domain Computers security group, but the Enable DirectAccess for mobile computers only option is selected. If you want to apply the DirectAccess client GPO only to computers that belong to a specific group, for example "DirectAccess Computers," create that group in AD DS. Next, assign the desired computers to that group as members, and then in the DirectAccess Client Setup dialog box, remove Domain Computers, and add the group you created. Clear the Enable DirectAccess for Mobile Computers Only check box, and click Next.

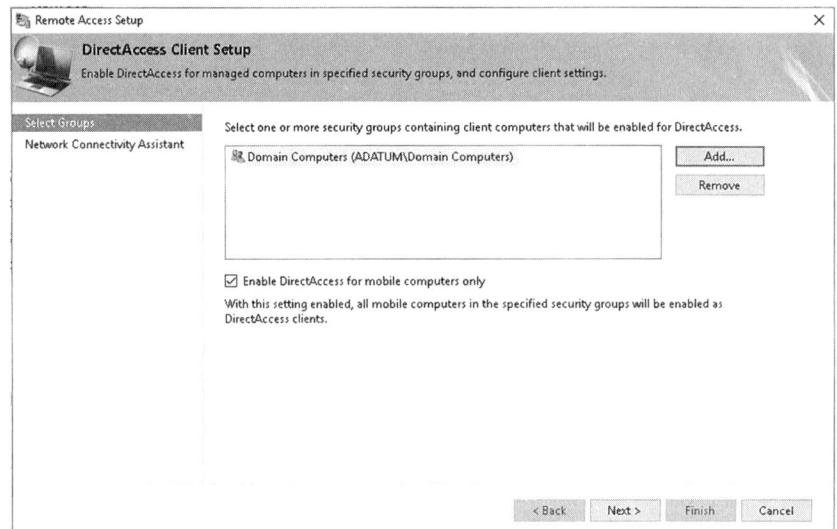

FIGURE 4-42 Selecting the client computers for DirectAccess

8. On the Network Connectivity Assistant page, define a DirectAccess connection name and then click Finish. This should be a name that is significant to your users and network administrators.

9. On the Review the Configuration Settings page, shown in Figure 4-41, optionally, next to GPO Settings, click Change. The GPO Names dialog box appears enabling you to change the names of the GPOs that will apply to DirectAccess servers and clients. There is no technical reason why you must do this, but you might opt to choose different names. The defaults are: DirectAccess Client Settings and DirectAccess Server Settings. If you change these, click OK.

10. On the Review the Configuration Settings page, click OK.

11. On the Remote Access Settings Will Be Applied page, click Finish. The DirectAccess configuration is applied. When prompted, click Close.

After you have completed the wizard, you can use the Remote Access Management Console to verify the configuration, as shown in Figure 4-43.

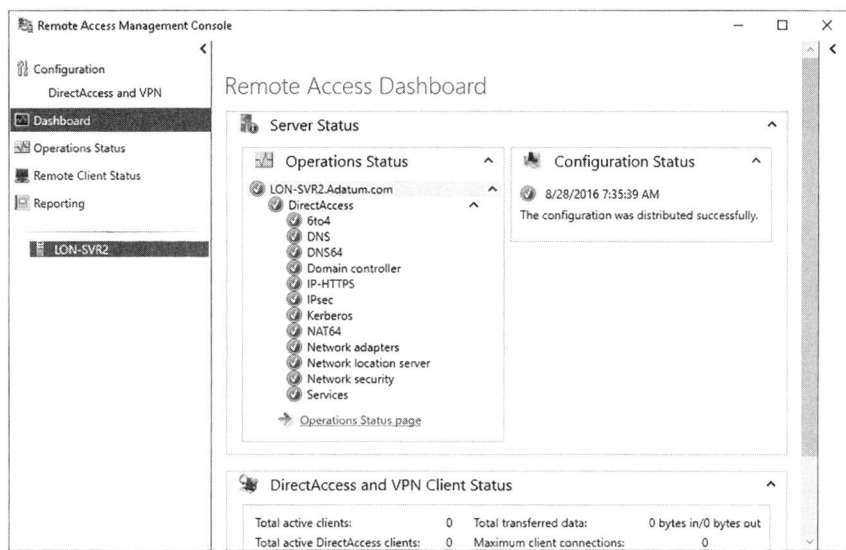

FIGURE 4-43 Verifying the DirectAccess configuration

You can use the Dashboard tab for a summary of all available information on your DirectAccess configuration. The Remote Client Status tab is useful for troubleshooting connectivity. This is discussed in the next section.

CHANGES MADE BY THE GETTING STARTED WIZARD

Using the Getting Started Wizard to configure and enable DirectAccess makes the following changes to your network infrastructure:

- The following DNS host records are created in your DNS zone:
    - directaccess-corpConnectivityHost
    - DirectAccess-NLS
    - directaccess-WebProbeHost
- Two GPOs are created (DirectAccess Client Settings and DirectAccess Server Settings) and applied to your domain. These are:
    - DirectAccess Client Settings. Settings in this GPO:
    - Configure DirectAccess clients to trust the self-signed certificates issued by the DirectAccess server.
    - Enable the IPsec ICMP protocol on the local firewall on the DirectAccess clients.
    - Enable outbound IP-HTTPS traffic on the local firewall.
    - Define the IPv6 address prefixes

- Define Kerberos authentication settings.
- DirectAccess Server Settings. Settings in this GPO:
- Enable the IPsec ICMP protocol on the local firewall on the DirectAccess server.
- Enable inbound IP-HTTPS traffic on the local firewall.
- Define the IPv6 address prefixes.
- Define Kerberos authentication settings.

WHEN NOT TO USE THE GETTING STARTED WIZARD

Using the Getting Started Wizard is the simplest way to configure and enable DirectAccess, but it does not suit all situations. If you want to support multiple locations, implement failover configurations, or you simply have Windows 7 client computers to integrate into your DirectAccess solution, you must implement an advanced DirectAccess configuration.

> ***NEED MORE REVIEW?*** **DEPLOY A SINGLE DIRECTACCESS SERVER WITH ADVANCED SETTINGS**
>
> To review further details about implementing an advanced DirectAccess infrastructure, refer to the Microsoft TechNet website at *https://technet.microsoft.com/library/hh831436(v=ws.11).aspx*.

Implement client configuration

Implementing DirectAccess clients is straightforward because this is done by the GPOs created when you run the Getting Started Wizard. You can verify that the settings are applied correctly by using GPO monitoring and troubleshooting techniques.

To determine whether the DirectAccess client settings are applying, start up a client computer that should be a DirectAccess client as defined by your settings, and sign in. From an elevated command prompt, run the **gpresult /r** command. Under the Computer Settings section, this command returns information about the GPOs that apply or do not apply to the client computer. If the computer is properly configured for DirectAccess, the DirectAccess Client Settings GPO should appear, as shown in Figure 4-44.

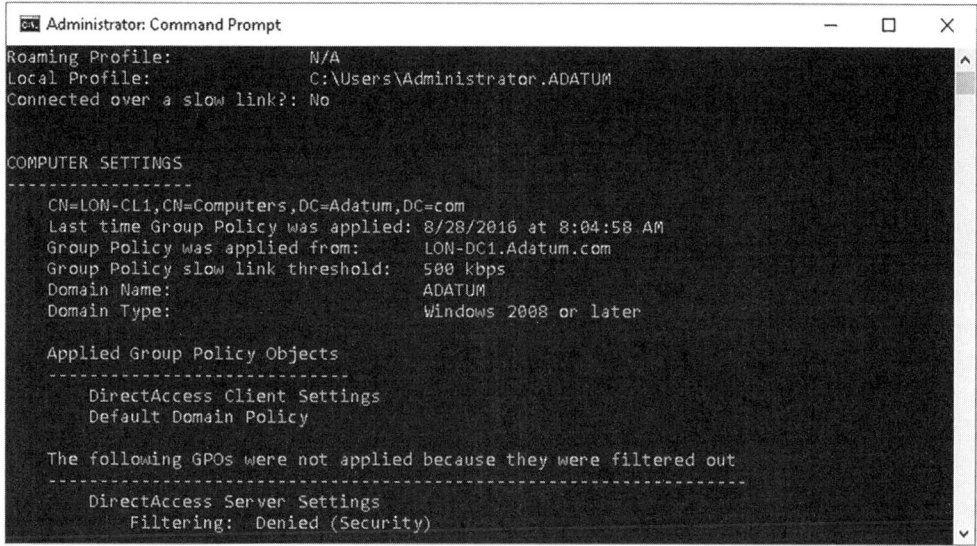

FIGURE 4-44 Checking the application of DirectAccess GPOs on a client computer

To test DirectAccess, you must move the computer to an external network. You can then use the Remote Access Management console to view the resultant DirectAccess connection, as shown in Figure 4-45.

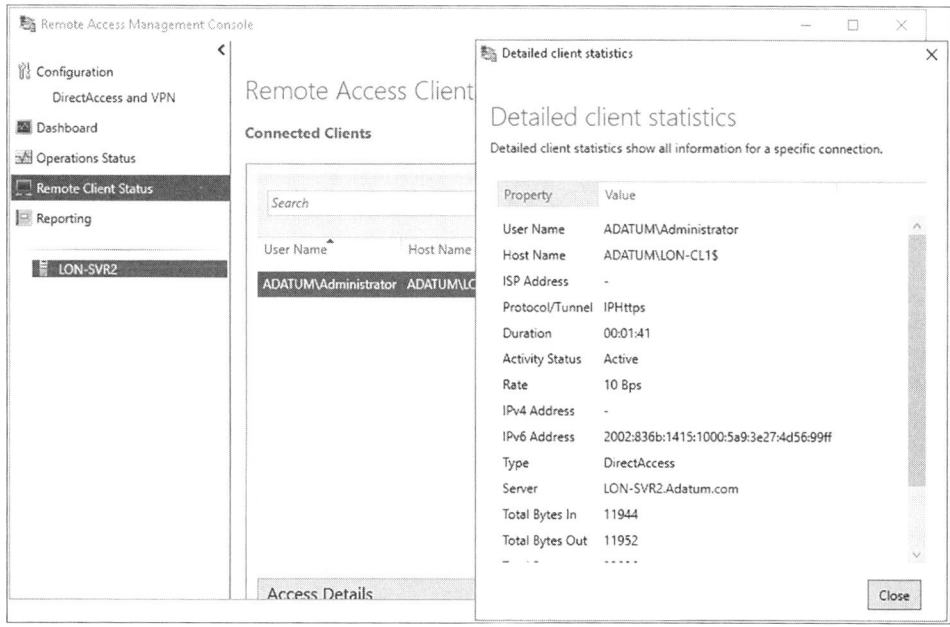

FIGURE 4-45 Checking the application of DirectAccess GPOs on a client computer

Troubleshoot DirectAccess

If your DirectAccess clients cannot connect to internal resources as expected, there are a number of things to check. Remember that because DirectAccess is based in the correct application of GPOs, it is important that you verify your GPO settings before you start to troubleshoot DirectAccess itself.

Start by verifying the following. On the DirectAccess client:

1. Verify that the DirectAccess Client Settings GPO is applied. You can use gpresult /r to check this. If the GPO does not apply, ensure that the computer is a member of any group you specified in the Getting Started wizard when you configured DirectAccess. Use standard GPO troubleshooting techniques to verify the correct application of the necessary client GPOs.
2. Verify connectivity to the DirectAccess server
   - Check that the client has a IPv6 address beginning with 2002. Use the IPconfig.exe command line tool to verify. This address is used to communicate with the DirectAccess server.
   - Open the **Settings** app, and in **Network & Internet**, click the **DirectAccess** tab. As shown in Figure 4-46, it should show that the DirectAccess connection is active (the name shown is the one you define in the Getting Started Wizard), and that the location is set up correctly for DirectAccess.

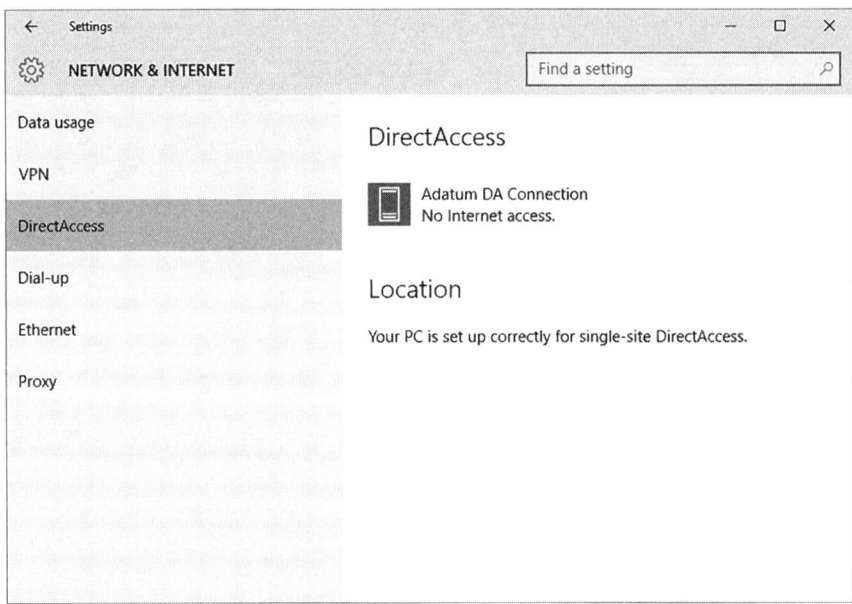

FIGURE 4-46 Verifying the DirectAccess setting on a Windows 10 client

- Use the Netsh name show effectivepolicy command at an elevated command prompt. This should return a list of policies when correctly connected to the DirectAccess server, as shown in Figure 4-47.

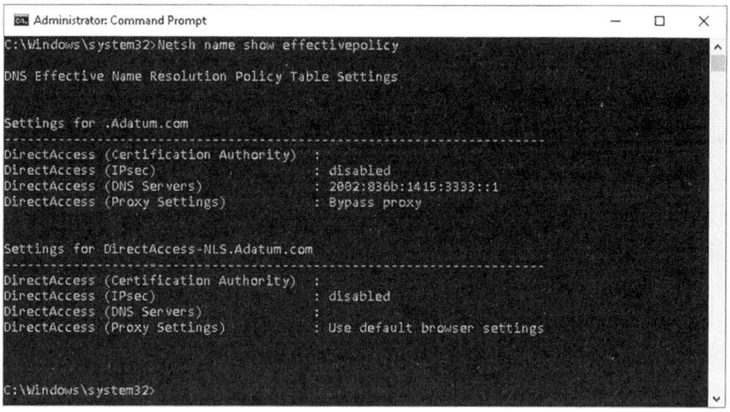

FIGURE 4-47 Viewing the effective policy with netsh.exe

If these tests do not identify the cause of the problem, use basic network troubleshooting tools to verify the client computer's configuration.

Skill 4.3: Implement NPS

It is essential that you understand NPS, its policies and how to enforce them, and how to implement RADIUS. These are important skills for any IT professional responsible for providing secure remote access to his organization's networked resources.

Configure RADIUS

RADIUS is a widely adopted authentication protocol used by many different vendors. RADIUS is used to help to secure remote access solutions by providing authentication. You can configure the Windows Server 2016 NPS role as a RADIUS server or RADIUS proxy.

The NPS role

In earlier versions of the Windows Server platform, IT administrators managed their users' remote access connections through a Remote Access Server, with dial-in permissions configured on a per-server basis. This was fine so long as the administrator did not need to manage too many remote clients and more than a couple of remote access servers.

Because remote access has become more prevalent, it has become necessary to centralize configuration and management of remote access servers and the clients they support. The NPS role enables you to do this by providing policy-based management of remote access, as shown in Figure 4-48.

The NPS role provides authentication, authorization, and accounting through a centralized point for the following situations:

- Dial-up remote access
- VPN remote access
- Wireless access
- 802.1X access
- Internet access
- Extranet access from partner organizations

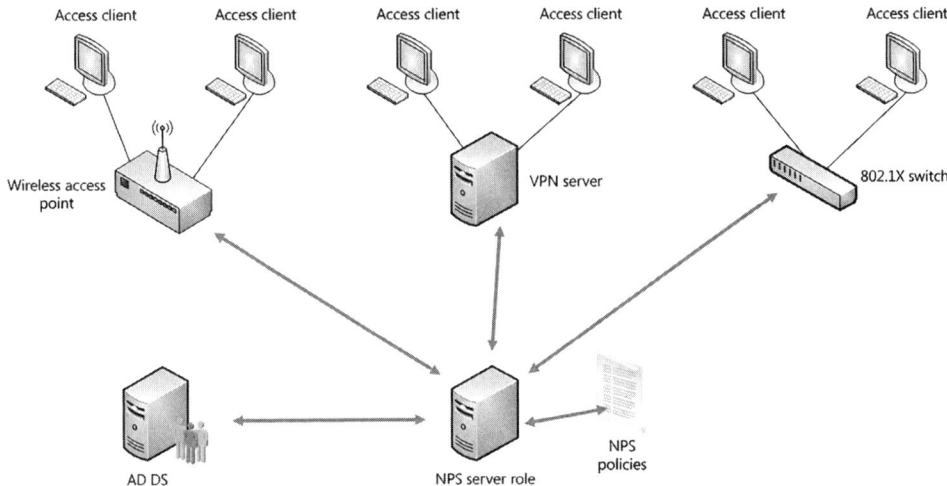

FIGURE 4-48 A typical deployment of the NPS server role

To deploy the NPS role, complete the following tasks:

1. In Server Manager, click Manage, and then click Add Roles And Features.
2. In the Add Roles And Features Wizard, on the Server Roles page, select the Network Policy and Access Services role, and when prompted, add the required features necessary to support the role.
3. Complete the wizard to install the role, and then, when prompted, click Finish.

You can now use the Network Policy Server console to configure and manage the role.

EXAM TIP

You can also deploy the role by using the Windows PowerShell Install-WindowsFeature -Name npas -IncludeManagementTools command.

> **NEED MORE REVIEW? NETWORK POLICY SERVER**
>
> To review further details about the NPS role, refer to the Microsoft TechNet website at *https://technet.microsoft.com/library/cc732912(v=ws.11).aspx*.

Configure a RADIUS server

NPS is Microsoft's implementation of a RADIUS server. When you configure NPS as a RADIUS server, you can add RADIUS clients, such as wireless access points, network access servers, and VPN servers—all of which can use the NPS role as their configured RADIUS server. After configuring the RADIUS clients, you must create and configure NPS policies that are used to authenticate and authorize connection attempts.

If you install the NPS role on a computer that is a member of an Active Directory Domain Services (AD DS) domain, you can use the AD DS user and group accounts to provide authentication. This allows your users to sign in to your network resources remotely by using the same user account with which they sign in when locally connected to those resources.

The NPS role gathers statistics relating to remote access authentication, authorization, and other data, and can store this logged data either locally, or in a central location on an accounting server, depending on configuration. A typical RADIUS server scenario is shown in Figure 4-49.

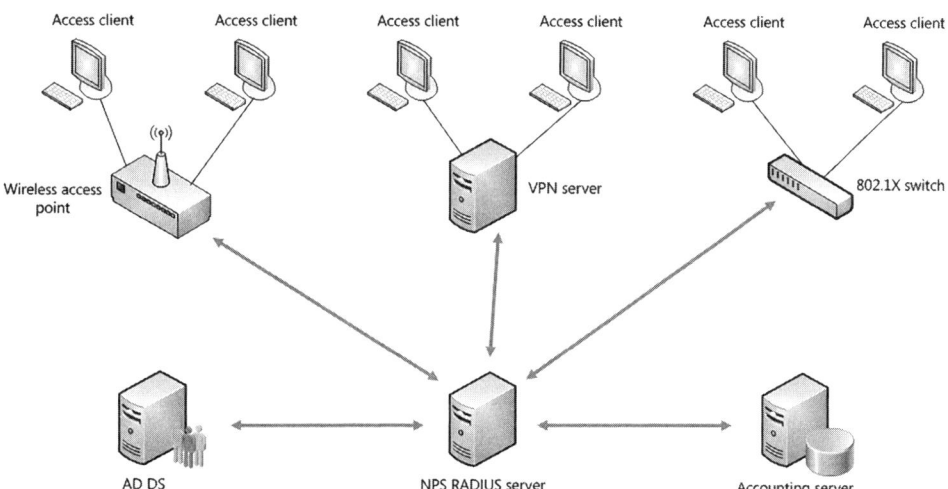

FIGURE 4-49 A typical NPS RADIUS server deployment

After you have deployed the NPS role, you must configure it either as a RADIUS server or a RADIUS proxy. These are not specific selectable roles. Rather, they are implied in how you configure the relationship between the various NPS role computers in your organization.

To deploy the NPS role as a RADIUS server, you must define the required RADIUS clients and configure the necessary network policies. To do this, complete the following high-level tasks:

1. Install the NPS role, as described in the preceding section.
2. Open the Network Policy Server console.
3. In the Network Policy Server console, shown in Figure 4-50, create and configure the required network policies.

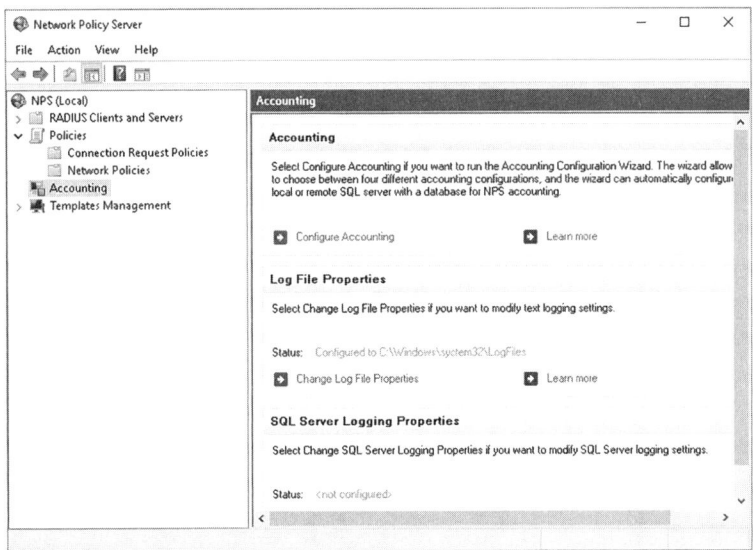

FIGURE 4-50 The Network Policy Server console

4. Select the RADIUS Clients and Servers node, and then right-click the RADIUS Clients node.
5. Click New, and then add the required RADIUS clients. This process is discussed in a subsequent section.

You can also use the Windows PowerShell New-NpsRadiusClient cmdlet to add RADIUS clients or RADIUS proxies.

> **NEED MORE REVIEW?** **RADIUS SERVER**
>
> To review further details about implementing NPS as a RADIUS server, refer to the Microsoft TechNet website at *https://technet.microsoft.com/library/cc755248(v=ws.11).aspx*.

Configure a RADIUS proxy

You can deploy NPS as a RADIUS proxy. In this configuration, the NPS role forwards connection request attempts from remote access clients to the configured RADIUS server for authentication and authorization. You can use connection request policies to determine which connection requests are handled locally, and which are forwarded to a RADIUS server.

A typical RADIUS proxy configuration based on the Windows Server NPS role is shown in Figure 4-51.

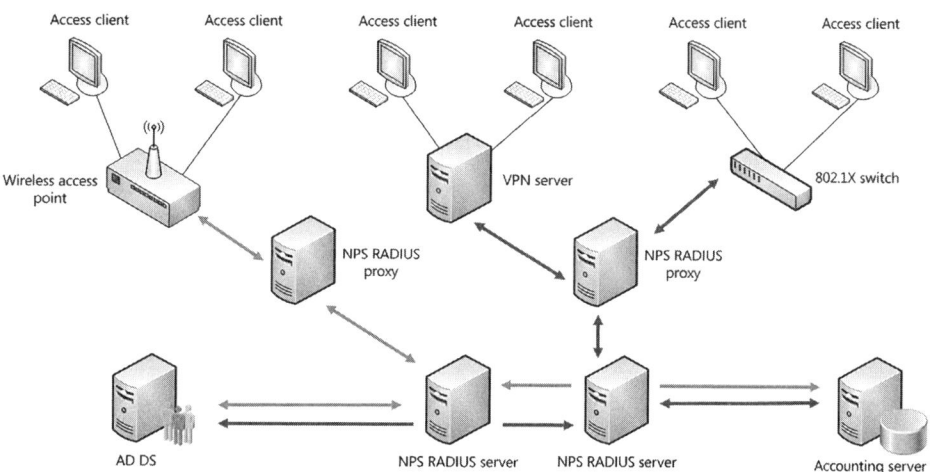

FIGURE 4-51 A typical NPS RADIUS proxy deployment

To deploy the NPS role as a RADIUS proxy, you must define the local NPS role's relationship with the RADIUS servers in your organization. To do this, use the following procedure:

1. Install the NPS role, as described earlier.
2. Open the Network Policy Server console.
3. Select the RADIUS Clients and Servers node, and right-click the Remote RADIUS Server Groups node.
4. Click New, and then in the New Remote RADIUS Server Group dialog box, type the name for the group of RADIUS servers. Even if you only have one RADIUS server, it must reside in a group.
5. Click Add, and in the Add RADIUS Server dialog box, as shown in Figure 4-52, type the name or Internet Protocol (IP) address of the RADIUS server.

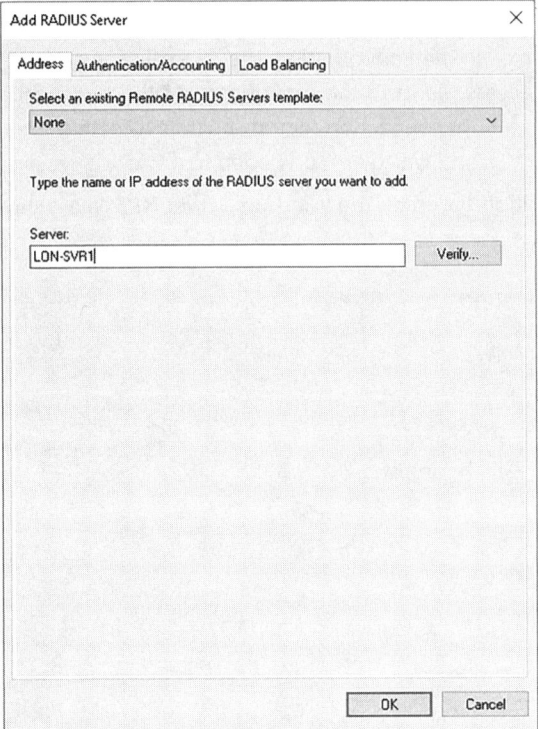

FIGURE 4-52 Adding a RADIUS server on a RADIUS proxy

EXAM TIP

You can use NPS templates to define RADIUS servers. You can then select those servers by using the Select An Existing Remote RADIUS Servers Template option.

6. On the Authentication/Accounting tab, shown in Figure 4-53, you can configure the settings required to link the RADIUS proxy to the RADIUS server for authentication. This includes defining a shared secret (a password) and an authentication port (the default is 1812). You also can define the accounting port (the default is 1813), and shared secret with which this RADIUS proxy will authenticate itself to the RADIUS accounting server.

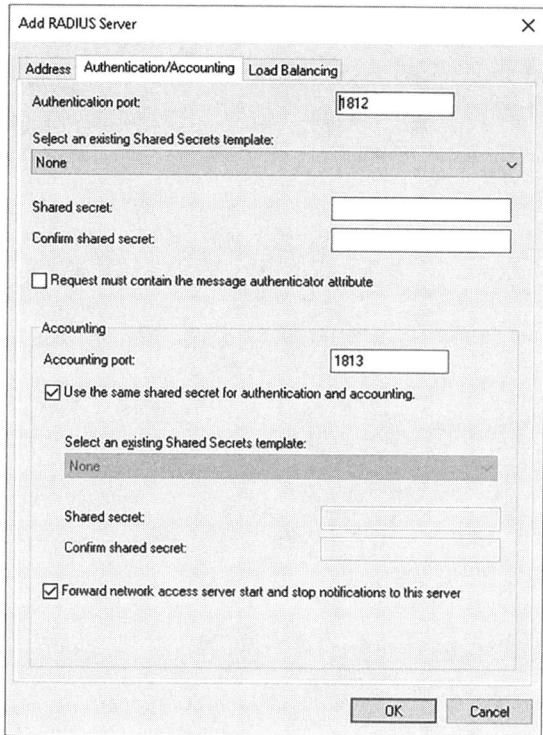

FIGURE 4-53 Configuring authentication and accounting options for a RADIUS proxy

EXAM TIP

You can use NPS templates to define RADIUS Shared secrets. You can then select those shared secrets by using the Select An Existing Shared Secrets Template option.

7. On the Load Balancing tab, shown in Figure 4-54, you can configure weighting and priority values for this server in the group. A Priority value of 1 is the highest. The Weight value is used when the priorities are equal. Use these options to determine which server, in a group of RADIUS servers, should be used in preference to others in the same group.

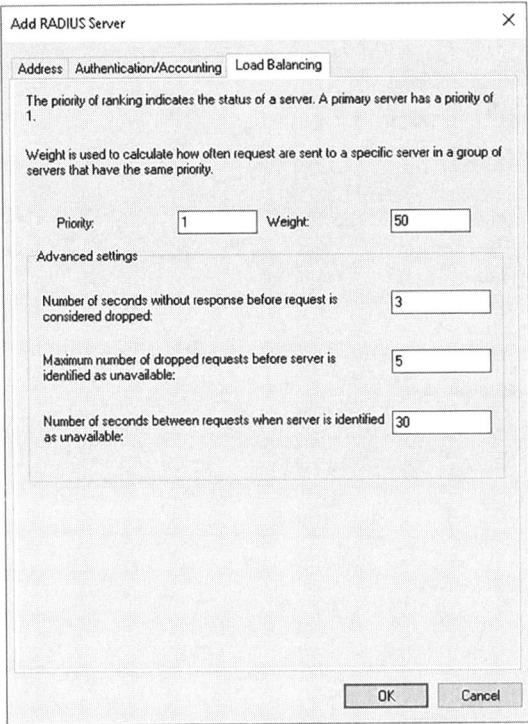

FIGURE 4-54 Configuring Load Balancing options for a RADIUS proxy

8. Repeat the process to add additional servers to this group.

After you have added the necessary server groups, you must define the RADIUS clients that this RADIUS proxy will support. To do this, complete the following steps:

1. In the Network Policy Server console, select the RADIUS Clients and Servers node, and then right-click the RADIUS Clients node.
2. Click New, and then add the required RADIUS clients. This process is discussed in a subsequent section.

> **NEED MORE REVIEW? RADIUS PROXY**
>
> To review further details about implementing NPS as a RADIUS proxy, refer to the Microsoft TechNet website at *https://technet.microsoft.com/library/cc731320(v=ws.11).aspx*.

Configure RADIUS clients

RADIUS clients are those devices and server components that service remote client connection attempts. These connections might be from wireless clients, VPN clients, or devices connected to 802.1X switches. Consequently, a RADIUS client can be considered to be a device, such as a VPN server or wireless access point, which supports the RADIUS protocol for authentication and accounting.

EXAM TIP

RADIUS clients are not remote access clients or devices attempting to connect to a wireless access point or VPN server.

CONFIGURE A RADIUS CLIENT ON THE NPS ROLE

The NPS role does not function as a RADIUS client, but supports RADIUS clients. However, it is necessary to configure RADIUS clients on RADIUS servers, or RADIUS proxies. To add a RADIUS client on your RADIUS server or proxy, complete the following procedure:

1. In the Network Policy Server console, expand the RADIUS Clients and Servers node, and then right-click the RADIUS Clients node.
2. Click Add, and then in the New RADIUS Client dialog box, shown in Figure 4-55, on the Settings tab, type a friendly name for the RADIUS client, and then type its IP address or fully qualified domain name (FQDN). Optionally, specify a shared secret to authenticate with the RADIUS client.

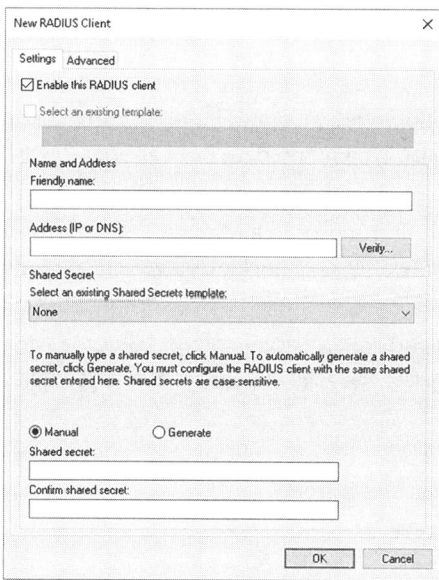

FIGURE 4-55 Adding a RADIUS client

3. Click the Advanced tab, and then define whether to use RADIUS standard protocol, or choose from a list of vendors for your specific device type.

EXAM TIP

You can use NPS templates to define RADIUS clients. You can then select those clients by using the Select An Existing Template option on the Settings tab.

CONFIGURE THE RADIUS CLIENT

The final step is to configure the RADIUS client itself. This procedure varies depending on the device being used, and the vendor that provided the device. However, the process is broadly similar.

To configure RADIUS authentication from a device such as a wireless access point, open the management tool for the device. Select the RADIUS option for authentication and then specify the FQDN or IP address of the RADIUS proxy or RADIUS server, as appropriate, that you want to use. The default ports for authentication and accounting are 1812 and 1813 respectively. Obviously, you must already have configured this RADIUS client on the RADIUS server or proxy.

> *NEED MORE REVIEW?* **RADIUS CLIENT**
>
> To review further details about RADIUS clients, refer to the Microsoft TechNet website at *https://technet.microsoft.com/library/cc754033(v=ws.11).aspx*.

Configure RADIUS accounting

RADIUS accounting enables you to gather and view statistics relating to RADIUS authentication and authorization. You can choose to configure accounting data to be gathered locally on each RADIUS server, or else you can centralize accounting data from all your RADIUS servers and proxies.

You can log RADIUS accounting data to text files and/or to a Microsoft SQL Server database. For most simple NPS deployments, using text files is sufficient. However, larger deployments benefit from SQL Server.

To configure accounting in NPS, in the Network Policy Server console, click the Accounting node and then click Configure Accounting. Use the following procedure to complete the configuration:

1. In the Accounting Configuration Wizard, on the Select Accounting Options page, choose how you will log accounting data. Select from:
   - Log to a SQL Server database.
   - Log to a text file on the local computer.
   - Simultaneously log to a SQL Server database and to a local text file.
   - Log to a SQL Server database using text file logging for failover.
2. On the Configure Local File Logging page, shown in Figure 4-56, specify what you will log, and where you will store the text log files. If you chose SQL Server logging, then specify the SQL Server name and Instance name, and specify what events you will log.
3. Complete the wizard to enable logging.

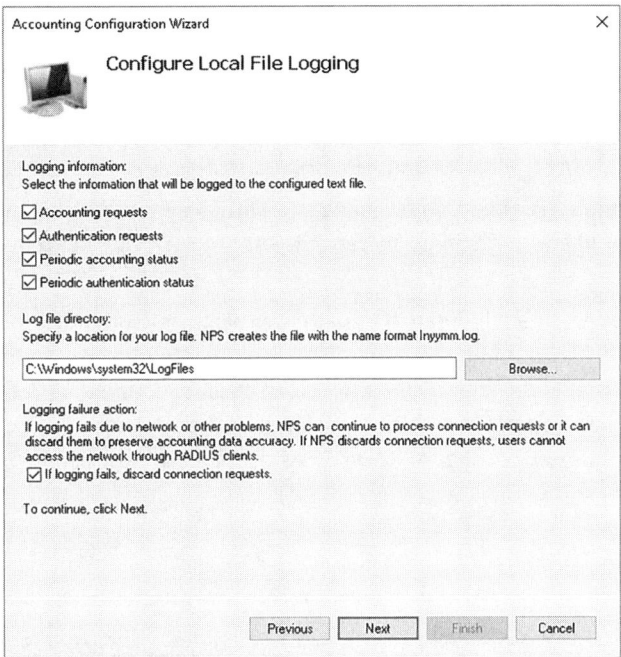

FIGURE 4-56 Enabling accounting

> **NEED MORE REVIEW? RADIUS ACCOUNTING**
>
> To review further details about implementing RADIUS accounting, refer to the Microsoft TechNet website at *https://technet.microsoft.com/library/cc725566(v=ws.11).aspx*.

Configure NPS templates

When you configure the NPS role, you are required to specify the relationship between the RADIUS servers, proxies, and clients that make up your network policy infrastructure. You can use NPS templates to help to make this process quicker and easier.

Create NPS templates

You can use the Network Policy Server console to create and manage NPS templates. In the navigation pane, expand NPS (Local), and then click the Templates Management node, as shown in Figure 4-57.

Using a template saves you from having to repeatedly restate the same information when configuring NPS. For example, if multiple RADIUS servers support connections from a number of RADIUS clients, by using a RADIUS Client template, you can quickly configure the relationship on the RADIUS server.

You can create the following types of template:

- **Shared Secrets**   Enables you to establish a shared secret that you can use to help secure connections between the RADIUS servers, proxies, and clients.
- **RADIUS Clients**   Enables you to create a RADIUS client object and define its properties: friendly name, IP address, vendor name, and shared secret.
- **Remote RADIUS Servers**   Enables you to define a RADIUS server and its properties such as server name or IP address, shared secret, authentication port, and accounting port.
- **IP Filters**   Enables you to create IP filters that permit or block network traffic based on specified conditions. This might include factors such as whether traffic is inbound or outbound, the source and destination IP networks or addresses, and the protocol being used, such as Transmission Control Protocol (TCP) or User Datagram Protocol (UDP). IP Filters are not used to configure RADIUS. Instead, they are used in NPS policies, discussed in the next section.

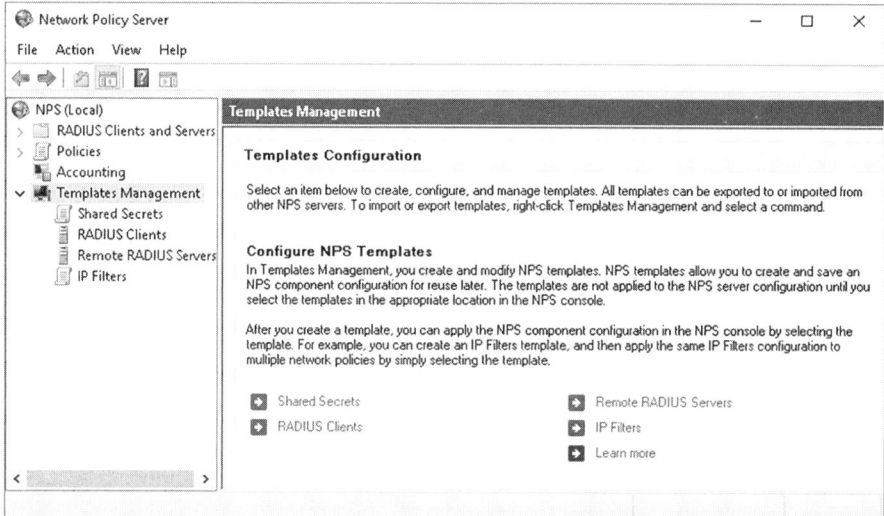

FIGURE 4-57   The Templates Management node

To create a Shared Secrets template, use the following procedure:

1. Click the Templates Management node, right-click Shared Secrets.
2. Click New.
3. In the New RADIUS Shared Secret Template dialog box, shown in Figure 4-58, in the Shared Secret and Confirm Shared Secret text boxes, type the password you want to use and then click OK.

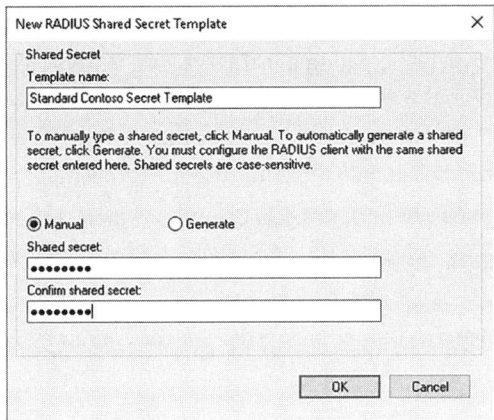

FIGURE 4-58 Configuring a Shared Secrets template

To configure a RADIUS Client template:

1. Click the Templates Management node, right-click RADIUS Clients.
2. Click New.
3. In the New RADIUS Client dialog box, shown in Figure 4-59, type the Friendly Name for the device, type its IP Address or FQDN, and then define the Shared Secret for the device. You can, as shown in Figure 4-59, use a previously defined Shared Secrets template.
4. If necessary, on the Advanced tab, define the Vendor Name. This ensures that the device uses the correct RADIUS version. Consult your device's documentation for the required value, and click OK.

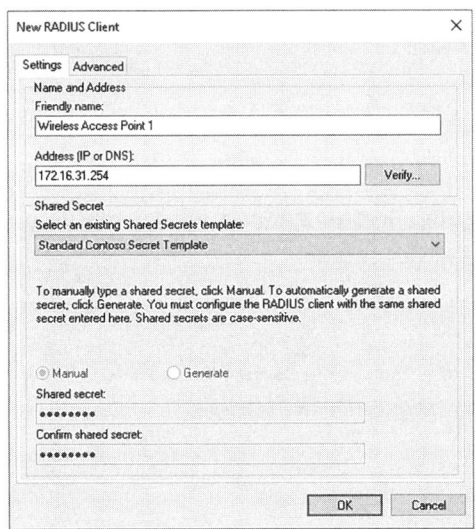

FIGURE 4-59 Configuring a RADIUS Clients template

Creating Shared Secrets, RADIUS Clients and Remote RADIUS Servers is broadly similar.

Apply NPS templates

Applying NPS templates is straightforward. When creating a RADIUS Client or Remote RADIUS Server definition, as described earlier in this section, select the option to use an existing template.

For example, to configure a RADIUS client based on a template, use the following procedure:

1. In the Network Policy Server console, right-click RADIUS Clients and then click New.
2. In the New RADIUS Clients dialog box, shown in Figure 4-60, enable the Select An Existing Template check box.
3. If necessary, change the Friendly Name. All other properties are configured by the template. Click OK.

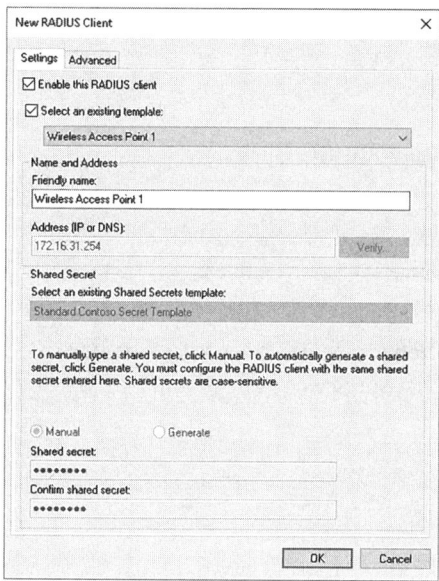

FIGURE 4-60 Adding a RADIUS client using a template

The procedure for applying templates to the creation of RADIUS servers is broadly similar. We look at applying IP Filters templates in the next section.

> **NEED MORE REVIEW? NPS TEMPLATES**
>
> To review further details about using NPS templates, refer to the Microsoft TechNet website at *https://technet.microsoft.com/library/dd759185(v=ws.11).aspx*.

Configure NPS policies

NPS policies enable you to determine which remote access clients are able to successfully connect to your organization and which RADIUS server is responsible for processing the connection attempt. NPS supports two types of policies. These are:

- **Network Policies**   Enable you to control whether a remote client's connection attempt is successful.
- **Connection Request Policies**   Enable you to determine whether the local, or a remote, server processes remote client connection attempts.

Configure network policies

You use Network Policies to determine whether a remote user's connection attempt is successful. Each network policy consists of four groups of properties. These are:

- **Overview**   This contains the policy's name and fundamental elements of the policy:
  - Whether the policy is enabled
  - What the access permission is for clients that match the properties of the policy: Grant access or Deny access
  - The type of network connection: Unspecified, Remote Desktop Gateway, or Remote Access Server (VPN-Dial up)
- **Conditions**   Contains the basic properties of a connection. You can define multiple conditions. For the policy to apply, the remote client must match *all* of the conditions specified in the policy. These include:
  - Membership of Windows groups
  - Day and time restrictions
  - IP address of the remote client
  - Authentication type
  - RADIUS client properties, such as IP address or friendly name

> *EXAM TIP*
>
> If the conditions are met, the policy applies and no further policies are processed. If, however, the conditions are not met, then the NPS role processes the next policy, if multiple policies are defined.

- **Constraints**   Similar to conditions, a constraint is a characteristic of the connection attempt. You can define multiple constraints in a policy, and for the connection attempt to be successful, the remote client must comply with all constraints. Constraints include:
  - Authentication methods
  - Idle and session timeout values
  - Day and time restrictions

EXAM TIP

Like conditions, if a client does not meet the constraints of a policy, the NPS role rejects the connection attempt. However, unlike conditions, the NPS role does not process further policies.

- **Settings** Assuming that both the conditions and constraints of a policy are met, and the policy's access permission is granted, the settings of the policy determine the characteristics of a connection attempt, including:
  - Encryption requirements
  - IP filters
  - IP settings, such as the IPv4 or IPv6 address used by a client
  - If applicable, RADIUS attributes, such as vendor

If you define multiple policies, NPS processes them as follows:

1. Starting at the policy with the highest lowest processing order value (generally, the first in the list), it compares the properties of the connection attempt with the conditions of the policy.

2. If the policy conditions are not met, NPS processes the next policy in turn. It continues processing policies in this way until a policy's conditions match the connection attempt profile. If none match, access is denied.

3. If the policy conditions are met, no further policies are checked. NPS then verifies that the constraints match. If they do not, the connection attempt is rejected. If the connection attempt profile matches the constraints, then:
   A. If the policy access permission is deny, the connection is dropped.
   B. If the policy access permission is grant, the connection is accepted.

EXAM TIP

You can configure a user account's Dial-in properties in AD DS. You can set three possible values: Allow Access, Deny Access, and Control Access Through NPS Policy. If the Dial-in permission for a user is Deny Access, then all connection attempts are rejected. If the Dial-in permission for a user is Allow Access, then NPS allows the connection attempt even if no matching policy exists.

When planning NPS policies, it's important that you create the required policies with the appropriate conditions, and ensure they are placed in the correct order in the policy list in the NPS console. For example, you must create two polices if you want users to be able to connect remotely, but only during out-of-office hours, or if you want administrators to be able to connect at any time, but only when using strongly encrypted connections:

- **Out-of-office hours** This policy requires that users attempt to sign in only during out of office hours and belong to the Domain Users group.

- **Strong encryption** This policy requires strong encryption to be configured on the remote client. This policy also has a condition of membership of the Domain Admins security group.

Now, if policies are set so that out-of-office hours is first in the list, when an administrator attempts to connect with strong encryption during office hours, the out-of-office policy does not apply. NPS processes the next policy in turn. The strong encryption policy applies, and the administrator is granted access.

If a standard user attempts to sign in during office hours, neither policy applies and the user is denied access. If the same user attempts a sign in after work, then the first policy applies, and the user is granted access.

To create a new network policy, in the Network Policy Server console, right-click the Network Policies node and then click New. Then complete the New Network Policy wizard:

1. Enter a meaningful name for the policy and click Next.
2. On the Specify Conditions page, click Add and select and configure a condition for the policy. If you want multiple conditions, repeat this process. Figure 4-61 shows two policy conditions. Click Next.

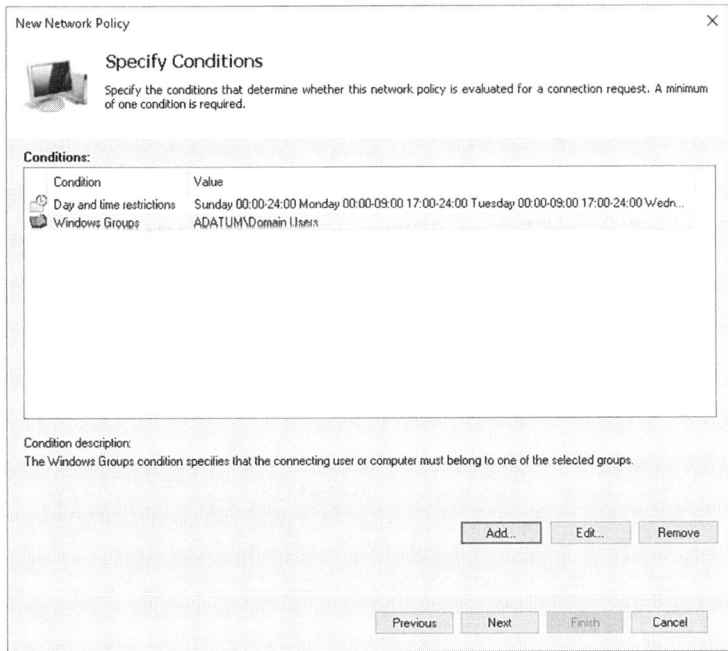

FIGURE 4-61 Defining NPS Network Policy conditions

3. On the Specify Access Permission page, choose either Access Granted, Access Denied, or Access Is Determined By User Dial-in Properties. Click Next.

4. On the Configure Authentication Methods page, define what authentication methods are allowable. Options include:
   - PAP
   - Shiva PAP (SPAP)
   - CHAP
   - MS-CHAP
   - MS-CHAP-v2
   - EAP
   - Protected EAP (PEAP)
5. Click Next.
6. On the Configure Constraints page, define one or more characteristics of remote connections. Remember that all constraints must be matched for a connection attempt to be allowed. Figure 4-62 shows the available options. Click Next.

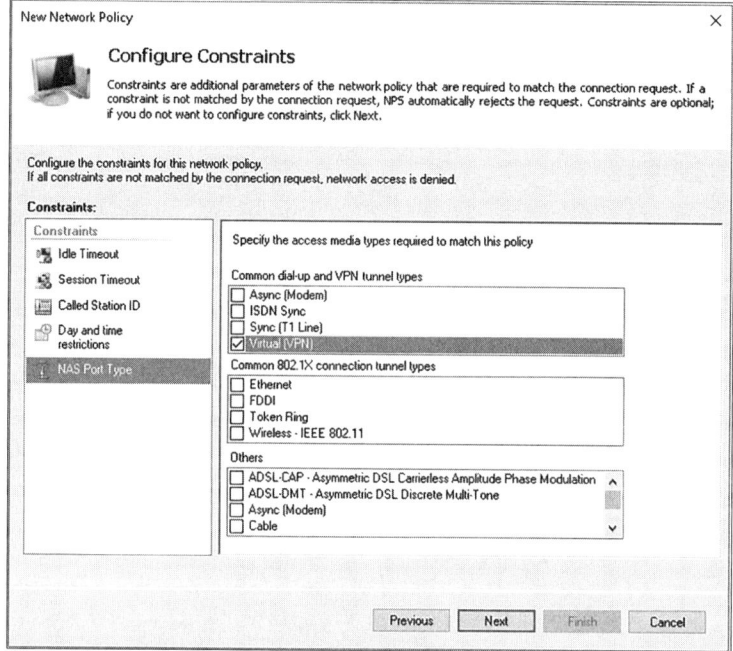

FIGURE 4-62 Defining NPS Network Policy constraints

7. Finally, on the Configure Settings page, you can define connection characteristics. These are only applied if both conditions and constraints are matched, and the policy grants access. Commonly, IP Filters are used to define the type of traffic that can be used over a connection. For example, you could restrict traffic flow to use only HTTP or HTTPS by defining a filter for TCP traffic over ports 80 and 443. Figure 4-63 shows the IP Filters node. Click Next.

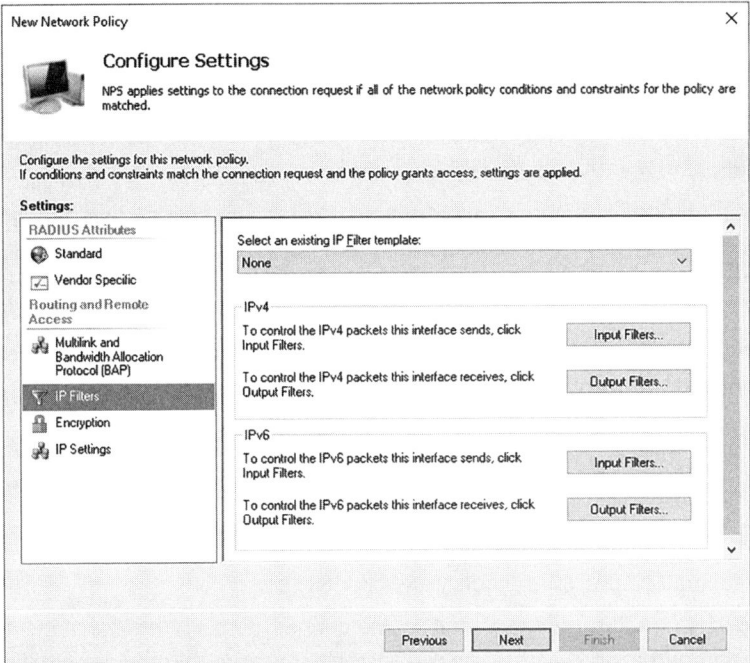

FIGURE 4-63 Defining NPS Network Policy settings

8. On the Completing New Network Policy page, click Finish after you have reviewed the settings.

The processing order of the new policy is assigned the value of 1, which means the policy applies first. After you have created any additional policies, you might want to change the order. Note that you might need to disable or remove the default policies.

EXAM TIP

Two default network policies are created when you install the NPS role: Connections to Microsoft Routing and Remote Access server and Connections to other access servers. These both deny access by default.

Configure connection request policies

You only use connection request policies when you have deployed multiple instances of the NPS role. The connection request policy determines which RADIUS server processes network policies for connection attempts received on another RADIUS server. In essence, if a connection request policy defines a remote server for processing network polices, then the local server is a RADIUS proxy in that scenario.

Connection request policies can forward all, some, or none of the connection attempt requests based on a number of factors, including:

- Day and time restrictions
- The connection type being requested
- The IP address of the RADIUS client

This means that you can configure multiple connection request policies, and depending on settings, different RADIUS servers could be used to process different connection attempts. A default connection request policy with a very low processing order exists after you deploy the NPS role. You can disable this policy, or even delete it. However, any other policies have a higher processing order and would take precedence over the default. The default policy does not forward connection attempts and processes them locally. This might be appropriate for smaller NPS deployments where few, or one, NPS role is deployed.

To create a connection request policy, use the following procedure from within the Network Policy Server console:

1. Right-click the Connection Request Policy node and then click New.
2. Type a meaningful name for the policy and click Next.
3. On the Specify Conditions page, click Add and define the characteristics of the connection attempt that you want to check. These are similar to those you can define on a network policy. You can define multiple conditions, all of which must be matched by the connection attempt for the policy to apply. When you have defined all the conditions, click Next.
4. On the Specify Connection Request Forwarding page, shown in Figure 4-64, define the remote RADIUS server group to which the request should be forwarded, or choose the default Authenticate Requests on This Server. Click Accounting and define whether accounting requests should be forwarded to a remote RADIUS server group and then click Next.

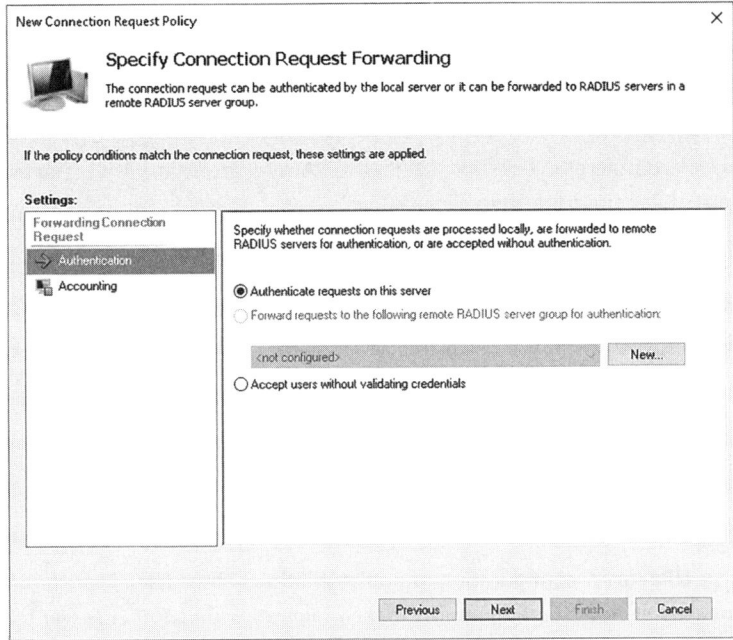

FIGURE 4-64 Defining on which servers to authenticate connection requests

5. On the Specify Authentication Methods page, you can accept the default that the network policy determines any authentication settings. Alternatively, choose Override Network Policy Authentication Settings, and then define any authentication settings for the policy. Click Next.
6. On the Configure Settings page, you can define realm name or RADIUS settings that are applied to connection requests.
7. Review your settings, and click Finish to create the policy. If required, you can reconfigure the precedence order of multiple policies.

> **NEED MORE REVIEW? POLICIES IN NPS**
>
> To review further details about configuring NPS policies, refer to the Microsoft TechNet website at *https://technet.microsoft.com/library/cc772279(v=ws.11).aspx*.

Import and export NPS policies

If you have multiple NPS roles deployed on multiple Windows Server 2016 computers, you can use the same NPS policies on all of them. You can do this by exporting the NPS configuration and the importing that configuration on another server. Use the following procedures to export and import the NPS configuration.

EXPORT NPS CONFIGURATION

To export the NPS configuration, in the Network Policy Server console, right-click the NPS (Local) server and then:

1. Click Export Configuration.
2. In the Export shared secret dialog box, select the I Am Aware That I Am Exporting All Shared Secrets check box, and then click OK.
3. Specify a location to store the export. This is an XML file. Click Save.

IMPORT NPS CONFIGURATION

To import the NPS configuration, in the Network Policy Server console, right-click the NPS (Local) **server and then:**

1. Click Import Configuration.
2. Locate the XML file that contains the exported configuration and double-click it.

EXAM TIP

You can export the NPS server configuration using the Windows PowerShell Export-NpsConfiguration cmdlet. You can then import that configuration on another server by using the Windows PowerShell Import-NpsConfiguration cmdlet.

Configure certificates

You can configure a number of authentication methods in NPS, including PAP, SPAP, CHAP, MS-CHAP and MS-CHAP-v2, EAP, and PEAP. Some of these authentication methods support the exchange of passwords. Although password-based authentication is widely adopted, it is not as secure as certificate-based authentication.

Overview

It is especially important for remote access scenarios that you choose the most secure form of authentication that your remote access infrastructure can support. The following authentication methods always use certificates for server authentication:

- EAP with Transport Layer Security (EAP-TLS)
- PEAP with TLS (PEAP-TLS) or MS-CHAP v2 (PEAP-MS-CHAP v2)

When you use EAP with a strong EAP type, such as TLS (using either smart cards or certificates), you enable mutual authentication in which both the remote access client computer and the NPS server use certificates to identify one another. The certificates you use must match the intended purpose. That is, you must configure a certificate that you use for a client's authentication with the Client Authentication purpose, or a server's authentication with the Server Authentication purpose. If the purpose for the certificate does not match its usage, authentication fails.

> **EXAM TIP**
>
> If you deploy the Active Directory Certificate Services (AD CS) server role to provide certificates for NPS, by default, the AD CS Computer certificate template supports both the Client Authentication and Server Authentication purpose.

To enable authentication for NPS using certificates, you require a number of certificates. These are described in Table 4-4.

TABLE 4-4 CERTIFICATES REQUIRED BY NPS

Certificate	Usage
Certificate Authority (CA) root certificate. This must be placed in the Trusted Root Certification Authorities store for the Local Computer and Current User. This certificate is deployed automatically to computers that are members of an AD DS domain. If a computer does not belong to the appropriate AD DS domain, you must manually import the certificate.	■ This certificate is required for EAP-TLS, PEAP-TLS, and PEAP-MS-CHAP-v2 authentication.
Client computer certificate. All domain member computers enroll this certificate automatically. For computers that do not belong to a domain, you must manually enroll this certificate. If the client computer certificate is deployed on smart cards, you do not need to install the certificate on the computer.	■ Required for EAP-TLS and PEAP-TLS. ■ It is not required for PEAP-MS-CHAP-v2 because user authentication is password-based.
Server computer certificate. This must reside on the NPS server. You can deploy this certificate using AD DS to all members of the RAS and Information Access Service (IAS) servers group. The NPS server send his certificate to client computers who use the certificate to identify the NPS server.	■ This certificate is required for EAP-TLS, PEAP-TLS, and PEAP-MS-CHAP-v2 authentication.
User certificate on a smart card. For EAP-TLS and PEAP-TLS, user certificates on smart cards are required unless you auto-enroll client computer certificates.	■ Required for EAP-TLS and PEAP-TLS. ■ It is not required for PEAP-MS-CHAP-v2 because user authentication is password-based.

> **NEED MORE REVIEW?** **CERTIFICATES AND NPS**
>
> To review further details about configuring certificates for NPS, refer to the Microsoft TechNet website at *https://technet.microsoft.com/library/cc772401(v=ws.10).aspx*.

Configure certificate authentication with NPS

When you create an NPS policy, you can define the authentication method and type, as shown in Figure 4-65. You can select one or more of these authentication methods within your policy. If the connecting client computer does not support or is not configured to use the specified method, the policy does not apply.

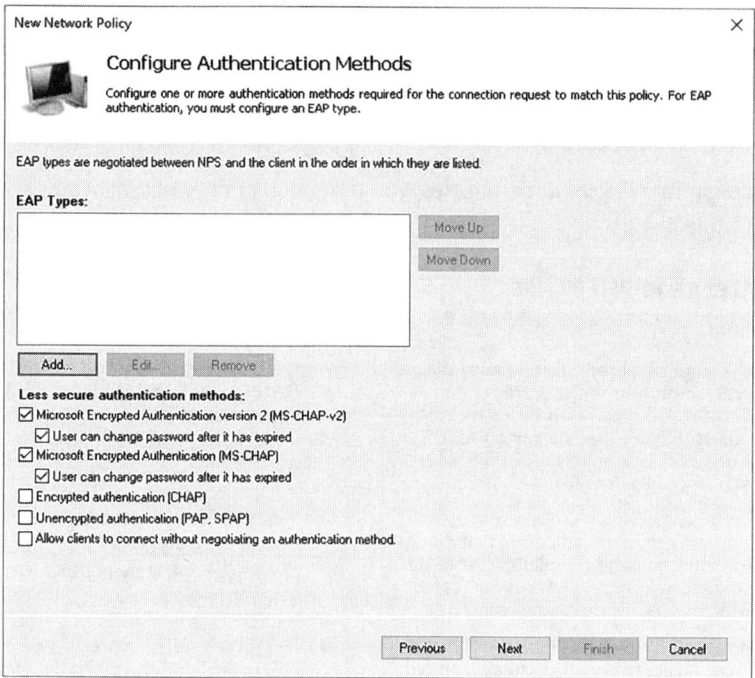

FIGURE 4-65 Configuring authentication

To configure certificate-based authentication, choose EAP, and then select an EAP type. To configure an EAP type:

1. In the New Policy Wizard, on the Configure Authentication Methods page, under EAP Types, click Add.

2. In the Add EAP dialog box, shown in Figure 4-66, choose the authentication method you want. For example, click Microsoft: Secured password (EAP-MSCHAP v2) and click OK.

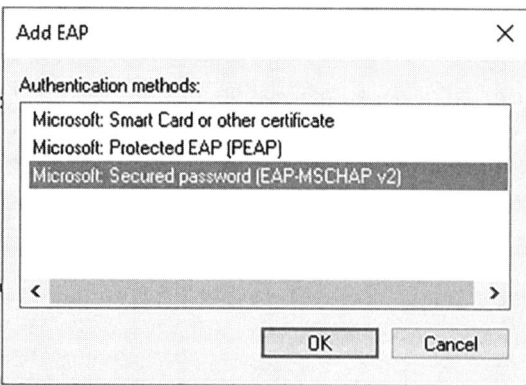

FIGURE 4-66 Configuring authentication

3. Complete the New Policy Wizard in the usual way.

You must now configure the client computers with the required authentication settings. You must also distribute the required certificates to both the client and server computers.

Chapter summary

- NAT enables you to connect devices that have private IPv4 addresses to the public Internet.
- NAT is installed as part of the Routing role service, which is part of the Remote Access server role.
- The NAT service can provide name resolution and DHCP allocated IPv4 addresses for internal clients, if desired.
- The Windows Server 2016 NAT service enables you to publish internal services which are located on the private network to clients on the Internet.
- You can implement both site-to-site and remote access VPNs using Windows Server 2016.
- Windows Server 2016 supports the creation of VPNs based on the PPTP, L2TP/IPsec, SSTP, or IKEv2 protocols.
- VPN reconnect requires an IKEv2-based VPN.
- Site-to-site VPNs in Windows Server 2016 can be configured as demand-dial interfaces with packet filters, available hours, and persistency settings.
- A DirectAccess server must be domain-joined, but cannot be a domain controller.
- GPOs are used to distribute DirectAccess client settings.
- You can implement NPS as a RADIUS server or a RADIUS proxy, but not a RADIUS client.
- When you configure a connection request policy on an NPS computer, and define a remote RADIUS server, you define the local server as a RADIUS proxy.
- You can log RADIUS accounting data to either a text file, or to a SQL Server database, or both.
- NPS templates enable you to more quickly configure shared secrets, RADIUS client, remote RADIUS servers, and IP filters for use in NPS policies.
- If a network policy's conditions are met, even if the policy denies a connection attempt, NPS does not process further policies.
- You can export and import an NPS computer's configuration by using the Network Policy Server console or Windows PowerShell.

Thought experiment

In this thought experiment, demonstrate your skills and knowledge of the topics covered in this chapter. You can find answer to this thought experiment in the next section.

You work in support at facilities management company. As a consultant, answer the following questions about network connectivity within your customers' networks:

1. You have a customer with a branch office that has about twenty staff, each with a personal computer running Windows 10. The branch office has a single Windows Server 2016 computer that provides basic network services. How would you configure Internet network connectivity for this branch office using the server? What are the requirements of your solution?

2. How will you configure clients at this customer site with the correct IP address settings so that they can connect to the Internet?

3. Your customer wants to make a web server available to users on the Internet. How could you make this configuration change?

4. You have been tasked with planning a DirectAccess deployment for A Datum. Only users in the Sales department will be using DirectAccess. Using the Getting Started Wizard, how could you configure this?

5. After applying your strategy to the above requirement, you find that not all sales computers are able to access internal resources when connected externally. What should you do?

6. You are responsible for planning a remote access solution for A. Datum's sales team. The remote users will connect using VPNs. You know that at certain times of the day, many users will attempt to connect to resources at the head office. You decide to implement multiple NPS servers to help distribute the load of these connection attempts. How might you achieve this?

7. You find yourself frequently configuring the same RADIUS clients for your RADIUS proxies. How could you more quickly configure these RADIUS clients on your RADIUS proxies?

8. What are IP Filters templates used for in NPS?

Thought experiment answers

This section contains the solution to the thought experiment. Each answer explains why the answer choice is correct.

1. You can install NAT by adding the Routing role service on the server. This requires two network adapters in the server, one connected to the private network and one to the Internet. You could configure the NAT service so that it provided DHCP and DNS name resolution for internal clients.

2. After installing NAT, if you opt to use the DHCP allocator in NAT, there is nothing further to do, because the clients are configured to use the NAT server as their default gateway. However, if you opted to manually configure networked clients, you must manually assign the private IPv4 address of the NAT server as the default gateway for all clients on the private network.

3. You can modify the configuration of the NAT server so that it published the HTTP port. To complete this task, you must know the private IPv4 address of the server on the internal network. You can then use the Services and Ports page of the Internet interface of the NAT server to define the location of the internal web server.

4. You can create a global security group called Sales_Computers. Next, you can add the computers for all sales users to that group. Next, in the Getting Started wizard, you can modify the Remote Clients settings to use only the newly-created group.

5. Use standard network troubleshooting techniques to determine whether those computers are obtaining an appropriate IPv6 address. Next, verify correct application of the DirectAccess Client Settings GPO by using the gpresult command. Finally, run the *Netsh name show effectivepolicy* command to verify whether DirectAccess settings are being applied.

6. To achieve load balancing for remote access connection attempts by using NPS, you must deploy multiple NPS computers. Configure connection request policies on some of these NPS computers such that remote RADIUS servers are used to perform authentication for remote connection attempts. This creates a deployment scenario based on RADIUS servers and RADIUS proxies.

7. You can create a number of RADIUS client templates and use these on the RADIUS proxies when adding a RADIUS client.

8. You use IP Filters templates in NPS to define the characteristics of network traffic in terms of protocol and port, and whether that traffic is allowed or blocked. After you define these templates, you can use them in network policies to control the type of traffic permitted by selecting the appropriate IP Filters template on the Configure Settings page in the New Policy Wizard.

CHAPTER 5

Implement core and distributed network solutions

At the heart of any properly implemented network infrastructure is a firm foundation based on core network solutions and, where necessary, distributed network solutions. Core networking starts with a properly planned and implemented Internet Protocol version 4 (IPv4) and Internet Protocol version 6 (IPv6) infrastructures. In Windows Server 2016, you can implement distributed network solutions by using features such as BranchCache and the Distributed File System (DFS).

Skills in this chapter:

- Implement IPv4 and IPv6 addressing
- Implement DFS and Branch Office solutions

Skill 5.1: Implement IPv4 and IPv6 addressing

To configure Windows Server 2016 networking settings correctly, you must understand how to implement IP addressing. This includes being able to implement both IPv4 and IPv6 subnetting and routing. The 70-741 Networking Windows Server 2016 exam also covers how to configure the Border Gateway Protocol (BGP), and how to configure IPv4 and IPv6 interoperability by using Intra-Site Automatic Tunnel Addressing Protocol (ISA-TAP), 6to4, or Teredo.

Implement IPv4 addressing

Before you can configure more advanced network settings, you must have a grasp of the IPv4 fundamentals, including how to plan and implement IPv4 addressing.

Configure IPv4 addresses

IPv4 is a mature networking protocol and is widely used on almost all Internet-connected devices. You must assign each device on an IPv4 network a unique IPv4 configuration that identifies that device. This configuration is based on a number of elements.

- **An IPv4 address** IPv4 uses a 32-bit binary address, which is divided into four octets (or groups of eight digits), each of which is converted to a decimal number. Thus: 1100 000010101000000100010000001 becomes 11000000.10101000.00010001.00000001 and converts to: 192.168.17.1.

- **A subnet mask** A subnet mask is also a 32-bit binary string, entered as four decimal digits, and is used to indicate the client's unique identity, known as the host ID, and the subnet where the client resides, known as the network ID. By convention, subnet masks use high order contiguous bits. For example: 11111111.11111111.00000000.00000000. This binary string converts to 255.255.0.0 in decimal. Often, subnet masks are expressed as the number of contiguous 1 bits. In the preceding example, the mask would be expressed as /16 because there are 16 contiguous 1s in the mask.

- **A default gateway address** To facilitate communications between network segments, or subnets, each device is assigned the IPv4 address of a router in the local network that is used to forward network traffic destined for devices in other subnets.

- **A Domain Name System (DNS) server address** DNS enables the device to resolve names into IPv4 or IPv6 addresses. It also enables devices to determine the location of services on the network, including authentication services.

PUBLIC AND PRIVATE ADDRESSING

Devices, or hosts, that connect directly to the Internet require a unique public IPv4 configuration. However, due to a limitation of the 32-bit addressing scheme of IPv4, there is a limit to the number of hosts that can be connected to the Internet using a public configuration. To alleviate this potential but significant problem, many organizations use private IPv4 configurations for their network devices, only using public IPv4 configurations for Internet-facing devices, such as routers.

The Internet Assigned Numbers Authority (IANA) has defined the address ranges shown in Table 5-1 as being available for private use. A technology, such as network address translation (NAT), is used to allow devices using private IPv4 configurations to communicate with the Internet.

TABLE 5-1 Private IPv4 address ranges

Class	Mask	Range
A	10.0.0.0/8	10.0.0.0–10.255.255.255
B	172.16.0.0/12	172.16.0.0–172.31.255.255
C	192.168.0.0/16	192.168.0.0–192.168.255.255

Generally, you assign devices within your organization an IPv4 address from one of these private address ranges, with the exception of Internet-facing devices. Most smaller organizations select the Class C 192.168.0.0 range, while larger organizations with more hosts opt for the Class B or Class A ranges, subnetting where appropriate within the private address space.

Configure IPv4 subnetting

A subnet is a network segment. One or more routers separate the subnet from other subnets. Each subnet within an organization's network infrastructure has a unique ID, just as each host within a subnet has a unique ID. You must use the 32 bits of an IPv4 address to define both the host's ID and the subnet ID in which that host resides.

SIMPLE NETWORKS

Remember that each 32-bit IPv4 address is divided into four octets. In simple IPv4 subnetting, whole octets are reserved for defining the subnet portion of the IPv4 address, as shown in Figure 5-1. Consequently, the remaining whole octets are available for defining the host portion of the address.

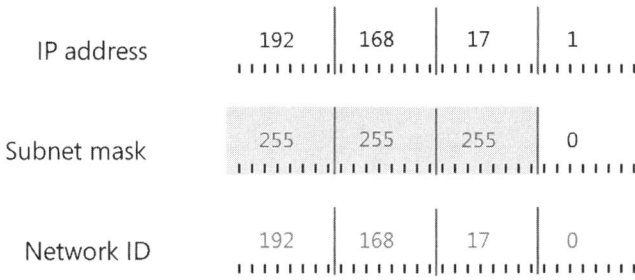

FIGURE 5-1 An IPv4 address using a simple Class C network addressing scheme

This simple subnetting is referred to as classful addressing, by which the address class, A, B, or C, defines the number of octets reserved for host and subnet IDs. Table 5-2 shows how this works.

TABLE 5-2 Characteristics of the default IPv4 address classes

Class	First octet	Default subnet mask	Number of networks	Number of hosts per network
A	1 to 127	255.0.0.0	126	16,777,214
B	128 to 191	255.255.0.0	16,384	65,534
C	192 to 223	255.255.255.0	2,097,152	254

> **NOTE OTHER ADDRESS CLASSES**
>
> There are also class D and class E addresses. Class D addresses are used for multicasting when a client device is part of a group. Class E addresses are reserved and are not used for hosts or subnets.

COMPLEX NETWORKS

For some situations, using a classful addressing scheme can be ideal. But for many situations, it might be important to have more flexibility over the number of bits allocated to the subnet address portion of an IPv4 address. For example, instead of using 8, 16, or 24 bits for the subnet, you can use 12 or 18. Indeed, you can use almost any number of bits.

Bear in mind that the more bits you allocate to subnetting, the fewer bits remain for the host portion of the IPv4 address. That is, you can have more subnets, each containing fewer hosts, or you can have few subnets, each containing many hosts. Figure 5-2 shows how changing the subnet mask changes the subnet ID without changing the octets that define the whole IPv4 address. This scheme is often referred to as classless addressing, or Classless Interdomain Routing (CIDR).

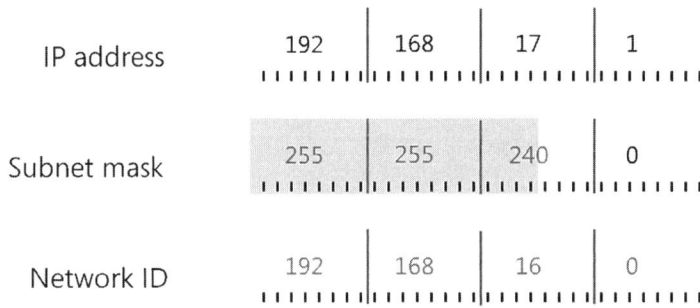

FIGURE 5-2 An IPv4 address using a classless network addressing scheme

In Figure 5-2, notice how changing the subnet mask from 255.255.255.0 to 255.255.240.0 shifts the device from subnet 192.168.17.0 to 192.168.16.0. In this case, by shifting the mask to the left, we have allocated more bits to describe hosts in each subnet, with correspondingly fewer subnets. You can see that to express a host's IPv4 configuration properly, not only must you state the IPv4 address, but you must also state the subnet mask. For example, in Figure 5-2, this host has an IPv4 configuration of 192.168.17.1/255.255.240.0.

EXAM TIP

You often see devices with IPv4 configurations shown as 192.168.17.1/20. The number after the slash denotes the number of contiguous binary 1s in the subnet mask (20 in this instance). If the mask were 255.255.248.0, that would be represented as /21.

Consider the following example:

- **Host 1**   IP address: 192.168.16.1/24
- **Host 2**   IP address: 192.168.17.1/24

Using the mask /24, or 255.255.255.0, these hosts are in different subnets. That is, Host 1 is in 192.168.16.0 while Host 2 is in subnet 192.168.17.0. Now, if we adjust the subnet mask by four bits, it becomes /20, or 255.255.240.0. This places both hosts in the same subnet: 192.168.16.0/20.

DETERMINING THE SUBNET MASK

You must choose a suitable subnet mask for your organization when planning an IPv4 intranet. To calculate a subnet mask, use the following process:

1. **Determine the number of subnets you need** When making this determination, consider the following:
   - **Number of physical segments** The number of physical segments determines the minimum number of subnets required.
   - **Number of hosts per segment** More hosts require more bits in the IPv4 address. More host bits means fewer subnet bits.
2. **Convert the number of subnets into binary** For example if you require 12 subnets, it is expressed in binary as 1100. This is four bits. In other words, you require four bits of binary to express 12 subnet IDs.
3. **Convert these four bits to high order contiguous bits in an octet** That is, 11110000. This is where some people get confused. "How does 1100 convert to 1111?" they ask. It doesn't. The process we use in step 3 determines the *number* of bits we need. It's worth noting that we need the same number of bits to express 14 (which is 1110).
4. **Convert this octet to decimal** In this case, 240. This is your decimal mask.
5. **Apply your decimal mask to your chosen network ID** For example, if you are using the network ID of 172.16.0.0, and you calculated the mask as 240, the full mask is 255.255.240.0 because 172 is a class B address.

DETERMINING THE SUBNET ADDRESSES

After you have calculated your subnet mask, you must determine the address of each subnet. This process is usually done in binary but, in fact, you can use a simple decimal cheat. Let's continue with the example of using a mask of 240. In Table 5-3, the possible permutations of those four bits are listed.

TABLE 5-3 Calculating subnet IDs

Binary mask	Subnet address
00000000	0
00010000	16
00100000	32
00110000	48
01000000	64
01010000	80
01100000	96
01110000	**112**
10000000	**128**
10010000	**144**
10100000	**160**
10110000	**176**
11000000	**192**
11010000	**208**
11100000	**224**
11110000	**240**

If you look at these numbers, you can see that each one is 16 more than the preceding one. This is the decimal value of 00010000; that is, the lowest value bit in the mask. So, if you know what the lowest value in the bit mask is, you can quickly calculate, in decimal, the subnet IDs.

Here's another example. Imagine your mask is 224. The lowest value bit in the mask if expressed in binary is 00100000. As a decimal, this is 32. Therefore, they increment by 32. The first subnet ID is 0, the next 32, the third is 64, and so on.

DETERMINING THE HOST ADDRESSES FOR EACH SUBNET

When you have determined your subnet IDs, you must determine the available host IDs in each subnet. The first host is always one binary digit higher than the subnet ID, and the last possible host is two binary digits lower than the next subnet ID. In our example, for subnet 172.16.16.0/20, the first host ID is 172.16.16.1, and the last is 172.16.31.254. Table 5-4 shows the rest of the range of host IDs for all subnets in our example.

EXAM TIP

One binary digit lower than the next subnet ID is the broadcast address for the current subnet. Thus, 172.16.31.255 is the broadcast address for subnet 172.16.16.0/20 and cannot be allocated to a host.

TABLE 5-4 Host IDs

Binary bit values	Decimal value	Beginning range	End range
00000000	0	x.x.0.1	x.x.0.254
00010000	16	x.x.16.1	x.x.31.254
00100000	32	x.x.32.1	x.x.47.254
00110000	48	x.x.48.1	x.x.63.254
01000000	64	x.x.64.1	x.x.79.254
01010000	80	x.x.80.1	x.x.95.254
01100000	96	x.x.96.1	x.x.111.254
01110000	112	x.x.112.1	x.x.127.254
10000000	128	x.x.128.1	x.x.143.254
10010000	144	x.x.144.1	x.x.159.254
10100000	160	x.x.160.1	x.x.175.254
10110000	176	x.x.176.1	x.x.191.254
11000000	192	x.x.192.1	x.x.207.254
11010000	208	x.x.208.1	x.x.223.254
11100000	224	x.x.224.1	x.x.239.254
11110000	240	x.x.240.1	x.x.240.254

SUPERNETTING

Supernetting uses bits that are normally assigned to the network address to mask them as host bits. For example, rather than allocate a class B network address to an organization, several class C addresses can be assigned. Eight class C subnets gives 2,032 hosts.

However, this means complicated routing with many entries in the route tables because there are now eight networks instead of one. CIDR is used to collapse these routing entries into single entry.

> **NEED MORE REVIEW?** **IPV4 ADDRESSING**
>
> To review further details about IPv4 subnetting and addressing, refer to the Microsoft TechNet website at *https://technet.microsoft.com/library/dd379547(v=ws.10).aspx*.

Plan an IPv4 addressing scheme

You must plan your IPv4 network addressing scheme carefully.

CONSIDERATIONS

Before choosing a scheme, consider the following factors:

- **Whether you need a public or private addressing scheme** For almost all organizations, a private IP addressing scheme is used internally, and public IP addresses are used only on those devices with a physical connection to the Internet.

- **How many networks you need** This is largely determined by how many locations you have, what infrastructure is used to connect them, and how many physical segments you have at each location.
- **How many subnets you need** The same factors mentioned earlier determine how many subnets you need, but you must also consider network bandwidth. The more devices you connect to a subnet, the more network traffic you have. Using subnets is one way to split network traffic.
- **How many hosts per subnet you envisage** This is largely determined by the maximum network bandwidth available; more hosts equals more traffic.
- **Your subnet mask** Try to implement a single subnet mask across your organization.

A SUGGESTED PROCESS

The planning process consists of the following steps:

1. Select an address class that gives you sufficient subnets and hosts per subnet. A class B address should be fine for almost anyone's needs. Smaller organizations can manage with class C.
2. Work out how many subnets you need (remember to include WAN connections).
3. Modify the default mask for your chosen address class to your needs.

EXAM TIP

Remember, the way to do this is: convert the number of subnets you think you need (plus a little for growth) into binary. See how many binary bits are needed to express that number. Add that number of bits to the default mask. For example, suppose you need 12 subnets in a class B network. In binary that is 1100, which is four bits. Adding four bits to the default class B mask means 20 bits in total. The mask now becomes 255.255.240.0.

4. Determine your subnet IDs.
5. Determine the host ranges for each subnet.
6. Implement your plan by using static IP configuration, or by using DHCP.

Configure an IPv4 host

You must assign each Windows Server 2016 host on an IPv4 network a unique IPv4 configuration that identifies that server. You can manually configure the IPv4 address, or use DHCP to assign the required configuration.

To configure IPv4 on a Windows Server computer, right-click Start, and then click Network Connections. Right-click the appropriate network interface card, and then click Properties. Double-click Internet Protocol Version 4 (TCP/IPv4). Then configure the required information, as shown in Figure 5-3.

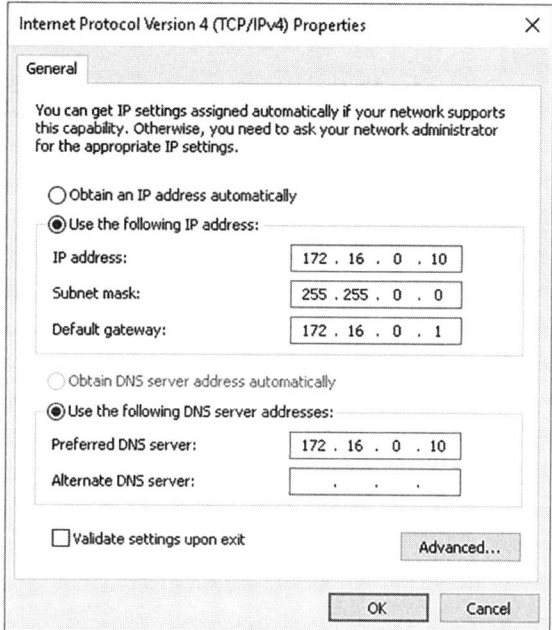

FIGURE 5-3 Configuring an IPv4 host

Alternatively, you can use the Windows PowerShell New-NetIPAddress cmdlet. For example:

```
New-NetIPAddress -InterfaceAlias "Ethernet" -IPAddress 172.16.16.10 -PrefixLength 20 -DefaultGateway 172.16.16.1
```

Implement IPv6 addressing

As with IPv4, you must be able to implement an IPv6 addressing scheme within your organization before you can progress to implementing services that rely on IPv6, such as DirectAccess.

An overview of IPv6

IPv6 offers a number of advantages over IPv4 and, as a consequence, many organizations are beginning to implement this protocol. The main benefits of using IPv6 are:

- **Increased address space** Because IPv6 uses 128 bits to express an address, it offers an almost limitless address space. Where currently, IPv4 private addresses and NAT are used to circumvent the limits of a 32-bit address, with IPv6, each node on the Internet could have an individual public address.
- **Improved routing** In some ways, IPv4 has evolved rather than been designed. Nowhere is this more true than with routing. The IPv4 address space is not optimized for routing because it does not contain hierarchical information that enables network

packets to be routed efficiently. IPv6 is different, with part of the address space used to indicate the routing infrastructure.

- **Simpler configuration**   With IPv4, network administrators must use DHCP to allocate IPv4 configurations. Otherwise, hosts must be manually configured. With IPv6, an administrator can choose between using DHCPv6 to provide stateful autoconfiguration, or router announcements to provide for stateless autoconfiguration, or even hybrid solutions, where both stateful and stateless autoconfiguration is used.
- **Improved security**   In order to secure IPv4 network traffic, additional components, such as Internet Protocol security (IPsec), are used. IPv6 provides for built-in authentication and encryption.
- **Better real-time data delivery**   In order to support some apps, IPv6 provides for improved, built-in Quality of Service (QoS).

EXAM TIP

IPv6 uses Stateless Address Auto Configuration (SLAAC) to provide simple plug and play networking.

Determine and configure appropriate IPv6 addresses

As we mentioned, an IPv6 address consists of 128 bits. It can be difficult to express an address of this size, even in decimal. Consequently, IPv6 addresses are expressed in hexadecimal, or Base 16.

IPV6 ADDRESS FORMAT

It can be daunting when you begin to work with IPv6 addresses, but in fact, the process is similar to using IPv4 addresses. With IPv4, the 32-bit binary address is broken into four octets, or groups, of eight binary digits:

11000000.10101000.00010001.00000001

Each octet is then converted to decimal, and separated by a period:

192.168.17.1

With IPv6, the 128-bit binary address is broken into eight groups of 16 binary digits. Each block of 16 binary digits is separated into four groups of four bits. For example, here are the first three blocks:

0010 0000 0000 0010 : 0000 1101 1011 0101 : 0000 0000 0000 0000

Each group of four bits is then converted to hexadecimal. Each 16-bit group is separated by a colon from the next group:

2 0 0 2 : 0 D B 5 : 0 0 0 0

When all blocks are converted, you have an eight-part address, with each part separated by colons. The following is an example of a complete IPv6 address:

2002:0DB5:0000:1D4B:01BC:0000:1123:1234

Even this address is quite long. To mitigate this, a process known as zero compression is used to further shorten the address. With zero compression, leading zeros in a 16-bit block are not expressed. In addition, whole contiguous blocks of zeros are replaced with double colons:

2002:DB5::1D4B:1BC:0:1123:1234

Notice that the second block of contiguous zeros (prior to 1123) is not all removed. This is because they are non-contiguous with the preceding 0000 block. However, they are reduced to a single 0. Note that double colons can only be used once in a compressed address without compromising the meaning.

ADDRESS SCOPES AND TYPES

IPv6 uses three scopes of address. These are:

- **Unicast**   Identifies a single interface on a host. There are several types of unicast address in IPv6:
    - **Global unicast addresses**   Much like public IPv4 addresses, these are globally accessible on the Internet. The first three bits of a global unicast address start 001. Consequently, all global unicast addresses begin with a hexadecimal 2 or 3. The next 45 bits of a global unicast address represent an organization's site, with the subsequent 16 bits available for subnetting within the organization. The last 64 bits express the host interfaces.
    - **Unique local addresses**   Similar to private IPv4 addresses, these addresses are routable throughout an organization, but not the Internet.
    - **Link-local addresses**   Link-local addresses behave like IPv4 Automatic Private IP Addressing (APIPA) addresses. They are non-routable and automatically generated.

EXAM TIP

Link-local addresses, unlike APIPA addresses in IPv4, perform a useful function in IPv6 connectivity. For example, they are used by IPv6 hosts when communicating with a DHCP server. In IPv4, this communication is performed with broadcasts.

- **Special addresses**   These include unspecified addresses and loopback addresses.
- **Compatibility or transition addresses**   Used for interoperability between IPv4 and IPv6 environments, typically when an organization is in transition between the two.
- **Multicast**   Identifies multiple interfaces on multiple hosts. Multicast addresses are used by apps on multiple hosts that communicate with many hosts simultaneously, such as deployment software.
- **Anycast**   Identifies multiple interfaces on multiple hosts. Packets addressed to an anycast address are routed to the nearest interface identified by the anycast address.

EXAM TIP

IPv6 addresses always identify interfaces rather than nodes. A node is identified by any unicast address assigned to one of its interfaces. The interface identifier is based on the media access control (MAC) address of the network adapter, or it is assigned by DHCPv6, or is randomly generated.

Configure IPv6 subnetting

As we have seen, an IPv4 address consists of a network ID, a subnet ID, and a host ID. The same is true of an IPv6 address. The most significant bits—those at the beginning of the address—are called the *prefix* and represent the IPv6 network and subnet IDs. The number of bits allocated to the prefix is indicated by a similar notation to that used in CIDR with IPv4. For example, 2002:DB5::/48 is a route prefix, and 2002:DB5:0:1D4B::/64 is a subnet prefix.

When you assign a unicast IPv6 address to a host, you use a 64-bit prefix. This leaves 64 bits in the address, which are allocated to the *interface identifier*. This identifies the host on that network. You can identify the type of unicast address by its prefix:

- Global unicast addresses have the prefix of 2000::/3.
- Unique local addresses have an address prefix of FD::/8.
- Link-local addresses have a prefix of FE80::/64.

Implement IPv6 stateless addressing

IPv6 supports both stateful and stateless autoconfiguration. Stateful autoconfiguration requires a DHCP server configured with IPv6 scopes.

EXAM TIP

Configuring a DHCPv6 scope is covered in Chapter 2, Implement DHCP: "Implement IPv6 addressing using DHCPv6."

Stateless autoconfiguration relies on Router Advertisements messages. During stateless IPv6 autoconfiguration, an IPv6 host uses the following process, shown in Figure 5-4, to configure a valid IPv6 address:

1. Creates a unique link-local address.
2. Discovers routers on the network.
3. Determines which prefixes have been configured on any discovered routers.
4. Applies those prefixes locally.
5. Contacts a DHCP server to obtain other IPv6 configuration information, but only if either the *Managed Address Configuration* or *Other Stateful Configuration* flags are set. These two flags are used by routers in combination to instruct IPv6 hosts on how to complete their IPv6 configuration:

- **Both flags are 0** There is no DHCP, and hosts must rely on router advertisements and manual configuration for their settings. This is known as stateless autoconfiguration.
- **Both flags are 1** This is known as stateful autoconfiguration, where hosts use DHCPv6 for both addresses and other IPv6 configuration settings.
- **The Managed Address Configuration flag is 0 and the Other Stateful Configuration flag is 1** Known as DHCPv6 stateless. In this scenario, hosts do not use DHCPv6 to obtain addresses, but only to obtain other configuration settings.
- **The Managed Address Configuration flag is 1 and the Other Stateful Configuration flag is 0** In this scenario, hosts use DHCPv6 to obtain an address but not for other settings. This is not often used because hosts need to be configured with other settings, such as DNS details.

6. The host applies the DHCPv6 settings according to the flags set in the router advertisement.

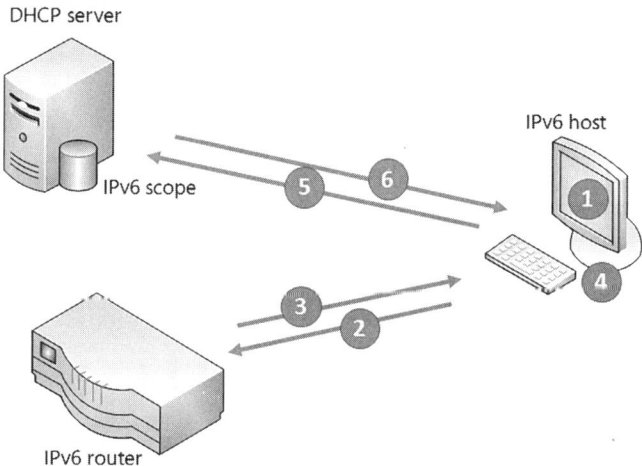

FIGURE 5-4 Obtaining a stateless IPv6 configuration

> **NEED MORE REVIEW? IPV6**
>
> To review further details about IPv6 addressing, refer to the Microsoft TechNet website at *https://technet.microsoft.com/library/cc755011(v=ws.10).aspx*.

Configure an IPv6 host

You must assign each device on an IPv6 network a unique IPv6 configuration that identifies that device. You can do this by using manual configuration of your IPv6 hosts, by using stateful autoconfiguration, and also by using stateless autoconfiguration.

Compared with IPv4 hosts, which are usually assigned a single IPv4 address, most IPv6 hosts are assigned multiple IPv6 addresses. Typically, an IPv6 network interface is assigned at least two addresses:

- A link-local address, used for traffic on the local link.
- A unicast address (either a global or a unique local), used for traffic routed outside the local link.

However you choose to implement IPv6, each host configuration is based on a number of elements, as shown in Figure 5-5.

- An IPv6 address
- A subnet prefix length
- A default gateway address
- A Domain Name System (DNS) server address

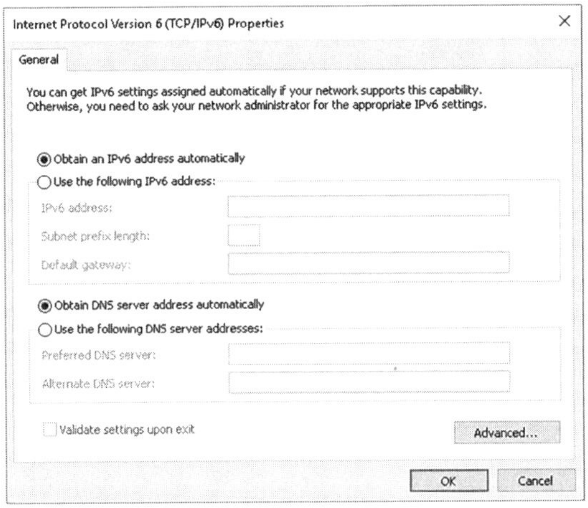

FIGURE 5-5 Configuring an IPv6 host

To configure IPv6 on a Windows Server computer, right-click Start, and then click Network Connections. Right-click the appropriate network interface card, and then click Properties. Double-click Internet Protocol Version 6 (TCP/IPv6).

Alternatively, you can use the Windows PowerShell New-NetIPAddress cmdlet. For example:

```
New-NetIPAddress -InterfaceAlias "Ethernet" -IPAddress
2002:DB5::1D4B:1BC:0:1123:1234 -PrefixLength 64 -DefaultGateway
2002:DB5::1D4B:1BC:0:DC0B:ABCD
```

Configure interoperability between IPv4 and IPv6

Because many organizations still use IPv4 as their primary networking transport protocol, and implementing IPv6 only as and when needed, it might be necessary for you to configure interoperability between these two network transport protocols. You can achieve this by implementing tunneling between the two environments. This section explores the methods available for implementing IPv4 and IPv6 interoperability.

Overview of IPv4 and IPv6 interoperability

Although IPv6 offers many advantages over IPv4, it is unlikely that your organization can move to a wholly IPv6-based network infrastructure now. This is because many apps and services still rely on IPv4.

However, it is increasingly likely that you might implement apps and service that require IPv6. Consequently, you must be able to configure your hosts and infrastructure to support both network protocols.

When considering how best to implement IPv6 in a predominantly IPv4-based network infrastructure, you have a number of options, including implementing both protocols on some or all hosts and devices, or implementing a tunneling solution.

IPv6 over IPv4 tunneling encapsulates IPv6 packets in an IPv4 packet, as shown in Figure 5-6, so that the IPv6 data can be routed through a predominantly IPv4-based infrastructure.

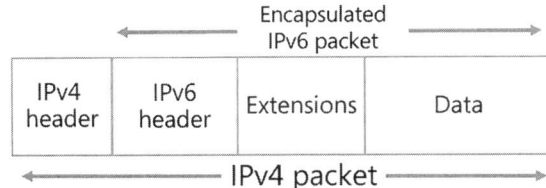

FIGURE 5-6 Encapsulated IPv6 packet

You can implement a tunneling solution in Windows Server 2016 by using:

- **ISATAP**   Enables connectivity over an IPv4 intranet between IPv6/IPv4 hosts.
- **6to4**   Enables connectivity between IPv6 hosts over the Internet.
- **Teredo**   Enables connectivity between IPv6 hosts over the Internet, but supports NAT.

Configure and implement ISATAP

You use ISATAP to enable IPv6 communications between configured hosts in an IPv4 Intranet. Hosts are configured with both IPv4 and IPv6.

EXAM TIP

Hosts enabled with both protocols are referred to as *IPv6/IPv4 nodes*. Hosts configured only with IPv4 are referred to as *IPv4 nodes*, while those configured only with IPv6 are *IPv6 nodes*.

When you enable ISATAP, as shown in Figure 5-7, configured ISATAP hosts can communicate:

- Over an IPv4 intranet
- Through an ISATAP-configured router to IPv6 nodes on an IPv6-only network

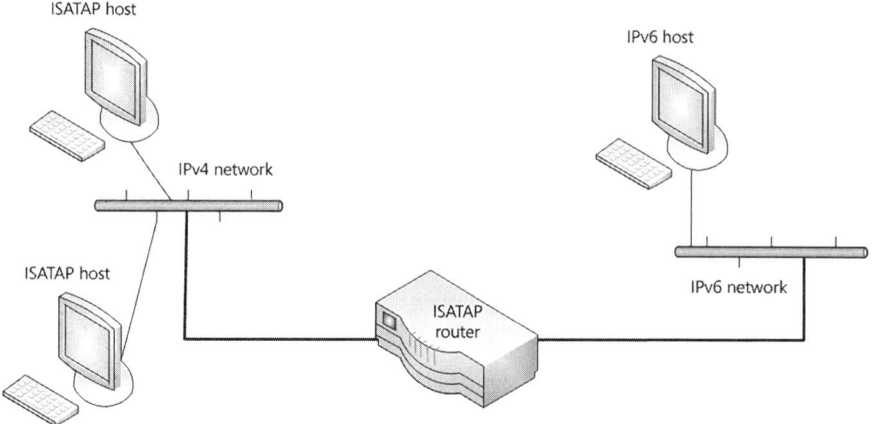

FIGURE 5-7 An ISATAP scenario

When configured, an ISATAP host has an ISATAP address that includes its IPv4 address. If your IPv4 hosts are using a private IP address, the IPv4 element is prefixed with 0:5EFE. Consequently, it looks something like this: [64 bit unicast prefix]:0:5EFE:w.x.y.z.

If your hosts are using public IPv4 addresses, the IPv4 address in the ISATAP address is prefixed with 200:5EFE. As a result, the ISATAP address looks like this: [64 bit unicast prefix]:200:5EFE:w.x.y.z.

For example:

- **Based on private IPv4 address**   FD00::5EFE:172.16.16.10.
- **Based on public IPv4 address**   2002:DB5::200:5EFE:131.107.16.10.

You do not need to manually configure hosts to enable ISATAP. You can rely on automatic configuration through router advertisements. An ISATAP router advertises the required IPv6 prefix for ISATAP hosts to use.

You can enable ISATAP using one of the following methods:

- **Configure an ISATAP host record in DNS**   This record enables clients to resolve the IPv4 address of the configured ISATAP router.

EXAM TIP

Windows Server 2016 DNS servers are configured to block ISATAP resolution by default. You must disable this behavior by removing ISATAP from the global query block list. On the DNS server, use the dnscmd /config /globalqueryblocklist wpad command.

- **Windows PowerShell** The Set-NetIsatapConfiguration -Router x.x.x.x. cmdlet enables ISATAP.
- **Use Group Policy Objects** Configure the ISATAP Router Name Group Policy setting.
- **Netsh** Use the Netsh Interface IPv6 ISATAP Set Router x.x.x.x command.

Configure and implement 6to4

A 6to4 router enables IPv6 connectivity through the IPv4 Internet. As shown in Figure 5-8, you can use 6to4 to enable IPv6 communications between:

- Two IPv6 sites
- An IPv6 host and an IPv6 site

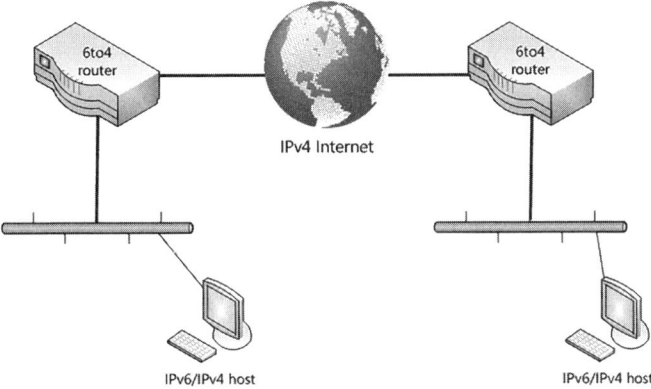

FIGURE 5-8 A 6to4 implementation

EXAM TIP

You cannot use 6to4 in situations requiring NAT.

You must configure a 6to4 router with:

- A public IPv4 address on the Internet-facing interface
- A 6to4 IPv6 address on the internal interface

The configured router then advertises the required addressing information to internal clients. Any client computer using the 6to4 network address is referred to as a *6to4 host*. These 6to4 hosts send 6to4 packets to the router for onward delivery through the IPv4 Internet to other 6to4 sites.

EXAM TIP

The IPv6 address used for 6to4 is based on the IPv4 address of the Internet-facing interface on the IPv6 router and starts with 2002. If your external router interface has the IPv4 address 131.107.20.21, this is converted to hexadecimal and used in the 6to4 address. For example: 2002:836B:1415::836B:1415, where 83 is hex for 131, 6B is hex for 107, 14 is hex for 20, and 15 is hex for 21.

There is no need to configure a Windows Server 2016 computer to use 6to4. If the server is configured with a private IPv4 address, Windows assumes that a NAT is being used, and 6to4 is disabled. If a public IPv4 address is configured on the server computer, Windows configures 6to4 automatically.

To configure a Windows Server 2016 computer as a 6to4 router, use one of the following options:

- **Enable Internet Connection Sharing (ICS) on the server**   When ICS is enabled, the server is automatically configured as a 6to4 router.
- **Windows PowerShell**   Use the Set-Net6to4Configuration -State enabled command to modify the current 6to4 configuration.
- **Netsh**   Use Netsh to create and configure a 6to4 router.

Configure and implement Teredo

Teredo works in a similar way to 6to4, but supports scenarios requiring NAT. Therefore, if you need to enable IPv6 connectivity through the internet, but are using private IPv4 addresses within your organization, choose Teredo as your transition technology, as shown in Figure 5-9.

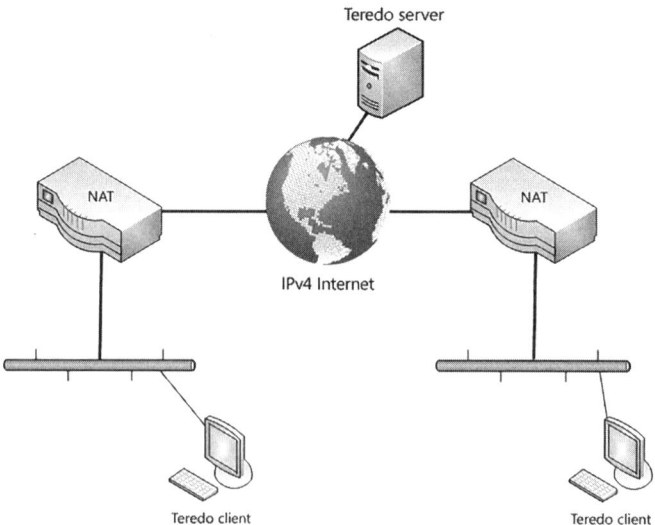

FIGURE 5-9 A Teredo implementation

> **EXAM TIP**
>
> A Teredo server is required to implement this solution. The Teredo server resides on the Internet and is used to initiate communications between Teredo hosts. A number of public Teredo servers are available for this purpose, including teredo.ipv6.microsoft.com, used by default on Windows Server and Windows 10.

As with the other tunneling technologies, Teredo uses specific addressing for clients. A Teredo address uses the 2001::/32 prefix. The remaining 96 bits are used to express the following information:

- The Teredo server address
- Communications options
- Obscured external port
- Obscured external IP address

To configure Teredo on Windows Server 2016, use the Windows PowerShell Set-NetTeredoConfiguration cmdlet.

> **NEED MORE REVIEW?** **IPV6 TRANSITION TECHNOLOGIES**
>
> To review further details about IPv6 transition technologies, refer to the Microsoft TechNet website at *https://technet.microsoft.com/library/dd379548(v=ws.10).aspx*.

Configure IPv4 and IPv6 routing

To deliver network packets from one subnet to another, you must enable and configure routing. You can configure Windows Server 2016 as both an IPv4 or IPv6 router to connect multiple IP subnets.

Routing is the process of managing the flow of network traffic between subnets. In essence, a router only passes traffic that is required to be passed. When a host wants to communicate with another host, the IP layer in the local host examines the source and destination IP addresses for the traffic. The source is the local host's IP address, and the destination is the address of whichever host the local host wants to communicate with. The network and subnetwork IDs of the two addresses are compared.

- If they are different, the local host examines its local routing table to determine an effective route to the destination subnet:
    - If a route is found, IP routes the packet to the next router in sequence.
    - If a route is not found, IP routes the packet to its configured default gateway.
- If the source and destination networks match, no routing is required. IP uses the address resolution protocol (ARP) to determine the MAC address of the destination host and the packet is merged onto the media for local delivery.

Most hosts do not maintain a lengthy or complex routing table, and so almost invariably, an IP host forwards all remotely addressed packets to its configured default gateway.

However, routers do maintain more complex routing tables. These routing tables contain information about what networks exist, and how to reach those networks. The information in the routing table might also contain data about the *cost* of using a particular route and other options. The routing tables can be manually maintained by an administrator, or else automatically configured by the routing protocol itself, depending upon which routing protocols are in use.

There are a number of routing protocols available, including:

- **Routing Information Protocol (RIP)**   Used in small to medium-sized network environments. RIP uses a distance vector to calculate the shortest path to a destination network. It is simple to deploy and configure, but does not scale well to large networks. Routing tables are maintained automatically through the use of router announcements. RIP is an interior gateway protocol (IGP) and is used to distribute routing information within an autonomous system, such as an organization's intranet.

- **Open Shortest Path First (OSPF)**   Used in larger network environments, OSPF is a link-state routing protocol. Each router maintains a database of router advertisements from other routers called Link State Advertisements (LSAs). These LSAs consist of a router, networks attached to the router, and the configured costs of those routes. OSPF scales well to large networks, but can be more difficult to deploy and configure than simple protocols like RIP. OSPF is also an IGP. Windows Server 2016 does not support OSPF when configured as a router.

- **Border Gateway Protocol (BGP)**   Designed for large, enterprise-networked systems. Unlike RIP and OSPF, BGP is an exterior gateway routing protocol and is used to distribute routing information between autonomous systems on the Internet.

A Windows Server 2016 server computer is not the ideal router platform. However, you can enable and configure routing on a Windows Server 2016 computer fairly easily.

Enabling a routing protocol

On Windows Server 2016, to enable routing, use the following procedure:

1. Install the Remote Access server role with Server Manager. When prompted by the Add Roles And Features Wizard, on the Select Role Services page, select the Routing check box.

2. After installation, in Server Manager, click Tools, and then click Routing And Remote Access.

3. In Routing And Remote Access, right-click your server, and then click Configure, and Enable Routing And Remote Access.

4. In the Routing And Remote Access Server Setup Wizard, choose Custom Configuration, and then choose LAN Routing.
5. Complete the wizard and start the LAN Routing service when prompted by clicking Start Service.

After you have installed the Routing and Remote Access service, you must enable and configure the required routing protocols. For example, to add and configure the RIP protocol, use the following procedure:

1. In Routing And Remote Access, expand the IPv4 node, right-click the General node, and then click New Routing Protocol.
2. Click RIP Version 2 For Internet Protocol, as shown in Figure 5-10, and then click OK.

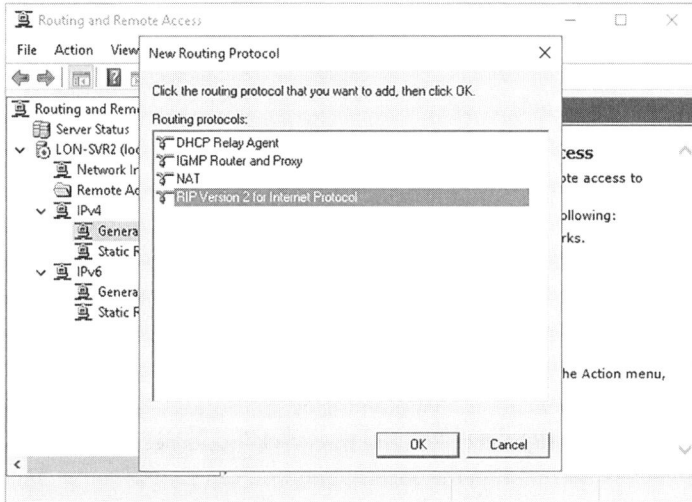

FIGURE 5-10 Adding RIP Version 2

3. In the navigation pane, right-click RIP, and then click New Interface.
4. Select the appropriate interface, and then click OK.
5. The RIP Properties dialog box is displayed, as shown in Figure 5-11.

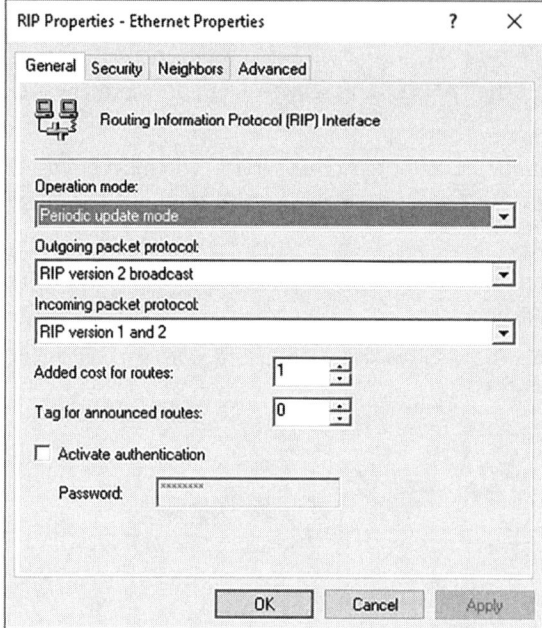

FIGURE 5-11 Configuring RIP for an Ethernet interface

6. If you want to use the default values, click OK. These are generally appropriate. Add any additional network adapters.

7. If you want to customize logging or configure the list of routers with which this server can exchange information, right-click RIP, and then click Properties. You can configure logging on the General tab, and on the Security tab, you can control router announcements.

Configuring routes

Although many routing protocols support dynamic routing table updates, you can also manually configure routes in Windows Server 2016. To modify routing tables, you can use:

- Windows PowerShell
- The route.exe command-line tool
- The Routing And Remote Access console

USING WINDOWS POWERSHELL

Table 5-5 lists the typical routing table functions and the Windows PowerShell cmdlets needed to perform them.

TABLE 5-5 Windows PowerShell routing cmdlets

Function	Cmdlet	Example
View the routing table	Get-NetRoute	Get-NetRoute –AddressFamily IPv4
Add a new route	New-NetRoute	New-NetRoute –InterfaceIndex 10 –DestinationPrefix 10.0.0.0/8 –NextHop 172.16.16.1
Change a route's metric	Set-NetRoute	Set-NetRoute –RouteMetric 257

USING THE ROUTE COMMAND

To use the Route.exe command, open an elevated command prompt. You can then use the following command to add a route:

`Route add 10.0.0.0 netmask 255.0.0.0 172.16.16.1 metric 2`

To display existing routes, use the `route print` command.

USING THE ROUTING AND REMOTE ACCESS CONSOLE

Using the Routing And Remote Access console, to view routes, use the following procedure:

1. Expand the local server, and then expand IPv4.
2. Right-click Static Routes, and then click Show IP Routing Table.

To add a route:

3. Under the IPv4 node, right-click Static Routes, and then click New Static Route.
4. Configure the static route with the appropriate Interface, Destination, Network Mask, and Gateway, and then click OK.

Configure BGP

BGP is used for large, enterprise-level networked systems. It is often implemented by cloud service providers (CSPs) to connect to their tenants' networked sites.

> **EXAM TIP**
>
> BGP reduces your need to configure manual routes on your routers. This is because it is a dynamic routing protocol. It automatically learns routes between sites that are connected with site-to-site Virtual Private Network (VPN) connections.

When you enable and configure BGP on a Windows Server 2016 RAS Gateway in multitenant mode, BGP enables you to manage the network routing between your tenants' networks and their remote sites. You also can implement BGP in single tenant RAS Gateway deployments, and when you deploy Remote Access as a LAN router.

> **NEED MORE REVIEW?** **RAS GATEWAY**
>
> To review further details about using RAS Gateway, refer to the Microsoft TechNet website at *https://technet.microsoft.com/windows-server-docs/networking/remote-access/ras-gateway/ras-gateway*.

To use BGP, first install the Routing role service of the Remote Access server role, or the Remote Access Service (RAS) role.

When you install RAS Gateway, you must specify whether BGP is enabled for each tenant by using the Windows PowerShell Enable-RemoteAccessRoutingDomain –Type All command.

To install a BGP-enabled LAN router without multitenant capabilities, use the Windows PowerShell Install-RemoteAccess –VpnType RoutingOnly command.

> **NEED MORE REVIEW?** **BORDER GATEWAY PROTOCOL**
>
> To review further details about Border Gateway Protocol, refer to the Microsoft TechNet website at *https://technet.microsoft.com/library/mt626647.aspx*.

Skill 5.2: Implement DFS and branch office solutions

Branch offices typically support fewer users, and consequently have less network infrastructure. Often, resources such as file servers and databases are located centrally. Branch office users might be expected to connect to these resources over lower bandwidth connections, posing challenges for the IT department.

Common issues facing IT support staff when implementing branch offices include:

- **Small number of users**   When a branch office has a handful of users, it is hard to justify deploying the same servers, services, and apps to the site as are deployed to the head office.
- **No local IT support**   Often, branch offices have no local IT support, and organizations must rely on remote administration features to support deployed servers and services.
- **Low bandwidth connections**   Many branch offices have slower links to the Internet and to the head office. Sometimes, these links are less reliable than others that support larger numbers of users.
- **Physical security of site**   Branch offices sometimes lack the physical security of the head office. Servers might be placed in the general office rather than in dedicated, secured computer rooms.
- **Use of head office resources**   Despite the fact that links from branches might be unreliable or slow, branch offices tend to reply upon services and apps at the head office. This means that the link becomes more critical.

Windows Server 2016 provides a number of features that can help you to support the specific needs of your branch office users. These features include DFS and BranchCache.

Install and configure DFS namespaces

You can use DFS to replicate files and folders between file servers distributed across your organization. You can implement DFS in a number of configurations to help support the specific needs of your branch and head office users, including using DFS to distribute synchronized copies of files and folders.

What is a DFS namespace?

A DFS namespace provides a virtualized representation of your shared folder structure. For example, let's say that you have three file servers in three cities: London, New York, and Sydney. Each file server has a shared folder called Sales, as shown in Figure 5-12.

Users in the Sales department in Adatum.com want to access all shared sales content on all servers. Currently, your users would need to remember three UNC names for these shared resources: \\LON-SVR1\Sales, \\NYC-SVR1\Sales, and \\SYD-SVR1\Sales.

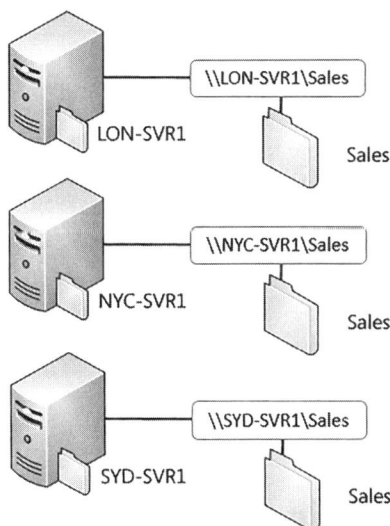

FIGURE 5-12 Distributed shared folder structure

However, if you deployed a DNS namespace—a domain-based namespace in this instance—you could consolidate this distributed structure into a simplified structure that requires only a single UNC: \\Adatum.com\Sales. Each of the shared folders on each of the three servers then becomes a subfolder beneath the \\Adatum.com\Sales UNC shared folder, as shown in Figure 5-13.

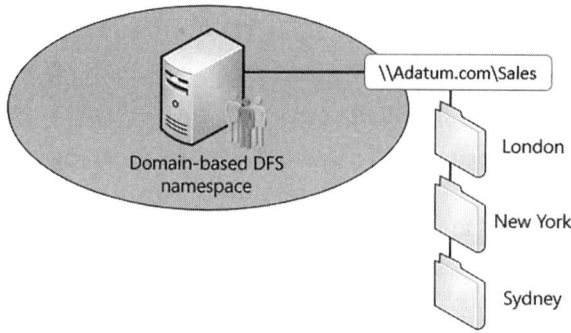

FIGURE 5-13 Consolidated shared folder structure using DFS namespace

Adding the DFS Namespaces role service

You deploy DFS Namespaces by choosing to install the DFS Namespaces role service. This is part of the File Services server role. You can deploy DFS Namespaces by using Server Manager, or by using Windows PowerShell.

To deploy DFS Namespaces with Server Manager, use the following procedure:

1. In Server Manager, click Manage, and then click Add Roles And Features.
2. In the Add Roles And Features Wizard, on the Server Roles page, in the Roles list, expand File And Storage Services, expand File And iSCSI Services, and then select the DFS Namespaces check box.
3. Click Add Features, and then click Next.
4. When prompted, click Install, and when installation is complete, click Finish.

To deploy DFS Namespaces with Windows PowerShell, run the following command:

```
Install-WindowsFeature FS-DFS-Namespace -IncludeManagementTools
```

Configuring DFS Namespaces

DFS Namespaces supports two configurations:

- **Domain-based**   The key advantage of a domain-based DFS namespace is that you can replicate the namespace to provide for high availability.
- **Standalone**   Organizations might consider using a standalone DFS namespace if the organization has not deployed AD DS. Alternatively, if you choose to provide for high availability of your DFS namespace by using a Windows Server failover cluster, you must choose a standalone DFS namespace.

To configure a DFS namespace, you must perform the following procedure:

1. Deploy the DFS Namespaces role service.

2. Create a namespace by using the DFS Manager console, or by using the Windows PowerShell New-DfsnRoot cmdlet. During the namespace creation, you must specify the following information:
   - The name of the server that hosts the namespace.
   - The namespace name.
   - The namespace type (domain-based or standalone).
   - Whether the namespace is enabled for Windows Server 2008 mode. This option provides for additional features and should generally always be selected.

> **NEED MORE REVIEW?** **DFS NAMESPACE CMDLETS**
>
> To review further details about using Windows PowerShell to manage DFS Namespaces, refer to the Microsoft TechNet website at *https://technet.microsoft.com/library/jj884270.aspx*.

3. Define a folder in the namespace that holds the content you want to publish.
4. Add folder targets. These are the UNC names for shared folders on file servers in your organization that you want to make available in the namespace.

For example, to deploy a domain-based DFS namespace, use the following procedure:

1. In Server Manager, click Tools, and then click DFS Management.
2. In the DFS Management console, shown in Figure 5-14, right-click Namespaces, and then click New Namespace.

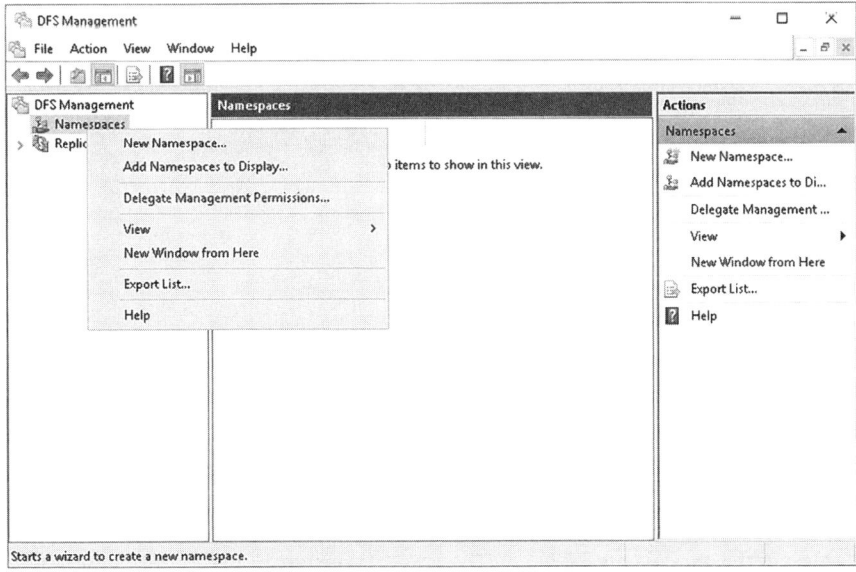

FIGURE 5-14 Adding a new DFS namespace

3. n the Namespace Server page, in the Server box, type the name of the server that host the namespace, and then click Next.

4. On the Namespace Name And Settings page, in the Name box, type the name for the namespace. This is the name that appears after the server or domain name (depending whether you choose standalone or domain-based) in the DFS namespace UNC name. For example, if you type Sales for the domain-based DFS namespace in the domain Adatum.com, the full DFS namespace name is \\Adatum.com\Sales. DFS creates a shared folder with the name you specify. You can click Edit Settings to manually control this behavior.

5. Click Next.

6. On the Namespace Type page, shown in Figure 5-15, click either Domain-Based Namespace, or click Stand-Alone Namespace. Optionally, select the Enable Windows Server 2008 Mode. Click Next.

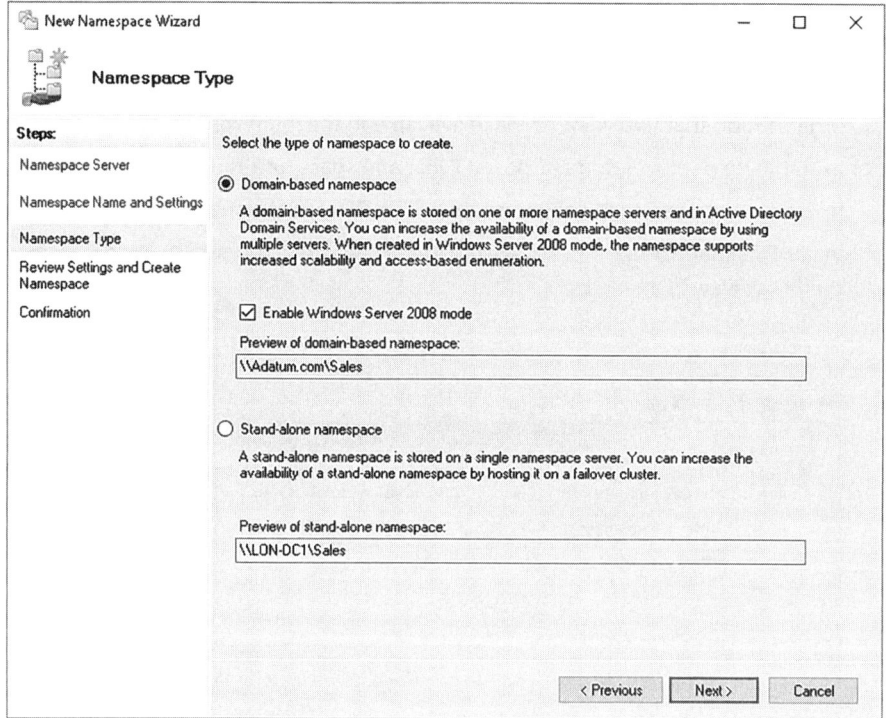

FIGURE 5-15 Defining the namespace type

7. When prompted, click Create, and then click Close.

After you have created the domain-based namespace, you can add namespace servers to it. To complete this process, in the DFS Management console, right-click the new namespace, and then click Add Namespace Server. Enter the name of the new namespace server, and click

OK, as shown in Figure 5-16. A new shared folder is created on the new namespace server automatically, although you can click Edit Settings to manually control this.

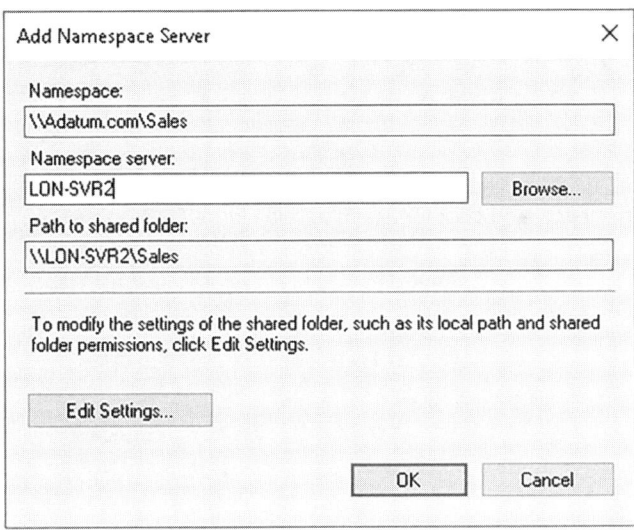

FIGURE 5-16 Adding a namespace server

From the DFS Management console, you can view the configured namespace servers and their status. In the console, click the appropriate namespace in the navigation pane, and then click the Namespace Servers tab, as shown in Figure 5-17.

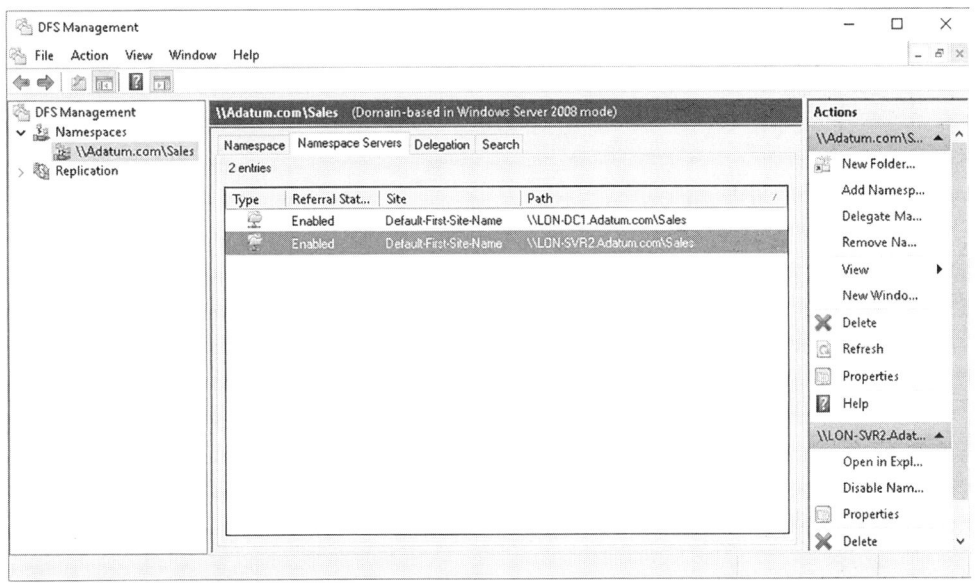

FIGURE 5-17 Viewing the namespace servers

Skill 5.2: Implement DFS and branch office solutions CHAPTER 5 255

Adding folders and folder targets

A folder is the UNC path to a shared folder on a file server in your organization. To create a folder, in the DFS Management console:

1. Right-click the namespace object in the navigation pane, and then click New Folder.
2. In the New Folder dialog box, type the folder name.
3. Then click Add.
4. In the Add Folder Target dialog box, type the UNC path to the shared folder you want to make available in the namespace, and click OK, as shown in Figure 5-18.

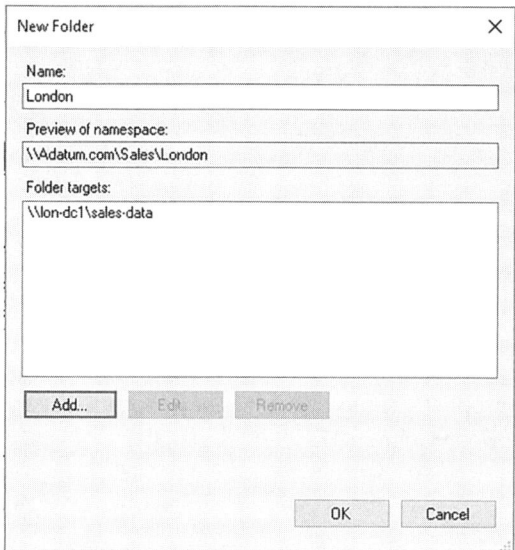

FIGURE 5-18 Adding a folder

Configure DFS replication targets

If you only want a single target for your folder, you have finished. But you can add multiple targets. For example, suppose you wanted two targets for the London folder, one accessible through LON-DC1 and another on a second server, LON-SVR2, as shown in Figure 5-19.

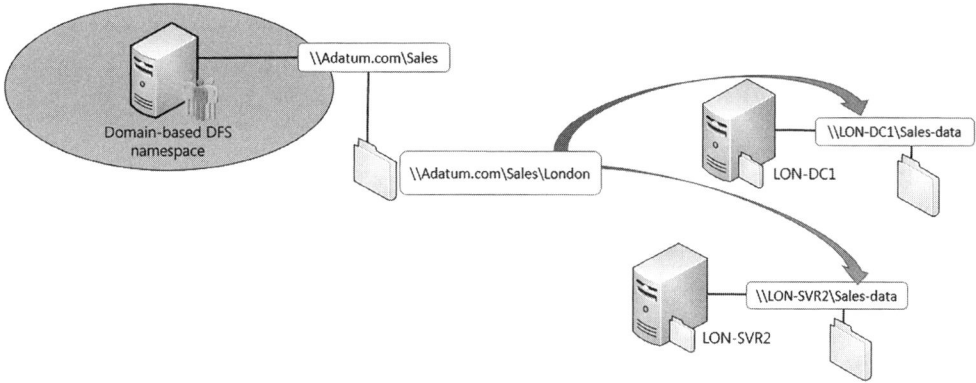

FIGURE 5-19 A domain-based DFS with two folder targets

When users access the \\Adatum.com\Sales\London UNC name, they are directed to one or other of the folder targets: \\LON-SVR2\Sales-data or \\LON-DC1\Sales-data. To configure this, use the following procedure:

1. In the DFS Management console, right-click the folder for which you want to add another folder target. Click Properties, and then click Add.
2. Define the UNC path to another shared folder on another server. Click OK.
3. Your folder targets are configured, as shown in Figure 5-20.

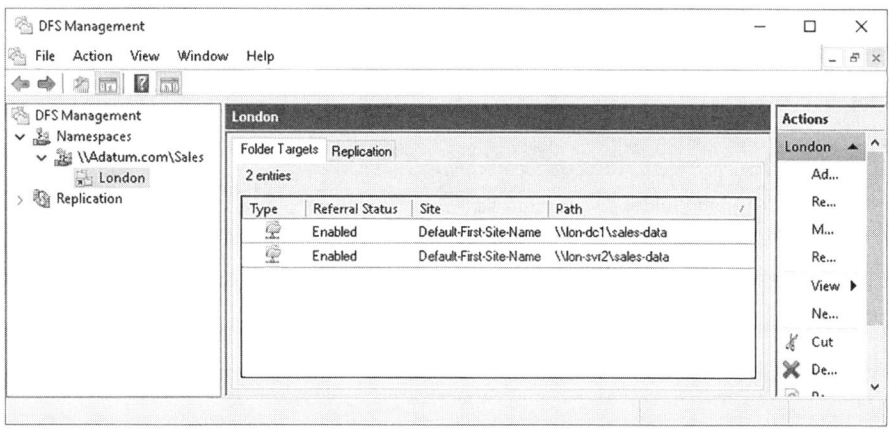

FIGURE 5-20 Configuring folder targets

If you choose to define multiple folder targets, you can configure referrals. A referral is a list of folder targets that a client computer receives when attempting to connect to a DFS namespace. When the client receives this referral, it tries to access the first target in the list. If that target is not available, it tries the next target.

Using multiple folder targets enables you to provide multiple copies of the same data. You must use DFS Replication to synchronize these folder targets. To replicate data between targets, in the DFS Management console, as shown in Figure 5-20, click the Replication tab, and then click the Replicate Folder Wizard link. DFS replication is covered in the next section.

To configure referrals for a particular folder, right-click the folder, and then click Properties. On the Referrals tab, shown in Figure 5-21, you can configure the ordering method and the clients fail back to preferred targets option.

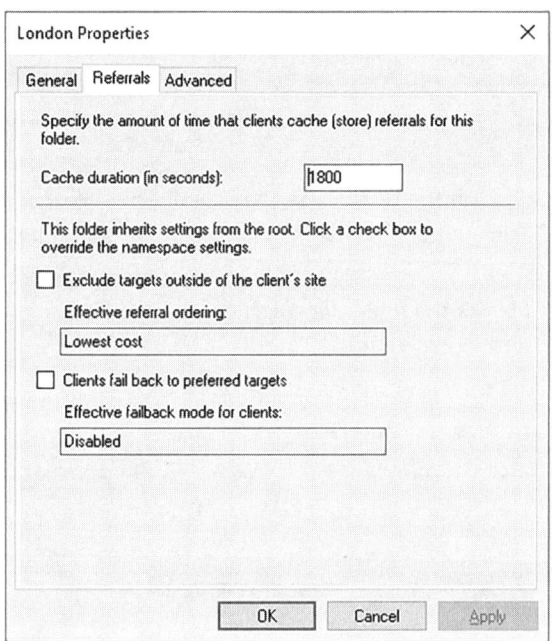

FIGURE 5-21 Configuring folder target referrals

You can also control the ordering method for targets outside the client computer's AD DS site by using the Referrals tab in the Namespace Properties dialog box, as shown in Figure 5-22.

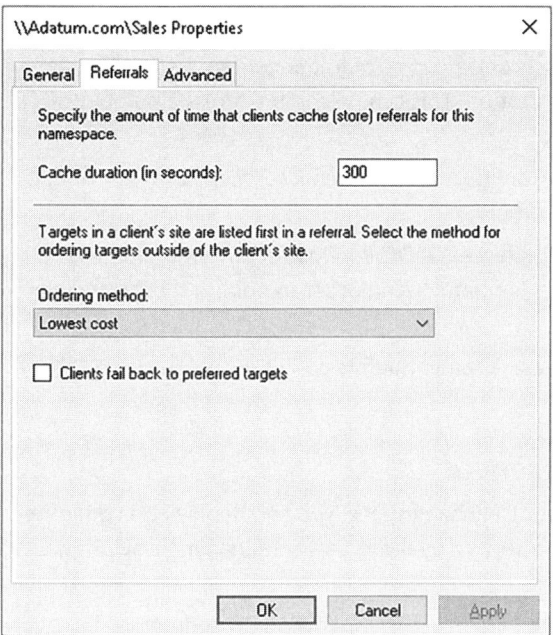

FIGURE 5-22 Configuring namespace folder target referrals

You can choose the following ordering methods:

- Lowest Cost
- Random Order
- Exclude Targets Outside Of The Client's Site

EXAM TIP

By default, the referral lists targets in the client's site first.

NEED MORE REVIEW? **SET THE ORDERING METHOD FOR TARGETS IN REFERRALS**

To review further details about configuring namespace referral, refer to the Microsoft MSDN website at *https://msdn.microsoft.com/library/cc732414(v=ws.11).aspx*.

Configure DFS replication

DFS Replication (DFSR) enables you to synchronize copies of folder content between instances of folder targets throughout your organization. This can help you address a number of scenarios when supporting branch offices:

- **Collecting data from branches**   Configure DFSR to replicate files from branch offices to a hub, perhaps at the head office.
- **Distributing data to branches**   Implement a DFSR infrastructure where data is replicated from a central location to the branches in order to publish the latest files throughout your organization.
- **Sharing data throughout branches**   Create multiple copies of files by using DFSR to synchronize the copies.

Adding the DFS Replication role service

After you have created and configured your DNS namespace, you can deploy and configure DFSR. You can add the DFS Replication role service by using Server Manager, or by using Windows PowerShell.

To deploy DFS Replication with Server Manager, use the following procedure:

1. In Server Manager, click Manage, and then click Add Roles And Features.
2. In the Add Roles And Features Wizard, on the Server Roles page, in the Roles list, expand File And Storage Services, expand File And iSCSI Services, and then select the DFS Replication check box.
3. Click Add Features, and then click Next.
4. When prompted, click Install, and when installation is complete, click Finish.

To deploy DFS Replication with Windows PowerShell, run the following command:

```
Install-WindowsFeature FS-DFS-Replication -IncludeManagementTools
```

Create a replication group

Before you can add replication targets, you must create a replication group. When you create the replication group, you must provide the following information:

- **Replication Group Type**   The group type defines what you use the group for. The option you select determines the subsequent configuration options that are available. You can select:
    - **A Multipurpose Replication Group**   Supports synchronization between folder targets for generic content sharing and publishing.
    - **A Replication Group For Data Collection**   Defines a relationship between two servers, such as a branch server and a head office hub server.

- **Replication Group Members** Define which servers are part of this replication group. You can add additional members after you create the group.
- **Topology** The topology defines how the data is synchronized between member servers. Available options are:
    - **Hub And Spoke** You require three or more member servers for this topology. This is the best option for when you wish to replicate from a central location out to branch offices.
    - **Full Mesh** Enables you to synchronize content from any member server to any other member server.
    - **Custom** This enables you to choose your own topology after deployment of DFSR.
- **Replication Group Schedule And Bandwidth** Enables you to define when replication occurs between group members, and how much network capacity can be used by the replication process. Options are:
    - **Schedule** Choose between Replicate Continuously, or Designate Specific Times Of The Day And Week When Replication Can Occur.
    - **Bandwidth** Choose between Full, in which all available bandwidth is used during a replication cycle, or Designate The Bandwidth To Use From 16 Kbps Through 256 Mbps.
- **Folders** You must define which folders are part of a replication topology. You can add folders to the topology during or after you create the replication group.

You can create a replication group with the DFS Management console, or by using the Windows PowerShell New-DfsReplicationGroup cmdlet.

> **NEED MORE REVIEW? DFS REPLICATION CMDLETS**
>
> To review further details about using Windows PowerShell to manage DFS replication, refer to the Microsoft TechNet website at *https://technet.microsoft.com/library/dn296591.aspx*.

To create a multipurpose replication group using the console, use the following procedure:

1. In the DFS Management console, in the navigation pane, right-click the Replication node, and then click New Replication Group. As shown in Figure 5-23, click Multipurpose Replication Group, and then click Next.

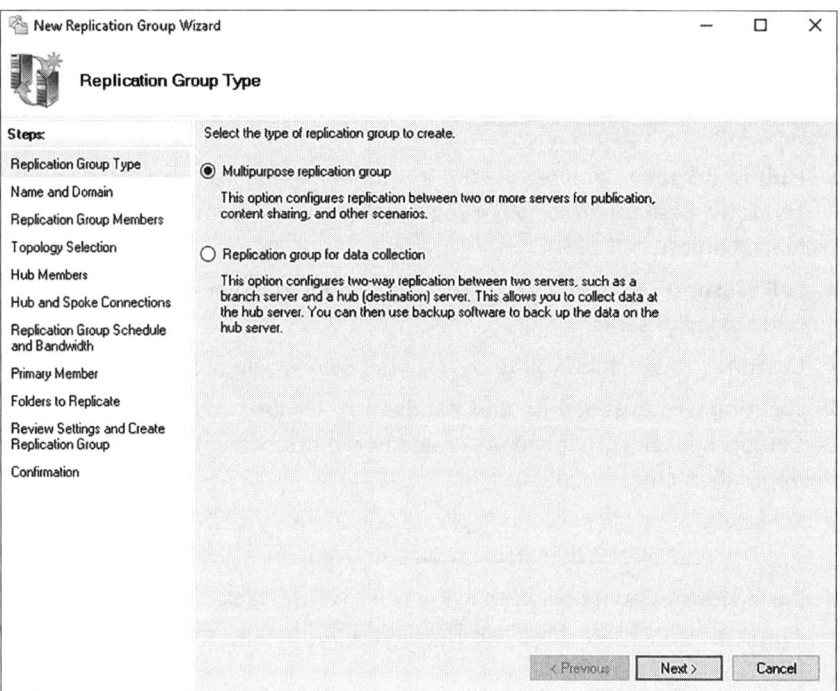

FIGURE 5-23 Defining the DFS replication group type

2. On the Name And Domain page, type the name and a description for the replication group, select the AD DS domain of which this group is a member, and then click Next.

3. On the Replication Group Members page, add the servers that are to be members of the group, and then click Next.

4. On the Topology Selection page, choose either Hub And Spoke, Full Mesh, or No Topology; this last option enables you to define the topology later. For example, click Hub And Spoke, as shown in Figure 5-24, and then click Next.

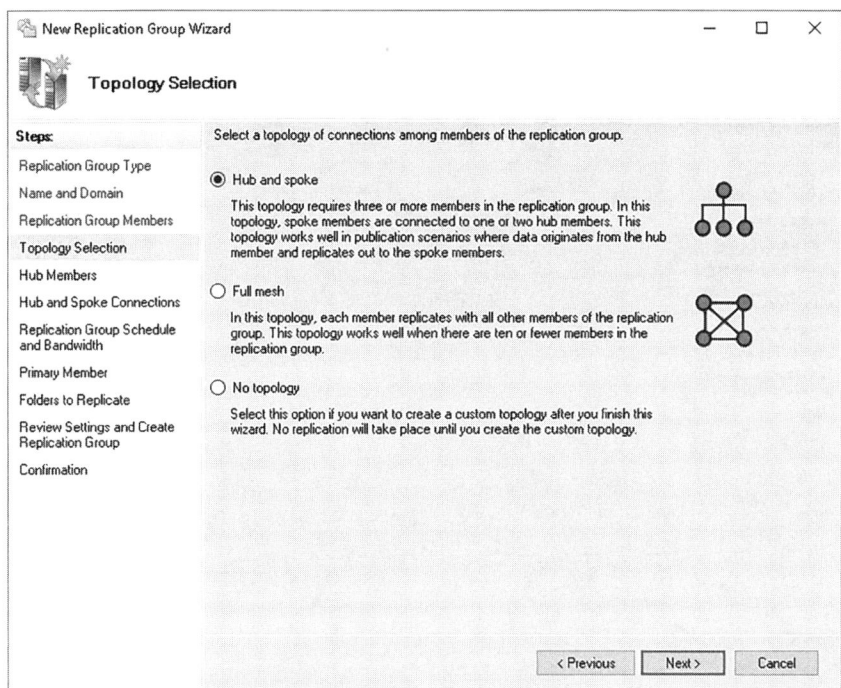

FIGURE 5-24 Selecting a DFS replication topology

EXAM TIP

You can reconfigure the replication topology after it is created. In the DFS Management console, right-click the replication group, and then click New Topology.

5. On the Hub Members page, click the Add> button to move servers in the group from the Spoke members list to the Hub members list, as shown in Figure 5-25. Click Next.

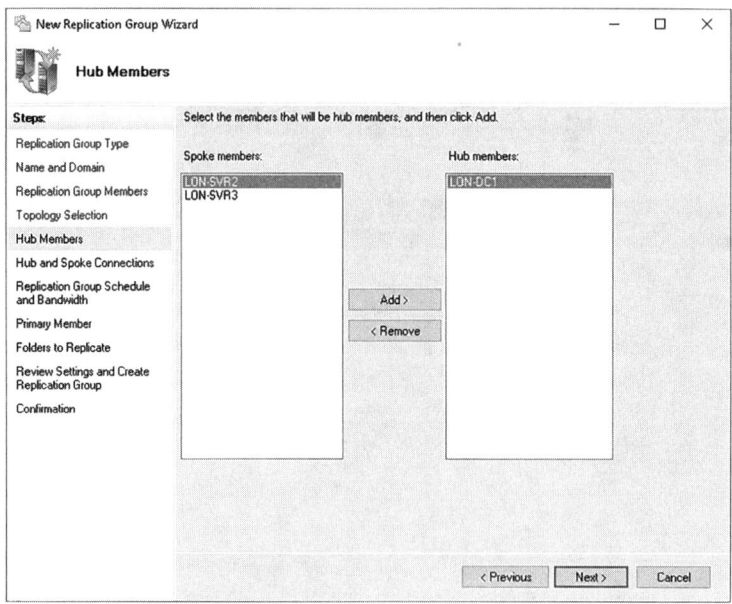

FIGURE 5-25 Configuring DFS replication group members

6. On the Hub And Spoke Connections page, review the current configuration. If you want to make changes, click Edit. Otherwise, click Next.

7. On the Replication Group Schedule And Bandwidth page, configure the required replication schedule, as shown in Figure 5-26, and then click Next.

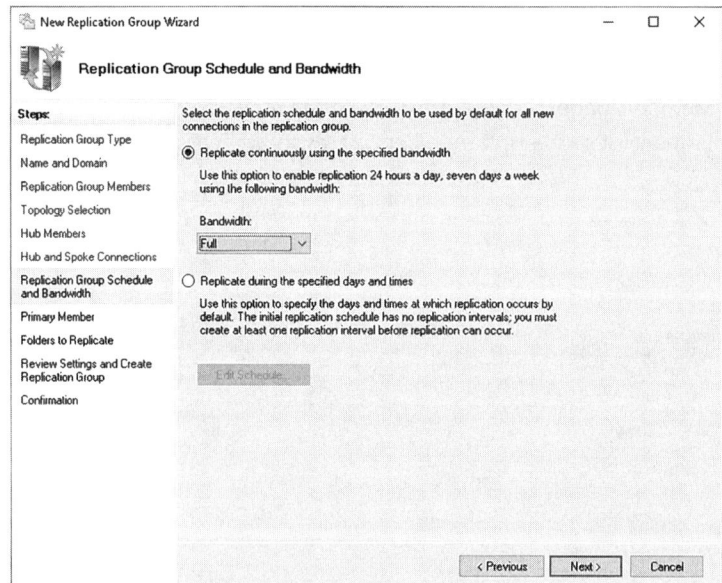

FIGURE 5-26 Configuring the DFS replication schedule and bandwidth

8. On the Primary member page, define which server acts as primary. The copies of folder content on the primary server are used as authoritative during initial replication. Click Next.
9. On the Folders To Replicate page, add the folders that you want to replicate, and then click Next. This folder exists on the primary member.
10. On the Local Path On Other Members page, define the path for the folder on the target servers. If the folder does not exist, it is created. Click Next.
11. Review your settings, as shown in Figure 5-27, click Create, and then click Close.

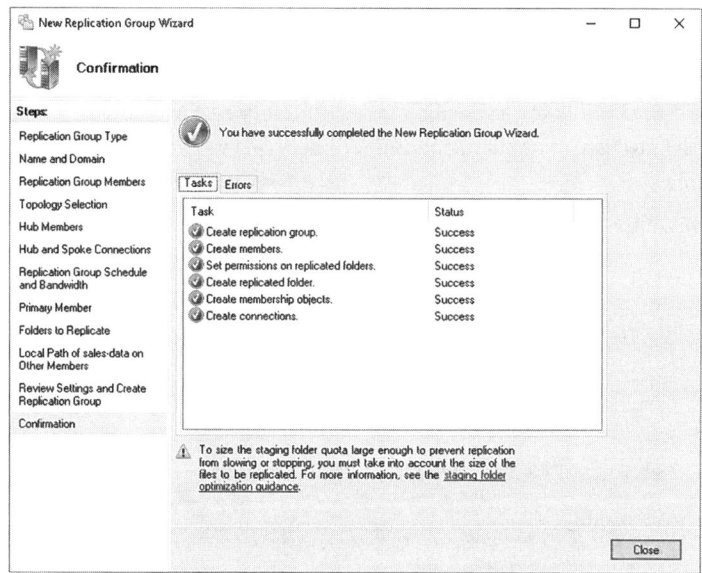

FIGURE 5-27 Verifying creation of the DFS replication group

Configure replication scheduling

As part of the process of creating a replication group, you define the scheduling. After creation, you can reconfigure these settings using the DFS Management console, or with the Set-DfsrGroupSchedule Windows PowerShell cmdlet.

To modify the schedule using the console, use the following procedure:

1. Click the Replication node in the DFS Management console, right-click the appropriate replication group, and then click Edit Replication Group Schedule, as shown in Figure 5-28.
2. Define the new schedule and optionally bandwidth for the whole group.

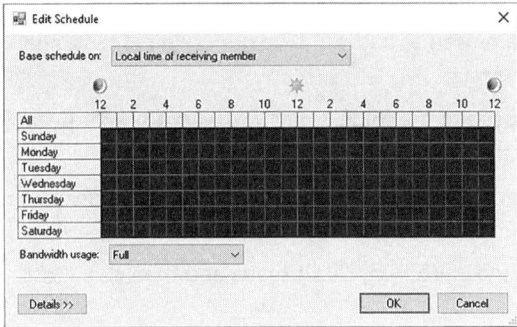

FIGURE 5-28 Editing the replication schedule for a DFS replication group

If you want to edit the schedule for a specific connection between two servers in the group, you can use the Set-DfsrConnectionSchedule Windows PowerShell cmdlet. Otherwise, you can use the console:

1. In the DFS Management console, click the Replication Group node in the navigation pane.
2. In the Details pane, as shown in Figure 5-29, click the connection you want to configure.

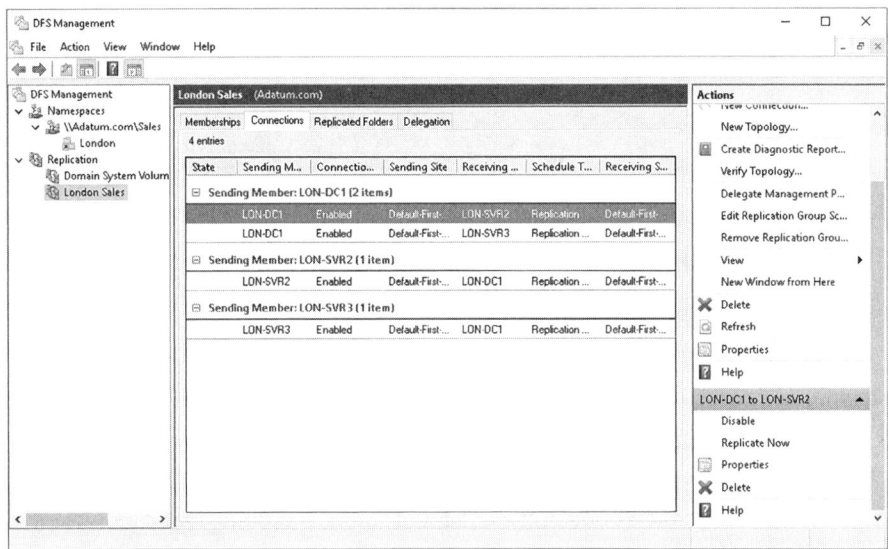

FIGURE 5-29 Viewing replication connections

3. In the Action pane, click Properties.
4. As shown in Figure 5-30, click the Schedule tab, and then click Custom Connection Schedule.

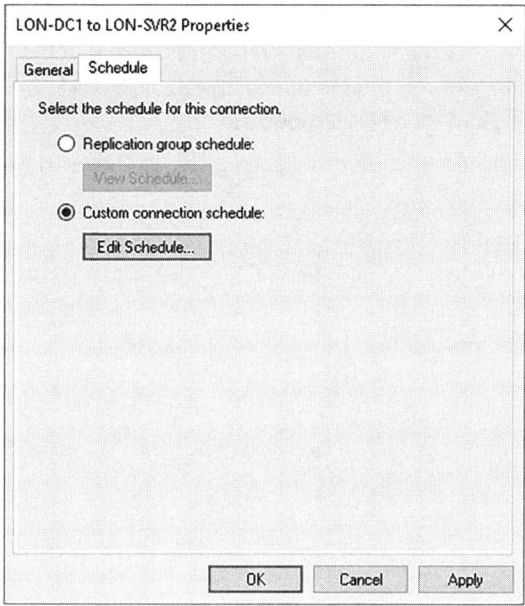

FIGURE 5-30 Reconfiguring the replication schedule for a specific connection

5. Click Edit Schedule, and then reconfigure the schedule for this server to server connection within the group, and then click OK twice.

Configure staging

To help optimize DFS replication, a staging folder is used. DFSR uses this staging folder to cache new or edited files until they can be replicated.

When replication occurs, you can consider one server to be a sending server, and another to be the receiving server in a given instance of replication. When a receiving server petitions a sending server for changes, the sending server stages any modified or new files. This involves creating a compressed version of these files and storing them in the staging folder. The sending server then sends those staged files.

The receiving server downloads the compressed files and stores them in its own staging folder. After the files are received, they are decompressed and placed in the replicated folder.

EXAM TIP
Each replicated folder has its own staging folder. By default, the staging folder for a replicated folder is in the DfsrPrivate\Staging subfolder.

To configure staging, use the following procedure:

1. In the DFS Management console, click the appropriate replication group in the navigation pane, and then in the details pane, on the Memberships tab, right-click the member server you want to configure, and then click Properties.

2. In the Server (folder) Properties dialog box, click the Staging tab, as shown in Figure 5-31.

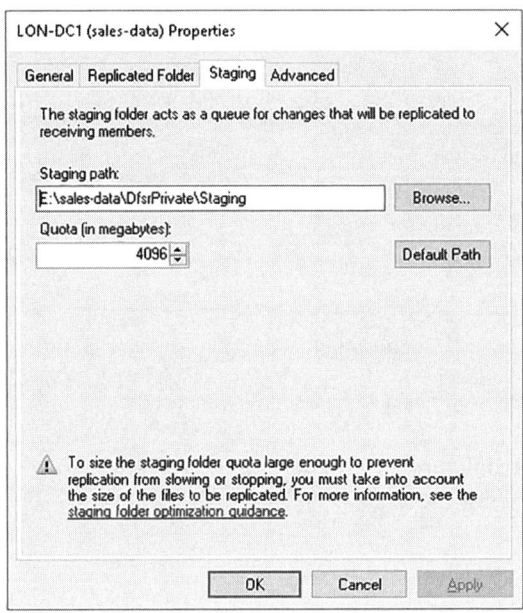

FIGURE 5-31 Reconfiguring staging for a replication folder

3. Enter a new Staging path value and Quota value, and then click OK.

Configure remote differential compression settings

DFS replication uses remote differential compression (RDC) to help to optimize replication between member servers in a replication group. RDC identifies changes to blocks in files rather than to entire files, and DFS replication only replicates the changed blocks, and not entire files.

EXAM TIP

By default, DFS replication only uses RDC for files that are 64 KB or larger.

To configure enable or disable RDC, use the following procedure:

1. In the DFS Management console, click the appropriate replication group in the navigation pane, and then in the details pane, on the Connections tab, right-click the connection that you want to configure, and then click Properties.

2. In the Server To Server Properties dialog box, on the General tab, shown in Figure 5-32, select or clear the Enable Remote Differential Compression (RDC) check box, and then click OK.

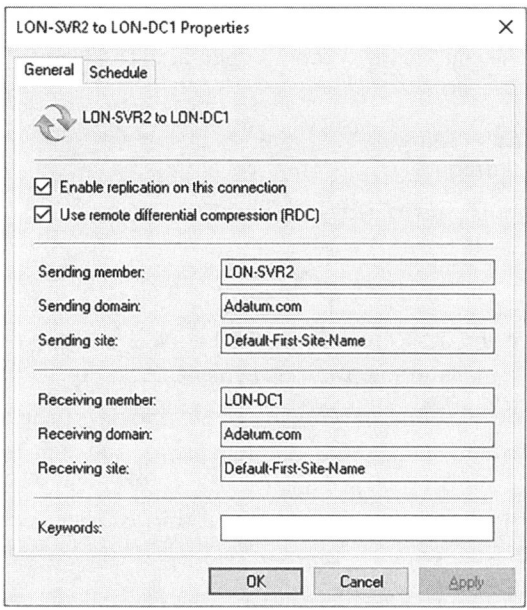

FIGURE 5-32 Enabling remote differential compression

Optimize DFS replication

There are a couple of things that you can do to optimize DFS replication. These are:

- **Multiple Hubs**   For larger DFSR deployments, consider using multiple hubs. This reduces the load on a single point, and can improve throughput.
- **Add RAM**   DFSR is affected by low memory, especially on busy hub servers. Adding memory is a very effective way of improving DFSR performance.
- **Increase Staging Quota**   If the staging quota is large enough for a folder, the DFSR server must restage replicating files less frequently, significantly reducing workload. In a perfect world, the staging quota would match the folder size, but that's almost certainly impractical. You can check the event logs for information about staging performance. Event IDs 4202, 4206, 4208 and 4212 signify potential issues with staging, and indicate that DFSR might fail due to lack of staging space.

> **NEED MORE REVIEW? TUNING REPLICATION PERFORMANCE IN DFSR**
>
> To review further details about using optimizing DFS replication, refer to the Microsoft TechNet website at *https://blogs.technet.microsoft.com/askds/2010/03/31/tuning-replication-performance-in-dfsr-especially-on-win2008-r2/.*

Configure DFS fault tolerance

DFS provides for namespace fault tolerance in two ways.

- **Domain-Based Namespace** You can create multiple copies of a namespace by implementing a domain-based namespace and adding additional namespace servers. Creating a DFS namespace was covered in the section "Configuring DFS Namespaces" earlier in this chapter.
- **Failover Cluster** Alternatively, you can deploy a standalone namespace and implement Windows Server failover clustering.

Fault tolerance for folder content in DFS is provided through DFS replication.

Manage DFS databases

DFS uses databases to manage content and replication. There are a number of database management tasks that you can use to help manage your DFS deployment. These are:

- **Cloning a Database** When you establish a new replica of a DFS folder, the initial replication can be very time-consuming and resource-intensive. You can mitigate these issues by cloning the database. To clone a database, use the Windows PowerShell Export-DfsrClone and Import-DfsrClone cmdlets. For example, the following procedure clones the database to a new DFS server:
    A. On the existing DFS server, run the Export-DfsrClone -Volume C: -Path "C:\Dfsrdatabase" command.
    B. Copy the contents of C:\Dfsrdatabase to the target server.
    C. On the target server, run the Import-DfsrClone -Volume C: -Path "C:\Dfsrdatabase" command.

> **NEED MORE REVIEW? EXPORT A CLONE OF THE DFS REPLICATION DATABASE**
>
> To review further details about exporting a clone, refer to the Microsoft TechNet website at *https://technet.microsoft.com/library/dn482443.aspx*.

- **Recover A Database** If DFS detects a problem in its database, it attempts to rebuild the database. However, files in the ConflictAndDeleted and Preexisting folders cannot be automatically recovered. To recover these folders, use the Windows PowerShell Get-DfsrPreservedFiles and Restore-DfsrPreservedFiles cmdlets.

> **NEED MORE REVIEW? DFS NAMESPACES AND DFS REPLICATION OVERVIEW**
>
> To review further details about DFS Namespaces and DFS Replication, refer to the Microsoft TechNet website at *https://technet.microsoft.com/library/jj127250(v=ws.11).aspx*.

Implement BranchCache

You can enable client computers at your branch offices to use cached copies of network files and folders. You can configure these files to be cached on each branch office computer, or on a file server within the branch office. By using cached copies of files, reliance on the network link is reduced making BranchCache ideal for branch offices with low bandwidth or unreliable connections.

Implement distributed and hosted cache modes

You can deploy BranchCache in two modes:

- **Distributed Cache Mode**   More suited to smaller branch offices, there is no local BranchCache server installed. Instead, as users access files from cached shared folders in the head office, copies are cached on each client computer that accesses the files. If other users attempt to access those same files, they retrieve the cached versions from other client computers at the branch office rather than downloading the file from the head office. This mode only supports per-subnet configurations. In other words, all the clients must reside in the same subnet. For a small branch office, this probably won't be an issue.

    If you configure client computers to use distributed cache mode, client computers use a multicast protocol, WS-Discovery, to locate content cached on other local client computers. To support this mode, you must enable the following ports on the local client computers' firewalls:

- HTTP (TCP port 80)
- WS-Discovery (UDP port 3702)

EXAM TIP

Clients' computers configured for distributed cache mode still search for a hosted cache server. If they locate a server, they reconfigure as hosted cache mode clients automatically.

- **Hosted Cache Mode**   For larger branch offices, you can consider deploying a Windows Server 2016 file server. You can then choose to implement BranchCache in hosted cache mode. In this mode, accessed files are cached on the local server for other client computers.

EXAM TIP

To support hosted cache mode, the server you deploy must be running Windows Server 2008 R2 or newer.

    In hosted cache mode, client computers search for a host server to retrieve cached content. You can use AD DS Group Policy Objects (GPOs) to configure hosted cache mode by defining the FQDN of the hosted cache servers, or by enabling auto-discovery by defining service connection points for those servers.

EXAM TIP

In both modes, BranchCache uses the HTTP protocol to transfer between client computers and/or the cache server. Therefore, you must configure client firewalls to enable incoming HTTP traffic.

Install and configure BranchCache

To enable BranchCache for file services, complete the following high-level tasks:

- On the host running Windows Server 2016, install either:
    - The BranchCache feature
    - The BranchCache For Network Files role service
- On client computers, configure BranchCache by either:
    - Using GPOs
    - Running the netsh branchcache set service command
    - Running the Enable-BCDistributed or Enable-BCHostedServer Windows PowerShell cmdlets

EXAM TIP

You do not need to install BranchCache on client computers; it is installed by default on Windows 7 and newer operating systems. However, you must enable it.

To cache content on a file server using BranchCache, complete the following high-level tasks:

- Install the BranchCache for the Network Files role service
- Configure hash publication for BranchCache
- Create BranchCache-enabled file shares

IMPLEMENT BRANCHCACHE FOR WEB, FILE, AND APPLICATION SERVERS

BranchCache supports caching of a number of different server content types. These are:

- **Web server** To enable BranchCache for a Windows Server 2016 web server, install the BranchCache feature. You do not need to perform any additional web server configuration.
- **File server** Install the BranchCache for the Network Files role service of the File Services server role. After this role service is installed, configure each shared folder to enable BranchCache.
- **Application servers** For an application server using BITS protocol, the configuration is the same as for a web server.

To install and configure BranchCache on a file server, use the following procedure:

1. In Server Manager, click Manage, and then click Add Roles And Features.
2. On the Select server roles page, expand File And Storage Services, expand File And iSCSI Services, as shown in Figure 5-33, select the BranchCache For Network Files check box, and then click Next.
3. Complete the wizard, and when prompted, click Install. When installation completes, click Close.

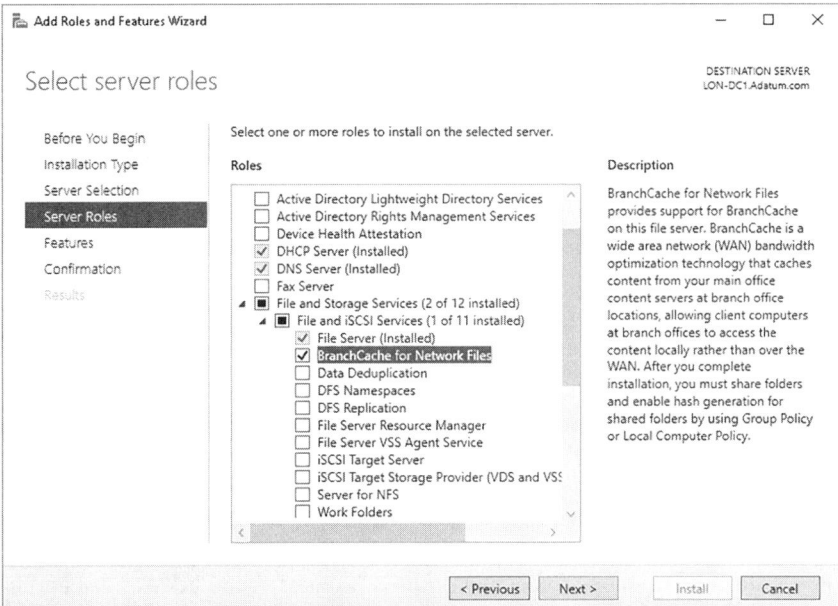

FIGURE 5-33 Installing the BranchCache for Network Files role service

After adding the role service, you must configure the hash publication for BranchCache and create BranchCache-enabled file shares. To do this, use the following procedure:

1. On a domain controller, open the Group Policy Management console.
2. Create and link a GPO to a domain container that reflects the computers that you want to configure. For example, create a GPO called BranchCache File Servers and link it to an organizational unit (OU) that contains all server computers that cache content for branches.
3. Open the GPO for editing.
4. In the GPO, browse to Computer Configuration\Policies\Administrative Templates\Network\Lanman Server.
5. Enable the Hash Publication For BranchCache setting and then select Allow Hash Publication Only For Shared Folder On Which BranchCache Is Enabled, as shown in Figure 5-34.

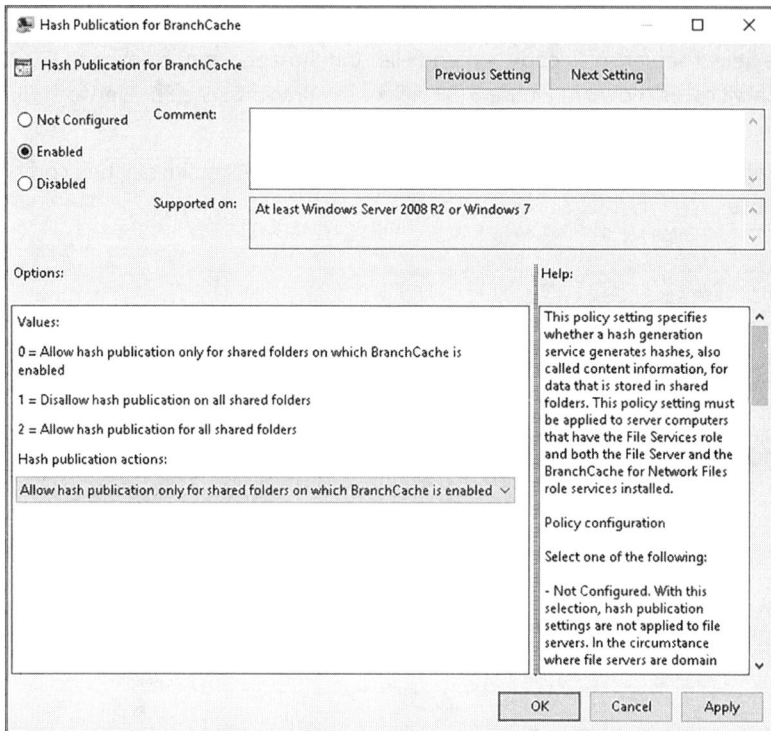

FIGURE 5-34 Configuring the Hash Publication settings for Branch Cache

6. Finally, to cache a shared folder, in Windows Explorer, right-click a folder, and then click Properties.
7. In the folder Properties dialog box, click the Sharing tab, and then click Advanced Sharing.
8. In the Advanced Sharing dialog box, select the Share This Folder check box, and then click Caching.
9. In the Caching dialog box, select the Enable BranchCache option, as shown in Figure 5-35.
10. Click OK twice, and then click Close.

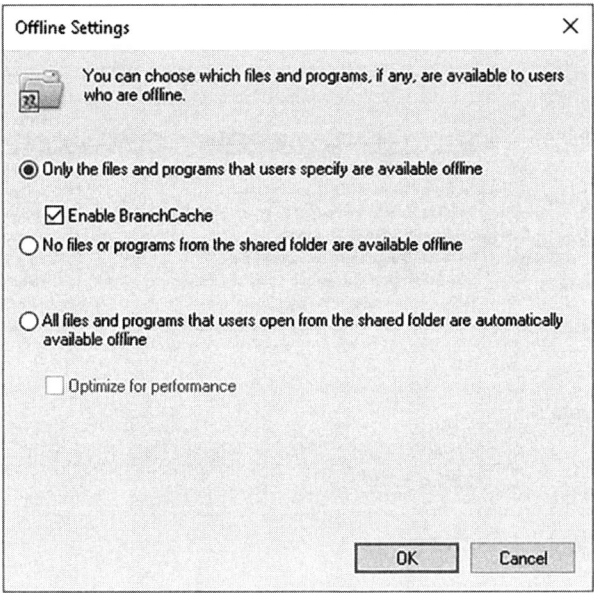

FIGURE 5-35 Configuring Offline Settings

CLIENT COMPUTERS

To enable BranchCache on a client computer, use the following procedure:

1. On a domain controller, open the Group Policy Management console.
2. Create and link a GPO to a domain container that reflects the computers that you want to configure. For example, create a GPO called Branch Offices, and link it to an organizational unit (OU) that contains all branch office computers.
3. Open the GPO for editing.
4. In the GPO, browse to Computer Configuration\Policies\Administrative Templates\Network\BranchCache.
5. Enable the Turn On BranchCache setting in the GPO, as shown in Figure 5-36.

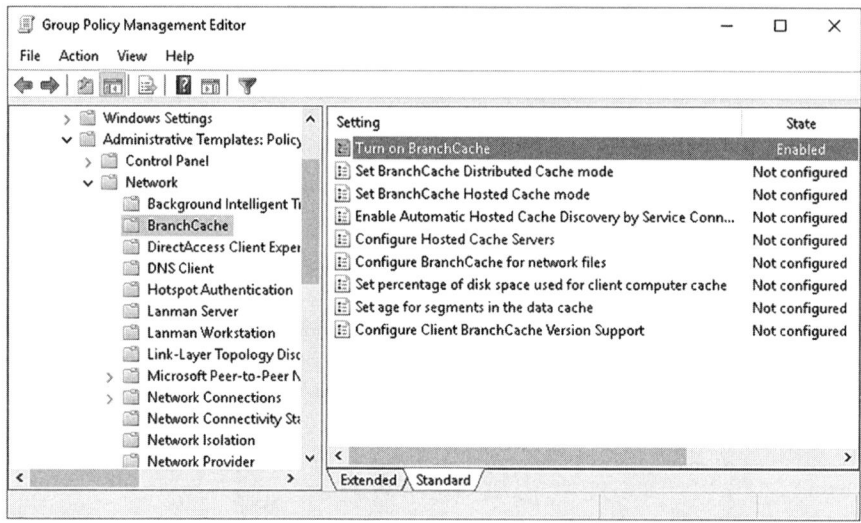

FIGURE 5-36 Enabling BranchCache with GPOs

To configure BranchCache on a client computer for distributed or hosted cache mode, use the following procedure:

1. On a domain controller, open the Group Policy Management console and locate the GPO you used to enable BranchCache. Open the GPO for editing.
2. In the GPO, browse to Computer Configuration\Policies\Administrative Templates\Network\BranchCache.
3. Enable either the Set BranchCache Distributed Cache Mode or the Set BranchCache Hosted Cache Mode setting in the GPO.

You can also use Windows PowerShell to enable and configure BranchCache on client computers. For example, to enable hosted cache mode on Windows 10 clients using the LON-SVR3.adatum.com server as the hosted cache server, run the following command:

```
Enable-BCHostedClient -ServerNames LON-SVR3.adatum.com -UseVersion Windows10
```

EXAM TIP

Remember to reconfigure the client firewall. You can use GPOs to achieve this, too.

Troubleshoot BranchCache

BranchCache relies on core Windows Server technologies, such as Group Policies, client firewall settings, and file sharing options. It also relies on the underlying network infrastructure.

When troubleshooting BranchCache, ensure that common networking issues are not the root cause of any problems. Then, use the following procedure to try to determine where the problem lies:

- **Verify client status** Open a command prompt on the client computer and run the netsh branchcache show status all command. This shows the status of the service, and if working, what the local cache status and publication status is, as shown in Figure 5-37.

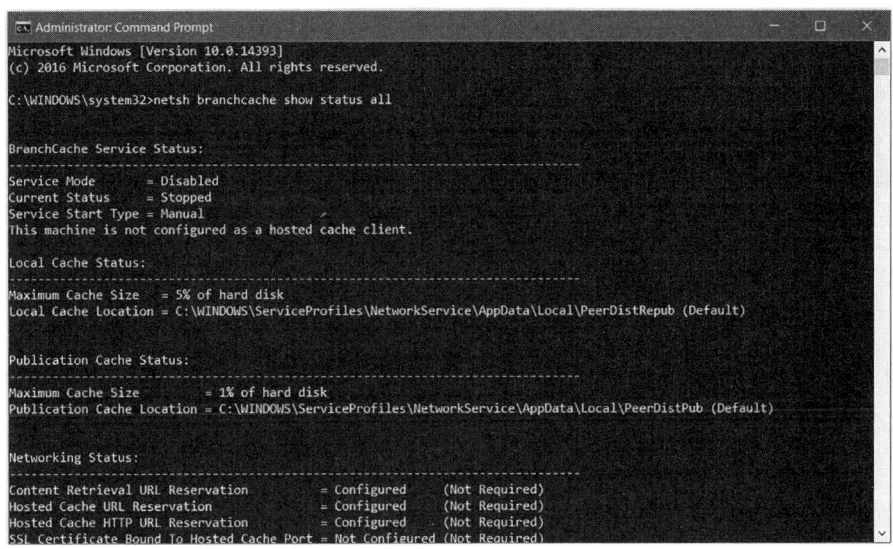

FIGURE 5-37 Using Netsh to check the BranchCache client settings

- **Check throughput of BranchCache by using Performance Monitor** Switch Performance Monitor to a report view, and then add the BranchCache object to the report. **Local cache** values should increase with time, as should SMB: bytes from cache and SMB: bytes from server. If they do not, then BranchCache is not working.
- **Verify the correct configuration and application of GPOs by using Group Policy troubleshooting procedures** Use the `gpresult.exe /h` command-line tool to determine which GPOs are applying. You can also see which settings are applied, and by which GPO. Any problems with your GPO configuration should be visible.
- **Check the local firewall configuration** Incoming TCP port 80 and UDP port 3702 must be open on client computers. Remember, this setting can be configured through GPOs.
- **Check the event logs** BranchCache has both an operational log and a security log. The operational log appears in Event Viewer at Applications And Services Logs\Microsoft\Windows\BranchCache\Operational. Investigate any errors or warnings.

> **NEED MORE REVIEW? BRANCHCACHE**
>
> To review further details about BranchCache, refer to the Microsoft TechNet website at *https://technet.microsoft.com/library/mt613461.aspx*.

Chapter summary

- Most organizations implement private IPv4 addressing within their intranets.
- CIDR enables you to use a variable length subnet mask.
- There are three types of IPv6 unicast addresses. These are global unicast, unique local addresses, and link-local addresses.
- IPv6 stateless autoconfiguration relies on router advertisements.
- 6to4 tunneling enables connectivity between IPv6 hosts over the internet, but does not support NAT configurations.
- You can configure routes in Windows Server 2016 by using Windows PowerShell, the route command-line tool, or the Routing And Remote Access console.
- A domain-based DFS namespace provides for high availability of the namespace through replication.
- Target referrals provide a means for a DFS client to connect to a suitable instance of a DFS folder.
- If you create multiple instances of a folder, it is sensible to use DFS replication to synchronize these instances.
- When configuring DFSR, you can choose between two topologies: Hub And Spoke and Full Mesh.
- The default replication schedule for DFSR is always using full bandwidth.
- Configuring the staging quota can have a significant impact on DFSR throughput.
- You do not need to install BranchCache on client computers, but you must enable and configure it.
- To make a web server's content available through BranchCache, install the Windows Server 2016 BranchCache feature.
- To make a file server's content available with BranchCache, install the Windows Server 2016 BranchCache for Network Files role service.

Thought experiment

In this thought experiment, demonstrate your skills and knowledge of the topics covered in this chapter. You can find answers to this thought experiment in the next section.

You work in support at A. Datum Corporation. As a consultant for A. Datum, answer the following questions about implementing core and distributed network solutions within the A. Datum organization:

1. You have been given the task of configuring IPv4 subnets for a new branch office. You examine the documentation for A. Datum's network and determine that the next available subnet is 172.16.24.0/21. What is the first IPv4 host address that you can assign in this subnet?

2. What is the last available host that you can assign in subnet 172.16.24.0/21?

3. You are troubleshooting an IPv6 deployment. You use `ipconfig /all` to verify the configuration of an IPv6 host. The command returns a value for one of the network interfaces of FE80. What type of IPv6 address begins with FE80?

4. You are in the process of installing an application that requires IPv6. Most of the networked devices in A. Datum are IPv4 based. You decide to implement an IPv6 transition technology. When would ISATAP be a good choice?

5. You are choosing a routing protocol. When would BGP be a suitable choice?

6. Your branch office users modify data files that must be collated at the head office. How can you achieve this?

7. Branch office users access website content from the head office. The content changes infrequently. You want to make the access to this content quicker, but the link between the branch and head office is slow and sometimes unavailable. How could you address this issue? What specific steps must you take?

Thought experiment answers

This section contains the solution to the thought experiment. Each answer explains why the answer choice is correct.

1. 172.16.24.0/21 uses 21 bits for the subnet mask. This means that the mask, expressed in decimal, is 255.255.248.0. Consequently, the first subnet ID is 172.16.8.0, the next is 172.16.16.0, the third is 172.16.24.0, and the fourth is 172.16.32.0. The first host in a subnet is 1 binary digit higher than the subnet ID. Therefore, the first host in 172.16.24.0/21 is 172.16.24.1/21.

2. The last host in any subnet is 2 binary digits lower than the next subnet ID. The next subnet ID in this instance is 172.16.32.0. Therefore, the last host in subnet 172.16.24.0/21 is 172.16.31.254/21.

3. Link-local addresses begin FE80.

4. ISATAP is suitable for IPv6/IPv4 transition when all devices are located on an intranet.

5. BGP is an exterior gateway protocol. It is used to support large enterprise networked environments. It is ideal for supporting a CSP with multitenant networks.

6. To collate data files from branch offices, you could implement DFSR. When setting up the replication group, select a replication group for data collection in the New Replication Group Wizard.

7. Consider implementing BranchCache on the web server at the head office. Install the BranchCache feature on the Windows Server 2016 server computer hosting the website. Then, use GPO to configure the branch offices computers to use distributed cache mode. You must reconfigure the client computers' firewall settings. You can also do this with GPO.

CHAPTER 6

Implement an advanced network infrastructure

In this chapter, you learn about the advanced networking features of Windows Server 2016, including how to implement high performance network solutions, and how to determine scenarios and requirements for implementing software defined networking (SDN).

Skills in this chapter:
- Skill 6.1: Implement high performance network solutions
- Skill 6.2: Determine scenarios and requirements for implementing SDN

Skill 6.1: Implement high performance network solutions

Many large organizations connect their on-premises network infrastructure to the cloud and interconnect their datacenters. While these interconnections are highly desirable, they can lead to a reduction in network performance.

Windows Server 2016 includes a number of features that you can implement to enable and support high performance networking. These features can help to alleviate performance problems, and include:

- Network interface card (NIC) teaming and switch embedded teaming (SET)
- Server Message Block (SMB) 3.1.1
- New Quality of Service (QoS) options
- Network packet processing improvements

In addition, Windows Server 2016 introduces a number of improvements in the networking architecture of Hyper-V, including:

- Expanded virtual switch functionality and extensibility
- Single-Root I/O virtualization (SR-IOV)
- Dynamic virtual machine queuing
- NIC teaming for virtual machines

Implement NIC teaming or the SET solution and identify when to use each

NIC teaming enables you to combine multiple network adapters and use them as a single entity; this can help improve performance and add resilience to your network infrastructure. In the event that one of the network adapters in the NIC team fails, the others continue functioning, thereby providing a degree of fault tolerance.

You can use SET instead of NIC teaming in environments that include Hyper-V and SDN. SET combines some NIC teaming functionality within the Hyper-V virtual switch.

Implementing NIC teaming

Windows Server 2016 enables you to combine between one and 32 network adapters in a NIC team.

> **NOTE SINGLE NETWORK ADAPTERS**
> If you add only a single network adapter to a team, you gain nothing in terms of either fault tolerance or network performance.

When you implement NIC teaming, you must configure the teaming mode, load balancing mode, and standby adapter properties:

- **Teaming mode** You can select from three teaming modes. These are:
    - **Static teaming** This is also known as generic teaming. If you choose this mode, you must manually configure your physical Ethernet switch and the server to correctly form the NIC team. You must also select server-class Ethernet switches. This mode is based on 802.3ad.
    - **Switch independent** If you choose this mode, you can use any Ethernet switches and no special configuration is needed.
    - **LACP** Supported by most enterprise-class switches, this mode supports Link Aggregation Control Protocol (LACP) as defined in 802.1ax. LACP identifies links between the server and a specific switch dynamically. If you select this mode, you must enable LACP manually on the appropriate port of your switch. This mode is also known as dynamic teaming.
- **Load balancing mode** If you are using NIC teaming to achieve load balancing, you must choose a load balancing mode. There are three load balancing modes:
    - **Address Hash** Distributes network traffic across the network adapters in the team by creating a hash from the address elements in the network packets. Packets with a particular hash value are assigned to one of the adapters in the team. Note that outbound traffic is load-balanced. Inbound traffic is only received by one adapter in the team. This scenario works well for servers that handle mostly outbound network traffic—such as web servers.

- **Hyper-V Port** Distributes traffic across the teamed adapters using the MAC address or port used by a virtual machine to connect to a virtual switch on a Hyper-V host. Use this mode if your server is a Hyper-V host running multiple virtual machines. In this mode, virtual machines are distributed across the NIC team with each virtual machine's traffic (both inbound and outbound) handled by a specific active network adapter.
- **Dynamic** This is the default mode. It automatically and equally distributes network traffic across the adapters in a team.
- **Standby adapter** If you are implementing NIC teaming for failover purposes, you must configure a standby adapter. Select the second adapter in the team, and if the first becomes unavailable, the standby adapter becomes active.

If you are using Hyper-V, both the Hyper-V host and Hyper-V virtual machines can use the NIC teaming feature. To enable NIC teaming, use the following procedure:

1. In Server Manager, in the navigation pane, click Local Server.
2. In the details pane, next to NIC Teaming, click Disabled, as shown in Figure 6-1. The NIC Teaming Wizard loads.

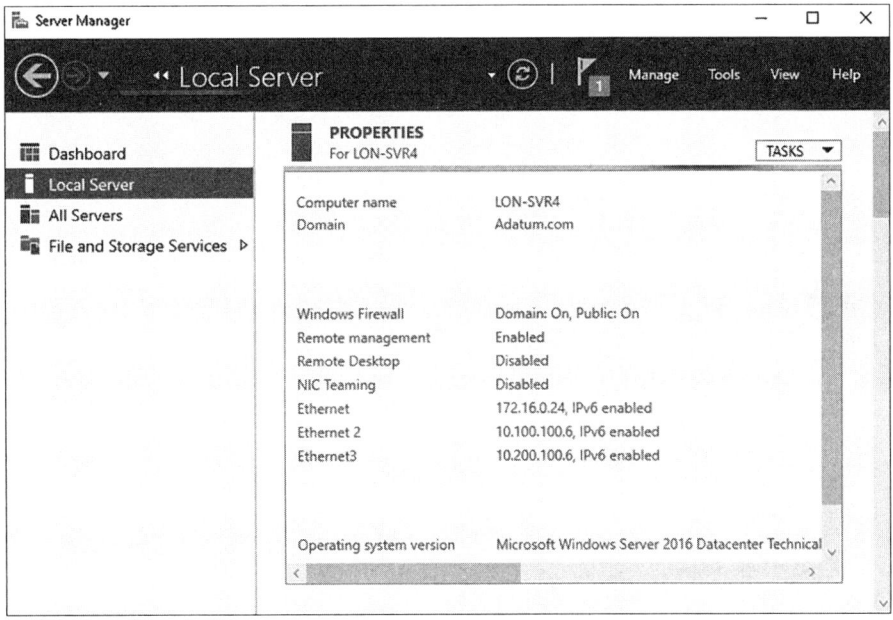

FIGURE 6-1 How to enable NIC teaming

3. In the NIC Teaming dialog box, under the Adapters And Interfaces heading, select the adapters you want to add to a team, as shown in Figure 6-2, and then, in the Tasks list, click Add To New Team.

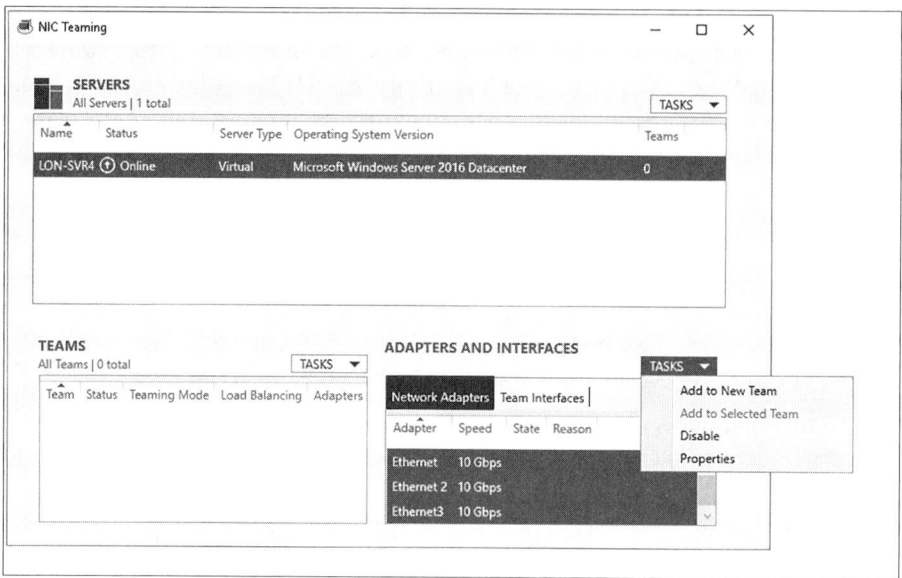

FIGURE 6-2 Creating a new NIC team

4. In the NIC Teaming Wizard, in the Team Name box, type a suitable name for your NIC team, and then click Additional Properties, as shown in Figure 6-3.

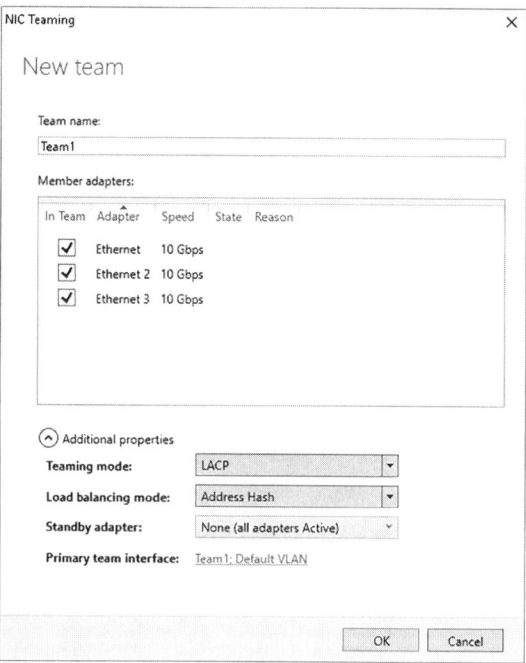

FIGURE 6-3 Configuring NIC team properties

5. Under Additional Properties, configure the Teaming Mode, Load Balancing Mode, and Standby Adapter Settings, and then click OK.

After you have established the NIC team, you can configure its properties by using the NIC Teaming console, as shown in Figure 6-4, or by using Windows PowerShell. To reconfigure a team, right-click the team under the Teams heading, and then click Properties. You can then reconfigure the Teaming Mode, Load Balancing Mode, Standby Adapter, and you can allocate member adapters to the team.

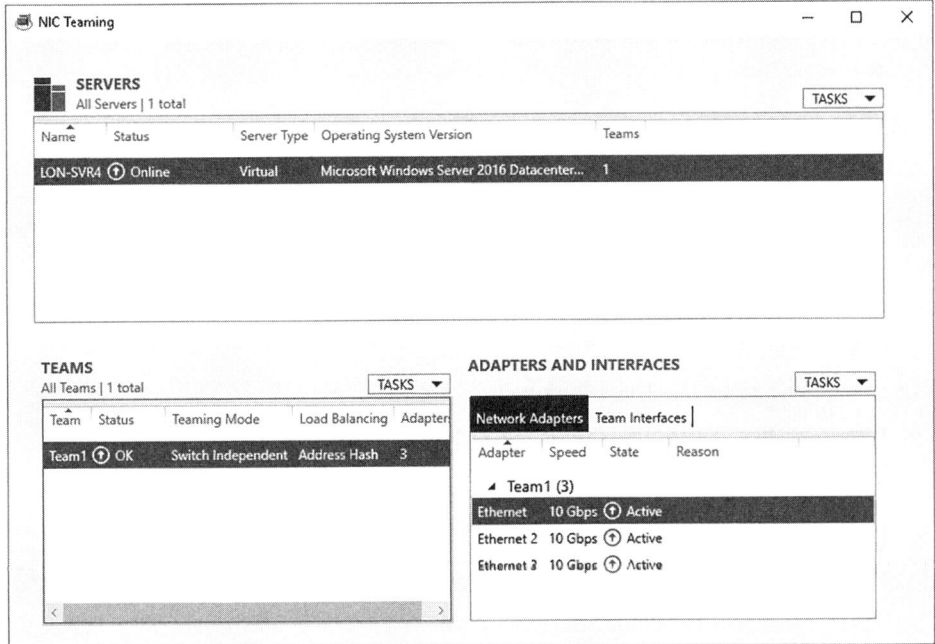

FIGURE 6-4 Viewing NIC Teaming status

> **NEED MORE REVIEW?** **NIC TEAMING CMDLETS IN WINDOWS POWERSHELL**
>
> To review further details about using Windows PowerShell to configure NIC teaming, refer to the Microsoft TechNet website at *https://technet.microsoft.com/library/jj130849.aspx*.

Implementing SET

With SET, you can group between one and eight physical Ethernet network adapters into one or more virtual network adapters. These software-based virtual network adapters provide support for high throughput and enable failover options.

> **NOTE SET MEMBERS**
>
> You must install all SET member network adapters in the same physical Hyper-V host in order to place them in the same team.

Although SET provides similar functionality to NIC teaming, there are some differences, including during setup. For example, when you create a SET team, you do not define a SET team name. In addition, the notion of standby mode is not supported; in SET, all adapters are active. It is also worth noting that while there are three teaming modes in NIC teaming, there is only one in SET: Switch Independent.

> **NOTE SWITCH INDEPENDENT MODE**
>
> In Switch Independent mode, the switches do not determine how to distribute network traffic. This is because the switch to which you connect your SET team is not aware of the SET team. It is the SET team that distributes inbound network traffic across the SET team members.

When you implement SET you must define the following:

- **Member adapters** Define up to eight identical network adapters as part of the team.
- **Load balancing mode** There are two load balancing modes:
    - **Hyper-V Port** Distributes traffic across the SET team member adapters using the MAC address or port used by a virtual machine to connect to a virtual switch on a Hyper-V host.
    - **Dynamic** Outbound traffic is distributed based on a hash of addressing information in the packet stream. Inbound traffic is distributed as per Hyper-V port mode.

To create and manage a SET team, you should use System Center Virtual Machine Manager (VMM), but you can also use Windows PowerShell. For example, to create a SET team with two network adapters called Ethernet and Ethernet 2, use the following command:

```
New-VMSwitch -Name TeamedvSwitch -NetAdapterName "Ethernet","Ethernet 2"
 -EnableEmbeddedTeaming $true
```

> **NEED MORE REVIEW? MANAGING A SET TEAM**
>
> To review further details about implementing SET with Windows PowerShell, refer to the Microsoft TechNet website at *https://technet.microsoft.com/en-us/library/mt403349.aspx#Anchor_11*.

> **NEED MORE REVIEW? NIC AND SWITCH EMBEDDED TEAMING USER GUIDE**
>
> To review further details about using NIC teaming or SET, download the user guide at *https://gallery.technet.microsoft.com/Windows-Server-2016-839cb607*.

Enable and configure Receive Side Scaling (RSS)

When network packets are received by a host, they must be processed by the CPU. Limiting network I/O to a single CPU creates a potential bottleneck, and under high network loads, network throughout can be seriously restricted. RSS helps improve network throughout by distributing the load of network I/O across multiple CPUs rather than using only one.

> **NOTE RECEIVE SIDE SCALING**
>
> To implement RSS, your network adapters and adapter device drivers must support this feature. This is now routinely the case for most physical server network adapters and for all virtual network adapters.

RSS has been part of the Windows Server operating system family for some time and is enabled in the operating system by default. However, not all network adapter vendors enable RSS by default on their drivers. Therefore, you must know how to enable and configure RSS.

Enable and configure RSS

Use the following procedure to enable RSS:

1. Open Device Manager.
2. Locate and right-click your network adapter. Click Properties.
3. On the Advanced tab, in the Property list, as shown in Figure 6-5, click Receive Side Scaling and in the Value list, click Enabled.
4. Optionally, configure the following values:
   - **Max Number Of RSS Processors** Determines how many CPUs should be used for RSS on this network adapter.
   - **Maximum Number Of RSS Queues** To fully utilize the available CPUs, the number of RSS queues must be equal to or greater than the configured number of RSS processors.
   - **RSS Base Processor Number** Identifies which processor to start counting from. For example, if you assign this value 0, and identify that the adapter should use 4 processors, it uses processors 0 through 3.
   - **RSS Profile** You can assign an RSS profile to the adapter. Available options are:
   - **Closest Processor** Can significantly reduce CPU utilization.
   - **Closest Processor Static** As for Closest Processor, but without load balancing.
   - **NUMA Scaling** Windows Server assigns RSS CPUs to each NUMA node on a round robin basis enabling applications running on multi-NUMA servers to scale well.
   - **NUMA Scaling Static** NUMA Scalability is used but RSS does not perform load balancing.
   - **Conservative Scaling** RSS uses as few processors as possible.

EXAM TIP

Not all adapters and device drivers offer all of these settings.

5. Click OK.

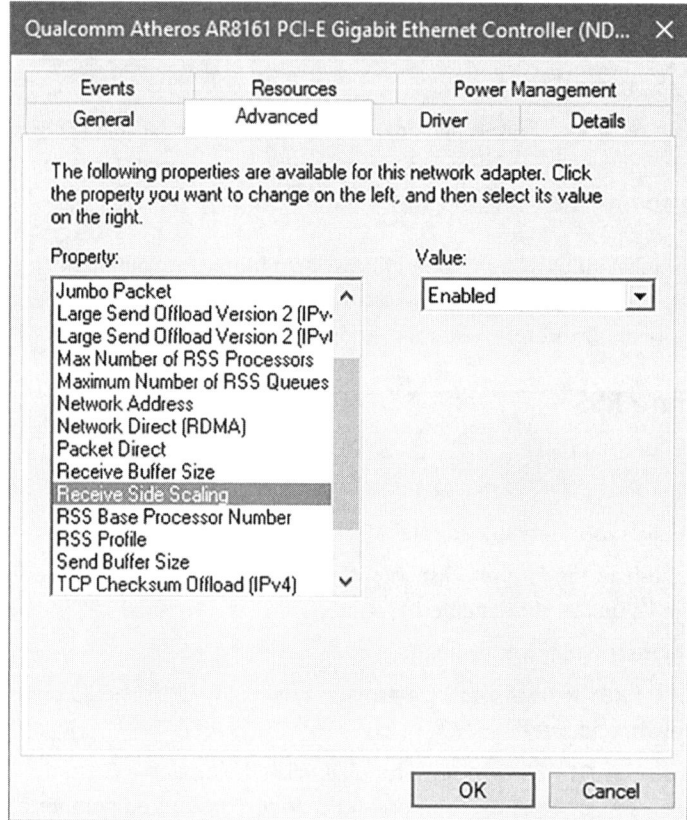

FIGURE 6-5 Enabling RSS on a physical network adapter

You can enable and configure RSS by using Windows PowerShell. For example, to enable RSS, use the following command:

```
Enable-NetAdapterRSS -Name "Ethernet"
```

You can then use the Windows PowerShell Get-NetAdapterRSS cmdlet to view RSS settings, and the Set-NetAdapterRSS cmdlet to configure RSS settings.

> **NEED MORE REVIEW? RECEIVE SIDE SCALING (RSS)**
>
> To review further details about RSS, refer to the Microsoft TechNet website at *https://technet.microsoft.com/library/hh997036.aspx*.

Enable and configure virtual RSS

Virtual RSS enables the network I/O load to be distributed across multiple virtual processors in a virtual machine and provides the same benefits as does RSS. You can enable and configure virtual RSS in your virtual machine in the same way as you do with your physical servers, as shown in Figure 6-6.

> **EXAM TIP**
>
> The physical network adapter in your host computer must support Virtual Machine Queue (VMQ). If VMQ is unavailable, you cannot enable virtual RSS.

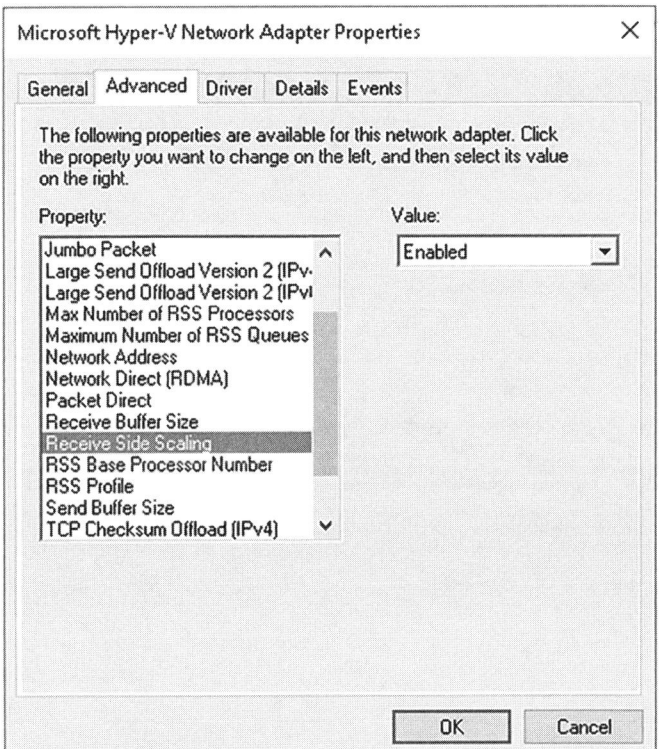

FIGURE 6-6 Enabling virtual RSS

> **NEED MORE REVIEW?** **VIRTUAL RECEIVE SIDE SCALING**
>
> To review further details about Virtual RSS, refer to the Microsoft TechNet website at *https://technet.microsoft.com/library/dn383582.aspx*.

Enable and configure Virtual Machine Multi-Queue (VMMQ)

Virtual Machine Queue VMQ uses hardware packet filtering to deliver external network packets directly to virtual machines; this helps to reduce the overhead of routing packets by avoiding copying them from the host management operating system to the guest virtual machine. To enable VMQ on your virtual machine, use the following procedure:

1. Open Hyper-V Manager.
2. In the Virtual Machines list, right-click the virtual machine you want to configure and click Settings.
3. In Settings, locate the network adapter for which you want to enable VMQ and then click the Hardware Acceleration node, as shown in Figure 6-7.
4. Select the Enable Virtual Machine Queue check box and click OK.

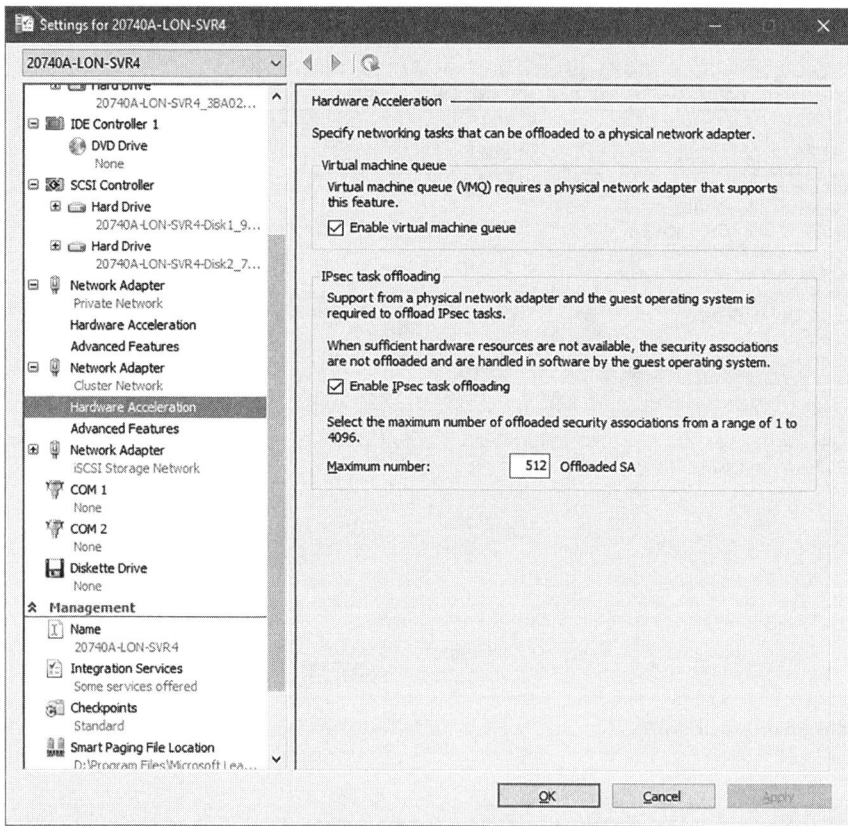

FIGURE 6-7 Enabling VMQ

VMMQ is an extension of VMQ and is integrated with virtual RSS in the hardware and enables virtual machines to sustain a greater network traffic load by distributing the processing across multiple cores on the host and multiple cores on the guest virtual machine.

EXAM TIP

VMMQ enables physical network adapters to offload some of the network traffic processing from virtual RSS into a traffic queue stored on the physical network adapter. VMQ should be used only if the network link on the physical card is 10Gbps or greater. If less than 10Gbps, it is disabled automatically even if it shows as being enabled in settings.

Enable and configure network QoS with Data Center Bridging (DCB)

QoS can help manage your network traffic by enabling you to configure rules that can detect congestion or reduced bandwidth, and then to prioritize, or throttle, traffic accordingly. For example, you can use QoS to prioritize voice and video traffic, which is sensitive to latency.

DCB provides bandwidth allocation to specific network traffic and helps to improve Ethernet transport reliability by using flow control based on priority. Because DCB is a hardware-based network traffic management technology, when you use DCB to manage QoS rules to control network traffic, you can:

- Offload bandwidth management to the physical network adapter.
- Enforce QoS on 'invisible' protocols, for example, Remote Direct Memory Access (RDMA).

EXAM TIP

To implement this environment, your physical network adapters and your intermediate switches must all support DCB.

To enable QoS with DCB, you must perform the following steps:

1. Enable DCB on your physical switches. Refer to your vendor's documentation to complete this step.
2. Create QoS rules. Use the new-NetQoSPolicy cmdlet to create the required rules. For example, as shown in Figure 6-8, the following command creates a QoS rule for SMB Direct traffic over TCP port 445 with a priority of 4:

```
New-NetQosPolicy "SMB Direct Traffic" -NetDirectPort 445 -Priority 4
```

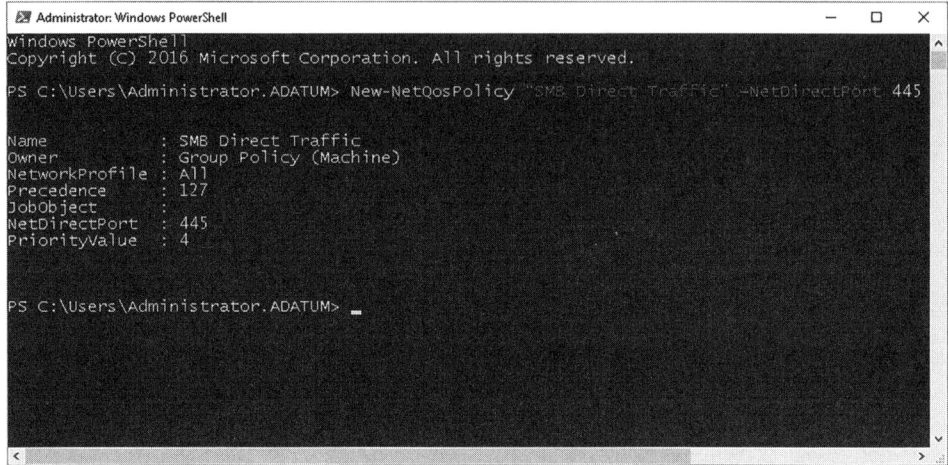

FIGURE 6-8 Creating QoS rules

3. Install the DCB feature on your server(s). Use Server Manager, as shown in Figure 6-9, to add the Data Center Bridging feature. Alternatively, use the Install-WindowsFeature PowerShell cmdlet.

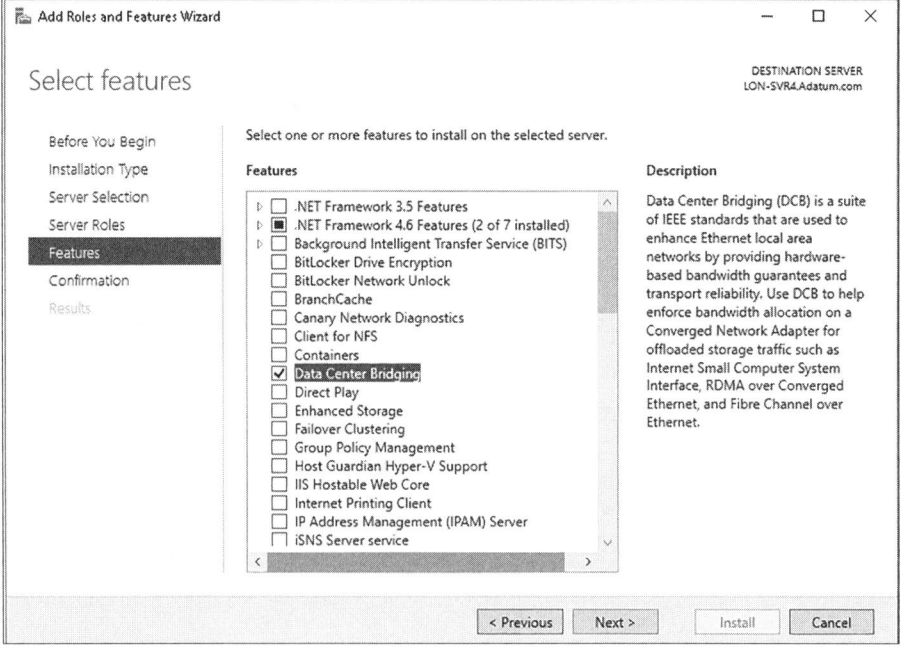

FIGURE 6-9 Enabling the Data Center Bridging feature

4. Use Windows PowerShell to define the traffic classes. Use the New-NetQoSTrafficClass PowerShell cmdlet. Each class you create must match the previously created QoS rule. For example, as shown in Figure 6-10, the following command creates the required traffic class for the SMB Direct Traffic rule and assigns a bandwidth of 30:

   ```
   New-NetQosTrafficClass 'SMB Direct Traffic' -Priority 4 -Algorithm ETS -Bandwidth 30
   ```

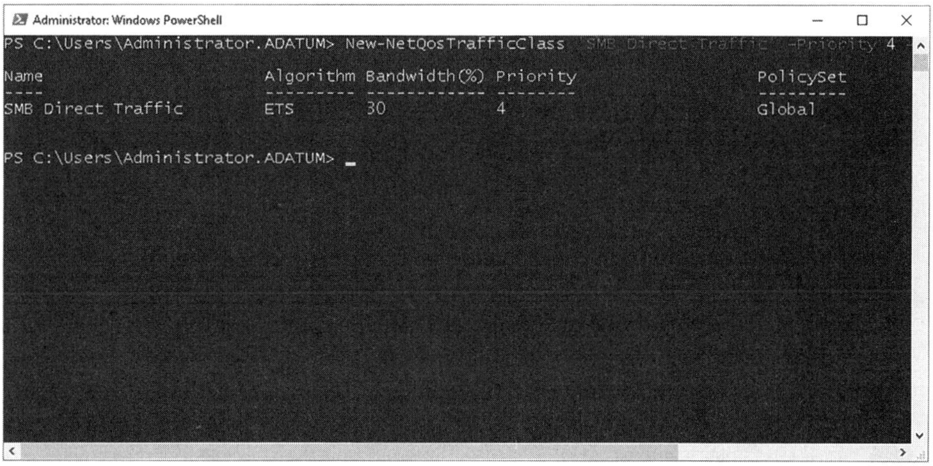

FIGURE 6-10 Defining traffic classes

5. Enable the DCB settings. Use the Windows PowerShell Set-NetQosDcbxSetting cmdlet. For example, the following command enables the DCB settings and the -willing $true parameter enables the adapter to accept remote DCB configuration from remote devices via the DCBX protocol, as well as from the local server:

   ```
   Set-NetQosDcbxSetting -Willing $true
   ```

6. Enable DCB on your network adapters. Use the Enable-NetAdapterQos cmdlet. For example:

   ```
   Enable-NetAdapterQos 'Ethernet 2'
   ```

> **NEED MORE REVIEW?** **DCB QOS CMDLETS IN WINDOWS POWERSHELL**
>
> To review further details about implementing QoS with DCB using Windows PowerShell, refer to the Microsoft TechNet website at *https://technet.microsoft.com/library/hh967440(v=wps.630).aspx*.

Enable and configure SMB Direct on RDMA-enabled network adapters

SMB Direct is implemented automatically in Windows Server 2016 on network adapters that support RDMA. NICs that support RDMA run at full speed with very low latency, and use very little CPU.

SMB Direct provides the following benefits:

- **Increased throughput**   Uses the full throughput of high-speed networks.
- **Low latency**   Provides fast responses to network requests, helping to reduce latency.
- **Low CPU utilization**   Uses less CPU resource, leaving more CPU resource available to service other apps.

> **NOTE SMB DIRECT**
> Windows Server 2016 automatically enables and configures SMB Direct.

To check whether your network adapter is RDMA-enabled, use Windows PowerShell Get-NetAdapterRdma cmdlet, as shown in Figure 6-11.

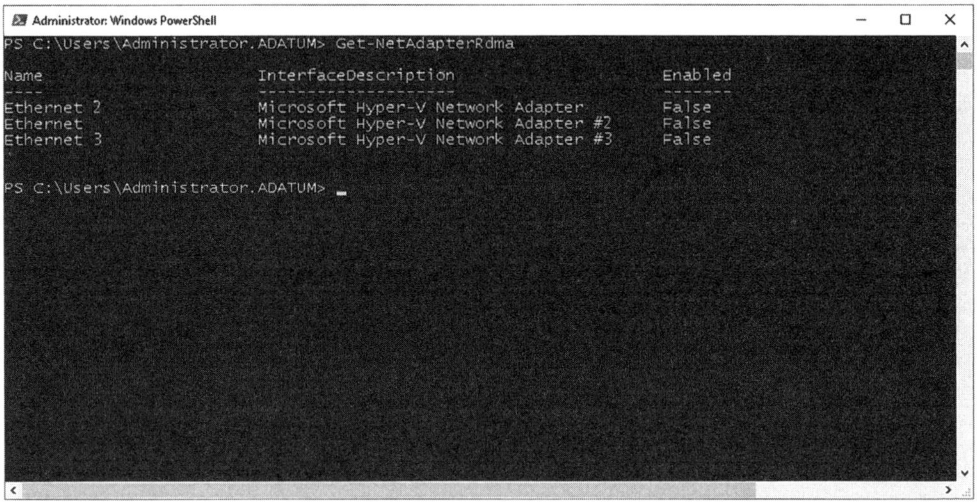

FIGURE 6-11 Checking RDMA settings

You can enable RDMA on your network adapter, assuming they are RDMA-capable, by using the Windows PowerShell Enable-NetAdapterRdma cmdlet. Alternatively, you can use Device Manager, as shown in Figure 6-12. Open the network adapter you want to configure, and enable the Network Direct (RDMA) value. Click OK.

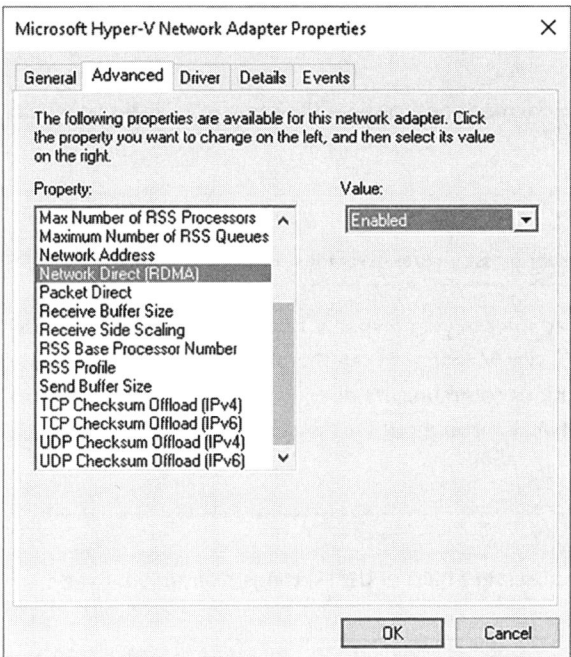

FIGURE 6-12 Enabling RDMA by using Device Manager

EXAM TIP

Do not add RDMA-capable network adapters to a NIC team if you want to use the RDMA capability of those adapters. When teamed, the network adapters no longer support RDMA.

Enable and configure SMB Multichannel

SMB Multichannel is the component in Windows Server that detects whether your installed network adapters are RDMA-capable. Using SMB Multichannel enables SMB to use the high throughput, low latency, and low CPU utilization offered by RDMA-capable network adapters. As SMB Multichannel is enabled by default in Windows Server, there is nothing to configure.

The requirements for SMB Multichannel are:

- Two or more computers running Windows Server 2012 or newer, or Windows 8 or newer.
- One of the following network adapter configurations:
    - Multiple NICs
    - One or more RSS-capable NICs
    - One or more NICs configured as part of a NIC team
    - One or more RDMA-capable NICs

Enable and configure SR-IOV on a supported network adapter

With SR-IOV, you can enable multiple virtual machines to share the same PCI Express physical hardware devices.

> **EXAM TIP**
>
> Only 64-bit Windows and Windows Server guest virtual machines support SR-IOV.

When enabled, the physical network adapter in your Hyper-V host is accessible directly in the virtual machines. You can even use Device Manager to see the physical network adapter. What this means is that your virtual machines communicate directly with the physical network hardware. Using SR-IOV can improve network throughput for demanding virtualized workloads.

> **EXAM TIP**
>
> You might need to enable SR-IOV in your server's BIOS or UEFI settings. Consult your vendor's documentation.

To enable SR-IOV, you must create a new Hyper-V virtual switch. To do this, open Hyper-V Manager, and then complete the following procedure:

1. In Hyper-V Manager, in the Actions pane, click Virtual Switch Manager.
2. In the Virtual Switch Manager dialog box, in the What Type Of Virtual Switch Do You Want To Create? section, click External, and then click Create Virtual Switch.
3. In the Name box, type a descriptive name.
4. In the Connection Type area, click External Network, and then select the appropriate network adapter.
5. Select the Enable Single Root I/O Virtualization (SR-IOV) check box, and then click OK.

296 CHAPTER 6   Implement an advanced network infrastructure

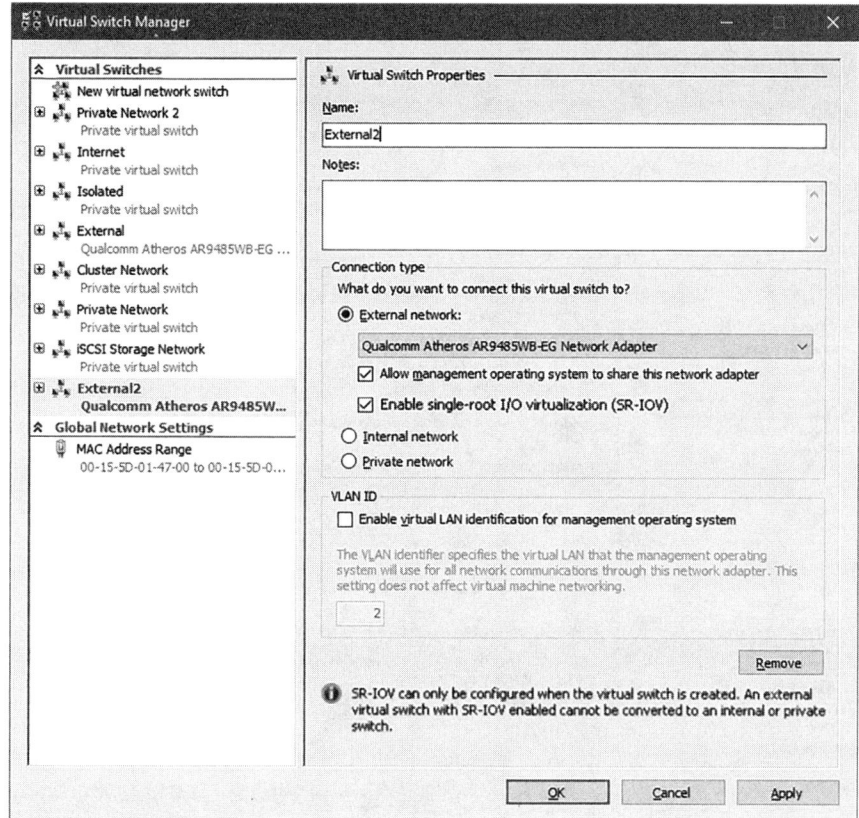

FIGURE 6-13 Enabling SR-IOV on a virtual switch

EXAM TIP

You cannot add SR-IOV to an existing virtual switch.

After you have enabled the SR-IOV setting on your virtual switch, you must configure the advanced settings for the network adapter within the virtual machine. Use the following procedure:

1. Open Hyper-V Manager.
2. In the Virtual Machines list, right-click the virtual machine you want to configure, and click Settings.
3. In Settings, click the network adapter for which you want to enable SR-IOV.
4. In the details pane, in the Virtual Switch list, click the virtual switch you just created.
5. Click Apply, and then click the Hardware Acceleration node, as shown in Figure 6-14.
6. Select the Enable SR-IOV check box, and click OK.

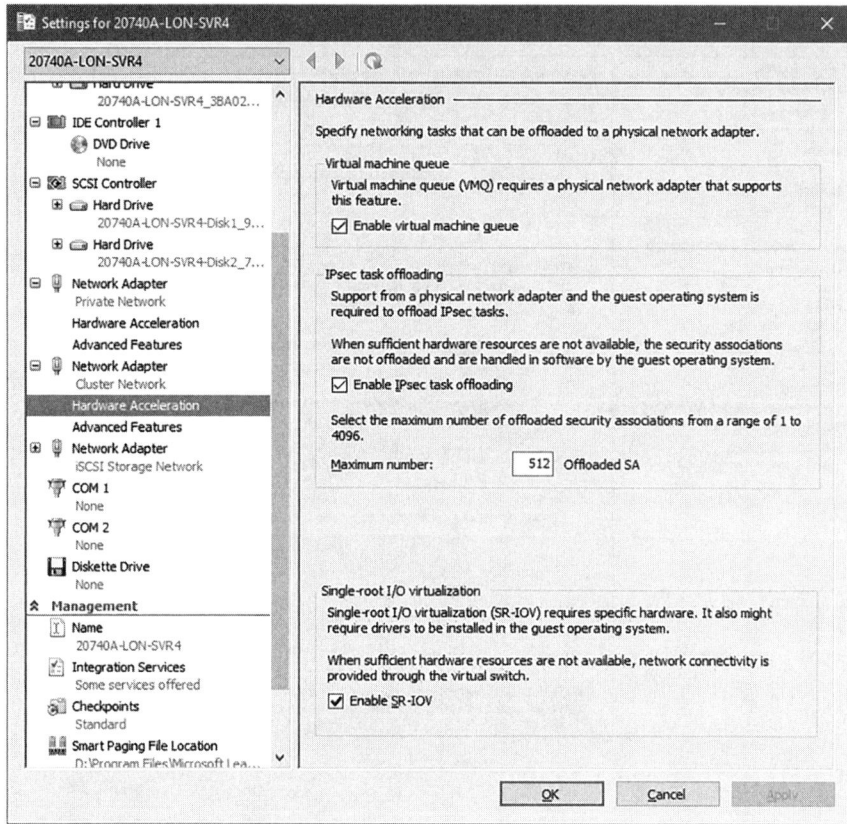

FIGURE 6-14 Enabling SR-IOV

Skill 6.2: Determine scenarios and requirements for implementing SDN

Using SDN bypasses the limitations imposed by physical network and implements a software abstraction layer that enables you to manage your network dynamically. Using SDN enables you to implement a cloud-based network infrastructure, overcoming limitations of your on-premises infrastructure, and offers the following benefits:

- **Efficient** Abstract hardware components in your network infrastructure by using software components.
- **Flexible** Shift traffic from your on-premises infrastructure to your private or public cloud infrastructure.
- **Scalable** Extend, as needed, into the cloud, providing far broader limits than your on-premises infrastructure can support.

When you implement SDN, you:

- **Virtualize your network**   Break the direct connection between the underlying physical network and the apps and virtual servers that run on it. You must virtualize your network management by creating virtual abstractions for physical network elements including ports, switches, and even IP addresses.
- **Define policies**   Define these policies in your network management system and apply them at the physical layer enabling you to manage traffic flow across both the physical and the virtual networks.
- **Manage the virtualized network infrastructure**   Provide the tools to configure the virtual network objects and policies.

Microsoft implements SDN in Hyper-V in Windows Server 2012 and newer by providing the following components:

- **Hyper-V Network Virtualization (HNV)**   Enables you to abstract the underlying physical network from your apps and workloads with virtual networks.
- **Hyper-V Virtual Switch**   Enables you to connect virtual machines to both virtual networks and physical networks.
- **RRAS Multitenant Gateway**   Enables you to extend network boundaries to the cloud so that you can deliver an on-demand, hybrid network infrastructure.
- **NIC Teaming**   Enables you to configure multiple network adapters as a team for bandwidth distribution and failover.
- **Network Controller**   Network Controller is a new feature in Windows Server 2016 and provides centralized management of both physical and virtual networks.

You can integrate SDN with Microsoft System Center to extend SDN. Microsoft System Center provides a number of SDN technologies in the following components:

- **System Center Operations Manager**   Enables you to monitor your infrastructure.
- **System Center Virtual Machine Manager**   Enables you to provision and manage virtual networks and provides for centralized management of virtual network policies.
- **Windows Server Gateway**   A virtual software router and gateway that can router traffic between your physical and virtual networks.

Determine deployment scenarios and network requirements for deploying SDN

Before you can deploy SDN, you must ensure that your network infrastructure meets the following prerequisites. These prerequisites fall into two broad categories:

- **Physical network**   You must be able to access all of your physical networking components, including:
    - Virtual LANs (VLANs)
    - Routers
    - Border Gateway Protocol (BGP) devices

- DCB with Enhanced Transmission Selection if using a RDMA technology
- DCB with Priority-based Flow Control if using an RDMA technology that is based in RDMA over Converged Ethernet (RoCE)

■ **Physical compute hosts** These computers are installed with the Hyper-V role and host the SDN infrastructure and tenant virtual machines and must:

- Have Windows Server 2016 installed.
- Have the Hyper-V role enabled.
- Have an external Hyper-V Virtual Switch created with at least one physical adapter.
- Be reachable with a management IP address assigned to the management host virtual NIC (vNIC).

TYPICAL SDN DEPLOYMENT

After you have verified that your infrastructure meets the requirements for SDN, you can plan your SDN deployment. The components of a typical SDN deployment are shown in Figure 6-15.

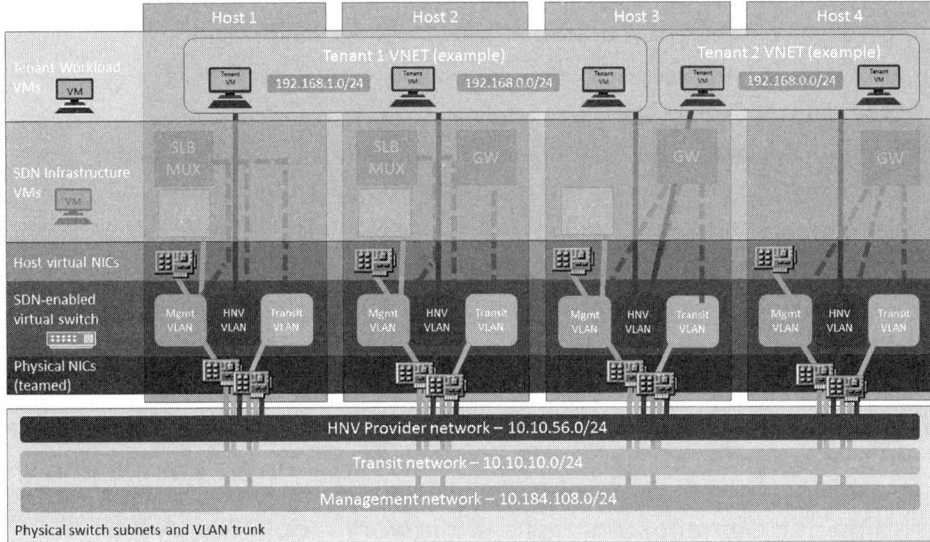

FIGURE 6-15 A typical SDN deployment

A typical SDN deployment consists of the following components:

■ **Management and HNV Provider logical networks** Physical compute hosts must have access to the Management logical network and the HNV Provider logical network. Consequently, each physical compute host must be assigned at least one IP address from the management logical network; you can assign a static IP address or use DHCP.

> **EXAM TIP**
> Compute hosts use the management logical network to communicate with each other.

- **Logical networks for gateways and the software load balancer** You must create and provision logical networks for gateway and Software Load Balancing (SLB) usage. These logical networks include:
    - **Transit** Used by SLB multiplexer (MUX) and RAS Gateway to exchange BGP peering information and North/South (external-internal) tenant traffic.
    - **Public virtual IP address (VIP)** Must have IP subnet prefixes that are Internet-routable outside the cloud environment and are the front-end IP addresses that external clients use to access your virtual networks.
    - **Private VIP** Do not need to be routable outside of the cloud. Used for VIPs that are only accessed from internal cloud clients, such as Generic Route Encapsulation (GRE) gateways.
    - **GRE VIP** Used to define VIPs that are assigned to gateway virtual machines running on your SDN fabric for server-to-server (S2S) GRE connection type.
- **Logical networks required for RDMA-based storage** You must define a VLAN and a subnet for each physical adapter in your compute and storage hosts if you use RDMA-based storage.
- **Routing infrastructure** Routing information for the VIP subnets is advertised into the physical network by using internal BGP peering. Consequently, you need to create a BGP peer on the router that your SDN infrastructure uses to receive routes for the VIP logical networks advertised by the SLB MUXs and HNV Gateways.
- **Default gateways** You must configure only one default gateway on the physical compute hosts and gateway virtual machines; this is usually the default gateway on the adapter that is used to connect to the Internet.
- **Network hardware** Your network hardware has a number of requirements, including those for network interface cards, switches, link control, availability and redundancy, and monitoring.

> **NEED MORE REVIEW? PLAN A SOFTWARE DEFINED NETWORK INFRASTRUCTURE**
> To review further details about planning SDN, refer to the Microsoft TechNet website at https://technet.microsoft.com/windows-server-docs/networking/sdn/plan/plan-a-software-defined-network-infrastructure.

Determine requirements and scenarios for implementing HNV

You can use network virtualization to manage network traffic by creating multiple virtual networks, logically isolated, on the same physical network, as shown in Figure 6-16.

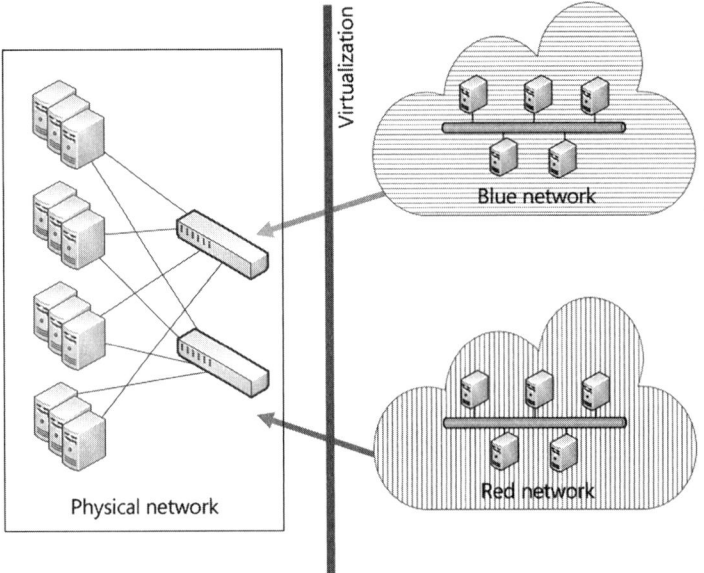

FIGURE 6-16 Network virtualization

Because network virtualization abstracts the physical network from the network traffic it carries, it provides the following benefits:

- **Compatibility**   Avoids the need to redesign your physical network to implement network virtualization.
- **Flexible IP address use**   Isolates virtual networks, enabling IP address reuse. Your virtual machines in different virtual networks can use the same IP address space.
- **Flexible virtual machine placement**   Separates the IP addresses assigned to virtual machines from the IP addresses used on your physical network enabling you to deploy your virtual machines on any Hyper-V host, irrespective of physical network constraints.
- **Network isolation without VLANs**   Enables you to define network traffic isolation without requiring VLANs or needing to reconfigure your physical network switches.
- **Inter-subnet live migration**   Enables you to move virtual machines between two Hyper-V hosts in different subnets using live migration without having to change the virtual machine IP address.

In Windows Server 2016, the Hyper-V Virtual Switch supports network virtualization. Windows Server 2016 Hyper-V uses either Network Virtualization Generic Route Encapsulation (NVGRE) or Virtual Extensible LAN (VXLAN). HNV with VXLAN is new in Windows Server 2016.

Implementing HNV with NVGRE encapsulation

If you implement network virtualization with NVGRE, when a virtual machine communicates over a network, NVGRE is used to encapsulate its packets. To configure NVGRE, you start by associating each virtual network adapter with two IP addresses: the customer address (CA) and the provider address (PA), as shown in Figure 6-17.

- **CA** Used by the virtual machine and configured on the virtual network adapter in the virtual machine guest operating system.

- **PA** Assigned by HNV and used by the Hyper-V host.

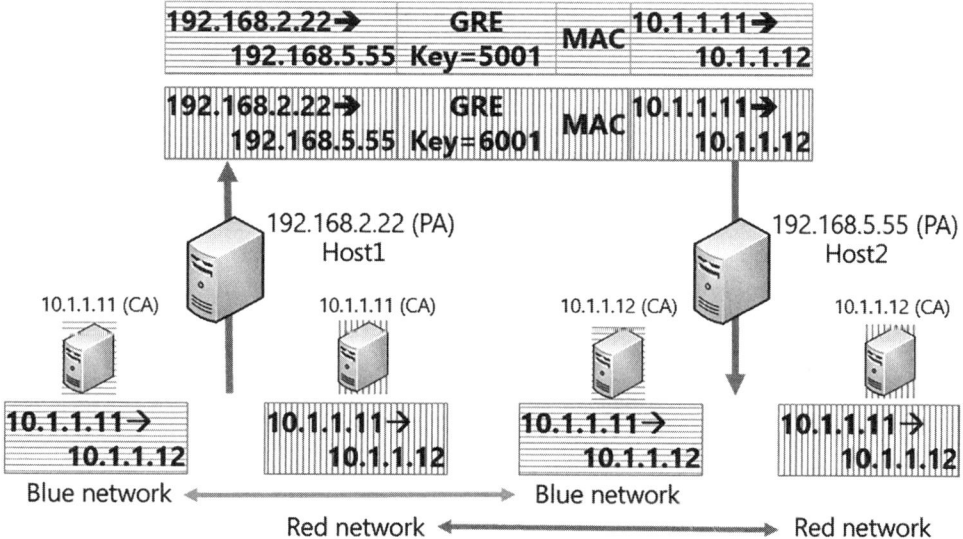

FIGURE 6-17 HNV using NVGRE

Let's discuss the example, shown in Figure 6-17. You see that each Hyper-V host is assigned one PA address: Host1: 192.168.2.22 and Host2: 192.168.5.55. These PAs are used for tunneling NVGRE traffic between the physical subnets: 192.168.2.0/24 and 192.168.5.0/24. This tunneling occurs on the physical network.

Each virtual machine is assigned a CA address, for example, 10.1.1.11 or 10.1.1.12. These addresses are unique on each virtualized network. Traffic between them is tunneled using the NVGRE tunnel between the hosts. To ensure separation of the traffic between the two virtualized networks, a GRE key is included in the GRE headers on the tunneled packets to provide a unique Virtual Subnet ID, in this case 5001 and 6001, for each virtualized network.

As a result of this configuration, you have two virtualized networks, red and blue, isolated from each another as separate IP networks, but extended across two physical Hyper-V hosts, each of which is located on a different physical subnet.

SET UP HNV WITH NVGRE

To set up HNV with NVGRE, you must complete the following high-level steps:

- Define PAs for each Hyper-V host
- Define CAs for each virtual machine
- Configure virtual subnet IDs for each subnet you want to virtualize

You can use either System Center VMM or Windows PowerShell to complete these tasks. For example, to configure the Blue Network shown in Figure 6-17 with Windows PowerShell, complete the following tasks:

1. Enable the Windows network virtualization binding on the physical NIC on each Hyper-V host.

   ```
   Enable-NetAdapterBinding Ethernet -ComponentID ms_netwnv
   ```

2. Configure Blue subnet locator and route records on each Hyper-V host.

   ```
   New-NetVirtualizationLookupRecord -CustomerAddress "10.1.1.12" -ProviderAddress
   "192.168.2.22"    -VirtualSubnetID "6001" -MACAddress "101010101105" -Rule
   "TranslationMethodEncap"
   New-NetVirtualizationLookupRecord -CustomerAddress "10.1.1.12" -ProviderAddress
   "192.168.5.55"    -VirtualSubnetID "6001" -MACAddress "101010101107" -Rule
   "TranslationMethodEncap"
   New-NetVirtualizationCustomerRoute -RoutingDomainID "{11111111-2222-3333-4444-
   000000000000}" -VirtualSubnetID "6001" -DestinationPrefix "10.1.1.0/24" -NextHop
   "0.0.0.0" -Metric 255
   ```

3. Configure the PA and route records on Hyper-V host1.

   ```
   $NIC = Get-NetAdapter Ethernet
   New-NetVirtualizationProviderAddress -InterfaceIndex $NIC.InterfaceIndex
   -ProviderAddress "192.168.2.22" -PrefixLength 24
   New-NetVirtualizationProviderRoute -InterfaceIndex $NIC.InterfaceIndex
   -DestinationPrefix "0.0.0.0/0" -NextHop "192.168.2.1"
   ```

4. Configure the PA and route records on Hyper-V host2.

   ```
   $NIC = Get-NetAdapter Ethernet
   New-NetVirtualizationProviderAddress -InterfaceIndex $NIC.InterfaceIndex
   -ProviderAddress "192.168.5.55" -PrefixLength 24
   New-NetVirtualizationProviderRoute -InterfaceIndex $NIC.InterfaceIndex
   -DestinationPrefix "0.0.0.0/0" -NextHop "192.168.5.1"
   ```

5. Configure the virtual subnet ID on the Hyper-V network switch ports for each Blue virtual machine on each Hyper-V host.

   ```
   Get-VMNetworkAdapter -VMName BlueVM1 | where {$_.MacAddress -eq "101010101105"} |
   Set-VMNetworkAdapter -VirtualSubnetID 6001
   Get-VMNetworkAdapter -VMName BlueVM2 | where {$_.MacAddress -eq "101010101107"} |
   Set-VMNetworkAdapter -VirtualSubnetID 6001
   ```

Next, repeat this process for the Red Network.

> **NEED MORE REVIEW?** **STEP-BY-STEP: HYPER-V NETWORK VIRTUALIZATION**
>
> To review further details about implementing HNV with NVGRE, refer to the Microsoft TechNet website at *https://blogs.technet.microsoft.com/keithmayer/2012/10/08/step-by-step-hyper-v-network-virtualization-31-days-of-favorite-features-in-winserv-2012-part-8-of-31/*.

HNV with VXLAN encapsulation

HNV over VXLAN is the default configuration in Windows Server 2016. VXLAN uses UDP over port 4789 as its network transport. To create the tunnel, in the UDP datagram after the header, a VXLAN header is added to enable network packets to be routed correctly. In Windows Server 2016, you must deploy the Network Controller feature in order to implement VXLAN for HNV.

> **NEED MORE REVIEW?** **NETWORK VIRTUALIZATION THROUGH ADDRESS VIRTUALIZATION**
>
> To review further details about implementing HNV with VXLAN, refer to the Microsoft TechNet website at *https://technet.microsoft.com/en-us/library/mt238303.aspx#Anchor_3*.

Deploying Network Controller

With Network Controller, a new feature in Windows Server 2016, you can manage and configure both your virtual and physical network infrastructure, as shown in Figure 6-18.

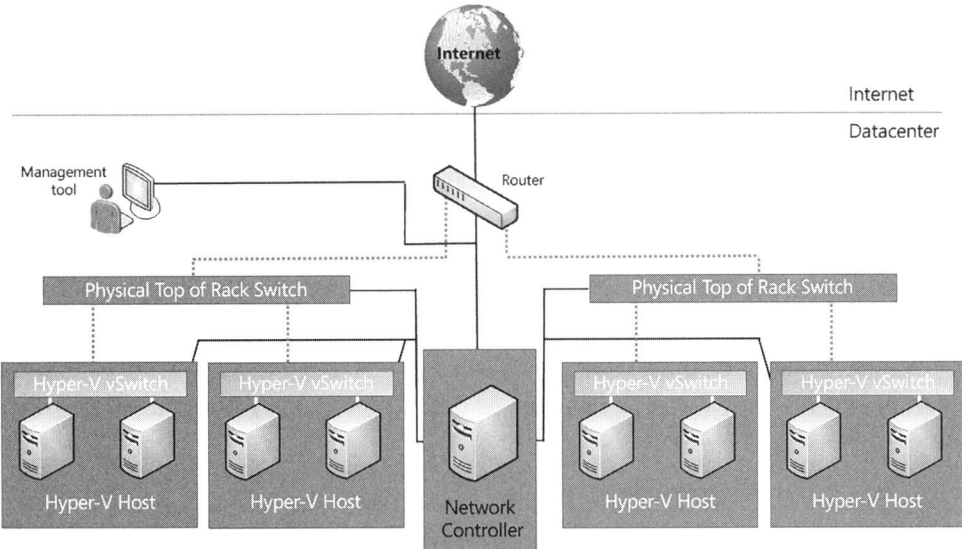

FIGURE 6-18 A Network Controller deployment

You can also automate the configuration of your network infrastructure. You can use Network Controller to manage the following physical and virtual network infrastructure:

- Hyper-V virtual machines and virtual switches
- Datacenter Firewall
- RAS Multitenant Gateways, Virtual Gateways, and gateway pools
- Load balancers

Network Controller is a Windows Server 2016 server role that provides two programming interfaces (APIs):

- **Northbound** Enables you to collect network information from Network Controller with which you can monitor and configure your network. The Northbound API enables you to configure, monitor, troubleshoot, and deploy new devices on the network by using:
  - Windows PowerShell
  - Representational state transfer (REST) API
  - System Center VMM or System Center Operations Manager or similar non-Microsoft management UI
- **Southbound** Network Controller uses the Southbound API to communicate with network devices, services, and components. With the Southbound API, Network Controller can:
  - Discover devices on your network.
  - Detect configuration of services.
  - Collect network data and statistics.
  - Send information to your network infrastructure, such as configuration changes you have made.

Prerequisites for deployment

You can deploy Network Controller on physical computers or virtual machines, or both. Since Network Controller is a Windows Server 2016 server role, the requirements are not complex. They are that you must:

- Deploy Network Controller on Windows Server 2016 Datacenter edition.
- Install your Network Controller management client on a computer or virtual machine running Windows 10, Windows 8.1, or Windows 8.
- Configure dynamic DNS registration to enable registration of the required Network Controller DNS records.
- In an AD DS domain environment:
  - Create a security group for all the users that require permission to configure Network Controller.

- Create a security group for all the users that require permission to manage your network with Network Controller.
- Configure certificate-based authentication for Network Controller deployments in non-domain joined environments.

DEPLOYING NETWORK CONTROLLER

To deploy Network Controller, you must perform the following high-level steps:

1. Install the Network Controller server role   Use Windows PowerShell Install-WindowsFeature -Name NetworkController –IncludeManagementTools command, or Server Manager, as shown in Figure 6-19.

2. Configure the Network Controller cluster   To do this, complete the following steps:

    A. **Create a node object**. You must create a node object for each computer or virtual machine that is a member of the Network Controller cluster. The following command creates a Network Controller node object named NCNode1. The FQDN of the computer is NCNode1.Adatum.com, and Ethernet is the name of the interface on the computer listening to REST requests.

    ```
    New-NetworkControllerNodeObject -Name "NCNode1" -Server "NCNode1.Adatum.com"
    -FaultDomain "fd:/rack1/host1" -RestInterface "Ethernet"
    ```

    B. **Configure the cluster**. After you have created the node(s) for the cluster, you must configure the cluster. The following commands install a Network Controller cluster.

    ```
    $NodeObject = New-NetworkControllerNodeObject -Name "NCNode1" -Server
    "NCNode1.Adatum.com" -FaultDomain "fd:/rack1/host1" -RestInterface "Ethernet"
    Install-NetworkControllerCluster -Node $NodeObject -ClusterAuthentication
    Kerberos
    ```

3. Configure Network Controller. The first command creates a Network Controller node object, and then stores it in the $NodeObject variable. The second command gets a certificate named NCEncryption, and then stores it in the $Certificate variable. The third command creates a cluster node. The fourth and final command deploys the Network Controller:

    ```
    $NodeObject = New-NetworkControllerNodeObject -Name "NCNode01" -Server "NCNode1"
    -FaultDomain "fd:/rack1/host1" -RestInterface Ethernet
    $Certificate = Get-Item Cert:\LocalMachine\My | Get-ChildItem | where {$_.Subject
    -imatch "NCEncryption" }
    Install-NetworkControllerCluster -Node $NodeObject -ClusterAuthentication None
    Install-NetworkController -Node $NodeObject -ClientAuthentication None
    -RestIpAddress "10.0.0.1/24" -ServerCertificate $Certificate
    ```

> **NEED MORE REVIEW? DEPLOY NETWORK CONTROLLER USING WINDOWS POWERSHELL**
>
> To review further details about deploying Network Controller with Windows PowerShell, refer to the Microsoft TechNet website at *https://technet.microsoft.com/library/mt282165.aspx#bkmk_app*.

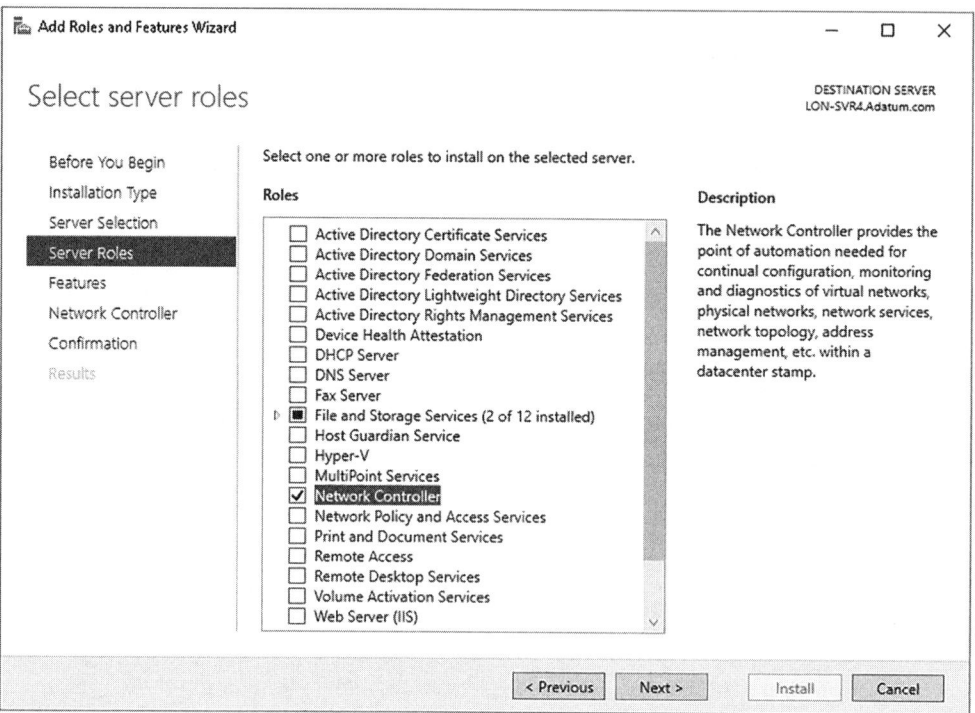

FIGURE 6-19 Installing the Network Controller server role

EXAM TIP

You can deploy Network Controller in both AD DS domain and non-domain environments. If you deploy in an AD DS domain environment, Network Controller authenticates users and devices using Kerberos. If you deploy in a non-domain environment, you must deploy digital certificates to provide for authentication.

After you have deployed and configured Network Controller, you can use it to configure and manage both virtual and physical network devices and services. These are:

- **SLB management**   Configure multiple servers to host the same workload to provide for high availability and scalability.
- **RAS gateway management**   Provide gateway services with Hyper-V hosts and virtual machines that are members of a RAS gateway pool.
- **Firewall management**   Configure and manage firewall Access Control rules for your virtual machines.
- **Virtual network management**   Deploy and configure HNV. This includes:

- Hyper-V Virtual Switch
- Virtual network adapters on individual virtual machines
- Virtual network policies

> **NEED MORE REVIEW? DEPLOY A NETWORK CONTROLLER USING VMM**
>
> To review further details about deploying Network Controller with VMM, refer to the Microsoft TechNet website at *https://technet.microsoft.com/en-us/system-center-docs/vmm/manage/deploy-a-network-controller-using-vmm*.

Software Load Balancing

You can use SLB in SDN to distribute your network traffic across your available network resources. In Windows Server 2016, SLB provides the following features:

- Layer 4 load balancing for both North-South and East-West TCP and UDP traffic.
- Public and internal network traffic load balancing.
- Support for dynamic IP addresses (DIPs) on Hyper-V virtual networks and VLANs.
- Support for health probe.
- Maps Virtual IP addresses (VIPs) to DIPs. In this scenario:
  - VIPs are single IP addresses that map to a pool of available virtual machines; they are IP addresses available on the Internet for tenants (and tenant customers) to connect to tenant resources in the cloud.
  - DIPs are assigned to tenant resources within your cloud infrastructure and are the IP addresses of the virtual machines that are members of a load-balanced pool.

SLB INFRASTRUCTURE

The SLB infrastructure consists of the following components, as shown in Figure 6-20.

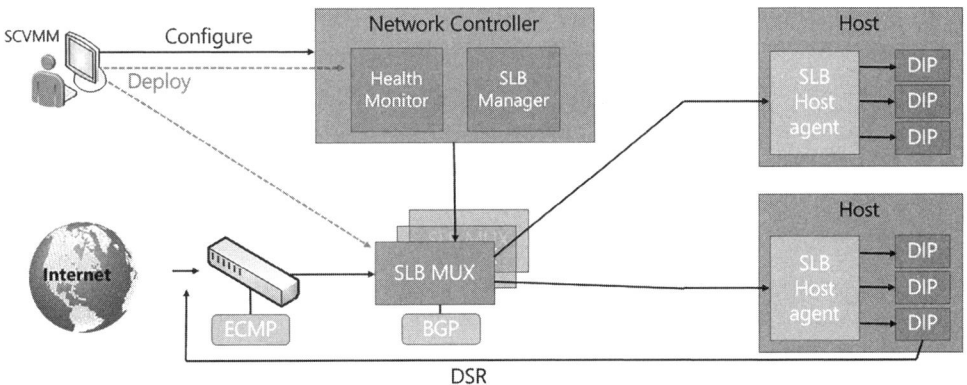

FIGURE 6-20 An SLB deployment

- **VMM** Used to configure Network Controller, including Health Monitor and SLB Manager. You can also use Windows PowerShell to manage Network Controller.
- **Network Controller** Performs the following functions in SLB:
    - Processes SLB commands that arrive from the Northbound API from VMM, Windows PowerShell, or other management app.
    - Calculates policy for distribution to Hyper-V hosts and SLB MUXs.
    - Provides health status of the SLB infrastructure.
    - Provides each MUX with each VIP.
    - Configures and controls behavior of the VIP to DIP mapping in the MUX.

> **NEED MORE REVIEW? NETWORK CONTROLLER CMDLETS**
>
> For more information on the Windows PowerShell cmdlets that you can use to manage Network Controller, refer to the Microsoft TechNet website at *https://technet.microsoft.com/library/mt576401.aspx*.

> **EXAM TIP**
>
> You define load balancing policies by using Network Controller, and the MUX maps VIPs to the correct DIPs with those policies.

- **SLB MUX** Maps and rewrites network inbound Internet traffic, so that it arrives at an individual DIP. Within the SLB infrastructure, the MUX consists of one or more virtual machines and:
    - Holds the VIPs.
    - Uses BGP to advertise each of the VIPs to routers.
- **Hosts that run Hyper-V** You use SLB with computers that are running Windows Server 2016 and Hyper-V.
- **SLB Host Agent** Deploy the SLB Host Agent on every Hyper-V host computer. The SLB Host Agent:
    - Listens for SLB policy updates from Network Controller.
    - Programs rules for SLB into the Software Defined Networking–enabled Hyper-V virtual switches that are configured on the local computer.

> **NOTE VIRTUAL SWITCH AND SLB COMPATABILITY**
>
> For a virtual switch to be compatible with SLB, you must use Hyper-V Virtual Switch Manager or Windows PowerShell commands to create the switch. Then you must enable Virtual Filtering Platform for the virtual switch.

EXAM TIP

You can install the SLB Host Agent on all versions of Windows Server 2016 that support the Hyper-V role, including Nano Server.

- **SDN–enabled Hyper-V Virtual Switch**   The virtual switch performs the following actions for SLB:
    - Processes the data path for SLB.
    - Receives inbound network traffic from the MUX.
    - Bypasses the MUX for outbound network traffic, sending it to the router by using direct server return.

EXAM TIP

You can run the virtual switch on Nano Server instances of Hyper-V.

- **BGP-enabled router**   Allows routers to:
    - Route inbound traffic to the MUX by using equal-cost multi-path routing (ECMP).
    - For outbound network traffic, use the route provided by the host.
    - Listen for route updates for VIPs via the SLB MUX.
    - Remove SLB MUXs from the SLB rotation if Keep Alive fails.

> **NEED MORE REVIEW?** **SOFTWARE LOAD BALANCING INFRASTRUCTURE**
>
> To review further details about SLB, refer to the Microsoft TechNet website at *https://technet.microsoft.com/library/mt632286.aspx#bkmk_infrastructure*.

Implementing Windows Server gateways

If you implement network virtualization using the Hyper-V Virtual Switch, the switch operates as a router between the various Hyper-V hosts in your network; network virtualization policies define how traffic is routed between those hosts. But a virtual switch cannot route to external networks when you use network virtualization.

If you do not use network virtualization, you could connect your virtual machine(s) to an external switch enabling the virtual machine(s) to connect to the same networks as the Hyper-V host.

But when you implement network virtualization, you have a number of additional considerations:

- You can have multiple virtual machines running on a Hyper-V host that are all using the same IP addresses.
- You can move the virtual machine to any host in your network without interrupting network connectivity.

To address these considerations, you must implement a solution that is multitenant-aware to connect your virtualized networks to the Internet in order that traffic to external networks is correctly routed to the internal addresses that the virtual machines use. The RAS Gateway in Windows Server 2016 provides a solution to these issues.

EXAM TIP

RAS Gateway is referred to as Windows Server Gateway in System Center.

OVERVIEW OF RAS GATEWAY

RAS Gateway is a software-based, multitenant, BGP-capable router and provides the following features:

- **Site-to-site VPN**   Connects two networks at different locations using the Internet with a site-to-site VPN connection.
- **Point-to-site VPN**   Enables employees to connect to your organization's network from remote locations.
- **GRE tunneling**   Enables connectivity between external and tenant virtual networks.
- **Dynamic routing with BGP**   Automatically learns routes between sites that are connected by using site-to-site VPN connections.

SCENARIOS FOR USE

You can implement RAS Gateway in a number of different configurations:

- **Multitenant-aware VPN gateway**   Configured as a VPN gateway that is aware of the virtual networks deployed on the Hyper-V hosts. Although the RAS Gateway operates like any other VPN gateway, the main difference is that it is multitenant-aware. This means you can have multiple virtual networks with overlapping address spaces located on the same virtual infrastructure. Deploying RAS Gateway like this means you can connect to the RAS Gateway by using:
    - A site-to-site VPN from a remote location
    - Remote VPN access to the RAS Gateway
- **Multitenant-aware network address translation (NAT) gateway for Internet access**   Provides virtual machines on virtual networks with access to the Internet. You configure the RAS Gateway as a NAT device. In this configuration, all virtual networks behind the RAS Gateway can connect to the Internet, even if they use overlapping address spaces because the RAS Gateway is multitenant-aware.
- **Forwarding gateway for internal physical network access**   Provides access to internal network resources located on physical networks. For example, if you have servers that are deployed on physical hosts, when you configure RAS Gateway as a forwarding gateway, it enables computers on the virtual networks to connect to those physical hosts.

NETWORK CONTROLLER WITH RAS GATEWAY

If you use Network Controller to manage Hyper-V hosts and virtual machines that are members of a RAS Gateway pool, you can provide RAS Gateway services to your tenants. In this scenario, you use Network Controller automatically to deploy virtual machines running RAS Gateway to support the following features:

- Site-to-site VPN gateway connectivity using Internet Protocol security (IPsec)
- Site-to-site VPN gateway connectivity using GRE
- Point-to-site VPN gateway connectivity
- Layer 3 forwarding
- BGP routing

Distributed firewall policies

The Datacenter Firewall in Windows Server 2016 can help you to install and configure firewall policies that can help protect your virtual networks from unwanted network traffic. You manage the Datacenter Firewall policies using Network Controller Northbound APIs, as shown in Figure 6-21.

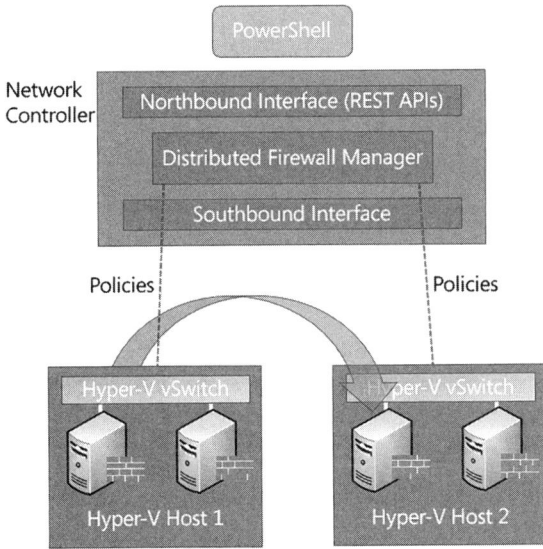

FIGURE 6-21 Distributed firewall policies

BENEFITS FOR CLOUD PROVIDER

For cloud service providers, the Datacenter Firewall provides these benefits:

- A software-based firewall solution which is scalable and manageable.
- Protection to tenant virtual machines regardless of the tenant guest operating system.

- The ability easily to move tenant virtual machines to different physical hosts without interrupting tenant firewall configuration because:
  - You deploy as a vSwitch port host agent firewall.
  - Policies are assigned to vSwitch host agent firewalls on tenant virtual machines.
  - Irrespective of the host that runs the virtual machine, firewall rules are configured in each vSwitch port.

BENEFITS FOR TENANTS

For tenants, the Datacenter Firewall provides the ability to:

- Define firewall rules that can protect Internet-facing resources on their virtual networks.
- Define firewall rules that can isolate and protect network traffic between tenant virtual networks at their service provider and their on-premises networks.
- Define firewall rules that can protect traffic between virtual machines on the same L2 virtual subnet but also protect traffic between virtual machines on different L2 virtual subnets.

Network security groups

A network security group (NSG) contains a list of Access Control List (ACL) rules that allow or block network traffic to your virtual machines in a virtual network. You can associate NSGs with subnets or individual virtual machines within a subnet.

When you associate an NSG with a subnet, the ACL rules apply to all the virtual machines in that subnet. You can further restrict network traffic to an individual virtual machine by associating an NSG directly to that virtual machine.

> ***NEED MORE REVIEW?*** **WHAT IS A NETWORK SECURITY GROUP?**
>
> To review further details about implementing NSG, refer to the Microsoft TechNet website at *https://azure.microsoft.com/en-gb/documentation/articles/virtual-networks-nsg/*.

Chapter summary

- You can choose between NIC teaming and SET to combine network adapters to help improve network throughput.
- You can implement RSS on compatible network adapters to distribute the CPU load on a server.
- QoS enables you to prioritize network traffic that is latency sensitive.
- SR-IOV enables multiple virtual machines to share the same PCI Express hardware devices.
- Network Controller is a new Windows Server 2016 features that you can use to easily configure and maintain both your physical and virtual network infrastructure.
- You can implement HNV with both NVGRE and VXLAN.

Thought experiment

In this thought experiment, demonstrate your skills and knowledge of the topics covered in this chapter. You can find answers to this thought experiment in the next section.

You work in support at A. Datum. As a consultant for A. Datum, answer the following questions about advanced network infrastructure features within the A. Datum organization:

1. You are configuring NIC teaming. You have chosen to implement Static teaming as the teaming mode. What is your next step?
2. When you are configuring SET in a test network, you can only use one Teaming mode. What is it?
3. You try to enable RSS in a virtual machine running Windows Server. You are unable to do so. What could the possible reason(s) be?
4. You decide to implement QoS over DCB. What are the high-level steps that you must complete?
5. What Windows PowerShell cmdlet can you use to enable RDMA on your server's network adapter?
6. What is the main purpose of using network virtualization?

Thought experiment answers

This section contains the solution to the thought experiment. Each answer explains why the answer choice is correct.

1. Static teaming requires that your Ethernet switches must be configured for NIC teaming per the 802.3ad standard.
2. Switch independent mode is the only supported teaming mode in SET.
3. In order to enable RSS on a virtual machine, your network adapters must support the VMQ feature.
4. The high-level steps are:
    A. Enable DCB on your physical switches
    B. Create QoS rules
    C. Install the DCB feature on your server(s)
    D. Define the traffic classes
    E. Enable the DCB settings
    F. Enable DCB on your network adapters
5. You can enable RDMA on your network adapter, assuming they are RDMA-capable, by using the Windows PowerShell Enable-NetAdapterRdma cmdlet.
6. You can use network virtualization to manage network traffic by creating multiple virtual networks, logically isolated, on the same physical network.

Index

A

Access Control List (ACL) 314
access policies 142, 144–146
access scopes 142, 144, 146–147
Active Directory
    primary zone integration 37–39
Active Directory Certificate Services (AD CS) 221
Active Directory Domain Services (AD DS) 3, 59
Add-ADGroupMember cmdlet 21
Add-DhcpServerv4Failover cmdlet 88
Add-DhcpServerv4MulticastScope cmdlet 67
Add-DhcpServerv4Policy cmdlet 74
Add-DhcpServerv4Reservation cmdlet 69
Add-DhcpServerv4Scope cmdlet 64
Add-DhcpServerv4Superscope cmdlet 66
Add-DhcpServerv6Scope cmdlet 77
Add-DnsServerConditionalForwarderZone cmdlet 8
Add-DnsServerForwarder cmdlet 7
Add-DnsServerPrimaryZone cmdlet 29
Add-DnsServerResourceRecord cmdlet 45, 49
Add-DnsServerRootHint cmdlet 11
Add-DnsServerStubZone cmdlet 41
Add-DnsServerZoneDelegation cmdlet 36
Add-IpamRange cmdlet 122
address resolution protocol (ARP) 245
AD DS forests
    managing multiple, with IPAM 141
AD DS-integrated zones 37–39, 40, 41
Add-VpnConnectionTriggerApplication cmdlet 177
Add-WindowsFeature cmdlet 60
anycast addresses 237
app-triggered VPNs 176–177
ARP. *See* address resolution protocol (ARP)
auditing
    IPAM 147–152

authentication
    certificate configuration 220–223
    IPv6 236
    password-based 220
    SQL 105–106
    VPN 166, 167
    Windows 105–106
Automatic Private IP Addressing (APIPA) addresses 58, 92, 237

B

bandwidth allocation 291–293
BGP. *See* Border Gateway Protocol
BOOTP forwarding 78
Border Gateway Protocol (BGP) 246
    configuration of 249–250
BranchCache 271–277
    client computers 275–276
    configuration 272–276
    distributed cache mode 271
    hosted cache mode 271–272
    installation 272
    server types supported by 272
    troubleshooting 276–277
branch office solutions 250–277
    BranchCache 271–277
    Distributed File Share 251–270
broadcast IPv4 addresses 76

C

cache locking 18
Certificate Authority (CA) 221
certificates
    configuration of 220–223
    digital 166

Certification Authority (CA)

Certification Authority (CA) 19
Challenge Handshake Authentication Protocol (CHAP) 167, 176
CHAP. *See* Challenge Handshake Authentication Protocol (CHAP)
classful addressing 229
client address conflicts 92
client computer certificates 221
client subnet 20
cloud service providers (CSPs) 168
CNAME records 43
comma separated value (CSV) files 124
conditional forwarding 7–8
  stub zones and 40–41
conditions, policy 213
Configuration Manager 178, 180
Connection Manager Administration Kit (CMAK) 178–179
connection profiles
  creation and configuration of 177–179
connection request policies 217–219
Connect To A Workplace Wizard 174
constraints, policy 213–214

D

DANE. *See* DNS-Baed Authentication of Named Entities
Data Center Bridging (DCB) 291–293
Datacenter Firewall 313–314
data encapsulation 166
data encryption 166
DCB. *See* Data Center Bridging
debug logging 22–23, 51
default gateway address 228
delegated administration 21
delegation
  DNS 34–36
demand-dial connections 181–189
demand-dial interface 181
denial-of-service (DOS) attacks 18
deployment
  connection profiles 179–180
  DirectAccess server 190–191
  IPAM 106–107
  Nano Server 5–6
  Network Controller 305–309
  Software Load Balancing 309–311
DFS Namespaces role service 252

DFS Replication (DFSR)
  adding role service 260
  configuration of 260–269
  optimization of 269
  remote differential compression settings 268–269
  replication group creation 260–265
  scheduling 265–267
  staging configuration 267–268
DHCP. *See* Dynamic Host Configuration Protocol
DHCPACK packets 58
DHCP Audit Logging 93–94
DHCPDISCOVER packets 58
DHCP Event Logs 94–95
dhcp.mdb file 89
DHCPOFFER packets 58
DHCP Post-Install Configuration Wizard 60–61
DHCP Relay Agent
  configuration of 78–79
DHCPREQUEST packets 58, 72
DHCP scopes 57
  configuration of 130–132
  creating 130–131
  creation and configuration of 61–68
  managing, with IPAM 127, 130–132
  multicast 65, 66–68
  options configuration 69–73
  replicating 88–89
  split scopes 82–85
  superscopes 65–66
  using Windows PowerShell to manage 136
DHCP servers 57–58
  auditing changes on 148–149
  authorization of 60–61
  export and import of 80–81
  installation and configuration 59–61
  managing, with IPAM 127–130
  manually provisioning for IPAM 110–111
  migration of 81
  options configuration 70–71
  policy configuration 132–134
  using Windows PowerShell to manage 136
DHCP Split-Scope Configuration Wizard 84
DhcpSrvLog - Day.log file 94
digital certificates 166
DirectAccess 155, 168, 189–199
  clients 189
  configuration 196–197
  install and configure 192–196

318

Dynamic Host Configuration Protocol (DHCP)

internal resources 189, 190
required components 189–190
server 189
    deployment options 190–191
    requirements 191
topology 193
troubleshooting 198–199
tunneling options 190
directory partitions 38
distributed cache mode 271
Distributed File System (DFS) 250–270
    adding folders and folder targets 256
    database management 270
    fault tolerance 270
    namespaces
        adding role service 252
        configuration of 252–255
        defined 251–252
    replication configuration 260–269
    replication targets 256–259
DNS. *See* Domain Name System
DNS Analytical events 52–53
DNS Audit events 51–53
DNS-Based Authentication of Named Entities (DANE) 19
DNSCMD.exe command-line tool 17
DNS delegation 34–36
dnsperf tool 25
DNS policies 51
DNS Policy 19–20
DNS records
    configuration of 42–49
    managing, using IPAM 138–140
DNS scopes
    configuration of 50–51
DNSSEC
    configuration of 14–17
    implementing 14–17
DNS servers
    auditing changes on 148–149
    managing properties, using IPAM 136–138
    manually provisioning for IPAM 111–112
    using Windows PowerShell to manage 140
DNS zones
    configuration of 27–42
        delegation 34–36
        records 42–49
        secure dynamic updates 40
        zone scavenging 45–47

GlobalNames zone 42
managing, using IPAM 138–140
overview of 26–27
primary zones 27–31, 37–39
secondary zones 31–34
stub zones 40–41
using Windows PowerShell to manage 140
domain-based DFS namespaces 252
domain controllers
    manually provisioning for IPAM 112
Domain Name System (DNS) 1–56
    cache locking 18
    deployment
        Nano Server 5–6
    global settings 26
    logging 22–23
    managing, with IPAM 136–140
        in multiple Active Directory forests 141
    monitoring 51–54
    name resolution 2–3
    options configuration 72–73
    performance tuning 23–25
    policies 19–20
    response rate limiting 18
    round robin 49
    server address 228
    server role 1–26
        administration of 19–26
        advanced settings 13–19
        forwarders configuration 6–8
        installation 3–5
        recursion configuration 12–13
        root hints configuration 8–12
    socket pool 17
    using Windows PowerShell to manage 140
Dynamic Host Configuration Protocol (DHCP) 57–100
    class options 71–72
    communication phases 58
    database
        backup and restore of 90–91
        overview of 89–90
    failover 83, 86–89
        configuration of, in IPAM 134–136
    high availability
        configuration, using DHCP failover 82–89
        options 82–83
    installation 59–61
    IPv6 addressing 76–77

dynamic updates

   managing, with IPAM 126–136
      in multiple Active Directory forests 141
   options configuration 69–73
   overview of 57–59
   policy configuration 73–75, 132–134
   prerequisites 59
   PXE boot configuration 79–80
   reservation configuration 68–69
   scopes 57, 61–73, 82–85
   troubleshooting 91–98
      common issues 91–92
      tools for 92–98
dynamic updates 43

E

EAP. *See* Extensible Authentication Protocol
EAP with Transport Layer Security (EAP-TLS) 220
Edge topology 190
Enable-NetAdapterRdma cmdlet 294
encapsulation 166
encryption 166, 215, 236
Event Catalog 150–152
Event Viewer 94–95
Export-DhcpServer cmdlet 80
Export-NpsConfiguration cmdlet 220
Extensible Authentication Protocol (EAP) 167, 175, 176

F

fault tolerance
   DFS 270
firewall policies 313–314
folders
   adding 256
forwarders
   configuration of 6–8
forward lookup zones 26–27
Fully Qualified Domain Name (FQDN) 30

G

Generic Route Encapsulation (GRE) 301
generic teaming 282
Get-DfsrPreservedFiles cmdlet 270
Get-DnsServerRootHint cmdlet 12
Get-DnsServerStatistics cmdlet 54

Get-IpamDhcpConfigurationEvent cmdlet 136
Get-IpamDhcpScope cmdlet 136
Get-IpamDhcpServer cmdlet 136
Get-IpamDhcpSuperscope cmdlet 136
Get-IpamDnsConditionalForwarder cmdlet 140
Get-IpamDnsResourceRecord cmdlet 140
Get-IpamDnsServer cmdlet 140
Get-IpamDnsZone cmdlet 140
Get-NetAdapterRdma cmdlet 294
Get-NetAdapterRSS cmdlet 288
Getting Started Wizard 192–197
Global access scope 144
GlobalNames zone 42
global unicast addresses 237
GRE. *See* Generic Route Encapsulation
Group Policy Objects (GPOs) 14
   for provisioning IPAM 107, 109, 113–114

H

hash values 282
high availability
   configuration, using DHCP failover 82–89
high performance network solutions 281–298
   Data Center Bridging 291–293
   NIC teaming 282–285
   receive side scaling 287–291
   SMB Direct 294–295
   SR-IOV 296–298
   switch embedded teaming 285–286
   Virtual Machine Queue VMQ 290–291
HNV. *See* Hyper-V Network Virtualization
hosted cache mode 271–272
host names 1, 2–3
host records 43
Hot Standby mode 86
Hyper-V 281
   port 283, 286
   SDN on 299
Hyper-V Network Virtualization (HNV) 299
   benefits of 302
   implementing 302–305
   with NVGRE encapsulation 303–305
   with VXLAN encapsulation 305
Hyper-V Virtual Switch 299, 311

I

ICS. *See* Internet Connection Sharing
IIPConfig.exe command-line tool 95–96
Import-DhcpServer cmdlet 81
Import-DnsServerRootHint cmdlet 11
Import-IpamAddress cmdlet 124
Import-IpamRange cmdlet 124
Import-IpamSubnet cmdlet 124
Import-NpsConfiguration cmdlet 220
installation
  BranchCache 272
  DHCP server role 59–61
  DNS server role 3–5
  Remote Access server role 157–158
Install-WindowsFeature -Name npas -IncludeManagementTools command 200
interface identifiers 238
Internet Assigned Numbers Authority (IANA) 156, 228
Internet Connection Sharing (ICS) 244
Internet DNS queries
  handling of 9–10
Internet Key Exchange Version 2 (IKEv2) 166
Internet Protocol security (IPsec) 236
Internet Protocol version 4 (IPv4) 1, 26, 57, 155
Internet Protocol version 6 (IPv6) 1, 26, 57
  addressing, using DHCPv6 76–77
  scopes 76–77
Invoke-IpamGpoProvisioning cmdlet 116
IP addresses
  assignment of 171
  DHCP reservations 68–69
  inventory 118
  IPv4 227–235
  IPv6 235–249
  managing blocks on 118–121
  pool depletion 65
  range groups 118
  ranges 118, 121–123
  scope 62, 67
  subnets 118
  usage trail 149–150
IP address management (IPAM) 101–154
  access policies 144–146
  access scopes 144, 146–147
  architecture 102–103
  auditing 147–152
    address usage trail 149–150
    DHCP lease events 150–152
    DNS and DHCP servers 148–149
    user logon events 150–152
  client 102
  database 102
    configuration of 108
  database storage using SQL Server 104–106
  deployment 106–107
  DHCP management with 126–136
    in multiple Active Directory forests 141
  DNS management with 136–140
    in multiple Active Directory forests 141
  IP blocks 118–121
  IP ranges 121–123
  migrating existing workloads to 124
  monitoring utilization of IP address space 123–124
  provisioning
    manual 107–112
    using GPOs 113–114
  RBAC in 142–147
  requirements for 103
  role-based access control 102
  role-based security groups 142
  roles 143–144
  scheduled tasks 102
  server 102
  server discovery configuration 114–118, 141
  tasks 101–102
  topologies for 104
  VMM integration 125–126
IPAM. *See* IP address management
IP configuration 3, 58
IP filters 210
IPv4 addresses 155–157, 161
IPv4 addressing 227–235
  address classes 229
  compared with IPv6 235–236
  host addresses 232–233
  host configuration 234–235
  interoperability between IPv6 and 241–245
  IPv4 address configuration 227–228
  public and private 228
  routing configuration 245–249
  scheme for 233–234
  subnet addresses 231–232
  subnet configuration 229–233
  subnet masks 231
  supernetting 233

IPv4 name resolution 2–3
IPv4 nodes 242
IPv6 addressing 235–249
    address format 236–237
    address scopes and types 237
    host configuration 240
    interoperability between IPv4 and 241–245
    IPv6 address configuration 236–238
    overview of 235–236
    routing configuration 245–249
    stateless 238–239
    subnetting configuration 238
IPv6/IPv4 nodes 242
IPv6 nodes 242
ISATAP 241–243

J

j5*.log file 89
j50.chk file 89
j50.log file 89
j50res00001.jrs file 89
j50res00002.jrs file 89

K

Key Signing Key (KSK) 15

L

LACP. *See* Link Aggregation Control Protocol (LACP)
Layer 2 Tunneling Protocol with Internet Protocol
        Security (L2TP/IPsec) 166
Link Aggregation Control Protocol (LACP) 282
link-local addresses 237
Link State Advertisements (LSAs) 246
load balancing 282–283, 301, 309–311
load sharing 86
local addresses 237
LockDown 178
logging
    debug 22–23
    DHCP audit logs 93–94
    DHCP event logs 94–95
    DNS 22–23
    IPAM audit logs 147–152
logging data 51–53
LSAs. *See* Link State Advertisements

M

mail exchanger (MX) records 43
managed servers 102
media access control (MAC) addresses 68, 238
Microsoft CHAP Version 2 (MS-CHAP v2) 167, 176
Microsoft Intune 178, 180
Microsoft Message Analyzer 96–98
Microsoft System Center 299
Minimum (Default) TTL value 30
MS-CHAP v2 (PEAP-MS-CHAP v2) 220
Multicast Address Dynamic Client Allocation Protocol
        (MADCAP) scopes 65
multicast addresses 237
multicast IPv6 addresses 76
multicast scopes 65, 66–68
multicast transmission 65
multimaster updates 37
multinets 65

N

name resolution 2–3, 25
Name Resolution Policy Table (NRPT) 14
name server (NS) records 29, 43
Nano Server
    DNS deployment on 5–6
NetBIOS names 2, 42
Netsh.exe command-line tool 81
network adapters
    combining multiple 282
    RDMA-enabled 294–295
    single 282
    SR-IOV 296–298
    standby 283
    virtual 285–286
Network Address Translation (NAT) 155–164
    enabling, in Remote Access 158–160
    implementing 157–163
    interface configuration 160–162
    monitoring 164
    node configuration 163
network connections
    naming 159
network connectivity
    connection profiles 177–180
    Network Address Translation 155–164
    routing configuration 164

Network Controller 299
   APIs 306
   Datacenter Firewall and 313–314
   deployment of 305–309
   prerequisites for 306–307
   SLB and 310
   with RAS Gateway 313
network interface card (NIC) teaming 281, 299
   implementing 282–285
   load balancing mode 282–283
   standby adapter 283
   teaming modes 282
network interfaces 169
network location server 189
network policies
   configuration of 213–217
Network Policy Server (NPS) 155, 199–223
   certificate configuration 220–223
   policy configuration 213–220
      connection request policies 217–219
      import and export policies 219–220
      network policies 213–217
   RADIUS configuration 199–209
   templates
      applying 212
      configuration of 209–212
      creation of 209–211
network security groups (NSGs) 314
network solutions
   BranchCache 271–277
   branch offices 250–277
   Distributed File Share 250–270
   high performance 281–298
   IPv4 addressing 227–235, 245–249
   IPv6 addressing 235–249
   software defined networking 298–314
   virtual networks 302–305
network virtualization 302–305
   firewall policies 313–314
   implementing Windows Server gateways 311–313
   network security groups 314
   with NVGRE 303–305
   with VXLAN encapsulation 305
Network Virtualization using Generic Routing Encapsulation (NVGRE) 303–305
New-DfsnRoot cmdlet 253
New-NetQoSTrafficClass cmdlet 293
no-refresh interval 46
NPS. *See* Network Policy Server

NPS servers
   manually provisioning for IMAP 112
NRPT. *See* Name Resolution Policy Table

O

Open Shortest Path First (OSPF) 246
OSPF. *See* Open Shortest Path First

P

Package Family Name 176
PAP protocol 167
Parent Domain Value 64
password-based authentication 220
PEAP with TLS (PEAP-TLS) 220
performance alerts 24–25
Performance Monitor 24
performance tuning 23–25
platform-as-a-service. *See* PaaS
pointer (PTR) records 26, 43
Point-to-Point Tunneling Protocol (PPTP) 166
Pre-Boot Execution (PXE) 79–80
primary zones
   Active Directory integration of 37–39
   creation of 27–31
private IPv4 addresses 155, 157
provisioning
   IPAM
      manually 107–112
      using GPOs 113–114
public IPv4 addresses 155–157, 161
public key infrastructure (PKI) 166
PXE boot
   configuration of 79–80

Q

Quality of Service (QoS) 291–293

R

RADIUS. *See* Remote Authentication Dial-In User Service (RADIUS)
RAS. *See* Remote Access Service
RAS Gateway 167–168, 250, 312–313
RBAC. *See* role-based access control
RDC. *See* remote differential compression

receive side scaling (RSS) 287–291
  virtual 289
recursion
  configuration of 12–13
  disabling 12, 25
  scope 13, 20
recursion scopes 50
refresh interval 46
Remote Access 165
  certificate configuration 220–223
  DirectAccess 189–199
  enabling NAT in 158–160
  RADIUS and 199–209
  server role
    installation of 157–158
  using RAS Gateway 167–168
  VPN
    determining when to use 169
    implementing 169–180
Remote Access Service (RAS) 250
Remote Authentication Dial-In User Service (RADIUS) 155, 169
  Client templates 210–211
  configuration of 199–209
    accounting 208–209
    clients 206–208
    proxy 203–206
    server 201–202
  NPS role and 199–201
  servers 210
remote differential compression (RDC) 268–269
Remote Direct Memory Access (RDMA) 291, 294–295
Remove-DnsServerRootHint cmdlet 11
replication
  AD DS 37
replication groups
  creation of 260–265
  folders 261
  members 261, 263–264, 265
  schedule and bandwidth 261, 264
  topology 261, 262–263
  types 260, 262
replication targets, DFS 256–259
resource records 42–44
  in zone scopes 50
  options 47–49
  preference, weight, and priority values 47–48
  time to live (TTL) value 48–49
  Unknown Records 49

response rate limiting 18
Restore-DfsrPreservedFiles cmdlet 270
reverse lookup zones 26–27
RIP. *See* Routing Information Protocol
role-based access control (RBAC) 125
  in IPAM 142–147
role-based security groups 142
roles 142, 143–144
root certificates 221
root hints
  configuration of 8–12
  editing 10–12
  use of 10
round robin 49
Route.exe command 249
Router Advertisements messages 238
router-to-router connections 165
routing
  configuration of 164
  IPv4 and IPv6 245–249
Routing And Remote Access console 249
Routing Information Protocol (RIP) 246
routing protocols
  configuration of 249–250
  enabling 246–248
  options for 246
routing tables 246, 248–249
RRAS Multitenant Gateway 299
RSS. *See* receive side scaling

S

scavenging 45–47
SDN. *See* software defined networking
secondary zones 31–34
secure dynamic updates 37, 40
Secure Dynamic Updates 73
Secure Socket Tunneling Protocol (SSTP) 166
security event log size 147
server clustering 82
server computer certificate 221
server discovery
  configuration of 114–118, 141
Server Manager
  DNS server role installation with 3–4
Server Message Block (SMB) 281
service location (SVR) records 43
Set-DfsrConnectionSchedule cmdlet 266

Set-DhcpServerv4OptionValue cmdlet   71
Set-DnsServer cmdlet   49
Set-DnsServerPrimaryZone cmdlet   31
Set-DnsServerResponseRateLimiting cmdlet   18
Set-DnsServerRootHint cmdlet   11
Set-DnsServerZoneAging cmdlet   47
Set-IpamRange cmdlet   122
Set-NetAdapterRSS cmdlet   288
Set-NetQosDcbxSetting cmdlet   293
settings, policy   214
Shared Secrets templates   210–211
Simple Mail Transfer Protocol (SMTP)   43
site-to-site connections   165, 169
site-to-site (S2S) VPNs   180–189
SLAAC. *See* Stateless Address Auto Configuration
smart cards   221
SMB Direct   294–295
SMB Multichannel   295
socket pool   17
software defined networking (SDN)   298–314
    benefits of   298–299
    components   299
    deployment   299–301
    firewall policies   313–314
    HNV implementation   302–305
    implementing Windows Server gateways   311–313
    Network Controller deployment   305–309
    network requirements for   299–300
    network security groups   314
    Software Load Balancing   309–311
Software Load Balancing (SLB)   301, 309–311
split scopes   82–85
SQL authentication   105–106
SQL Server
    IPAM database storage using   104–106
SR-IOV   296–298
staging folders   267–268
staging quota   269
standalone DFS namespaces   252
standby adapters   283
Start of Authority (SOA) records   29, 30, 41, 43
stateful autoconfiguration   238
Stateless Address Auto Configuration (SLAAC)   236
stateless autoconfiguration   238–239
static teaming   282
stub zones   40–41
    conditional forwarding and   40–41
    creating   41
subnet addresses   231–232

subnet IDs   232, 238
subnet masks   228, 231
supernetting   233
superscopes   65–66
switch embedded teaming (SET)   281, 282, 285–286
Switch Independent Mode   286
System Center Configuration Manager   180
System Center Virtual Machine Manager (VMM)   286

T

templates
    NPS   209–212
Teredo   244–245
time to live (TTL) value   48–49
tmp.edb file   89
traffic filters   178
Transport Layer Security Authentication (TLSA)   19
TrustAnchors zone   14

U

unicast addresses   237
Unknown Records   49
user certificates   221
User Datagram Protocol (UDP)   166
user logon events
    auditing   150–152

V

Virtual Extensible LAN (VXLAN)   305
Virtual Machine Manager (VMM)   286
    IPAM integration   125–126
virtual machine networks (VM networks)   125
Virtual Machine Queue (VMQ)   289
Virtual Machine Queue VMQ (VMMQ)   290–291
virtual network adapters   285
virtual networks   302–305. *See also* network virtualization
    firewall policies   313–314
Virtual Private Networks (VPNs)   155
    app-triggered   176–177
    authentication options   167
    client IP configuration   169
    connection profiles
        creation and configuration of   177–179
        deployment of   179–180

virtual RSS

    implementing remote access 169–180
    LockDown 178
    network interfaces 169
    overview of 165–166
    protocol options 166
    remote access and 165
    remote client configuration 174–176
    site-to-site 165, 169, 180–189
    traffic filters 178
    VPN reconnect 176
virtual RSS 289
virtual switches
    SLB compatability 310–311
VPN reconnect 176

W

WDS. *See* Windows Deployment Services
WID. *See* Windows Internal Database
Windows authentication 105–106
Windows Deployment Services (WDS) 79–80
Windows Internal Database (WID) 104–105
Windows Internet Name Service (WINS) 31
Windows PowerShell
    DHCP management using 136
    DNS global settings using 26
    DNS installation with 4–5
    DNS management using 140
Windows Server 2016
    high performance networking in 281–298
    implementing NAT with 157–163
    routing configuration 245–249
    server clustering 82
Windows Server gateways 311–313

Z

zone level statistics 53–54
zone scopes 20, 50–51
Zone Signing Key (ZSK) 15

About the author

ANDREW WARREN runs his own training and consultancy business in the UK. He has served as subject matter expert for Windows Server 2016 courses, technical lead for Windows 10 courses, and co-developer of TechNet sessions covering Microsoft Exchange Server. He has over thirty years of IT experience. He lives in rural Somerset in the UK.

Visit us today at

microsoftpressstore.com

- **Hundreds of titles available** – Books, eBooks, and online resources from industry experts

- **Free U.S. shipping**

- **eBooks in multiple formats** – Read on your computer, tablet, mobile device, or e-reader

- **Print & eBook Best Value Packs**

- **eBook Deal of the Week** – Save up to 60% on featured titles

- **Newsletter and special offers** – Be the first to hear about new releases, specials, and more

- **Register your book** – Get additional benefits

Hear about it first.

Get the latest news from Microsoft Press sent to your inbox.

- New and upcoming books
- Special offers
- Free eBooks
- How-to articles

Sign up today at MicrosoftPressStore.com/Newsletters

From technical overviews to drilldowns on special topics, get *free* ebooks from Microsoft Press at:

www.microsoftvirtualacademy.com/ebooks

Download your free ebooks in PDF, EPUB, and/or Mobi for Kindle formats.

Look for other great resources at Microsoft Virtual Academy, where you can learn new skills and help advance your career with free Microsoft training delivered by experts.

Microsoft Press

Tell us what you think!

Was it useful?
Did it teach you what you wanted to learn?
Was there room for improvement?

Let us know at https://aka.ms/tellpress

Your feedback goes directly to the staff at Microsoft Press, and we read every one of your responses. Thanks in advance!